PHIL JACKSON

PETER RICHMOND is the author of five other books, including *The Glory Game* (with Frank Gifford), which was a *New York Times* bestseller. His writing has appeared in *The New Yorker, Vanity Fair, Rolling Stone, The New York Times Magazine,* and *GQ.* He lives with his wife in Dutchess County, New York.

Praise for *Phil Jackson: Lord of the Rings*

"Richmond employs a folksy style that is both an homage to Jackson's nonconformist persona and a playful jab at his Zen master reputation. Thankfully for readers, Richmond favors personal evolution over hagiography, which is the difference maker in this in-depth and entertaining work."   —*Publishers Weekly*

Praise for *Badasses: The Legend of Snake, Foo, Dr. Death, and John Madden's Oakland Raiders*

"No NFL team ever strutted any better on the dark side than the Oakland Raiders of the 1970s. In *Badasses*, Peter Richmond chronicles the treacheries, debauchery, and yes, the winning, with appropriate literary gusto. Lock the doors, close the windows, send the kids to bed before reading."
                                       —Leigh Montville, author of *Ted Williams:*
                                                The Biography of an American Hero

"I always thought the Raiders were bad, but I never realized how bad—and how good—until I read Peter Richmond's smart, funny, rowdy tale."
                                  —Robert Lipsyte, former *New York Times* columnist and
                                                               author of *Center Field*

"Once upon a time, there lived a band of larger-than-life misfits who lorded over the NFL. Dirtbags! Castoffs! Has-beens! Deviants! You name 'em, John Madden's Raiders had 'em. And, thanks to Richmond's tireless reporting and vibrant prose, so does *Badasses*."

—Jeff Pearlman, *New York Times* bestselling author of *Boys Will Be Boys: The Glory Days and Party Nights of the Dallas Cowboys Dynasty*

"Richmond's book is a treasure trove of uproarious anecdotes skillfully woven into a seasonal chronicle spiced with sharp player profiles. . . . This rollicking read reminds us that football is a game that's meant to be played hard—and to be fun." —*Library Journal*

ALSO BY PETER RICHMOND

Badasses: The Legend of Snake, Foo, Dr. Death,
and John Madden's Oakland Raiders

The Glory Game: How the 1958 NFL Championship
Changed Football Forever
(as coauthor with Frank Gifford)

Fever: The Life and Music of Miss Peggy Lee

My Father's War: A Son's Journey

Ballpark: Camden Yards and the Building of an American Dream

PHIL JACKSON
LORD OF THE RINGS

Peter Richmond

★

A PLUME BOOK

PLUME
Published by the Penguin Group
Penguin Group (USA) LLC
375 Hudson Street
New York, New York 10014

USA | Canada | UK | Ireland | Australia | New Zealand | India | South Africa | China
penguin.com
A Penguin Random House Company

First published in the United States of America by Blue Rider Press,
a member of Penguin Group (USA) LLC, 2013
First Plume Printing 2014

THE LIBRARY OF CONGRESS HAS CATALOGED THE BLUE RIDER PRESS
EDITION AS FOLLOWS:

Richmond, Peter, 1953–
Phil Jackson : lord of the rings / Peter Richmond.
p.   cm.
Includes bibliographical references and index.
ISBN 978-0-399-15870-4 (hc.)
ISBN 978-0-14-218118-8 (pbk.)
1. Jackson, Phil.   2. Basketball coaches—United States—Biography.
3. Los Angeles Lakers (Basketball team).
4. Chicago Bulls (Basketball team).   I. Title.
GV884.J32R42   2013   2013039592
796.323092—dc23
[B]

Printed in the United States of America
10 9 8 7 6 5 4 3 2 1

Original hardcover design by Amanda Dewey

To David Milch, John Hersey, Tom McCormack and Ilena Silverman,
all of whom taught me to be a craftsman

PHIL JACKSON
LORD OF THE RINGS

PROLOGUE

"If the whole truth were told about any human being, he would inevitably emerge as the most depraved of criminals. I will not make any attempt to write your life even if you should counsel me to do it."

—S. N. Behrman to his friend Somerset Maugham after Maugham had asked Behrman to write Maugham's life story

Phil Jackson didn't counsel me to write this book, of course. By the time I decided that the story of the most successful coach in professional sports history might be worth exploring, said coach had already counseled someone else to help him write his own (latest) book. When I asked his agent whether Phil would be willing to participate in my own project, said agent smirked, if one can smirk over the phone, more or less saying, "Where were you a year ago when we were talking to writers about his next book? Good luck, dude. No, Phil will not be part of your project."

I plowed on. And then, when I got through to a lifelong friend of Phil's who graciously relayed to me, after talking to Phil, that Jackson wouldn't make any attempts to interfere—that he couldn't cooperate because he was working on his "own mess"—I felt relieved. Unburdened of having to see someone's life through that person's own particular lens, I was free to pursue my own mess: an attempt to chronicle, through the insights of those who had witnessed it firsthand, Jackson's extraordinary journey.

Like the college president who'd captained Princeton's basketball team before being recruited by the Yale Divinity School, and had performed

Phil's second wedding. Like the Woodstock rabbi who sent me a Lakota Sioux prayer that Phil had typed up for him after one of Phil's annual basketball workshops at the Omega Holistic Institute, founded on the principles of the Sufi mystic Pir Vilayat Inayat Khan.

Like the friend, Phil's first coauthor, whose PhD thesis sought to find a Dionysian allegory in the Canon's Yeoman's Tale in Chaucer's *Canterbury Tales*.

Like the former star of the Puerto Rican league's Fighting Cocks of Isabela. Like the former NBA player honored at the White House as the Wheelchair Athlete of the Year who, years earlier, had bonded with Phil over Ram Dass's "Be Here Now." Like another player who'd worn a dashiki to a White House ceremony, and then dressed down the President of the United States.

Like the dentist who endured Phil's elbow jabs in the regular game down at the Markle Residence for Women in Greenwich Village, run by the Salvation Army. Like the widow of one of Phil's best friends, who knows basketball better than most everyone who has ever *played* basketball.

From all of them, I was seeking enlightenment on two points: (1) How Phil Jackson became the best coach ever, championshipwise, and (2) Why. After all, he hardly possessed the requisite pedigree. He hadn't grown up reading the Big-Coach Hoop Manuals and attending their workshops. He'd digested, instead, the writings of, among others, P. D. Ouspensky, Black Elk, the anonymous fourteenth-century author of *The Cloude of Unknowyng*, and yes, L. Ron Hubbard.

But he'd retired as the greatest sports coach of all time, with the same number of rings as Pat Riley and Vince Lombardi combined. Now, obviously, this "greatest" label pertains only if your gauge of success is the ring. I myself always thought it was a pretty good barometer, but what did I know? So I asked an expert. "Sports is a strange animal," Earl Monroe told me, "in that you can make all the money in the world, but if you haven't won the championship, you don't have the same respect."

But I also wanted to know why a man who had shown, in my own handful of interviews with him, boundless curiosity about things spiritual and philosophic and cerebral (actually boundless curiosity about basically everything) could never, for his entire life, stay away from the basketball court. Why a man possessed by, in the words of critic Anthony Lane describing a tragic movie protagonist, "our unhealable human sickness: the need to know" could never put aside childish games.

Of course, like every other NBA fan, I also wanted to know whether Phil had simply been lucky. A lot of people think so. Scot Pollard, one of the most lovable wing nuts in the sport's history, enunciated the stance of the skeptic camp most succinctly when he said, "He's one of the most overrated coaches of our time. He's only had the greatest players of our era on his teams." On the other hand, other coaches had tried to coach Michael Jordan and Scottie Pippen; others had Shaquille O'Neal and Michael Jordan. Neither tandem ever won without Phil.

The late Baltimore Oriole manager Earl Weaver liked to say, "You make your luck." Clearly, Jackson's being lucky in terms of personnel was one element of his coaching successes. But both the Bulls and the Lakers had a whole lot of other players on those two decades' worth of championship rosters, none of them superstars. And somehow, Jackson alchemized them all into owners of diamond-sparkling and gold-glittering rings—an astounding eleven times. Luck doesn't give you double-figure titles.

As I sat down each morning to write, having first ignited dried sage leaves in a bowl on my desktop to smudge my workplace and free it of negativity (that's what Phil did for his locker and film rooms, and besides, the stuff grows like weeds in my wife's herb garden), I wanted to find out why a man with a BA in philosophy, psychology and religion who had considered joining the ministry chose instead to join a multibillion-dollar entertainment industry whose sideline-stalking supervisors generally look like coronaries waiting to happen, doing their jobs with all of the joy of someone who's just swallowed gravel—a corporation that, for several years, refused to admit him into their old-boys' club.

And, yes, because his critics enjoy harping on it, I wanted to know about the nature of his ego. Every head coach possesses one. Was his the aligned, sensible Freudian ego, which, filtering the id, allows your inner self-serving desires to mesh successfully with society's collective demands? Or was his of the current-day garden variety, as in Spike Lee sitting courtside at every Knick game ("Look at me!")?

To find Phil Jackson was not to go with the easy answers. Because with Phil, what you see is never what you get. "I've known him for thirty-five years," former Hunter College star Charley Rosen, that lifelong friend, assistant coach on the team that won Phil his first ring and twice Jackson's coauthor, told me. "And I still don't know who he is. You can't nail him."

By the time I was ready to write, I knew that defining Phil Jackson by way of the various labels affixed to him would be like trying to describe a Buckminster Fuller geodesic dome by looking at a single panel. Previously published takes on the man—including his own books about himself—had only hinted at answering the pressing question: How in hell did *Phil Jackson* coach more championship teams than any professional coach in the nation's history?

I did know that I was writing a biography of a man who had altered the landscape of a national subculture, even if the culture in question was pro sports, which should be a very small part of our world but is not. And I did know that my initial impulse—to certify my own lifelong distrust of convention by proving that a member of the counterculture could heroically triumph by beating Big Sport at its own game—was absurd and self-indulgent; there are no heroes in an entertainment industry in which dollars inevitably drive ethics.

As the biographer, I wanted to heed the dictum of an editor who once told me, "The truth of something is not to be found in the assemblage of the facts." It was the same editor who always instructed: "Surround the subject." I interviewed, I researched, I drew on personal experience. Most fun of all, I drove the Jackson trail, seven thousand miles of it round-trip, from New York to northwestern Montana and back, by way of North Dakota, Chicago and Albany, some of it on his favorite road, the Lincoln Highway (our first national road).

★

But I had no idea where to start the tale.

Definitely not at the beginning, where all biographies do, with something like, "In 1945, Anaconda, Montana, just west of Opportunity and north of Wisdom, was a burg abuzz with the energy of five thousand workers." Too ordinary. My subject was not.

Definitely not with a flashback to any given midseventies night when a stoned, surly rebel without a cause had bought a scalped yellow-seat Garden ticket five minutes before tip-off just to see Phil play. That would have been about *me* . . . looking at Phil through a retro-adolescently skewed lens.

Not with the last time we'd seen him as a Lakers coach, backhand-slapping Pau Gasol on his chest in the final playoff series in 2011. Again, too narrow a lens . . . as would have been beginning with the nadir that followed: the sneering disbelievers who jumped into the fray when it had ended, like the writer who used the national billboard of the Huffington Post to mock Jackson's "Buddha B.S." and "narcissistic grandiosity," calling him a "self-interest marketing fraud." While representing the extreme blowback, that scribe wasn't alone among the journalists who'd tracked Jackson's career close up; how else to explain Jackson winning a total of *one* Coach of the Year title . . . including *no* votes in 1992–93, when he won his *third straight title*? Whereas Riley earned three?

I didn't want to open with a former Jackson starter who told me how increasingly he wearies of hearing how "out of the box" Jackson was: "The players play the game, period."

Then, I also didn't want to begin with a former Bull and Laker who equated Phil with John Paul II, Desmond Tutu and the Dalai Lama.

★

And then, as happens in stories like this, I met someone who has known Phil Jackson for four decades, who guided me throughout the project. "There is no wrong place to start," Diane Mast told me. "But why not start with something good about him? That isn't about basketball? That no one knows?"

That sounded right to me.

★

An otherwise routine spring day at a medical base in South Vietnam: Blackhawk helicopters off-loading the wounded and the doomed; Blackhawks heading back out to gather more wounded. Captain Peter Pornish, whose previous claim to fame had been scoring three touchdowns for the University of North Dakota Sioux in their 1966 Pecan Bowl defeat of Parsons University, was supervising three companies of medics.

The difference between getting the first down and saving the life of a marine private was a fairly profound one. By now, Grand Forks, North Dokota, was a long way behind, in a lot of ways. Still, Pete vividly remembered those years, after failing to catch on with the Steelers and going overseas: beers back in '67 at Matt's Tavern, picking up girls at the college library. He'd not only been Phil's teammate at UND, but a high school teammate, too, on the western edge of the state in Williston.

Then one day, in the mail, came a letter from Jackson, postmarked New York. Pete wasn't its only recipient; Jackson was sending it to other former Sioux in Southeast Asia, too. Phil was sitting out the NBA season to recover from back surgery and said he thought he'd just check in with his friends, with the young men he'd played sports with, now stranded far from the banks of the Red River. The missives weren't heavy: just news about life in the States. Of the Knicks. Maybe some memories of Sigma Alpha Epsilon.

In the meantime, all the best, until the next letter.

"It didn't surprise me," Pete Pornish says now. "He was always a tremendously personable guy. Always had a philosophic side. And a friendly side. Even when I came back, and visited him in Greenwich Village, he always wanted to revisit with anybody he'd known before, and every kid on the street would say, 'Hi!' and he'd chat with every one of them. He would always take the time to talk to people. I don't know many celebrities, but I can't imagine many are like him: One of those people who's been true to himself and the people around him and never let it go to his head."

Pornish knows whereof he speaks when he talks of Phil these days; Jackson's attended the last few ten-year reunions at Williston High School, and only occasionally does his career come up.

Before the fortieth reunion, Jackson had had an angioplasty during the previous playoffs. And his old friend Barbara Sohlberg had to ask: "Phil, are you having heart problems, or is it just the stress of trying to keep up with that younger woman?"

"I think it's the latter," he said.

But we're getting ahead of ourselves.

ONE

By day, they'd spend long shifts at the foot of the 585-foot Anaconda Copper smelter stack in Anaconda, Montana, stoking the war effort. By night, they'd roam the saloons spending the company's money. Twice on Sunday and again on Wednesday night, there'd be salvation and repentance from Charles and Elisabeth Jackson, itinerant bringers of the Word at the Assembly of God church. When Elisabeth, the Sunday-evening-service pastor, pronounced, "Christ is the only answer," people tended to listen.

September 17, 1945, was a Monday. Elisabeth wouldn't have preached the night before in Anaconda; there was an impetigo epidemic in town, so she gave birth over in Deer Lodge, twenty-five miles away, to her third son, Philip Douglas Jackson. But it would be perfectly reasonable to assume that she was back spreading the word in Anaconda the following week, and fervently so.

Charles, the ordained minister, was strict enough in his beliefs about following the word of God. His wife's daily message was even more insistent: Listen to no one but Christ, or come the day when Gabriel rapturously blows that wild trumpet, be prepared to be left behind.

★

Shipbuilder John Jackson had come over from Bristol in the 1600s, settling in New England. John's grandson, a Tory, accepted the fifty thousand acres the king had deeded him in Ontario on the banks of the Ottawa

River. Some generations later, Charles Jackson quit school at the age of fourteen to work the Ontario farm and then married. He and his wife produced a daughter, Phil's half-sister Joan, but his wife died during her second pregnancy. Charles took this as a sign from God, dropped down across the border and became a lay preacher in western Montana.

In the meantime, Elisabeth Funk's grandfather, of Dutch stock, speaking "low German," had gone west to seek his fortune in Saskatchewan. His heritage proving a liability during the First World War, he moved the family to a plot outside Wolf Point, Montana. After captaining the girls' basketball team and coming up just short of valedictorian, Elisabeth taught in a one-room schoolhouse for a couple of years, burning cow chips for heat while looking for a truer calling. That curiosity drew her to Pentecostalism. After attending seminary at Central Bible College in Winnipeg, she and her brother and sister became a team of traveling evangelists . . . and when she met Charles Jackson, the die was cast.

"The Pentecostal movement changed regular church-going citizens into fanatics," Phil would write in his first book, while still a Knick, trying to distance himself not from his parents, whose love he would forever embrace, just from their immutable beliefs. As he'd later say, "They saw miraculous healings and they heard their neighbors speak in tongues."

They were a special kind of pilgrim, these carriers of the word in the snowcapped outback. "In the great, nearly empty stretches of northern Montana," Tom McGuane once wrote, ". . . some radicalized soothsayer would arise—a crop duster, a diesel mechanic, a gunsmith—then fade away, and the region would go back to sparse agriculture, a cow every hundred acres, a trailer house with a basketball backboard and a muddy truck. Minds spun in the solitude . . . the wind blew for weeks at a time, icy wind, and that, after a while, that constant wind would make you crazy."

The end of the war, coinciding with Phil's birth, gutted the copper town. The Butte, Anaconda and Pacific Railroad came to a halt in

Anaconda . . . six hundred miles short of the ocean. Today, the lonesome stack is still visible for miles.

The Jackson family odysseyed its way east, the youngest child trying to fathom the nature of the journey and to grow into normality—while falling asleep to the poster on his bedroom wall: "For God so loved the world that he gave his only begotten Son, that whosoever believeth in him should not perish, but have everlasting life."

Now on to Deer Lodge, another company town, location of the state prison, a turreted fortress, and nearby, the state hospital, holding two thousand psychiatric patients (the largest unincorporated gathering of people in the state). Several souls to be saved here, too.

Then it was on to Miles City, on the Tongue River (there's no record of it speaking), then a vibrant horse-trading town, home of Fort Keough, built after the Battle of the Little Bighorn by a man named Nelson Miles, who used the fort to complete the subjugation of the Native Americans of the area, although, as he would later say, whiskey brought him more trouble than the Indians. (Today a mural outside of the fairgrounds depicts a skeleton riding a bull, accompanied by the caption "Don't Let Meth Be Your Last Ride.") Miles City wasn't inhospitable by any means; it never got colder than 38 below in the winter.

Except for the omnipresence of the Creator, the Jackson household was like any other in one respect—older brothers Chuck and Joe fought and got whupped for it—but unusual in another: the male-female balance was healthier than most. Phil grew up with respect for women's equality. When Elisabeth Jackson preached on a Sunday night, Charles cooked the dinner.

Charles and Elisabeth's fame preceded their arrival. Whether Elisabeth actually performed a miracle on a boy born without eyes is clearly open to question. What is certain is that the apocalypse was due—not that the parents went out of their way to keep Phil healthy enough to meet it;

he saw no doctor until he was six. Today, in hip Montana restaurants, honey and deer lard would be an emulsion to slather onto an elk steak; back then, applied to Phil's chest, the salve would protect against chest colds. For an infection? A poultice of milk, oatmeal and bread crusts.

The youngest Jackson was bright but kinetic: "You used to wear out my apron," his mother once told him. One churchman suggested exorcism. Charles, fundamentalist but not insane, dissuaded the churchman. But no one doubted the Jacksons' compassion, parentwise. Phil was, yes, a PK—a preacher's kid, raised in a rigid way of life—but he never lacked for love at home. And being out there on the fringe, looking in, peerwise? There was no TV; card games were played with cards with no faces, because kings and queens suggested a mortal hierarchy that smacks of a golden calf; dancing or going to the movies was forbidden. What better perspective to have of what's possible within the pasture than from the fringe?

Add the geography, the view from the roads and rails leading into and out of Anaconda, Deer Lodge, Miles City: horizonless, a word not meant to imply "empty" but "without restraint."

The next Jackson family move was a like a wormhole voyage to another star system. When Phil was seven, his father took a position in Great Falls, the largest city in the state, as the supervisor of all of Montana's Pentecostal churches. The first settling point for the Paleo-Indians crossing the Bering Straight, fifteen millennia later, Great Falls had all the things that make a town a city: a state university branch, industry, pro baseball . . . and museums. Charles Jackson built a house, and as the kid grew like a bean sprout on steroids, Charles would plant a hoop in some cement. He knew secular talent when he saw it.

In the meantime, visiting his maternal grandfather's stable and boardinghouse in Wolf Point, Phil was given a view of Native America that mirrored every preconception of a European-blooded settler: "They were supposed to be dirt and weren't to be trusted and had no concept of civilization," Phil later wrote of the white man's attitude toward the Sioux in the area. His grandfather, lodging Native Americans in a boardinghouse, derided them as "shiftless drunks and thieves."

He learned now of the plight of Native American life. Little wonder that hereafter he'd turn to Native Americans for spiritual guidance; the Pentecostal thing wasn't finding traction, if the first speaking-in-tongues attempt was indicative. Chuck and Joe had passed with flying colors, but as Phil would later recall, "All of a sudden this thing was supposed to fall on you. Then you would turn to jelly and start speaking some kind of gibberish. Joe told me he had faked it. I tried to be very serious."

People laid on hands. Philip sat for hours. He cried. He stammered. But only in English. "He just about spoke in tongues," Elisabeth said. "I have faith that he will."

Possessed of his mother's athleticism and both parents' intellect, Jackson entered school a grade ahead of his peers. He hooped, he swam, he played hockey, he fished on a trip to the Middle Fork of the Flathead River, leading into the lake that is now his permanent residence. Hooking his first rainbow trout with a worm on a bamboo pole, Huck Finn–style, against the backdrop of a mountain called the Tea Kettle, the Great Northern tracks zigzagging their way across its face.

In the big city, new destinations beckoned, like the C. M. Russell Museum. That would be Charles Russell, one of the most celebrated Western artists (in 2005, a Russell sold for nearly $5.6 million). Picture Remington without the press. Russell's representational paintings of Native Americans so captivated the young man that he fantasized about living in Montana a century earlier, before the white man. Two Native American classmates in sixth grade lived down by the flats on the Missouri. He found himself drawn to their self-sufficiency (in contrast to the lost souls wandering around the grounds of the statewide revival meeting at which his mother was an annual speaker: "humming, wailing and praying").

As Bill Bradley recounted in his *Life on the Run*, those classmates had "spoken [to Phil] of a dis-attachment from material need. Wild food, from antelope to herbs, was enough to survive in brutal country." "Boys were taught the ways of animals," he told Bradley. "Storytellers passed on the traditions and history. The whole concept of life was how to stay in tune with your environment." He would later write of fantasizing about being an adopted Native American.

Adoption? By his eighth-grade year, the family structure had lost its center, his father often absent supervising Pentecostal outposts. Jackson and his two brothers—now fifteen and nineteen—were too much for the mother to manage alone. His half-sister, Joan, was away at seminary school.

His father thus resigned the Great Falls job . . . and now needed to find another church. The final destination was ninety miles farther east but this time across the state line, in the northwestern corner of the true outback: the empty state of North Dakota—specifically, the village of Williston, tucked into the top northwestern corner.

"This is where the Lord wants me to go," Charles said—to a state where, not so many years earlier, a windstorm had razed half of the capital. Where at the height of the drought-plagued Depression, women hung wet sheets across their windows, vainly trying to repel the flying dust that had been loosed by immigrant farmers tearing up the prairie grass for seasonal crops. Where in any winter, if you were out pumping water and your fingers were freezing, the best way to thaw them was in the snow.

Montana legend had it that North Dakota had no trees. Newsman Eric Sevareid, native of the midstate crossroads of Velva, put it more eloquently: "There wasn't much shade." But this monotonal terrain would provide enough soil for the man with eleven rings to grow.

TWO

It's a madhouse now, Williston, home of the Coyotes, who play in the Phil Jackson Fieldhouse, and getting madder with each new fracked well, each new itinerant, each new man camp. At last count, the wells numbered ten thousand. Hess and Halliburton and Baker Hughes (yes, *that* Hughes) are hoping for fifty thousand. Our latest boomtowners are perched atop the Bakken formation in RVs, mobile homes and tents. A half-million barrels of crude a day are being shipped out—east to refineries, west for shipment to China.

"Now Hiring" signs start popping up on Route 2 fifty miles east of town, the artery for the caravans of trucks bearing well-drilling equipment. By night the well flames dot the dark horizon like baby volcanoes. Motel rooms, once $39, now start at $300. An SUV parking space is $850 a month. And $60 a day gets you thirty-two square feet in a man camp, with three meals.

"Everyone from Halliburton except Dick Cheney is out here," says Jerry Zunich, now a Farmers Union Insurance rep. Jerry grew up a roughneck himself, so he's a "drill, baby, drill" guy: the more jobs, the better. Talk of crimes in the camps, in the parking lots where the workers reside? Rumors, says Jerry. The two out-of-state guys facing the death penalty for the murder of the schoolteacher? Best left undiscussed.

★

"It was the perfect place to grow up," Barbara Sohlberg, one of Jackson's high school friends, says now, "because it wasn't a place where you had to

be careful of anything. There wasn't anything to worry about. I don't remember any trouble in the high school. Ever. No violence ever. We were
allowed to be free. What did we do? Anything we wanted. Wander from
one end of town to another because the whole town was safe." They
savored the fragrant sanctuary of Keenan's Drive Inn, "The House of
Broasted Kitchen." Dittsworth's Charcoal Grill and Bowling Center was
equally alluring.

Not all of Phil's classmates spent money to find entertainment. "There
were those small hills, outside of town," Barbara says, "and we'd park the
car on the side of the hill and watch the lightning storms coming in from
Montana. And we used to have a creek [the Little Muddy] with a little
bridge, and in spring and early summer we could jump off the bridge.

"We'd meet at the pool, the drugstore. Remember: North Dakota has
always been at least ten years behind the rest of the world. North Dakota
was in the forties when the rest of the world was in the fifties."

Supervisors at the dances in the armory basement would separate the
kids who danced too close. Phil kept a greater distance: He wasn't allowed
to dance.

"They were innocent times," Sohlberg says now. "There were a few
accidental pregnancies, but there were actual virgins coming out of high
school."

"It was just like *American Graffiti,*" recalls Pete Pornish. "We used to
date all the girls who were waitresses at the drive-in, where you could always sneak kids in in the trunk. He didn't get to do any of those things.
But he was always present. He'd go to things . . . he just wouldn't dance. He
was such a great guy, he took it all in stride."

But it was a tough row to hoe. Assembly of God adherents are taught to
not be sociable. Christ is your only true friend. "We lived a rigid life, and it
was difficult to make friends," Phil later wrote. "We were like the Apos-
tolic church."

Reading? The Bible, of course. *Reader's Digest.* The most enchanting
home tomes? The ink-fragrant blue-and-crimson leather-bound volumes

of the *World Book Encyclopedia,* offering glimpses of the globe out there: from atomic bombs to Zagreb, with Mohammad to Montevideo and everything in between. In the library at school, where he was free of scrutiny, the novels of Pasternak and Dostoevsky were available, but he couldn't penetrate them. Yet.

Like any small town a hundred miles from the next high school, Williston loved its sports. Jackson was drawn to the court and the pitcher's mound. Sports could help raze the wall that separated a PK from the lay kids. Especially one so self-consciously thin that he'd only swim in a T-shirt, even though the lean physique packed some power. "When we'd practice, you get around Bones, and he'd go up for a rebound and one of his elbows cracked you on the head, you'd think you were dead," says Pornish. "He was all kneecaps and elbows. But he was just one of those things coaches were drooling about from the start."

By Jackson's own admission, he lacked one skill: being a leader. "I wanted very much to be one, and I guess I tried too hard to be liked," he would write. He began to skip church. He threw himself into the drama club (as King Neptune in the Coyote Capers' production of *Festival of the Gods,* towering in toga, holding his mighty staff). He was Moose in *Bachelor Father.* He was in the Pep Club. The Letterman's Club. (There is, however, no record of his having ever hung with Linda Morken, the winner of the Betty Crocker Award.) He *was* part of the broadcasting club, Coyote on the Air, run by Barbara, whose hiply cut hair, stockings and high heels in the hallways, when the blondes were saddle-shoed, made something of a statement.

At the end of the day, Jackson began to drift to the hardwood. A key to the gym allowed him to sneak in and work on that hook. In a league with no shot clock, where passing was paramount, his long arms, able to steal the ball, were important. When games finish 15–11, a guy who can intercept a pass—let alone score 10—is sort of important.

Only his father would watch games; athletes were popular, and for Elisabeth, the popularity thing was not in line with her version of Christianity. Still, she was a loving mother, sewing extra fabric into the sleeves of his shirts—at the elbow (even in his teens, those elbows were becoming famous).

His junior year launched Phil Jackson: Now popping the jumper after the extra work, he scored 44 in the state semis. The loss in the finals? Against Rugby, Class A's smallest school, two hundred miles east, led by the state's true neon all-star, Paul Presthus.

"It was quite a rivalry," Presthus says now, as polite as polite can be, a retired financial advisor living in the suburbs of Minneapolis. "Since there aren't many cities in North Dakota, high school basketball was big. I played him often—twice a year, and then in the States. I guess that since we were the dominant players for our teams, the two dominant big people, we were identified with those teams, but good competition is always what you look for in any game."

How'd he play you?

"Well, he had the same physical characteristics that stood him so well in college and the pros. He was more of an inside player, where I could move inside and outside, but he had a very nice game and played on a good team. He had a good supporting cast, as I did as well. We were the so-called 'stars' of the teams, but I knew that even then, we felt strongly about the team concept."

Hence the term "North Dakota nice."

How Jackson ever got any schoolwork done during his senior year remains a mystery, what with six-hundred-mile round-trips in the coaches' and parents' cars through blizzards and ice storms. After hours on a highway so straight that you could take a ten-minute power nap at the wheel, wake up and not have even nudged the shoulder, he'd disembark and quickly stretch in a gym whose windows were closed to defy the cold—until sweat began to flow during the game and coat the court, whereupon the maintenance guys opened the windows to lessen the heat, at which point gusts of subarctic air would freeze the moisture on the court.

And at the dance in the town after every game? Phil had to stand there, on the sideline.

The Williston home-court advantage was significant. Some 1,500 packed the Coyotes' home gym (not yet enwrapped by the brick skin of the Phil Jackson Fieldhouse, whose lobby today features Jacksonalia of all shapes and stripes, from ties worn during Bulls games to Coyote, Sioux and Knicks jerseys—44, 35, 18).

The Coyote offense was a one-three-one, with Phil hovering beneath the net. Coach Bob Pederson, a good Christian, was not a great inspiration. He was a good strategy man, not exactly a fiery leader. His reactions to a loss in the locker room? "Well, boys, that's too bad." Nor did Phil look up to the martinet football coach, for whom Phil played fall of his senior year, as he would say, "because I wanted to prove my manhood."

Principal Leon B. Olson was the man who spoke to him, metaphorically and literally. Olson had a passion for the native flora and fauna, despite the landscape's emptiness. His direct message to Phil's graduating class in the yearbook: "There are certain basic needs of every individual who has to cope as effectively as possible with the future. An individual needs to be a free man, a convertible worker, a continuing student, a creative spirit, and a Believer in a Power greater than himself. . . . His mind must be free—free externally from demands for the orthodox and denial of access to information, free externally from situations imposed by ignorance and inadequate thought process. . . . His basic education should be of such broad applicability that he can enter a variety of occupations and be in a position to profit from additional training if the need arises . . . equipped to learn on his own and aware of the necessity of doing so. As Margaret Mead said, 'In today's world, no one can complete an education.'"

It was the finest parade that North Dakota Route 2 had ever provided— although probably its only one. On a late afternoon in February 1963, the road had some traffic. The night before, the Coyotes had taken the States back east in Grand Forks, beating Rugby. In the final, Phil was within two points of beating Presthus's state record of 44 points in a tournament game when Pederson sat him down—and refused to let him back in. ("I'm glad it happened the way it did," Jackson would later say. "I realized that in the long run records don't count for anything." Well, it sounded good at the time.)

They were a good seventy miles from Williston when they saw a couple of cars on the shoulder, honking their horns. Then a few more, pulling out to pass the team, escorts for the royalty. "Pretty soon it was like a caravan," recalls guard Myron Oyloe. "Everyone was overwhelmed. It was unbelievable."

The destination? The armory. The problem? They were all asked to get up and speak. Athletes are seldom the most eloquent of spontaneous orators. Even class president Oyloe found himself at a loss: "Looking back, I'm sure what I said didn't make any sense at all. We all got up there and mumbled a few words.

"And then Philip got up there, and he was the only one who had the presence of mind to thank our parents. To thank the coaches. To thank the fans. And speak of all those things that none of us had remembered to. In later years, as I thought about how things had evolved afterward with him, I realized that we'd seen something special there. And that moment has stuck with me through all those years."

College recruiting in the Dakotas wasn't heavy; he'd had little national attention. Denison's Lefty Driesell was interested. Minnesota, a D-1 program, brought him in for a visit. "We visited [Minnesota] together during the recruitment period," Paul Presthus recalls. "I was pretty sure I was going to be going there. I wanted to play at the highest level. I had a feeling when we visited, though, that Phil was leaning toward North Dakota, although he didn't communicate that, which didn't surprise me . . . he's a deep thinker, but he doesn't always communicate."

Jackson would admit that much of the decision resulted from knowing that in Minnesota, if both he and Presthus were Gophers, comparisons would be intense and unending.

Down in Fargo, by his own account, North Dakota State had already offered Jackson $100 under the table in exchange for occasionally hanging out with jock-sniffing alumni. This was not Phil's kind of game.

At UND the ethics of the coach were obviously unimpeachable. The son of a marine drill sergeant, Bill Fitch had visited the victors' locker room to press the flesh. The team was readying for the tournament banquet at the Bronze Boot Steakhouse and Lounge, with its blinking neon boot beckoning beef lovers from miles around.

Trouble was, Jackson hadn't even brought a coat. "So I gave him my overcoat, and took him to the banquet," Fitch says now. "That's as aggressive [as a recruiter] as I ever got." At the banquet, Fitch gave a speech at the dais, then called Jackson over and pretended to handcuff him. "I'm not letting you get away," he said.

When Fitch had to drive across the state to get the official signing, the snow was flying on barren Route 2. "I was the only car to get across the state that day." Fitch laughs now. "It was nothing but snow, just miserable. If you saw any other cars, it was because you passed them in a ditch."

By the end of the day, though, two of the more intriguing future figures of the NBA had shaken hands. It was time for the younger one to head east.

THREE

There's another thing about flatness, especially when it's frozen: If you hit it with momentum, you can keep going. And going. Without friction, you can put a whole lot of distance between you and whatever's receding in the rearview mirror.

A six-foot-eight seventeen-year-old, Jackson, schooled in creationism, lined up for registration at the University of North Dakota, registered for some pre-law courses and was assigned to a stolid red-brick dorm called Walsh, which, unlike the girls' dorms, did not have a 10:00 curfew.

A few days later, at the convocation ceremony, an honorary doctorate was given to the guest speaker: John F. Kennedy. In seven weeks, he'd be dead. Just as convulsing to the young preachers' son was science class: The concept of evolution was tough to wrap your head around when you'd been raised to believe that the world had been created in six days.

To his eventual gratification, Jackson's ineligibility to play sports as a seventeen-year-old allowed him to begin to step outside of the jock mold, start to put the Pentecostal label behind him and return to the mind-engaging texts that had baffled him in earlier years. Before long, pre-law was a thing of the past. He fashioned a curriculum for a degree in psychology, philosophy and religion.

"My head was swimming with ideas that challenged my core beliefs," he recalled, citing first and foremost the works of Plato, whose cave metaphor couldn't have hit more fertile soil, with its thesis that people spend their lives shackled in caves (church?), mistaking shadow for substance—

until, released into sunshine (reality), they finally come to know them-selves.

His first exposure to meditation, in a class on Eastern religion, fur-thered the thought that self-realization was possible—and that the truth is in the moment, not in the Bible. That first year allowed him to mature, as well as absorb some pop-culture non-Lutheran music, thanks to the radio station down south in Fargo broadcasting from atop the nine-story sky-scraper of the Black Building, as well as hanging with another athlete who didn't have a car, African American Jimmy Hester out of Iowa. For Phil Jackson, borders were being breached.

In the meantime, Fitch was going through some tough times over in the gothic UND Field House. Sioux basketball hadn't won the conference in a decade. Students who stopped by were often simply taking the warmer route to the hockey rink. Sioux hockey, having just won the Frozen Four, was the pinnacle of entertainment in Les Grandes Fourches.

In Montana, a majestic mountain was always peeking over your shoulder to remind you of God's wonders. In North Dakota's eastern reaches, the horizons have retreated about as far as they can go, slathered in sunlight that seems unfiltered, as if coming from a source purer than anywhere else. Then the landscape also speaks of *men* here, not mountains and gods. Spend a few days amid the sunflowers, and you'll start to think the oppo-site of that old saw about one life not meaning a hill of beans—that out here one man could make a difference. "I would never have become presi-dent without my experiences in North Dakota," said Teddy Roosevelt, who'd ranched here a few years out of Harvard.

In a two-dimensional landscape, a man rising above the pack could start to see that he had some . . . well . . . standing. And it *was* two-dimensional: As Phil's friend and future NBA colleague Jimmy Rodgers puts it now, "In the East, if you go out and lie down, your nose is the high-est elevation for ten miles." That's because the SAC base—with the B-52s and the nukes—was a full sixteen miles west.

★

In his first year without sport, Jackson found himself footloose. He didn't feel comfortable unless he was "moving"; his head was bouncing among "all sorts of socialist philosophy."

Off campus? "Searching the churches"—trying to balance organized religion with sudden, boundless intellectual freedom. The Assembly of God churches in town began to disappoint him—redolent of low socioeconomic status and low intellect. Not to mention the poor grammar of the sermonizers.

"The blossom had definitely fallen off the rose of spirituality," he would write—but should have written "conventional religion." Because it was now that he came across William James's *The Varieties of Religious Experience*—a unique exploration of the nature of faith and how and when one finds it. In his thorough study of "the science of religion" through case studies of people upon whom conversion was visited in diverse and unpredictable ways, James spoke of how a shift in "personal energy" could take someone to a higher place—as if something that had been buried could be disinterred: one's individual self. James believed faith could be a force in your life without having to be strictly labeled and littered with presuppositions.

The college student supplemented James with the standard-bearers of the modern-era search for the nature of identity: Camus, Kierkegaard, Heidegger, all sensing that everything and anything should be questioned. Not for Jackson the rationalists and empiricists of centuries past, trying to find the "true" nature of worldly reality; he was searching within himself for his own path, his own reality, emerging from the cave of Pentecostalism into the light of the existential thinkers.

If Heidegger's required reading, *Being and Time,* was as dense as a thicket, it laid the groundwork for Jackson's lifelong habit of asking questions, turning down unforeseen paths, searching where no one else in the jockocracy had thought to look. A new friend named Mike Her Many Horses, from the Pine Ridge Lakota Sioux tribe in the southwest corner of

South Dakota, led him toward beliefs, he would eventually see, that over-lapped with his blossoming Buddhism in many ways.

Sportswise, Jackson hoped for a baseball career. He possessed no excep-tional talent for basketball other than height and desire; his fastball was a weapon on the baseball field, especially when it was wild. Before his Sioux career was over, Phil would pitch a one-hitter against Arkansas State after his brother Joe, a psychologist at the University at Buffalo with something of a New Age bent to his therapeutic approach, had hypno-tized him, apparently to lessen his anxiety about being able to hit the strike zone.

The big fish from small Williston Pond was finally able to suit up as a basketball player as a sophomore under third-year coach Fitch, the leg-endary disciplinarian still three years from his first gig in the NBA, where he would win two Coach of the Year awards (one more than Jackson). Today Fitch would like to clarify: "Discipline is important," he told me, "but only when you use it when you *need* to use it. Any time you're building a new program, one of the first things that has to be there for the founda-tion of what you're going to do is basic discipline.

"A lot of the time, it's not as harsh as it seems to be; it's just what's been missing where some of them came from. I didn't have to discipline [Jack-son] too much because he was a hard worker. That was the result of being raised by two great parents."

Fitch was the first to bring this sentiment but hardly the last. Fu-ture coaches Frank Hamblen and Rodgers—a collective fifteen years by his side as assistants—would cite the same thing: the upbringing. Fitch repeatedly emphasized Jackson's willingness to listen to, and re-tain, and then practice—"You could correct him, and you only had to do it once."

"I think he had a good mom," says Diane Mast, the wife of Eddie Mast, one of Jackson's closest friends in the NBA. "The family was a Christ-centered family. The interpretation of that gets so misguided, but when people live it every day, there's a value in everybody's spirit. Spirit has no flesh. The only flesh we have is what we carry. It's housed in female, it's housed in male. And I think there had to be tremendous respect by Phil's dad for Phil's mother. So that was a lesson taught, not like, 'You will respect me,' but as a lived way of being. The sixties being what they were, fraught with 'anything is OK,' to go from structure to no discipline needs that background of respect.

"I don't think Phil ever left that discipline. When you respect your parents, you never want to embarrass them, and if he had things he did or was curious about, he was never going to jeopardize what he had . . . for a flimsy roll of the dice one night."

For Fitch, what emerged in Jackson was his obvious sense of being a member of a team—"not just because he was well liked, and a lot of fun, with a good sense of humor. As a coach, you're always looking for an extra five minutes out of a ball club, and you're always looking for one to get everyone to go the extra mile. That was him."

After practices, Fitch would take Phil and his two point guards to a separate court for drills designed to help the guards learn how to beat a pressing defense: If they could get shots off against Phil's Spiderman arms, the various limbs seeming to unfold of their own accord, they could beat anyone.

And with Jackson, Fitch's third-year UND team turned the corner. Junior guard Paul Pederson was a natural: swift, agile, all-seeing. Phil? A "tiger on the boards," Fitch recalls. Thanks to Phil, the points piled up, if less than gracefully. The only extant photo of Phil dunking as a Fighting Sioux shows his hands curled around the rim after he's dunked the ball, the rest of him hanging straight down like a prisoner hanging from a dungeon wall. Those weren't dunking shoulders.

With Jackson starting as a sophomore, the "Nodaks" tore through the North Central Conference: 22-4 in the regular season, unbeaten in the conference. Jackson's flailing style, wherein his center of gravity seemed to shift at a whim, earned him the nickname the Mop, because he spent so much time on the floor.

After coasting through the D-II regionals, Fitch's men were derailed by a Southern Illinois guard from a segregated high school in Atlanta who'd learned to play basketball on a dirt court. Despite football offers— he was a quarterback—Walt "Clyde" Frazier had opted for basketball.

A few months later, anchoring the pitching staff of one Pinky Kraft, Phil put together a 5-1, 2.30-ERA record, despite weather cancellation of sixteen conference games due to snow, sleet, ice, toads and locusts. Why stay with baseball? A fastball and a deceptive delivery: "a lefthander whose long arms provided him with a confusing motion as he uncoiled," according to an in-house history of UND sports. On the other hand, as Fitch would later say, "Phil couldn't find home plate with a Geiger counter." Teammate Jerry Schultz, a three-year all-NCC baseball selection, laughs now. "He was wild. He was all arms and legs."

The next winter? Typically "Nodak." Fitch still owns a photo of a local standing on his roof, with his boxer dog, holding on to his chimney, his house buried, and vividly recalls having to get to the airport and copping a ride with a neighbor who had a tractor on skis. Nothing beat the blizzard of blizzards that trapped him in the field house. "I had two Canadian kids as student managers, and they knew nothing about basketball. One was named Sid. Sid and I got snowbound in the field house for three days, just the two of us. You can look it up." (I didn't have to. Pete Pornish recalls it vividly, and confirms: "Three days.")

"So to pass the time Sid and I'd play Horse, which was always a sure win for me. One game, Sid said, after I hit a few, 'My car against yours.' 'OK,' I say. And I was the owner of a car at the end of the night.

"Then they finally got us out, everything back to normal. I'm sitting at my desk. Sid comes in and throws his car keys on my desk, and says, 'It's yours.' I say, 'Come on, that was just a joke.' He says, 'No, it wasn't.' He'd already seen that when they were trying to plow us out, the snowplow had more or less cut his car in half.' "

"It wasn't so bad," Pornish recalls now. "Everyone in the fraternity went out to all the liquor stores with toboggans and loaded them with all the beer and liquor we could carry."

In Phil's junior year, Fitch molded the team into a true conference power. Behind Paul Pederson, and Phil and guard Jerry Schultz, Fitch found a way to mold disparate personalities. "God made us all different," Fitch says now. "But there's always something they share. It's the coach's job to find it."

By now, Fitch had brought in a new coach to help get his boys over the top—the Hawkeye graduate Rodgers. "Come on up and do some grad work," he said to Jimmy, a slick guard. Not only could he practice with the team, he could show it how the big boys in Division I played. And now Phil was playing for two men who would eventually be hired as head coaches by a cigar-smoking oligarch named Auerbach.

"Even then Phil was destined to be what he became," Rodgers tells me now. "At the time, I didn't think he was interested. But he sure had that strong competitive instinct."

And by now folks weren't just stopping by the field house to warm up. (Befitting the old-days balance between academics and sport, the Gothic lettering of GYMNASIUM above the main entrance is still the only clue that it isn't an academic building.)

On game night, the basketball court was brought in to cover the dirt track-and-field floor. Portable bleachers plugged both ends and extended the mezzanine seats down to courtside. The history book of Sioux athletics says the place could fit seven thousand (if some fans hung from the rafters, maybe), whose enthusiasm would guarantee a victory.

Then, the climate could intimidate as well. "We'd bring in some teams for home-and-home series," Rodgers recalls, "and if it was, say, Chico State, they had to warm up on the entry side of the field house, with the students coming in through open doors and the wind whipping in: thirty below."

This was the year when the Fighting Sioux would begin to be known as a hoop power as well as a hockey attraction. "Since it was a big agricultural community—except for the SAC base—the whole town revolved around sports," says Pornish, "and the city really began to support that team, especially with their pregame show."

Fitch allowed the team to be loose? "Oh, people forget how funny he was. The team used to do crazy stuff. During warm-ups, sometimes they pretended they were football players, hiking the basketball, with someone handing off and running through the line and jumping over the short guys and dunking it. They had all these routines. Fitch loved it."

But there was a time for fun and a time for the game. "The warm-up was also time for running our offense," says Schultz, "which was anytime you came down the court; whether you were two guards or three, you went straight to a spot, and then if you had to go to another spot, you knew what to do there, too."

(Triangle, anyone?)

"Everyone was always moving. We weren't wasting ten seconds to set up, because we might catch the other team out of position."

Phil? "He'd beat other guys down the court to get to the right-hand side, then a drop step, then taking the pass, crossing and shooting the left-hand hook. He could run the fast break like a guard, too."

★

The Sioux took the conference. Fortuitously, the Division II Midwest Regional was to be played in Grand Forks. Despite one of the worst storms in state history (four feet of snow, drifts reaching the telephone wires, says one account), the trains were running. In the title game, Jackson scored a UND-record 44 points against Valparaiso (supplemented by 16 rebounds).

But in the nationals, down in balmy Evansville, Southern Illinois beat UND again, even with Frazier on academic probation.

Jackson was named a first-team Division II Little All-American. The most enduring photograph of the year remains a portrait of number 34 flanked by a smiling Fitch and a grinning Rodgers. Unlike his Boy Scout posture in the Coyote yearbook back in high school, this time Jackson has clasped his hands behind his back, his head cocked slightly to the side, wearing an ironic kind of smile, his eyelids slightly closed. Between the two perfect-coach pose-and-grins, the look comes off as "This guy you're looking at, this Little All-American whose name will be in *Parade* magazine in the *Minot Herald*? He's a whole lot more than the guy you see wearing number 34 in this PR shot."

Or as a friend refers to that smile, "Like he's swallowed the canary just to get it out of the way."

Next year's 1965–66 team is remembered on the banks of the Red River as being one of its greatest. The secret, Rodgers says, was hardly the coaching. "As Red [Auerbach, his future boss] used to say, there are three things you need to win. First is talent. Second is talent. And third is talent."

It was Phil's team now, and he let it go to his head. After the Sioux were humiliated by DePaul in Chicago on December 3 in the season's second game, Jackson stomped off into the wind, found a bar, picked up a girl, and arrived back at the hotel two hours late. "I was swinging by then and didn't worry at all about being with women," he would later write. "I was cast as the super-stud."

Fitch stripped him of the captaincy. On a campus where, by all accounts, there was never really a BMOC, he'd begun to act like one. Fitch's disciplinary philosophy—"Use it when you need to"—paid off immediately. The Sioux took Loyola apart the next night. During the season, Jackson scored more than 50 twice. As would be the pattern of Phil's career, a slow start led to a middle-season comfort zone and then, with postseason looming, a ramp-up—as in the game against the University of Illinois-Springfield, when he scored 50 and took in 24 rebounds.

In the meantime, his immersion in the freedoms of college life didn't translate into a commonality with the seeds of revolution being sown on the coasts. He was supportive of bombing North Vietnam. Drugs? He stayed away from pot: "What if my true nature got out and, like the Wolf in *Steppenwolf,* never got back in?" he would later recall thinking. But he enjoyed his beer. And by his own admission, the girls.

"Phil kind of spread those big wings," says Rodgers now.

"Well," says Barbara Sohlberg, "he'd been *brainwashed,* the poor guy."

"I was totally involved in dualistic Western thought," he would recall, "and could find no intellectual home for myself."

But in the Division II Midwest Regional, UND ran into a wall in the semis in Normal, Oklahoma, where Louisiana Tech won going away (how could Phil ever prevail in a town named Normal?) thanks, in part, screamed the *Grand Forks Herald,* to "three unbelievably bad personal foul calls on Jackson." The first three came in the first six minutes, the fourth before the half. He still managed to score 21.

In the stands at this tournament sat two savvy NBA scouts: Red Holzman of the foundering Knicks and Jerry Krause, representing the Bullets, heading into their first season in Baltimore. After the game, Holzman walked into Fitch's office.

"Red asked, 'Can he play for me?' 'Yes, he can,' I said," Fitch recalls now. "Red turned around and walked out."

The consolation-game box score notes that Philip Jackson scored 51. By then, Krause and Holzman had escaped, on the same plane east. This is a retelling of the salient points of the conversation in the air, as Holzman recounted it in his memoir, *Red on Red*:

Krause, poker-faced: "So, what'd you think?"

Holzman, shrugging: "Eh."

"Yeah," says Krause, delighted; he'd be available in the third round for sure. Red hadn't seemed to be impressed.

★

Fitch left for Bowling Green: no snow. But not before the final ceremony, when UND took the day off to say good-bye to the coach who had turned the program around. Four years earlier, in the armory in Williston, Jackson had made his teammates proud. This time he didn't seize the day with a speech but with a book that Fitch literally keeps within reach of the phone: *Leaves of Gold: An Anthology of Prayers, Memorable Phrases, Inspirational Verse, and Prose.*

"Of all the things I have," Fitch says now, "I always end up looking at the book. It's got everything in it. My favorite is Browning." And here, I swear, Fitch leaves through the leaves, and finds it: "Grow old along with me! / The best is yet to be, / The last of life, for which the first was made: / Our times are in His hand / Who saith 'A whole I planned, / Youth shows but half; trust God: see all, nor be afraid!' "

(Jacksonologists, note: The final phrase, if it represents Jackson, means that the godhead is not to be feared, as the parents advised, just listened to.)

"They all signed it, so that's proof that they could all read and write." Fitch laughs now. But then he's back at it: "There's a chapter on faith. The definition is 'That which refines the pure essence of things from the circumstances around you.' There's another: 'The only way to have a friend is to be one.' And 'The Bible is a window in the prison of hope through which we look into eternity.' "

When I suggest that his choice of volume seems to indicate that Phil was still grounded in some of the axioms that his parents had instilled, Fitch laughs. "All I know is that I was one of the first to get a book. He gave out books for his players, too. That's why he could have been a great book salesman."

Rimshot.

*

Three weeks after the bestowal of the gift, NBA draft day turned out to be a very good one for its giver. The Knicks had limped into the playoffs with a 36-45 record before being ousted by the Celtics. But the Knick roster held promise; Holzman's scouting had produced Willis Reed, Cazzie Russell and Bill Bradley, although Bradley wouldn't be around until 1967 (someone named Rhodes had drafted him in England).

Detroit owned two of the top four picks. The Knicks would pick fifth. The Pistons took Jimmy Walker of Providence. Baltimore took Earl Monroe out of D-II Winston-Salem. The Bulls took Clem Haskins, and Detroit drafted Sonny Dove, "the Big Indian," out of St. John's. Frazier was available. The hundreds of thousands of miles of scouting over the last nine years, with the bottle of scotch (for medicinal purposes) and the rumpled raincoat, had paid off for Red. No matter how many courses he might have failed at Eastern Illinois, no one was ever court-smarter than Clyde.

In the second round, Krause's intelligence led the Bullets to pick Jimmy Jones out of Grambling. Four picks later, with the fifth pick in the second round, the Knicks took the Pentecostalist out of North Dakota. Holzman had sandbagged the little guy.

"I saw a lot of potential in him," Holzman would write, "even though he didn't look that effective in his senior year. However, he'd lost 20 pounds due to a virus. Other scouts didn't know this and gave up on him as a prospect." (Jackson himself made no mention of said virus in his own memoir. It's not hard to imagine Red asking, "Why you so thin, kid?" and the Pentecostalist doing a little fibbing.)

The absence of stars in Jackson's eyes allured Holzman as much as his talent. A first-generation American of Russian and Romanian roots who pushed a rag wagon through the streets of the garment district in Manhattan for $29 a week as a kid, Holzman was impressed by Jackson's worth ethic, his manners and—no small thing to Holzman—his work as a summer chaplain with the American Legion's local Boys State chapter. The kid's parents, Holzman thought, had obviously done their job.

Red flew back west to sign Jackson, but to save the Knicks money, they met down in Fargo, where John Lindsay, mayor of New York City, was giving a speech to . . . a Boys State chapter.

"Can you imagine?" Holzman said. "The mayor of New York is here and everybody knows it. And you're here getting signed and nobody knows it."

Red's later account of their presigning conversation:

Phil: "I'm very pleased that the Knicks thought so highly of me, but I'm having some second thoughts, Mr. Holzman. My original plans were to attend graduate school and become a minister. I still think about that."

Red: "I respect your frankness. But you're a young guy with a whole life ahead of you. Sign with the Knicks now. I have the contract with me. You'll be playing out of a great city and you'll have a fine career. And when you're finished with pro ball, you'll still be young enough to do whatever you want to do."

Phil: "I guess I can count on you, Mr. Holzman, to help me over the rough spots in New York."

The one-year deal was for $13,500. (That'd be $93,000 today . . . when a second-round pick, in a trade in advance of the draft, is worth $1.5 million.) Later, Phil would explain why he'd decided to stay in the game: "I expected that the adventure might . . . help me to locate the center of my soul."

Holzman flew back to New York. Jackson gathered his teammates, bought a keg of beer and reeled up a game film Holzman had left: Knicks-Lakers, October 28, 1966: a typical game in the big-time arena into which the kid had been welcomed. But they couldn't believe their eyes. They saw selfish shot selection, no set plays, and a lot of physical strength—especially when the game stopped being a game. Knick center Willis Reed, in his third year out of Grambling, having been manhandled in the paint, found himself being piled on by several Lakers—until, like some comic-book superhero, Reed shed his attackers and, one by one, started to take them out.

He punched John Block in the nose. Henry Finkel took one to the head. Rudy LaRusso was dumped to the court.

A man of few words, Red had decided to let a film tell Phil what, exactly, he was getting into. Subsequent years in New York would show that he'd absorbed the film tutorial.

Phil had a pretty good spring, all things considered. Lots of cash, and a prize steady. "[My girlfriend] Maxine and I were interested in intellectual pursuits," Jackson would write. "She was a good-looking girl, and really, really smart." Says a friend now, "You just knew she was someone Phil would gravitate to."

Forty-five years later: Did any of those Sioux see these eleven rings coming? "No idea," guard and baseball star Jerry Schultz laughs. "None of us did. I mean, the guy's a great guy. But nobody would have predicted what's happened. Once he got it going [as a coach], I'm thinking, *The guy has to be a great philosopher or psychologist . . . to coach those guys in the modern NBA.*"

FOUR

At the Northwest arrival ramp, the kid was hard to miss. "It looks like they squeezed him into the suit jacket," Selma Holzman said, "and forgot to take the hanger out." They piled into Red's new '67 Chevy convertible (Knick owner and Brooklyn kid Ned Irish must have thrown Red a bonus after draft day) and headed west on Queens Boulevard. Phil looked up at a pedestrian overpass to see a kid throw a pitch. The rock shattered the windshield.

The scout wisely drove on. "Sorry about the welcome wagon. But if you can take that, you'll do fine here."

He checked into the New Yorker Hotel, across from the strange cereal bowl saucer rising into the sky, nine months away from its first basketball game. In the meantime, he'd be debuting in slightly different surroundings.

On his first night in town, Red asked journeyman Neil Johnson to show him the town. Johnson said he had a date, shoved a $20 bill at Phil and suggested he go to the circus. Phil went back to the New Yorker, perhaps wondering whether the Phillips 66 team might have been a wiser choice, instead of this new world, featuring, eight blocks to the north, Times Square's needles, hookers and porn.

Holzman found Phil a new tutor: a New Yorker to the bone. They couldn't have been more diametrically opposed, rootswise. Mike Riordan, the

Knicks' twelfth-rounder from Providence the year before, grew up in Queens, son of a Railway Express guy out of that old Penn Station, working the graveyard shift. The highlight of Mike's all-hoop, all-the-time life? High school Catholic League games . . . in the *Garden*.

It wasn't just the intensity of Jackson's game that impressed Riordan. It was how comfortable he was immediately upon meeting Riordan's pack of friends. "He became one of the guys, real quick," Riordan says now, over coffee near his farm on Maryland's Eastern Shore. "I notice right away: Phil is very adaptable." As Buddha said, every moment's a new life.

Jackson moved in with Riordan in Great Neck, "a working-class community—row houses, narrow streets," Riordan says. "We'd play schoolyard ball every night at a public school, go out for a couple drinks. There were a lot of blue-collar, working-class neighborhood bars. This isn't the club scene of Manhattan. This is not the luxury suites at Staples Center. This is down-and-dirty neighborhood bars, and Phil, I swear, after the first introductions, he's just one of the guys. He *fits*.

"Then we'd go down to Long Beach on Long Island, play some ball there, then hang out at a beachside bar," Riordan recalls. "Those games were *real* intense. Phil got it right off. Held his own."

What he didn't get was the first *real* borough, on that isle of Mannahatta, as the natives had called it. He'd gone from true community, wherein the most important people were the folks in the house on each side of you, to a place wherein only the strong survived. "We're walking around in Manhattan early that first year," Riordan remembers, "and there's a bum in the street laying in the gutter. I don't even notice the guy. Phil goes, 'What are we gonna do about this?' I go, 'What?' 'This guy laying here,' he goes. I go, 'Phil, he's a bum. Keep on moving.' He's thinking, *What's wrong with this insensitive, inconsiderate New Yorker?* I said, 'Phil, it's none of your business. Get this: We're like millions of rats in a cage here, and the sooner you get that mentality, the more at ease and comfortable you'll be in this environment, OK?' I can see he isn't used to this at all."

His prior metropolis housed thirty-nine thousand. This one counted more than seven million rats in its tribe. "I was shocked at how everybody's hostility seemed to be so close to the surface," he'd write. "I couldn't stand the terrific amount of tension that was in the air."

No wonder he took so quickly to the Catskills, where he, Riordan and Johnson held a series of clinics in private Jewish camps that summer to drum up business. They comprised a curious triangle. Johnson thought his companions were rednecks. Riordan wasn't a fan of the steeply angled mountains.

But the Plainsman took to the mountain range, even if its peaks were on a human scale, not a godlike one. At the foot of these mountains sat hamlets with Mohawk names like Willowemac and Shawangunk, fertile land for Jackson, and not only for the Native American heritage—the camps happily struck him as being like small universities.

Before training camp, though, he had one more thing to accomplish. He flew back to North Dakota and got married. He and Maxine had, he later said, "talked about getting married, but we rarely talked about love." She would become pregnant with Elizabeth Jackson, and in March 1968, the papers would show a PR picture of a smiling Phil greeting Maxine with their infant outside the hospital. His jacket's too small. His smile is a tad posed.

He'd played in some intimate venues but never in a place like the old Garden in its forty-sixth year—a dark, cigar-smoky, beer-and-popcorn-butter-perfumed garage with boxing in its backbone and a back-scent of four decades of blood, sweat and tears invisibly painted on its dark, spooky walls.

Twenty-two years after VJ Day, thirty-four after the place had been packed to the girders for the Boycott Nazi Germany rally on March 27, 1933, Jackson pulled on the number 18 jersey and scored five points. Heard some boos, too. This was a betting parlor as much as an athletic emporium. With its overhanging balconies, its backboards attached to the mezzanine by wire, it was like playing basketball under a microscope. The old girl had five months of life to go when Phil first stepped onto its court. In the early sixties, when the woeful Knicks would file in before a game, sometimes the boxing ring would be still up.

"They were tough fans," recalls Darrell Imhoff, a Knick in the early sixties. "One game I got in my rookie year, got in and played hard, got in and scored a few—and I got booed. I thought, *What the heck?* I didn't know that they were such a heavy betting crowd. I was screwing up the point spread."

In the next six games—all losses—Phil amassed twenty points. But this was anything but a dismal start; the streak paved the way to the coaching replacement that would change Phil's life. Under coach Dick McGuire, a team expected to be much improved instead proved erratic, despite the arrival of their two immaculately clean-cut rookies (Frazier a half-inch of hair, Phil's short and parted neatly on the left). Reed, Dick Barnett, Walt Bellamy, Dick Van Arsdale, Howie Komives, Cazzie Russell and in December Bradley should have been a formula for success. But Bradley was at first a disappointment, missing too many shots on a team that had no real offensive system.

Meantime, the city's fans were beating Jackson's outweighed psyche to a pulp. "They seemed like vultures, picking at my flesh and demanding to know everything about my private life," he would write. They hounded him on the streets, where he was hard to miss. His skin was as thick as a moth's wing. He'd find refuge on the subway out at their place in Queens— sometimes. Three months after the riots in Newark claimed twenty-six lives, on the way into the game a large black man cleaning his nails with a knife looked at the North Dakotan and said, "You white motherfucker, I'll empty your guts out." He was not in Kansas anymore, Toto.

The fans, skeptical that their number two (when the draft went twelve rounds deep) was a thin D-II forward, wanted a big guy with a touch. ("I always say that the most dangerous play in basketball," Brooklyn kid

Chris Rock once said, "is the open white man. A white guy open behind the arc is frightening. The ball's going in, he's knocking it down.")

For New Yorkers, that tradition had been Komives and Van Arsdale, and later Bradley and Dave DeBusschere. Phil would never play white. Or black, either. More like a marionette whose puppeteer would pause to down the occasional tequila shot as the strings tangled up.

Now seven-time all-star McGuire had lost his team. "Former great players expect their teams to perform as well as they once did," Holzman once said, "and they get frustrated when their players don't perform at that level. Fringe players who go on to coach are naturally a bit more patient." Most baffling to Jackson, coming out of a Fitch-Rodgers tradition, was the lack of discipline. Players smoked cigarettes and wolfed hot dogs during halftimes of games in which they were getting blown out.

After their twenty-second loss in thirty-seven games, McGuire was out. Red was in—but only, he told GM Eddie Donovan, if he could return to scouting at season's end. He didn't take to the spotlight very well. Maybe if he hadn't been called Red, while another Red was earning deification in the northeast, history would have seen Holzman the coach for what he was: Coach Phil Jackson two decades earlier, without superstars or as many rings but gifted at reaching and motivating every one of his charges. In every subsequent Jackson ring, there was more than a little Holzman.

As a kid, Holzman would watch the Brooklyn Jewels host the Harlem Renaissance Five, known to history as the Rens, arriving at Arcadia Hall in Bed-Stuy in a $10,000 customized bus—in the middle of the Depression. It was a heady taste of what the game could bring to a man who played his cards (and his game) right, as the Rens did: disciplined and unselfish.

At City College, Holzman was a five-ten guard, learning at the feet of legendary coach Nat Holman, whose coaching attitude was to adopt a stance of "distant nearness" to his players; he knew where to occupy that elusive DMZ between "player's coach" and autocrat. Holman played an offense he called "five moving pivots"—no one held the ball for long. (See *triangle*.)

After a military-service pause (coaching Rizzuto's Ragamuffins in a Norfolk, Virginia, "morale unit" against a team coached by someone named Pee Wee), a part-time gig with the New York Gothams led to a full-time job with the Rochester Royals of the National Basketball League, whose owner, Les Harrison, needed a Jew for audience appeal. Wearing leather knee guards with felt linings, Red debuted against Sheboygan in Edgerton Park Arena, built in 1892 as a drill hall for delinquent boys, now best known for the exit door under one basket through which energetic players who'd driven too hard to the hoop would vault out into the snow-banks.

A two-time all-star, Red roomed with a guy named Dolly King: by some accounts the first black player in pro ball. In cities where Dolly was not allowed in the hotel dining room, he and Red would eat in their room. Dolly breakfasted on a raw egg stirred with sherry. Red had coffee.

In 1948, the front-running Basketball Association of America deigned to absorb four NBL teams: Fort Wayne, Rochester, Indianapolis and Minneapolis (and George Mikan). In '51 Red picked up his first coaching gig, the Milwaukee, then St. Louis, Hawks, and famously shouted at Bob Pettit, "Hit somebody, or you're going home to Baton Rouge!"—whereupon Pettit used an elbow (see *Jackson, Phil*) to clock one Vern Mikkelsen.

His coaching philosophy: Move the ball, hit the open man. "I let the players know their roles." They drafted Bill Russell in '56, but the average attendance for a game in Kiel Auditorium was less than the place had drawn for the second annual International Alcoholics Anonymous Conference the year before, so the owner traded Russell to the Celtics for Cliff ("Li'l Abner") Hagan and Ed ("Easy Ed") Macauley, who would later, as a deacon in the Catholic Church, write a book of sayings called *Homilies Alive,* the best known of which is "When you are not practicing, remember, someone somewhere else is practicing, and when you meet them, they will win." Unfortunately, apparently, he was right, at least when it came to Russell and Macauley.

Red got fired after a 14-19 start. When his friend Fuzzy Levane got the Knick head-coaching job in '58, Holzman became his scout: the perfect calling. "I was always concerned about guts, attitude, intelligence and unselfishness," he wrote. "I tried to find out how willing players were to sacrifice for a team."

His first head-coaching success was guiding Los Leones de Ponce from 1964 to 1966 in Puerto Rico, where he won three titles—a decade after a coach named Tex Winter had led the Lions to two of his own, and two decades before Jackson would follow in their footsteps.

Now, with McGuire's firing in 1967, Knick discipline changed dramatically. If a player was late, Holzman would fine him. He once let the plane take off without a tardy Bellamy. The discipline worked on Dick Barnett, former Laker, until then underachieving. He was now scoring 18 a game. Frazier now frequently spelled Komives; Red let Phil know what his exact role was, and he thrived. Having seen Jackson score 26 in an exhibition game, he began to give Phil more minutes. Team now overshadowed stats: As Jackson would later say, "The Knicks had to become *less* talented to be a better team."

Practices were now intense. The first forty-five minutes featured pressing defense: no plays, just the second unit—Jackson, Van Arsdale, Nate "the Snake" Bowman, Frazier and Emmette Bryant (Riordan was down in Allentown of the Eastern League) hounding the starters. Jackson's role? Befuddle in the passing lanes.

"The tendency on a pass is to whiz it by the defender's head," says Charley Rosen now, the future Boswell to Jackson's Johnson, "because his instinct is to get out of the way. But Phil had incredibly quick hands; he'd get that hand up there faster than anyone I ever saw and deflect the pass."

Playing someone else's wide-open offense—like Fitch's at Grand Forks—instead of Holzman's half-court pass-till-someone's-open offense, Jackson might have had better stats. But Holzman was hardly a my-way-or-the-highway guy. The defenses were Red's, but he'd often ask the likes of Bradley and DeBusschere during time-outs what they wanted to run on offense.

"The thing I liked about Red was the fact that he involved you in a lot of the decision making," says Monroe. "Whether he took it or not, the fact that he asked for it is what counted. By doing things like that, it got you to think more about how the game was played. Now you're thinking of the game in a different way. Now you're becoming more a student of the game. Inadvertently you pick up so much from just being around him, his demeanor and so forth, you, I guess, morph yourself into his being."

Team rules regarding practices and games were tough, but away from home, Holzman used the John Madden philosophy: a long leash breeds respect. If you get lucky on the road, he'd say, sleep *under* the covers; we don't need a cold the next day. There was no ban on drinking in the airport bar before the flight, no ban on drinking on the flight, no ban on poker games at thirty thousand feet in which Phil once lost $400 (that's $3,000 now) to Barnett in a hand of seven-card stud. (Money never changed hands in flight; civilians might be watching. Once Jerry Lucas came on board, he watched each game and kept irrefutable score. When they disembarked, they'd go to Lucas, the man who literally wrote the book on memory training. "Barnett down $37, Jackson up $21.")

"His biggest strength," says former center John Gianelli now, "was keeping levelheaded. Red treated everyone like a man. He didn't baby anybody. If you screwed up, he let you know. And he really was without ego. To him, the game was more like a chess match. He liked to have an answer to what the other guy was doing. Like if someone came in to foul one of our guys, he'd answer"—most often with Phil.

Treat them like grown-ups, they'll play for you. Act like their boss, as Bill Russell the coach painfully discovered, they won't.

In February 1968, the Knicks inaugurated the new place. The crenellated flying saucer signaled a new beginning. Colorful, classy, replete with five bars. Yes, as the *Times* reported, "In the new girder-free, no-overhang bowl, a huge proportion are high-priced seats." The priciest went for an unthinkable $7. Leonard Koppett was clearly suspicious: The baskets were "questionable to shoot at. The basket-and-backboard structure, stemming from a single pole like the new football goalposts, and with no guide wires at the top as in the old Garden, tends to vibrate every time a ball hits the rim or backboard."

On top of which, the court floor was eight feet longer! Perhaps it was that extra acreage that allowed Jackson, in a rout of the San Diego Rockets, to score eighteen. Only Willis Reed (listed as "left forward" in the box) had more points. True, the Rockets, with backup shooting guard Pat Riley, were headed for a 15-67 season.

The Knicks were headed for their first above-.500 season in a decade. Leaving the barn behind, letting Frazier and Bradley take over, the Knicks had shed the vestigial smoke-stained skin. For the first time in New York, with every seat sloping toward the bottom of the bowl, fans hopping on the bandwagon were given a theater in the round. Even up in the blue seats ($2 a ticket) the whole place felt intimate when it was full and rocking.

Jackson's game picked up as quickly as his curls grew, and the new wave of scribes known as the Chipmunks took to the rebel. One column described him as playing like "either like The Happy Hooker or Raggedy Ann." On one shot, said Larry Merchant in the *Post,* "he looked like a clumsy 6-foot-8-inch stork that suddenly winged away in a graceful arc." (Another Merchant-ism: "He plays like a Giacometti sculpture on roller skates.") While Bradley was intentionally issuing banalities so the writers would leave him alone, Camus and Kierkegaard found their way into Phil's interviews.

More to the point, Holzman opined, "He plays like he's seven feet. He may play lousy at times, but he won't ever play scared." The aggression soon earned him a reputation as a dirty player, after an elbow to Bill Bridges's nose brought blood—and boos. Rich Kelley, his future teammate on the Nets and lifelong friend, saw Phil's aggression slightly differently: "He knew he was dirty, but it wasn't dirty just to be dirty—it was to win the game." And Red knew the rest of the team would have his back. Once he tangled with rock-solid Paul Silas (not a very fair fight there), and after the oaken Silas took a unanimous decision, captain Reed stood Silas up with a forearm shiver. In practice, Holzman would caution his players to be careful around Jackson, the "bull in a china shop."

Leave it to the eloquent Bradley to script it in his *Life on the Run*. "When he ran or jumped or shot he seemed to be caroming off unseen opponents, able to right himself with just enough time to make the necessary move. It was as if his arms served as separate sides of a scale which never achieved equilibrium but fluctuated from side to side"—an apt metaphor for the man himself, as the next three decades of his life unspooled.

Philly knocked the Knicks out of the playoffs. Jackson scored a total of 20. In one game in the Garden, Chet Walker blocked a Jackson hook. The boos rained down.

At season's end, Jackson was named to the all-rookie team but, having earned seven technicals, didn't believe he deserved it. "I discovered that being a professional athlete provided me with no great thrill," he wrote in *Maverick*. "I thought it was something I could do for a while before going on with my 'normal' life. Maxine and I were interested in intellectual pursuits. We believed athletics to be little more than a primal struggle for dominance . . . that this kind of primitive competition should not exist."

Nevertheless, he admitted in the first book that it was "arrogance" to try to deny his competitive spirit. The inability to reconcile the two would become a pattern as he grew into the man he became, forever tugged by two poles. Did that friction forever ignite a spark, by osmosis, in his future teams? A question worth asking. But this was the first overt indication that he recognized the horns of his particular dilemma.

Jackson's rookie performance earned him a two-year contract worth $47,000. But job security was far from assured: The Knicks used their number-one pick on shooting forward Bill Hosket Jr. "We were as different as two people could be," the insurance salesman says now. "I read about Woodstock, whereas I think he probably went. But there was always common respect. We were competing for playing time, but we were different players. He was a much better defensive player and I was a little bit better shooter. But he was obviously a very bright guy. Both of us understood we were there for one reason: for the team to win."

In the season opener of year two, he had 10 off the bench, but the team subsequently wallowed—until late December, when Donovan and Holzman pulled off a trade for the ages: Bellamy and Komives to the Pistons for Dave DeBusschere: basketball incarnate. "Dave DeBusschere," Hosket once said, "was born a man." History will remember the era as belonging to Frazier, and Bradley because of the Princeton/Rhodes résumé. But it was Reed who led the team by example and DeBusschere who led it by skill.

DeBusschere had been entrusted with player-coaching the Pistons but admitted that he couldn't control a team with at least two players bringing guns to the locker room (the latter-day incarnation of the Fort Wayne Zollner Pistons were firing, just not on all basketball cylinders). The son of a bar owner from East Detroit, DeBusschere could find the open man, be the open man, bang for a rebound, and lay out a hard foul. With Barnett freed to be the true shooting guard and Reed playing more center, Jackson absorbed more passes and played more minutes. Riordan had now made the team and brought the plugger mentality that the Garden crowd adored. He also noticed a distinct difference in his friend.

"I'm riding in a car with him," Mike recalls. "He's driving like a New Yorker, a maniac, cutting people off, throwing the bird, hollering, matter-of-factly and comfortably. See, he's adapted again. He's another rat in the cage."

The discourse in the locker room was generally civil between the vets and the guy known as "Head and Shoulders." And how could his teammates not empathize with the rat by now? He'd posted two letters in his locker. The first: "You're one of the worst players ever." The second: "Last year I hoped you'd get hurt and you sprained your ankle. This year I hope you die."

In 1968–69, Jackson was averaging 13 points and 10 rebounds a game. He was heading for a more-than-respectable career. And if Johnson doesn't give him a shove in practice and he doesn't feel something pull, and then in the next game, if he doesn't come down hard on his right heel, perhaps his future takes a very different path.

The Knicks' physician, the well-liked Kazuo Yanagisawa ("He loved to play cards," Hosket recalls, "and they always said he carried a gun"), suggested a pulled muscle. The pain suggested otherwise. "Fortunately," Phil later wrote, "I was smoking pot at the time, so I was able to get loaded and just drift away." But in an interview with the *Times*, he admitted, "My leg felt like a piece of lead. It was frightening to me." The same piece described him as "an intelligent, articulate, concerned young man, whose interests range from existentialism to Dixieland jazz, with stopovers at modern literature, the New York City housing situation, the problem of the student-athlete in college life, and the ever present dilemma of what constitutes the 'good life.'"

"You might call me a pseudo-intellectual," Jackson said, clearly not shy at this point about selling his brand. If for the first time he couldn't crack a starting lineup, he could stake his own territory in other ways. "I am an athlete with an interest in intellectual matters," he said. "Many people think that the body and the mind are two separate quantities, but that doesn't have to be true."

But by midwinter he felt like a stranger. "Just being away a couple of weeks can do that," he told a *New York Post* writer—wearing, yes, an Edwardian suit. He gave *The Post* a running commentary on the game, as Frazier and Bradley and DeBusschere wove effortlessly. "In effect," wrote the *Post* writer, "Jackson was saying, 'They don't miss me.' Somebody else would have been resentful. Phil, son of a minister, a contemporary young man who reads Spinoza and Sartre, seemed thankful. He is a rare person." He obviously had 'em at Sartre. The Chipmunks were eager to shed the worship of baseball-card Potemkin athletes (Stanley Woodward: "Don't God them up"), while simultaneously establishing their own chops as writers. Jackson gave so many quotes in those early years, he almost seemed to be using the press as a sort of silent Freudian analyst to test out his new persona. Was this mask he'd created, he wondered, an artificial construct detached from who he really was?

In late February 1969, he resumed practicing, but he never made it back to the court in a game. By now, Cazzie had broken an ankle, and Bradley, starting, had found a groove. Frazier? Capable of turning a game around in a minute: stealing the ball, flying down the court for a layup, grabbing a rebound and, two passes later, backing a smaller guard into the paint and hitting a ten-foot fallaway.

The Knicks routed the Bullets in four in the first playoff round but lost to the Celtics in six, and Phil now underwent what any slip of the knife could have made a career-ending procedure: A four-inch piece of hipbone was grafted against three lower vertebrae. Then he was strapped to his bed, facedown.

"I had knee surgery at the same time," Hosket recalls. "So I've been there two days when Dr. Yana walks in and says, 'Get up and follow me down the hall.' I say, 'You don't care if I put weight on it?' 'Just follow me,' he says.

"We go into this room where Phil's been lying on his stomach for forty-eight hours. There are three nurses and an orderly, and they're getting ready to turn him over. 'You're the only one big enough to help,' says Yana. Phil looks up and says, 'No! Anybody but Hosket!'

"So we turn him over, and I'm thinking, *Here I am feeling sorry about my knee surgery, and this guy might never play again.*"

The surgery was successful. The physical healing began. Psychologically, he was thrashing. His marriage was on its deathbed. He felt "tied down," he'd later recount.

But if the operation derailed what might have been a more distinguished career as a player, the upside was inarguable: His coaching apprenticeship began. The league didn't allow for assistant coaches. Phil had to sit behind Red at home games. Holzman would send him ahead to cities, have him break down games on tape. Phil peppered Holzman with questions about subbing and the two-minute game, and he noted Red's calm postgame demeanor: "We played as well as we could. Tomorrow is another day."

"It's not rocket science," Red once told him. No, it was the early triangle—two guards, two men on the wing, and if the center gets the pass, strong-side guard and forward move into lanes. On defense, Red's three-word mantra: "See the ball." ("If you play good, solid defense, the offense will take care of itself," Jackson would tell me some years later. "You can't teach how to shoot. You can teach defense.")

Jackson saw that every man off the bench, from Dean Meminger to Nate the Snake, knew not only what was expected of them but *when* it would be expected. He got a new feel for Holzman's treatment of the final weeks of the season as preseason for the playoffs.

"During the season," Riordan told me, "Bradley was preparing for the presidency. Road trips, he was always meeting somebody, under the radar. But when the playoffs came, he put everything like that aside. After regular-season games, DeBusschere and I would have a cold one and B.S. the game. Come playoff time, the next thing you know, Bradley's with us in the hotel room with a cooler, dissecting the game and what adjustments to make for the next game."

That championship season, Red paired Phil with bench players on the road, to impart the Knick way of doing things: Team is all. He must have taught them well; when they won the title, eight players averaged more than twenty minutes a game in the playoffs.

It was not an easy seven months for Jackson. Knowing that you'll never dress, how can you give it your all? The result? A lot of weed, too much drinking. "I was using some of the popular head drugs at the time," he said. "My program was Know thyself." It was having limited success.

The team voted Phil a full share—$12,000—and the official photo of the World Champion Knicks shows Phil Jackson in a uniform he'd never donned in a game, standing next to Holzman.

★

In 1970–71, with Riordan, Cazzie, and Dave Stallworth—the Minutemen—playing ahead of him, Jackson, his gait now hampered, averaged ten minutes a game. Something in his head was keeping him from going all out (not to mention the defenders leaning on his lower back). But he be-friended a man who would guide him toward some equilibrium—his first true friend in the new world.

The Knicks had drafted Temple's Eddie Mast, the dominant player on the '69 NIT champ (22 rebounds in the final) and too talented a ballplayer to pursue his other passion: skillfully playing blues guitar. (Eddie not only knew the names of the studio musicians on Magic Sam albums; he knew the Latin genus names of the trees whose wood made up his guitars.)

Jackson would call him "the only friend I ever made in pro ball"—extreme, but heartfelt. Their bond? Belonging to a generation that be-lieved in change. Bradley never changed. Willis never changed. Frazier never changed: He had to be the center of attention, whether through clothes then or rhyming color commentary now. Eddie and Phil were still moving.

On a more mundane level, they both liked to move on motorcycles. Diane Mast had graduated high school and gone to work at Temple when Mast showed up on a motorcycle one day and Diane said she'd love to know what it was like to ride on a motorcycle. The rest was history.

And thus began a delightful couple of years for the two big men: fellow explorers—of open-air markets wherever they could find them, of beaches in San Diego, and of Baltimore pawnshops, looking for old guitars.

"Their friendship was based on truth," says Diane Mast. "Phil didn't have to be what Bradley or Willis or DeBusschere thought he should be. Phil didn't have to be somebody for Eddie. He could be completely who he was."

Both had been raised on the religious fringes, Mast amid Southern Baptists, the devil always there around the corner. And Eddie had loved the game as a teenager as much as Phil had. But instead of unlocking a field house in Williston, he'd hit the street courts of Philly, where the black kids would beat on him until they finally had to accept him. If he came home late, though, the beating would come from the father.

"At Temple, the basketball court gave him a new code to live by," says

Diane. "Eddie's life situation was stark because of economics and abuse. Phil's was stark because of the chosen, strict way of being for his parents. Eddie rejected his. I don't think Phil rejected his."

When I asked what they might have learned from each other, she answered, "It's not so much who taught who what. It was they were both in that moment together. Their dialogue was lively. Their mutual exchange of perspective was on the cutting edge."

And, of course, they had the competition disease in common. Diane recalls training-camp tennis games: "Enter that lanky dude with the white tennis shorts and a dimpled smile who was laughing at the world. Phil beat Eddie at tennis *way* bad all through that camp. In their last match, Eddie was so frustrated he took his racket and hit the court so hard it bent sideways. Phil kept laughing."

Mast opened Phil's ears up to reggae and blues: roots music. He loved to give Phil grief about classical music's absence of feeling. On the most significant level, Jackson would later admit, Mast seemed unencumbered by his self-worth being wrapped up in his basketball jones while Phil was still dueling with his dualities: Was winning all the time worth losing his religion? Or did they overlap?

"He could lose and live with himself without feeling like a chump," Jackson would write. Mast was the first moment-to-moment, breath-to-breath guy Jackson had ever played with. It was unusual to be enlightened enough to know that second place meant "first loser." Phil was searching for that quiet center where the journey mattered more than the destination. Eddie had already found it.

He also knew a rudimentary triangle. Knick owner Irish was good friends with Temple coach Harry Litwack, who used an offense analogous to the triangle, designed to break a zone defense. Jay Norman, the Temple coach emeritus, swears that when he saw Mast and Jackson talking on the bench that first year together, Mast was teaching Phil the fundamentals of the Temple offense. They'd continue the tutorial at any given tavern, where Eddie'd use his quarters for the jukebox while Phil used his to design backdoor screens on the bar.

★

The Knicks finished 52-30, second in the league behind Lew Alcindor's and Oscar Robertson's Bucks. But as Jackson would later tell it, in 1970–71, the defending champion "we's" had started to turn into "me's." They toasted the Hawks in five, but they now faced the Joe Frazier to their Ali: the Bullets, with Jack Marin the sharpshooter, Earl Monroe the magician and Wes Unseld the Ur–Charles Barkley.

Through the years, pat story lines offered up the Celtics as the hated rival for the Knicks, but for mutual by-the-throat basketball, this rivalry was one for the ages. The gritty port city was a town where a late-night walk through a deserted downtown could surprise a half-dozen bats from an abandoned building. The Bullets were playing in the sorry Baltimore Civic Center for the last time, before they fled down to the Beltway. This was the last time Baltimore would ever have a professional basketball team, and the Bullets were not about to go down without a kick and a scream.

In games in the Garden, all Marin remembers is what would happen if he got hot against Bradley. "They always ran Jackson in to pick a fight with me," Marin told me with an edge to his laughter. "He would beat me up with . . . let's say, the acquiescence of the officials. That's the way I saw it, anyway. He would just mug me. If the officials had called the game fair, I'd have gone to the line and he'd have gone back to the bench, but in the Garden that was to be expected. The fistfight was the intention. If it had been a straight game, I'd have gone to the line and he'd have fouled out, but that's not exactly the way it worked out."

Ever the political conservative, Marin has an interesting take on the Elbow of the seventies versus the Zen master of the new millennium, now comfortably ensconced in Hollywood. "Maybe it was a matter of necessity," Marin said. "Coaching in the CBA, he wasn't making a lot of money. But as a hippie he could have lived on nuts and berries. Phil is a capitalist pig at this point and has a great deal of dissonance he has to deal with on a daily basis." This is said mostly with tongue in cheek. Because he is also quick to praise the man as coach: "There are two guys in my era that I have the most respect for, Wes and Phil."

The hardest-working center in history being compared to Phil? Because it was never easy for either. "And Phil took the hard way there. I think he figured out where it was going to and what it took to get there, and he did it."

After the Knicks had taken a 3–2 lead, they were blown out down on 201 West Baltimore Street, and came home for a seventh game at the Garden. In stunning fashion, after Monroe shut down Frazier, the Knicks lost by two. Bradley had a shot to tie it at the buzzer—and missed.

(Alcindor and Robertson, unexpectedly, were gifted an exhausted foe for the finals. "We could beat everybody that year," says Bobby Greacen, a friend of Eddie Mast's, "but we could never beat the Knicks. We figured we'd coast through the West, but then . . . the Knicks? But then they lost to the Bullets, and that series wiped them out. And we swept them.")

★

And so, fittingly for a man who had to move, Phil took a journey "to ride away my blues." He hit the road, and ended up at a campground on the Flathead—the lake where he'd fished with the bamboo poles as a kid. Flanked by snowcapped Rockies. America the Beautiful? Flathead Lake. America's ancestors? The Salish and Kootenai tribes of the Flathead Reservation, who called themselves "the people." He was home. He'd buy land. He'd build. Today, the place on the lake is his spiritual center.

It was the first of dozens of memorable motorcycle odysseys that would bring him sacred moments of high-speed solitude, daring nature at high speed, finding a new universe around every corner. (In a posting on her Myspace site many years later, his daughter Chelsea would cite as one of her happiest memories "riding behind my dad on his motorcycle in Montana.")

He was not a Harley-Davidson sheep. This passion represented more of a Zen pull, where the journey is the destination. And thus did the man who'd spent hundreds of hours trapped in cars and buses going to games in the Plains find freedom in breaking down a boundary between man and nature.

The fascination began in Great Falls, when his older brother bought a Whizzer—a motorbike with a small engine that Phil and his brother tinkered with. First invented by an airplane-parts manufacturer in 1940, Chuck Jackson's never ran for long before dying. But it was a revelation, this whizzer, a bicycle that could drive itself. During the past season with the Knicks, his brother Joe, a psychology professor at SUNY Buffalo, picked up an old BMW. Phil was hooked. "On a bike," he would write two decades later, "you have to be continuously alert. You can never fall into the kind of trance that you often do when driving a car. The sunshine, the smells. The clouds, the wind, even the rain. You have to be totally present in the environment. It's a very Zen attitude." Not to mention what he called "the whole dance on the edge of danger."

He'd had a good year at in-flight poker. The winnings? Fifteen hundred dollars—a nice chunk of change when it represents more than 5 percent of your salary. He bought his own bike and hit the road. Joe was always worried about Phil's style of riding. He played basketball verging on out-of-control. Riding a motorcycle in mountain passes requires laser focus. It was on Lake Louise in Alberta, driving back to their campground with a bag of groceries between his legs, that he rounded a dirt-road curve at high speed and was just able to bail out before the bike did a half-dozen end-over-ends into a small canyon.

Phil was fine. The bike was wounded, but with bent handlebars and no headlight, he somehow made it back home. Would a nonathlete have been able to bail in time? Probably not. Would a nonathlete have been flooring it around a curve with a grocery bag of eggs between his legs on a dirt road, supremely confident that he'd never crash? Probably not.

The trip did more than satisfy Jackson's wanderlust. Campfire talks with Joe made him realize that he *was* holding back, as anyone would who'd been testing a fused spine in a brutal-in-the-paint game. If he wasn't going to commit to this game, it wasn't worth it. The same would soon be said of the marriage. And if there was anyone he'd listen to, it was brother Joe, the middle boy: the successful academic, the psychologist with a bit of New Age to him.

That summer Eddie and Diane visited Phil and Maxine. And while by now Elizabeth was four, the marriage was destined for dissolution. They divorced in 1972. As he would later write, he and his wife were "strangers." He still, he said, needed ego gratification that he wasn't getting. He was "sorry" about the end of the marriage, he wrote.

He rededicated himself to basketball. He averaged sixteen minutes and 7 points per game in 1971–72. Later, Jackson would assert that his improved play allowed Holzman, nine games into the season, to part with Riordan and Dave Stallworth in the trade that provided the last piece to the puzzle: Earl Monroe. The catalyst was the toxic relationship between the Bullets and Pearl. Two weeks earlier, Monroe had simply failed to show for the fourth game of the season, against the Knicks. There was no way the Bullets could *not* trade the guy.

"It's hard to say how he could be dissatisfied," Marin says now. "He had the ball all the time. I think his dissatisfaction lay in the fact that he preferred to be Joe Namath in New York. He wanted to go where the market would bear economic decisions. Put it this way, if it were the other way around, Earl would not have wanted to come to Baltimore."

Off the court, he was shy and thoughtful, a small-town guy whose college coach, Big House Gaines, was something of a minor-league Zenner himself. "He used to say stuff in the huddle like, 'Opportunity on every door doth knock, but it's never been known to pick a lock.'" Monroe laughs now. "You'd say, 'What?' Then you'd think about it and realize he was saying, 'Go out and make it happen yourself.'"

The truth is, if goateed Barnett came off as Kerouac/Beat cool, Monroe was the most laid-back of them all: watching, taking in. "You know what's funny?" he says now. "At that time, when I was coming to New York, I was looking for land, so all my people could come out and commune. I figured Phil would be one."

Jackson could now back up at his two best positions, and he played a major role in getting the Knicks to the finals: 7 points and 4 rebounds in sixteen minutes, and no Fu Manchu. He told writers, "I wanted to see what my face looked like." Merchant suggested it was probably because he was aiming for his sideburns but "fouled himself in the act of shaving." He grew back another, but it was one of the first examples of Jackson mask-morphing . . . to keep us guessing.

No guessing about the new aggression. The cameras didn't catch the actual punch, but they did find Marin prone, blood flowing from a cut above his left eye, the cut-man from the Bullets corner trying to stanch the bleeding. Jackson, with his halo of curly hair evocative of Harpo, still standing. It had been a right hand, said the writers. Jackson said he couldn't remember. But the Darksider moment hinted at an inner tripwire not seen before, the darkest part of the competitor let off the leash.

After the Knicks had knocked off the Celts in five, Jackson explained, "When I play for fun, when I'm loose, I don't play well. I [have] to concentrate very hard on what I'm doing. I have to be a little hostile."

The Knicks came up short in the finals. Behind a John Wooden–coached Gail Goodrich and an aging Wilt Chamberlain (thirty-five) and Jerry West (thirty-three), they'd put together a remarkable 33-game wining streak. Bill Sharman had led them to a record 69-13 mark, a percentage that no team would best until . . . the 1996 Bulls.

In the first game, in Los Angeles, Lucas befuddled Chamberlain, and Jackson hit for thirteen. But then the Lakers found a way to pick off Lucas with Jim McMillian and won the next four. Phil had ten in the finale. But there was no doubt about Jackson's ability to be a first man off the bench, to be able to throw a wrench into anyone's offensive rhythm.

★

But the college sweetheart had moved to the Upper West Side with their daughter. A friend said he gave it his best but that there was never a "burning affection. I think for a long, long time he tried."

★

And thus did that summer entail a very interesting motorcycle ride home, one that he dreaded: to tell his parents that the marriage was over. On the ride back to New York, he called Mast and told him it had been the most difficult thing he'd ever done.

But he was now, finally, free to try out the next fulfilling, if somewhat sensational, act.

FIVE

The High Line on the Lower West Side of Manhattan? Rusted, rotting, for sale. The West Side Highway? No bike lanes yet. Crumbling docks where the ocean liners used to berth. Chelsea was a neighborhood that was industrial by day, sketchy by night; West Nineteenth Street and Twelfth Avenue was a literally edgy piece of pavement, within a jump shot of the river. This was not SoHo, filling with artists whose parents could afford to put them in lofts. This was the *real* frontier.

You never would have figured that the building with the whining-air-wrench Big Bear shop on street level housed a pro basketball player, unless you noticed the Mercedes parked at curbside. (He did like his ride, although he didn't want to spring for the tape player.)

The loft was something of a metaphor for Jackson's mind: a boundariless home space, a hearth without border. High ceilings. No doorways to duck through. No room for escape. Room only for exploration—and room for soccer and tennis balls slammed against a brick wall.

Jackson had rented it from a guy named Hakim—"ex-tripper, ex-doper," before becoming a Muslim. Hakim had managed to burrow into Our Searcher's head. He was on his way to Egypt to study. In the meantime, he was advising Jackson that the man's spiritual core was obvious—but hoped he could straighten out his act.

"Although he didn't try to discourage me from smoking pot," Jackson would write, "he made his own opinions very clear: 'You can refine things by fire . . . but nothing is refined by smoke. Marijuana only confuses you and clouds up your head. . . . There will come a time, perhaps, when you won't need it anymore. But until that time comes, make sure you know exactly why you're doing it.' "

"I soon realized that I was smoking grass partly for the introspection it brought me," he wrote. "I knew, though, that smoking too much can make people depressed, but I also enjoyed the different outlooks on my surroundings and the intuitive feelings that marijuana seemed to produce."

That introspection included the growing sense that the persona he'd adopted was not his true self. Ready to take off the mask, he just wasn't sure what lay beneath it.

Hakim's analysis of Jackson? A childhood retreat from reality had produced "an ego shield." Jackson's own therapy? To break down and cry for a couple of days in the middle of the next season. By his own account, the self-induced solo Esalen retreat started to work: "I even learned to stop watching myself perform in front of other people."

He'd also learned to love again.

Her name was June Perry—a pretty, athletic, outdoorsy girl who radiated "strength, self-sufficiency and confidence." They'd met at a card game. She was a UConn grad with friends in SDS—the Students for a Democratic Society, the tamer Caucasian version of the Panthers but a forceful, organized protest organization, far more radical than it sounds now. Then, she also had a fondness for hiking. June's initial impressions of the man? "[He was] not nearly as radical as the people I knew in college," she would tell a *New York Times Magazine* writer some years later. "He never dropped out. He always had money."

Soon she'd be living in the loft. Phil and June would be together through the long, strange trip for the next thirty years.

★

Fifteen blocks north, in Madison Square (round) Garden's new raucous saucer? The 1972–73 season was as good as it would ever get. By the end of November, the Knicks were 20-4, including a 25-point defeat of the Lakers

(12 for Phil) and a 48-point defeat of Kevin Loughery's 76ers (destined to win 9 that year).

On the practice court, Jackson was apprenticing with the best: defending Bradley as an outside scorer and DeBusschere as an inside scorer (and trying to figure out ways to beat both of their defensive strategies). Off his previous year's performance, in a winning locker room, Phil had found his niche. Bradley and Barnett and he had real discussions about politics as Phil began to drift in from the right. (Jackson, as quoted by Bradley: "Both parties are controlled by the same interests." Barnett, nodding: "The rich always get richer and the poor always get poorer.")

The best re-creation of the Jackson-Barnett relationship, two rebels from different pods? From Bradley's first book: "Phil closes his book on Zen love, hangs up his plaid lumberjack shirt and Wrangler jeans, scratches his beard and replaces his wire-rim glasses with contact lenses. He puts on his jock, walks over to the taping table, and notices what Barnett is reading: *Building Black Business*.

"You believe in capitalism?" he asks.

"Why, Phil," interjects Lucas defensively. "Don't you?"

Phil smiles.

"Do I what?" Barnett asks.

"Do you believe in capitalism."

"No, Phil," Barnett says in exasperation. "I believe in love."

"The players were very outspoken about their sentiments among each other," Jackson would write a few years later, "but were private in public. We did have a few guys serving their country. . . . Bradley and I get into the ethics and morality of politics quite a bit. I used to be a die-hard Republican, but I'm becoming more and more liberal. When you live in an integrated society, as basketball is, with fellows who come from slum backgrounds, it has to have an effect on you."

He was still beating himself up for bad games (Eddie, traded to Atlanta, wasn't around to exorcise that demon) but he was playing confidently. "Red would send him in to get things riled up," says Jerry Lucas now. "He was a flailing, two-armed octopus, doing the thing he came in to do." As soon as Jackson took off the sweats and checked in at the scorer's table, the men out on the court knew that their formerly Euclidean universe was about to be visited by an agent of chaos theory.

"*Unorthodox* is the best way to explain it," says Lucas now. "Phil's game was unique to Phil. When Phil came in, you absolutely knew that something was going to happen. He might steal a ball four times in a row, or foul out in fifty seconds. Of course, he was a good teammate, obviously; selfishness did not exist on that team."

Take a February game against the Bullets in Baltimore (to which Clyde traveled in a full-length mink coat, a white fur hat and high-heeled red boots; Phil in a flowered shirt and Levi's). Phil whooshed a perfect hook, followed a few minutes later by a rebound—which he bounced off his knee and out of bounds. A *Post* columnist subsequently wrote that Phil was Woody Allen's idea of a basketball player: unpredictable, neurotic and instantly likable because of his human fallibility. Columnist Jim O'Brien's conclusion? "Jackson has what appears to be a fright wig for hair, a mustache and a skinny frame, but inside there's a warmth, an intelligence and a beautiful guy"—a guy who, like clockwork, O'Brien wrote, received every week a letter from someone calling herself "Miss Knick Fan," sometimes in verse, celebrating the man.

(Lucas and Jackson roomed one year. I asked Jerry what they'd talk about. Apparently, they didn't. Lucas liked to memorize phone books and license plates, mastering his universe. Phil's brain loved the idea that there *were* no answers. "I wasn't interested in philosophical searches," Jerry told me.)

Only believers in cosmic concurrence will find the events of that February 27 to be portentous. Two thousand miles away, at the site of the original Wounded Knee massacre, two hundred Lakota Oglala Sioux from the Pine Ridge Reservation, joined by other American Indian Movement activists, occupied the town of Wounded Knee, South Dakota, protesting the actions of a corrupt tribal chief and the United States government's refusal to honor treaties. Their actions were the beginning of an ultimately bloody two-month standoff against both federal marshals and the FBI. Soon, one federal agent and two Native Americans were dead, and a third protester was believed to have been murdered. It would be a few more months before the standoff/siege's effects would cross Jackson's life path.

Back east, on that night of February 27, 1973, before a delirious packed house in the Garden, the second-place 50-18 Knicks welcomed the 52-12 Celtics. The Knicks won easily, 123–91, because Lucas shut down Dave Cowens and Bradley harassed John Havlicek; Jackson, most unusually, was high scorer with 20 points. There is no record of whether Jackson knew that his old (and lifelong) friend Mike Her Many Horses had begun the occupation that day. But two days later, in Milwaukee, Jackson led the team again, with 22.

Soon after, a reporter asked Holzman which player had received the most trade inquiries that year. Jackson.

They finished second to the Celtics. Holzman's mantra entering the play-offs? "From here on in, it's defense." First up were the Capital Bullets, now a team without a city, transplanted to the Capital Centre, an ugly whale of an arena down in Maryland just outside of the Beltway. The Knicks handled them in five despite imp Riordan's fresh intelligence. In the decisive final game, a Knick rout; Jackson scored 13.

The Celtics were next, a seven-game series in alternating arenas: four in the old Garden, three in the new. The intimate Boston version was the ultimate intimidator, two balconies hanging right over the players' heads. Some of the magical 264 pieces of wood that made up the parquet court were quite dead, and well known by the home team, helping account for the Celtics having gone 35-6 at home that year. Not to mention Auerbach's habit of turning up the radiators in the visitors' locker room to about 122 degrees Fahrenheit.

Havlicek was averaging 24. Cowens, the league MVP, had epitomized in effort, if not talent, predecessor Russell. The Celts were deep (Paul Westphal was eighth in minutes), and Tommy Heinsohn, a former Celt, now in his fourth year, knew how to coach. In his first year they'd won 34. Then 44. Then 56. Now 68. He'd been named Coach of the Year.

Holzman had devised a possible key to dismantling Tommy's Machine. If Cowens, a court-savvy large forward in a small center's body, was always guarding the Knicks' slower centers, they couldn't hope to prevail. So Holzman developed a series of high-low pick situations in the hopes that, eventually, Monroe or Frazier could get free near the basket, where Cowens might not handle either guard one-on-one.

After a Celtic victory in Boston, in New York the Knicks stunned the favorites with a 129–96 laugher. Jackson scored 16, third behind Frazier and Reed. The tipping point of the series occurred two days later, when, up in Boston, behind dominant nights from the usual starting five, and dominant D, the Knicks won, 98–91.

In game four, in New York, with regulation time running out, Holzman replaced Bradley with Jackson. Amped, rotating his arms like a DC-3 prop, he foiled an inbounds pass, and the game went into overtime. Phil stayed in. With eleven seconds left in the first overtime, and the Knicks down by 2, the Celtics fouled Phil.

Now: One miss and the series would be tied, with two of the remaining games in Boston. No one who watched it (me, among we Knicklanders, on a small black-and-white TV in a college dorm room) will ever forget it. As soon as the ref handed him the ball, clearly not wanting to take the time to succumb to pressure—to vibe with Buddhic non-thought—he immediately hoisted an inordinately high-arcing swish.

As soon as he got the ball back, Jackson did it again: all instant instinct. Another high arc—and swish. Very Zen. The Garden went insane. Maybe the first triumphant Zen Basketball moment of his life.

In the second overtime, Jackson now worked himself free for two layups, stole a ball from Jo Jo White, pulled in two rebounds and drew a key offensive foul. The Knicks blew the Celtics away in the second OT and won going away, to take a 3–1 lead.

"I'd sure be sick if I missed them," he said afterward to a reporter watching him shave, who used the moment to ask Jackson about the letters he'd been getting.

"Her poetry leaves a lot to be desired," he said, "but you have to appreciate her zealousness."

That sounds like you, said the writer. Jackson agreed.

The next day's papers featured a more lyrical quote than usual from Bradley: "We won the game the way Phil Jackson runs—unpredictable, but it gets it done."

The Celtics took the next one up in Boston, cutting the Knick lead to 3–2—and two days later, stunned the Knicks at home, 110–100. While everyone was paying attention to Havlicek, holding him to nine, five other Celtics scored in double figures. Phil had seven points.

The seventh game, in Boston, promised to be ugly. It was—for Auerbach, who never got to light his phallic cigar. Holzman's defense swayed the day. The Knicks beat the Celtics, in their home arena, by the extraordinary score of 94–78. Phil scored nine. He'd averaged nine points and nineteen minutes a game in the slugfest series.

Now we go from the sublimely sporting setting of the Boston Garden to the most absurd arena in American sports history, a grandiosely becolumned place meant to evoke an ancient civilization whose own famous arena was filled for recreational Sunday shows involving executions of captured enemies and was built by an emperor of an empire hoping to conquer the world (although it did build pretty cool roads). The L.A. Forum had been built in the late sixties by the previous Lakers owner,

Virginia-horse-country fop and egotist extraordinaire Jack Kent Cooke, who once bought the Chrysler Building just for the hell of it. His Forum featured waitresses in togas.

Game One belonged to the Lakers, 115–112. Goodrich shot the lights out of the place. Red used Phil in his marauder role, but futilely. He fouled out, after dueling with seven-foot fencepost Mel Counts. "Have an over-sized flamingo and a pterodactyl ever thrown elbows at each other while wearing short pants?" wrote Larry Merchant, in prose as purple as those togas. "Jackson's elbows played on Counts' ribs like a glockenspiel when he reached toward the ceiling with his jump shot."

But in game two, Jackson hit his stride: 17 points in a 99–95 victory— the unexpected spark off the bench . . . and precursor to the Kerrs and Hansens and Horrys and Wenningtons who could come off the bench to turn championship-final-series future teams into the ultimate champions.

"I'm starting to make things happen on offense," he told writers that night. "When I used to shoot, I'd think, 'Oh no, here I am again, shooting.' But I realized suddenly that I'm not that bad a shooter, even if my body is all over the place. When the ball goes in the hoop, you don't look so bad."

Back home in game three, though, one of Counts's jousts elbowed a front tooth out of Phil's mouth, and a blow to the thigh from someone else began to hemorrhage the wound. He scored 8 in an 87–83 victory, as Reed and Lucas held Wilt to 5 points.

Jackson was hurting, but DeBusschere more than made up for it in game four in New York: 33 points, and a 103–98 victory. Now it was back to L.A., with the Lakers' back to the wall. They'd only lost ten at home all year. The Lakers led at the half, 41–39. And then, as in Boston, as in a whole lot of future Jackson-coached games, the third quarter made the statement. Reed and Lucas locked down on Wilt while Earl and Clyde went wild. The Lakers scored 18 in the quarter while the Knicks scored 32 en route to an easy 102–93 victory.

Two rings in four years. A Knick dynasty in the making.

Jackson's seventeen-minute, 8-point line in the championship game mirrored exactly his regular-season average: He had become that blueprint for future coaching success: the bench player, the role player, the guy who sits and watches and listens, and knows what it means to have twelve men coalesce and win.

"He was six-eight with a wingspan of a seven-two guy. His ability to cover and to disrupt in a semipressing situation was great," says Riordan now. "And he was the perfect role player for that team because he could give you minutes defensively, the hustle plays, the dish-off and dunk. He was only an average jump shooter, and his ability to put it on the ground you wouldn't say was outstanding, but he knew his strengths. He was very analytical, and he could sublimate himself, adapt and adjust, game by game, player by player."

"He was a great teammate to play with," Henry Bibby says, "and one of the dirtiest players out there. Walt was dirty, but Phil was dirty without even knowing he was dirty. He could make an open jump shot, but his game was to be an in-the-way player. He was able to use the talent he had, which was not a lot, but talent that fit into a team.

"I honestly wondered why Red didn't play him more, because he'd come in and bring intangibles on the court that the rest of us didn't have."

"I remember him coming in and lighting a spark," Dave DeBusschere once told me. "I also remember Red yelling at him, 'Don't dribble it!' And Phil would dribble it off his knee and the ball would go two rows deep into the stands."

But Jackson's account of that championship series two years later, in his first book? Virtually invisible. Instead, now a made man ringwise, he emphasized his "spiritual hassles." That night in Los Angeles, after the final victory, by his own account, a woman called Jackson's room. He agreed to meet her for breakfast. She was young; she was beautiful. Not long afterward, after (temporarily) splitting with June, back in Los Angeles, he and his new friend dropped LSD for breakfast and spent the day tripping on the beach. "It was all very symbolic for me, and I felt like a lion," he'd later recount. He also called the experience "at least as dramatic as the Knicks' winning the championship" and wrote that he sensed the "awe of God"—a significant statement for someone who in 1970 had said to a religious friend, "There is no God."

(Jackson's experiment, perhaps not incidentally, puts him in some elite company, from Steve Jobs to Francis Crick, who codiscovered the double helix structure of DNA, to Aldous Huxley, who was reportedly injected with the drug as he died. Explorers all.)

Jackson soon flew back home and asked June back to the loft, and their relationship began anew. And for real.

★

Now another door of illumination opened, accompanied by a different drug, Lakota Sioux tobacco, best smoked out of a sacred pipe—which, like the bag that held it, had to be blessed. Mike Her Many Horses asked him to give clinics at the beleaguered Pine Ridge Reservation to lighten the psychic load. He brought Bill Bradley and Willis Reed with him. They played and spoke at the old Porcupine High School, since burned to the ground.

The man christened Ohnahkoh Wamblee (Swift Eagle) in a naming ceremony by Edgar Red Cloud would return each summer. To the Lakota, the eagle represents a state of grace. If he couldn't be graceful, perhaps he could be full of grace—or at least, in Lakota terms, get closer to that dream state where leadership is ultimately the result of a vision.

The smoke? Holzman and trainer Danny Whelan had started giving Jackson a cigar to smoke with them after victories. (Take that, Auerbach.) With the Lakota Sioux, Phil's love of smoke began to take on new dimensions. The sacred pipe, made of sacred red clay found in Minnesota, was a prized artifact. The ceremony was all. (Phil's tobacco pouch would later be sanctified in a ceremony in Rapid City.)

"The Native Americans use tobacco in everything," he would later say. "There's a pinch of tobacco in every one of their religious relics, in every gift they offer to each other, in every pouch they wear around their necks.

Tobacco is indigenous to America, and the Native Americans feel it was given to them by the Great Spirit to help them talk freely, and to also help center their thoughts and their dreams into prayers. The smoke symbolizes their prayers rising to heaven.

"Smoking represents a combination of the elements of earth, fire and air, but it also signifies the hearth and the home and a means of protection against animals."

The tobacco was traditionally combined with medicinal and herbal barks in a mixture called kinnikinnick and used in a kind of communion—"a way of inviting an alien into the tribal circle." The Sioux and the Cheyenne would take long journeys just to trade the ingredients.

The billboard at a crossroads on South Dakota Route 18 that reads *"Wophi la unkenici yapi"* tells you that you've entered a reservation. The American translation lies printed below: "Suicide is 100 percent preventable." Then, a phone number for the Sweetgrass Suicide-Prevention Hotline.

Farther down Route 18 is a faded sign that says "Home of the Pine Ridge Thorpes—'86–'87 State A basketball champs." En route to the dirt road that will lead me to Virgil Bush's place I pass seven signs commemorating DUI deaths, although alcohol was illegal on the reservation until recently.

I take a left. Five miles of rolling dirt road later, I am standing in the middle of a 640-acre piece of heaven on which the Bush family's buffalo typically roam in the middle of the most utter, complete silence I have ever experienced. No wind rustles the tall buffalo grass.

I'm not going to say that I felt at that moment that I was in place more special than any I'd ever been in. But I am going to suggest the possibility.

Virgil apologizes that there are no buffalo in sight: They are allowed to roam free; it is their land. "We hold them in reverence," he tells me. His ponytail is braided down his back. "They are our clothing, our shelter, our pets." (Also not in evidence are the two-foot-long groundhogs.)

When I mention the suicide sign, Virgil nods. "We live to survive," he says. "We're plagued by poverty, negatives, suicide, domestic violence. We are passionate people. We honor our culture and our ceremonies, and the old ways." But when I bring up the Thorpes sign he smiles. The game, he explains, is a huge source of pride for the local tribes. In less than a month, Pine Ridge, in their red and black, would join a dozen other teams at the Lakota Nation Invitational tournament in Rapid City: twelve Native American teams, two non-LN teams.

"He is kind, a compassionate man," Rick Two Dogs tells me about Phil. Rick lives down the road from Virgil. "And I guess he adapted to our ways really easily because of that. I think what he saw is our philosophy: We live with everything in nature. If I say a prayer, it's not just for relatives or friends; when we pray, we're talking about all of creation."

The first time Rick met Phil was when, as the newly named head coach of the Chicago Bulls, Jackson wanted to participate in an *inipi* ("to make life within")—a sweat lodge ceremony. "Our belief," Rick told me, "is that you can take a shower and wash your body, but in order to purify your spirit, you need to go into the sacred sweat lodge, where we heat rocks. Our creation story says that all life sprang from the stone. We believe that you are going back to the beginning of time. It also represents the womb of our mothers and grandmothers. When we come out of the lodge, we are starting over."

When I asked whether he thought Lakota religion had influenced Jackson's success as a coach, he cut me off. "We don't have a word for religion. That doesn't mean we are not spiritual people. Our spirituality and religion are one, practiced on a daily basis. Phil saw that, for us, spirituality is in everything in life. Spirituality *is* everyday life."

I saw two more signs as I left the reservation by the BIA highway. The first was the historical marker at Wounded Knee, at the site of the original massacre, when one hundred fifty Sioux were killed, as well as twenty-five US troops, twenty of whom were awarded the Medal of Honor. The second sign was a work of spray-painted art showing eyes bugging out of a brain, with a coffin for its body, next to the words "Drugs Are Not Traditional. It's all About Choice. Choose life or meth." The word *Not* had been spray-painted out with an X.

Jerry Schultz, of UND, with whom Phil is still in touch, suggested that Phil's Native American trope was as important as the Zen thing. "I saw all those Sioux artifacts in the Berto Center, first time I visited," Jerry said. "And that LNI tournament is something."

Say again, Jerry?

"You know about the Lakota Nation Invitational, right?"

I allowed that I had for about a week.

"I have a granddaughter out there, eighth grade, and she's darned good. Her school was one of the two white schools to play in the tournament last December. And I could not believe how good these kids were. I mean, this was great basketball. I have no idea why they don't advance higher. I guess it's just the system."

Now, back in New York, Phil's stock was rising, publicly. Clothier Sy Syms hosted a luncheon for the man at Jimmy's, where a newly shorn and bearded Jackson signed autographs. "I've never been on an ego trip," he told a reporter. "I've always been able to control that."

SIX

Jackson was running wind sprints at training camp in Monmouth, New Jersey, when he turned to a new arrival, a big guy from Princeton, a lot bigger than Bradley, with whom Chris Thomforde had been hanging. "I hear you're going to be a minister," Phil said. Thomforde allowed as to how that would be true.

"Phil says, 'Let's get together and talk about your religious experiences,' and so we did," Thomforde says now, in the office of the president of Moravian College and Seminary in Bethlehem (Pennsylvania), founded on the tenets of a liberal Eastern European branch of Lutheranism. Thomforde, Princeton's captain in both 1969 and '70 as a six-nine center, was the twelfth-round Knicks pick in the 1970 draft but opted for academia, Yale Divinity School. Thomforde had a feeling that he had a calling: not to teach doctrine; to teach faith.

But in the fall of 1973, Demon Basketball was calling again. The Knicks' core was aging, so Red called Thomforde. "You know, we've never seen you play. Why don't you come on down to training camp?" Such is the pull of the roundball that he packed his Converses and made it down to Jersey— not only to test his court mettle, no risk, but also for a chance to reunite with Bradley, whom he'd met at a Fellowship of Christian Athletes meeting. They were each "sort of on the evangelical side" as youths, Thomforde says today, and by this time, like Jackson, were both looking for more realistic ways of defining "faith."

"As a result of Bill's experience as a Rhodes scholar, and mine at Princeton, we sort of shifted gears," Thomforde told me. "We believed in God, but in a god that must produce mercy, justice and kindness. Not self-righteousness, not 'I don't drink, eat, smoke or have sex or do anything bad.' Bill and I had a very strong relationship based on our sense of civil and civic responsibility."

Off the court, Thomforde had found his calling. Bradley? Not yet. In Harvey Araton's *When the Garden Was Eden,* Bradley describes the night a car brushed against him outside the Garden after a bad game and he entertained the oblique thought that this was meant as some sort of warning. He tried to disappear. Hence the bland quotes. Hence the work with kids in Harlem through the Urban League—anonymously. Hence the reported reluctance to do endorsements that came his way because of his race.

Phil's assessment of Bradley in that first book? That at first he'd been cold, but that the two would bond over questioning the foundations of Christianity. Of Thomforde, Phil wrote, "He suggested the truth I was seeking frantically was right there in front of my eye. 'Ask of the Father what you will.' It's as simple as that."

"The Phil I know," says Thomforde, "knows that faith is not a principle, a set of doctrines or dogmas that must be intellectually believed so you can get to heaven; faith is a passion about how to live one's life. That's his spirituality." On another level, such passion reflects his immersion in the principles of Buddha and the Lakota, who reconcile individualism with a universe of One.

A documentary crew happened to be following Bradley around at the camp, and Thomforde and Jackson batted about the themes that Bill was discussing on camera. "What would it mean to have moral courage? Phil and I didn't talk about *belief* in God, but what the moral consequences of such a belief would be, the responsibility."

Thomforde's Knicks experience ended when Red assembled the remaining, uncut players in the lobby of a Holiday Inn. "You're good, Chris, but you need to gain weight," he said in front of the rest of the squad. "Stick around with the team for a year; you can practice with us." Chris said he really *was* planning to be a Lutheran minister. "Oh, you should do that!" Red said. "That's something worthwhile. Plus, I think you'll be much better at it."

Chris and Phil corresponded. One weekend, he drove to New Haven to join Thomforde interning at a storefront church, up Dixwell Avenue—a neighborhood that Yalies assiduously avoided. Chris and Phil were the only white people in the room. The preacher's sermon went on for three hours. Then he said, "Let's sing some songs!" Phil stuck his hand in the air and said, "Lift Me Up to Higher Ground." And that's what they sang.

"So when I think of Phil Jackson now," says Thomforde, "I think of that song. What is the higher ground? How do we get there? What's the move involved? The Ten Basic Principles of Christianity or Buddhism? His search isn't to study them and see if they're true and see if we can do them. It's 'Let's try and see where these beliefs can intersect with other truths.'

"And so now, I think, it's 'Let's play basketball this way, and dedicate ourselves to each other, and see what happens. Let's pursue the fundamental rhythms and dynamics and see where that takes us.'

"He made me think: If Islam is a language, then Christianity and Judaism are languages, and within them are sublanguages—a taxi driver different than a don at Oxford—but they're all speaking English. If one understood religions like that—to be distinct without being parochial—how amazing would that be?"

★

Let's take another trip, down to Chelsea. Walk through the doorway next to the Big Bear. Beware the dog poop June would leave on the stairway to deter nighttime visitors when Phil was on the road.

Welcome to the party. Observe the trappings of a man free to be he.

Note, at different occasions over a few years, the hammock, the Spiro Agnew dartboard, a floor-to-ceiling crossword puzzle, an inverted parachute to collect roaches. On the roof? A skylight. In the floor? A hole big enough to see men changing brakes at daybreak.

A Jerry Garcia Chia Pet. The Dead, the Allmans. A *Whole Earth Catalog*. A bottle of wine. Someone playing piano in a corner. Phil's dirty socks stuck into boots.

The partygoers? For the most part, not basketball players. "None of my friends are basketball people," he brashly told his new acquaintance Charley Rosen for a *Sport* magazine piece. "You have to stop at a certain level. Playing basketball is just like everything else. They own your body, and they try to own your head.

"Pro basketball is dominated by black players, but the people who own the sport, pay to see it live, sponsor it on TV and write about it are white. So they all focused in on Bradley."

At this, Rosen reports, he "wiped his dirty hands on his pants. . . . He's the Knicks' media hippie," Rosen wrote. "It has gotten to the point where the hippie community expects him to trip for every game and to attend an obligatory number of rock concerts."

"Sometimes I feel like an amoeba on a slide," Jackson said. "But I just try to ignore all of these extraneous things as best I can—they're all so totally absurd. It's fun for people to have their superstars, but you can't take the cross off their backs and put it on yours." He was puffing on a good cigar.

"In *The Hobbit,* the grand wizard can blow smoke rings in different colors," he said. "He just sits there and blows them to the ceiling. I aspire to that."

A tad precocious, prideful and . . . premature.

★

As the 1973–74 season began, Phil's propensity for on-court encounters led to inevitable questions about aggression. "I'm really a very passive person who doesn't like getting riled up," he told the *Christian Science Moni-*

tor. "I've tried to eliminate technical fouls, and hostilities. I don't want to feel tensed up inside when I'm playing anymore. I want to feel calm."

He opened with a new look: shorter hair but a full beard. His minutes were up to twenty-five a game, his points to 11, his defense on clamp-down mode. "I once actually saw him block three consecutive inbound passes," Jim Drucker, son of revered official Norm, recalls. (Jim would be the commissioner of the Continental Basketball Association. His dad reffed Phil's last game in the old Garden and the first in the new.)

This season, on a trip to Los Angeles, he wasn't heading for hallucinogenic enlightenment; he was rereading James's *The Varieties of Religious Experience.* He was looking for "another mystical experience . . . [one] which would confirm the wisdom of my return to my spiritual roots."

He stopped playing cards. He stopped making "sweaty locker room talk." He was trying to distance himself from that competitive demon within, rationalizing that average ballplayers like him were not going to always have great games and that he should make peace with that. He even learned to speak in tongues. Well, sort of. He'd just sit in a comfortable chair, utter nonsense syllables as they came out, and enjoy this meditation with a mystical, atonal soundtrack.

This was still a solid, if aging, team. Gianelli was getting more minutes behind Reed, and the laid-back Californian enjoyed watching Phil grow into an integral member of the inner circle. "He wasn't physically gifted, but he had a knack for the game," Gianelli says now. "He always had his head in it. He and Bradley were great at setting other teams up. You played everybody eight times, so teams knew what you were going to run if you called out a play. So in the huddle, Phil or Bill would suggest we call out one play, then we'd run a different one. Bradley would do it to Havlicek all the time."

Holzman took them to 49-33, second in the division, to face the Bullets, without Marin (traded to Houston)—but with Elvin Hayes. This series presented a thrilling, less physical seesaw battle. With the Knicks ready to put the series away in New York, leading 3–2, and Jackson pouring in 14, Riordan, exploiting a defense he knew so well, hit for 23, to complement

Hayes's 31, in an ugly 109–92 rout. Game seven, though, featured that future Phil coaching mantra: Win the third quarter. The Bullets scored 10 in theirs. Hayes finished with 12. The final was 91–81.

The Celtics' roster was virtually the same, but Willis was hurting, and Gianelli was no match for Cowens. The Celts routed the Knicks in game one and took a 2–0 lead down in New York. In the third game, in Boston, Frazier decided he'd had enough, and poured in 38 to lead a 103–100 Knick victory, but the Celtics took the fourth, despite 17 for Phil.

Back in Boston, Jackson had his best playoff game ever: 27 points on 9 field goals, 9-for-9 from the free-throw line. But the Celtic defense slammed the door in the fourth quarter, holding the Knicks to 15 and rendering Monroe impotent, while Havlicek, now thirty-four but not about to go out meekly, scored 33.

Havlicek kept it up for seven more games, and despite Kareem's dominance, Tommy Heinsohn outcoached Larry Costello's Milwaukee Bucks guys, who had beaten Jerry West's last Lakers team. The Celtics took it in seven for their first title since the Bill Russell run.

SEVEN

In the spring of 1974, Thomforde, then assistant chaplain at Colgate, got a call from Phil: "June and I are getting married. Will you perform the ceremony?" Thomforde suggested Phil's father conduct the services. "Phil had a pithy answer: 'Nope.'" Thomforde agreed.

The 167-year-old Chapel of the Good Shepherd on the campus of the General Theological Seminary on Manhattan's Lower West Side is a soaring Episcopalian chapel with a huge stained-glass window backing the altar, a humbling and joyous space no matter what your faith. Brother Joe was the best man. At the reception, Thomforde was delighted to find himself seated, in the second floor of a nice restaurant, next to Muslims.

The following fall, Jackson picked up where he'd left off: on his game. He averaged twenty-nine minutes a game, 11 points and 8 rebounds. But Reed, his knees shot the previous season, was now gone, as was his symbolic leadership. For Phil, the search for the outer limits of experience endured. Like the evening in Houston when he and Bradley decided to go to the movies. *Chinatown* or *The Godfather: Part II*? No, the notorious 1962 Italian art-house film *Mondo Cane* (World of Dogs), featuring a gumbo of bizarre rituals from around the world. Jackson had already turned in the rental car when they discovered that the film was at a distant drive-in. So they took a taxi. The evening cost $45—the equivalent of $250 today.

★

Charley Rosen and Phil hit it off immediately, after being introduced by Stan Love, the Bullets' resident rebel. The plaque that read "Basketball isn't a metaphor for life; life is a metaphor for basketball" in Jackson's office years later? A Rosen quote. (For Rosen, Jackson once wrote, "Waiting to turn left, a truck was a 'moving pick.'") In truth, the six-nine, solid *Rosen* was a moving pick, though not on the court; at Hunter, guards hit his picks like Yugos hitting a diesel train.

Like Phil, he was tugged in two directions: the mind and the court. He was half hoop beast and half Renaissance scholar (literally). After being sent from his home to a summer camp for troubled youths at the age of nine, he learned the game on portable baskets set up in a neighborhood swimming pool in a sketchy section of the Bronx before hitting the street courts (and once getting beaten by his dad for tearing his pants). After starring at Hunter, he played in various leagues, including a season for Rotol Electric in Bridgeport in the Middletown City League.

The other pole? His master's thesis was on the Canon's Yeoman's Tale of Chaucer's *Canterbury Tales*, the story whose moral is that riches are not to be found through such shortcuts as alchemy and gold. The PhD dissertation, an allegorical interpretation of the *Tales'* General Prologue, wherein he argued that Saint Denis was a pseudo-Dionysus, never got off the ground. "It was all a metaphysical smokescreen," Rosen says now. Rosen was more comfortable writing in a different genre. His 1978 *Scandals of '51*, the tale of betting in college sports, and his novel *The House of Moses All-Stars* would both be critically acclaimed, the latter optioned for the screen.

Rosen's version of hoop heaven entailed assembling friends and college teammates to form the Woodstock Joneses, a roaming band of court warriors. Rosen loved nothing more than posting up, shoving, butting, grabbing a rebound and starting the break.

Off the court? "I was reading Native American stuff," he says now, "and [mystic Joel] Goldsmith [*The Infinite Way*]. But it was Phil who introduced me to the spiritual context of the sport. As a way to exercise all of myself. To bear witness." Rosen knew he didn't have great talent. But he did see the game's patterns as a constant push-and-pull wherein offense and defense are in perfect balance, a game so rhythmic and fluid that it bordered on art. That a team in cohesion would always beat five individuals mirrored society's main catalyst: tribal community . . . all the while allowing, when it was called for—as in dance, as in music—individual expression.

"It seems to be the simplest of sports, but it's the opposite," he says now, over sushi in his favorite restaurant south of Woodstock. "There are so many complexities that remain secret to people who can't see them. More than any other sport, it tests character. There are more opportunities to be selfish or unselfish than in any other sport. Which means that, seen by the right person, you can give a psychological profile of every player."

They checked out music stores. They went to Unitarian churches. They talked about P. D. Ouspensky, the Russian esotericist.

★

In the city, these were heady days: cigar-puffing, poker-playing, manly gym-rat days. The poker was at DeBusschere's regular game. ("My idol," Jackson called him once. "If I had his physical attributes, I would have styled myself after Dave.") Phil had found the right lady and was playing full-time hoop, not ten minutes a game: in the off-season, *all* game, beneath the buzzing wire-encased lights in the grotty United Nations gym, for a weekly "run" where Jackson's game stayed just as intense, or with pals against the Woodstock Joneses, home and away.

If there was competition to be had, he had to have it, whether backgammon with June to see who'd do the dishes, stickball with a Spaldeen on Nineteenth Street against Charley, or Monday nights in the basement of the Markle Evangeline Residence Center for Women.

"He played every game like it was seventh game of the playoffs," says Jackson's friend Danny Rudolph, whose West Village office features a photograph of the Monday-night gang—a photo that Diane Mast's daughter keeps in her phone. "If you got the elbow, he took no prisoners. He'd come down with Neal [Walk] or Rosen or Gianelli or Mast. When we picked teams, we'd always make sure that Phil played with the four worst guys. He just didn't want to lose."

Was his addiction to competition a way to find a mooring as a *normal guy* after a childhood of not being allowed to be one of the boys? Was his constant intellectual searching ever since Grand Forks a way to soften and/or balance that competitive mania?

Back at the Garden, where the stakes were higher but the competitive urge was collectively waning, the Knicks had started down the slippery slope of one of the great skids in modern sport: forty years and still counting. But for Jackson, this 1974–75 season was one to be cherished: With the departure of Mast, another brother from a strange planet crossed his radar early in the season, in December.

Neal Walk was no pseudointellectual. He was certifiably brilliant. He'd been the second pick in the 1969 draft by the bottom-feeding Suns—behind Lew Alcindor, under whose shadow he would always labor. In his second year, under Cotton Fitzsimmons, a triangle guy who had succeeded Tex Winter at Kansas State, he led the Suns to a 48-34 record, good but not good enough for the playoffs. In his third year, Walk averaged 16 points, the team finished *sixteen* games over .500 . . . and still missed the playoffs. Fitzsimmons was out. Jerry Colangelo traded Walk to the Jazz. Walk understood. He'd been drifting toward Far Eastern religion. Breakfast generally consisted of . . . bean sprouts. He was reading Lao-tzu and *The Book of Changes.*

In a game against the Jazz in late December, Holzman asked Phil what he thought of this guy who clearly listened to a different drummer. "I think we could use him" was Phil's answer. Jackson had a new spiritual buddy the first time he walked into Walk's New York hotel room and saw

Ram Dass's *Be Here Now*, the story of a Harvard psychiatrist who drops acid, drops out, and follows an Indian guru.

"I'd been exploring anything that was counter to the establishment," Walk recalls now. "Christianity is where Phil came from, but in the end . . . I wouldn't say he eschewed Christianity, but Buddhism, Taoism and Sufism are more to his speed—more than Judeo-Christian, where you get these neodeities. I mean, Christ was a cool kid, a nice Jewish kid, and they screwed him up. See, neither of us was into deities—just common sense. And I think Phil would go on to teach that to his players. Like, he wouldn't pose with people, believing that they should find their own light to validate them, not someone else."

They were both vegetarians. They were both left-handed. And soon they were neighbors. Walk moved down to Chelsea. On game days, they'd bike on the West Side Highway to loosen up. Then Phil would walk up to Neal's place and give his piercing whistle, and they'd walk uptown, unless they were late. They'd flag down a cop cruiser sometimes, and the officers would be happy to oblige. Once the cops even put on the siren and the lights.

Jackson soon was giving Walk guided tours of the historical landmarks of his newly adopted town: The Old Stone House (1699, Brooklyn). Trinity Church, down on Wall Street. Always by bike. "I kept thinking, *For a kid from Montana, he sure had gained a lot of knowledge about New York.* Then we'd get to Boston and Philly, and he knew those towns just as well. He was curious about everything. He just had to keep learning." In the loft, Walk enjoyed the brick tennis backboard and the roof access. "We'd sit up there, drink beers, listen to the sounds of the city."

In that first half-season, Walk immediately sensed that Jackson's future might be as a guy in charge. "Whenever Red addressed the team before or after a game, Phil would stand right in front, and when Red was finished, he'd ask, 'How'd I do, Phil?' They'd tap fingers, kind of a low five.

"Not that Red wouldn't get on your ass. He was on Phil's ass every day.

Then he'd get on mine. But Phil had watched Red coach a lot of games. Plus, add the practices. That's a lot of learning. And most of what he learned is that you win with defense."

(In 1987, Neal Walk suddenly found himself unable to stand straight—a tumor on his spinal cord was removed, but the surgery left him a paraplegic. Rather than plunge into self-pity, Walk took the opposite path. Legs get you from one point to another is all, he says. Meditation, he reasoned, can do the same thing. Within a year, Walk was playing for the Los Angeles–Phoenix Samaritans of the National Wheelchair Basketball Association. Within another year, George H. W. Bush was honoring him at the White House as the Wheelchair Athlete of the Year.)

"I consider him a brother, in every sense," Walk says. "I feel graced to have been traded to New York to meet him. He introduced me to Native American culture. He introduced me to a lot of things. It was a good fit."

Entering the final day of the season at 39-42, a slim shot at a playoff berth beckoned. The 49-33 Buffalo Braves were rocking the intimate Buffalo Memorial Coliseum, with the fifth-best attendance in the division. Bob McAdoo was averaging 34 a game, Randy Smith was peaking, and a couple of veterans named Jack Marin and Jim McMillian still had legs.

The Knicks had to win, but they then still needed the Bill Fitch–coached Cavaliers to lose to the Kansas City–Omaha Kings, who had split the season between Kansas City's Municipal Auditorium (c. 1936) and Omaha's Civic Auditorium (c. 1954). Led by Tiny Archibald and Jimmy Walker (no, not *that* Jimmy Walker), they were best known at that time for having players' names *beneath* the number on the back of the jersey.

Led by Frazier, Bradley and Monroe (starting, Phil had 9), the Knicks beat the playoff-locked Braves. Then, back at the loft, Phil and Charley watched the Cavaliers game, along with June and Charley's second wife and three-month-old Chelsea and six-month-old Darrell Rosen. They watched Fitch improvise a play at the last second, which failed, whereupon the Kings improbably beat the Cavs, and the Knicks had made it.

The phone rang immediately: Meet at Clyde's Upper East Side palatial apartment, ASAP. The bathtub in the master bedroom was loaded with champagne, beer and wine. A feast of Chinese take-out adorned the main dining table.

The Jacksons and the Rosens laid the kids down in the bedroom/coat room. It was all giddy, so *Clyde*—until Charley went to check on Darrell, and found Spider Lockhart of the Giants and Nate the Snake tossing his kid across the bed and, as Charley puts it, "weaving in a mild alcoholic haze. The kid is laughing and gurgling and having a great time, but I was a little worried about Nate Bowman's hands," Charley says now. "Lockhart's? No. Bowman? Definitely."

Charley sought out his buddy and expressed his concern. "He's round like a basketball," Phil said. "Don't worry. He won't drop the kid. Just don't let him dribble him."

The next day, the Knicks, presumably somewhat the worse for wear, flew to Houston, to drop the season. They lost to the Rockets, badly. Back in the Garden, they prevailed. But back in Houston, the Rockets won the decisive game by 32. Rudy Tomjanovich and Calvin Murphy went wild. Phil scored 6.

Jackson headed for Flathead Lake to clear land and earn his first byline in the *New York Times* after the Warriors and Bulls finals, accompanied by a posed shot of a flanneled, bespectacled Phil splitting logs with a long-handled ax. "Winning: It Means Not Losing" wouldn't have won any literary awards. On the other hand, it's a safe bet that none of the other players in the NBA were penning thoughtful *pensées* about the nature of competition for the Gray Lady that summer.

"Flathead Lake," the piece began. "Sometimes the beauty of it hushes the mind's activity and one can just be. . . . The woodpecker on my old pier piling creates the loudest noise in the morning as he seeks out insects."

The takeaway of the piece is explicit: In trying to balance competition with Zen-nature bliss, as a human, he would always give in to the mortal side. Competition is embedded in us. He wishes he were still playing that day. "Why?" he quotes June as chiding him. "You know how you love it out here."

"It's just being a part of winning and knowing that you are the best in basketball," he answers her. That night, he writes, he watched that seventh game—"watching winners. Winning doesn't make you a better person. Just look at Nixon. It also doesn't mean you're right. It means that you know for that brief second that you've won."

It's slightly off, the whole thing, considering Jackson's previous pronouncements, as if the *Times* had said, "We need an essay" and, when he'd suggested that nature was good enough, had vetoed it.

Would the *Times* have run it if he weren't eccentric Phil? Hell, no. Was he already marketing himself as the man who broke the mold? Phil's mother didn't raise no dummy.

★

Soon after they met, he told Rosen he wanted to do the book. The result appeared, to little notice, via Playboy Press, in autumn of 1975. (Rumor has it that when Jerry Krause finally hired Jackson into the bigs, twelve years later, he tried to buy up every extant copy, given its frankness about the weed and the acid and the women, mention of which would never again appear in subsequent Jackson volumes.)

Apparently, Jerry missed a few. As of this writing, six hardcovers of *Maverick* are available on Amazon, from $75 to $342.52. The cover shows a heavily bearded Jackson trying to control a ball. Not controlling it; trying to. Juggling the ball. Juggling life.

"We just wanted to tell the truth," says Rosen now. "Well, *he* wanted to tell the truth; I didn't know what the fuck the truth was." Was the wisdom of mentioning the acid trip ever discussed? No, Phil wanted it in the book. Any thought of future implications? Nope. Why would there be? Coaching wasn't yet on his radar. In 1974, this was a corporation he was not about to spend a lifetime in.

The editor sent it back because he wanted more from Phil on what he thought of his teammates. So: Bradley became "cold" and "a loner." Frazier had a "cocky aloofness." Barnett? "Unfortunately, he . . . felt that the name of the game was scoring and nothing else."

In *Life on the Run,* Bradley tried to see his teammates through their own eyes—a talent Jackson, at this point, lacked. *Maverick* was refreshingly unfiltered, if highly naive. That he went ahead with it can only speak of the folly of youth and a still adolescent ego. Remember, he didn't really become a regular kid until college; developmentally, he was behind the pack. As people from humble beginnings who hit the jackpot turn into the nouveaux riches, so did Phil, shooting from the verbal hip, seem to want to distance himself from all things mainstream, be they organized religion or organized sport.

But here's the takeaway of this tome: Yes, the drug passages stand out ("When I had been playing with the Knicks for several years and had turned into a long-haired, pot-smoking hippie, Red was always quick to needle me about my ministerial ambitions"). "But it's a thread, all that stuff," says Diane Mast. "Not the quilt of the man." More than anything, the book is a detailed, rational, fascinating digest of his ongoing search for faith outside organized religion. It should be required reading for Religion 101.

As Rosen says now, "We both had vague spiritual itches that we couldn't quite scratch to our respective satisfaction." Credit Rosen for reining in the cerebral wanderings: "He has, generally speaking, a very circular way of thinking. He starts somewhere, goes off on a little tangent, goes off there, and then comes back." In a circle.

"If I had a chance to do it all over again," Jackson told me some fifteen years later, "I would not. I regret it because it caused pain to some people who were close to me. I don't regret it for myself. I did think at some point that it held up the advancement of my career. Maybe it was something people could point their finger at, or snicker behind my back that I'd done something unsavory . . . [but] I don't regret it for myself. When you start seeing that of the eight senators who were running for the presidential nomination, five of them had said they'd used marijuana, let's face it, these are the products our generation experimented with. It's not something I'd do in this day and age, but I think it's something you do as a kid, and growing up you try it. I don't think it was unusual [in the NBA]. I think it's unusual that I'd admit it."

The 1975–76 season? The creaking had turned into crumbling. Spencer Haywood, of all people, had come in to stem the bleeding. He failed. The Knicks went 38-44. Jackson was relegated to fewer minutes. For the first time in his career, they didn't make the playoffs.

And 1976–77? Now *McAdoo* came in. They missed the playoffs again. Phil, now thirty-two, averaged 3 points a game but did provide a highlight for the national press in a bout with the 76ers' George McGinnis, who threw a vicious first punch. Phil dodged it, swung back. McGinnis wasn't even called. Less than two months later, Kermit Washington shattered Rudy Tomjanovich's face. Jackson's public reaction? He made a remark about how it took a punch to a white star to get the league exercised about violence: his first impolitic utterance. Not his last.

The next year, 1977–78, the final Jackson Knick year, Gulf & Western bought the team and the arena. Holzman was gone. Willis came in and took them to a 43-39 finish, but they were not a team. Phil averaged just over 2 points. The Buddha would have retired. Phil, the human, couldn't give it up. Competition still ruled over cognitive quiet.

In retrospect, though, hanging on had a huge benefit. He had a new teammate: quiet, unpretentious Jim Cleamons, a guard who'd been coached in Cleveland for six years by . . . Fitch. Unlike Jackson, Cleamons, an education major out of Ohio State, already had "teacher/coach" written all over him, though three years younger than Phil.

"Phil was completely unselfish as a player—I saw that right away," Cleamons says now. "Oddly enough, he had very good basketball skills." (But then, he'd been through Fitch's boot camp.) "A lot of players get a label that you can only do this or that in a game. But when you see what a guy can do on a practice floor . . . we were on the second unit. Athletically

I could appreciate what he could do. But more than that, a player's game tells you a lot about who he is as a person. And he was unselfish. His willingness to share was impressive."

Phil did not learn from Cleamons that silence could be golden. "A former teammate told me this year," Jackson said to a reporter midseason, "that we had, as a team, the collective intelligence of an orangutan. I cannot say that I disagree."

Nonetheless, Reed's Knicks managed to make it into the second round of the playoffs before getting swept by the 76ers. Phil told writers he'd likely retire.

★

It had been an impressive run, numbers-wise if not scoring-numbers-wise: 801 games, bested only by Bradley and Frazier. He'd never averaged more than eleven points a game, but by the end of that season, Pulitzer-winning columnist Dave Anderson called him "surely the most valuable National Basketball Association player who never was really a starter."

"An intelligent person on a very intelligent team," Jerry Lucas, Dr. Memory, told me. "I think that team may have been the most intelligent team to ever play the game of basketball. Not just IQ, but knowledge of the game. He fit right into the mode."

Not according to a conversation I had with Walt Frazier in the spring of 1990. "He could have been a better player if he'd applied himself to it more, as much as he applied himself to his books. He read those weird books. They were weird to us, anyway. No one else ever read them."

But the voice of reason? This is what Red Holzman would write: "More than anything, he always wanted the game to played right. . . . He probably wasn't as selfish as he should have been to be a great ballplayer."

The average fan's reaction? There were no average fans anymore. Not when Reed, Frazier et al had been replaced by the McAdoos, McMillians and Haywoods. The "we" seventies were verging on the "me" eighties. On Thirty-Third Street, it was "Win: now." The garden where Phil belonged was now growing on his land on the banks of Flathead Lake.

EIGHT

He couldn't retire. He'd tried. But grad school could wait, and Flathead wasn't going anywhere. When Nets coach Kevin Loughery asked Jackson to be an assistant, it was a no-brainer, even if, playing in the brand-new Rutgers Athletic Center a few miles west, the previous year New Jersey had averaged 4,850 and finished in last place in their division . . . and in attendance.

Loughery, a Bronx guy, knew his game and knew his man. He'd been a sub on the Bullet team that beat Jackson's guys in the '71 playoffs. "I knew he'd be an outstanding coach from the start," Loughery says now. "He had supreme confidence in himself, but he was also able to get along with people. He was ready then. He could have stepped into coaching anywhere."

Why? Can you distill it to one overwhelming reason? Loughery doesn't hesitate more than half a second: "Competition. Extreme desire to compete. *Unbelievable* competitor."

As with Holzman, when you think city game, you think Loughery. This move represented another valuable apprenticeship. "He was a really good game coach," Jackson would write. "I admired his ingenuity."

When forward Bob Elliott tore up a knee, GM Charlie Theokas (a Jersey guy) activated Phil as a player/coach. Jackson put in eighteen minutes a game in a season that produced twelve more wins than the year before and a playoff spot, before Dr. J, Julius Erving, shook them off like a rag doll. Phil scored two points in each game.

On the other hand, the Knicks didn't even make the playoffs.

The following season, Phil reported as a player. He was cut from one of the league's worst teams and returned to the bench, working with big men. And, of course, the ragtag Nets being the ragtag Nets, Phil was once again called upon to suit up—for just sixteen games. (Attendance? Still last in the league.) And thus did one of the arguably greatest sixth men in basketball history—and clearly its number-one Kierkegaard scholar—end his playing career not with a bang but a whimper.

The following year, he hooked on as color commentator for the team. The guttural, gravelly, basso profundo voice, sounding like a car trying to start in a Montana winter, was barely understandable on the air. And— surprise!—he was frank in his commentary. The Nets were promoting a player for Rookie of the Year. Jackson said that the guy wasn't good enough. End of media career.

"When he was broadcasting," Walk recalls, "I was playing with Italy and Israel, and I returned with a wife. She couldn't deal with New York. Phil's living in Jersey. I'd go to Net games with him, and I'd started playing with him in that game at the UN school. So one time he needed to move furniture from Jersey. I wanted out of the house."

They rented a Ryder truck, loaded it up, took off west and planned their stops according to baseball games. They'd grab a beer, listen to a game on the radio. But as Walk remembers it, the honorary tribal member objected when Neal asked if they could detour to Little Bighorn: "Nah, too much time." Walk waited for Jackson to fall asleep and made the detour anyway.

Other than a few diner meals where the locals surveyed the two goliaths pulling in in the bumblebee yellow truck and arched a few eyebrows, Walk remembers it as a great trip. In Montana, Phil's mom was living in the house—"burning stuff up, sparks flying out of the chimney, she was a pisser, a literally fiery Pentecostal," Neal recalls.

Walk met the brothers, Joe and Charlie. He accompanied Phil down to Pine Ridge for a clinic. His report: "Trust me: It was obvious that to Phil, the whole place, the whole thing, was pretty sacred."

Now came another shot at writing: an analysis of the upcoming season for the *New York Times*—at the beginning of the first season that Phil would not be playing the game since the age of fifteen. This time, the paper didn't get any Thoreau-ian musings. They got a serious, thoughtful examination of the NBA's waning popularity. He'd seen it firsthand.

"The season begins with a shakeup of divisions, large numbers of un-signed free agents and college draft choices, after a summer of unfortunate press stories about drug use within the league," wrote the former weeder. The league had gone from Cousy/Pettit/Schayes to Russell/Havlicek to Frazier/Reed to . . . an irrelevant (to the networks) distant Western anonymous champion and a whole lot of black guys. The *L.A. Times* had just run a cocaine-use exposé, of which Jackson first heard when a reporter had called when he was hammering nails. (Jackson told the reporter to do a survey of his own young colleagues, or of doctors, lawyers, actors, politicians, golfers or construction workers: 45 to 75 percent of them, he opined, had tried blow.)

In print, he went on to criticize the writer for taking what he considered a cheap shot at the league and for implying that the level of play had diminished. He was now defending the athletic institution that he had eagerly skewered in print. Then, the piece also disses the owners for bringing in another expansion to swell the coffers of a league on "thin ice"—what with the average salary now bloated to $180,000. He nailed agents, too, for asking for too much for their clients. In essence, it was a well-written, if hardly electric, manifesto, redolent of the old contrarian judging the mainstream from out on the fringe.

Jackson seemed poised to become a literary gadfly of the game he not only loved but also desperately needed. And it was never going to happen in front of the TV lights. But freelance journalism wasn't going to pay the bills.

October of 1982 found him stacking wood. He and June had opened a sports-and-fitness club named the Second Wind as he wondered which direction his own wind would come from. That feeler from the Albany Patroons of the Continental Basketball Association didn't float his boat. Minor league? Not after those major-league apprenticeships. What was left to prove?

This was a man versed in the thoughts of everyone from Black Elk to the Buddha, poised to live a life of the mind. In which arena? The ministry? Law school? A grad degree in psychology? Or write his own definitive philosophical tome?

It was time to put childhood games behind him. Wasn't it?

NINE

I t was probably on the highway from Albany to Detroit—the team's longest odyssey, mileswise, the only route that would have allowed for a five-hour version of the game that enlivened their endless treks down ribbons of highway from minor-league town to minor-league town. This much we do know: Patroons were packed knee to elbow in a twelve-passenger Dodge Ram van with a thirty-six-gallon fuel tank. Not patroons, as in "landholders granted certain feudal powers in New York under Dutch colonial rule," but Patroons, as in men who dreamed of playing in the NBA but at the moment were not doing so. The van had been donated by an Albany Dodge dealer in return for assurances he'd get advertising banners hanging at the Patroons' home court, the Washington Street Armory, built in 1898.

It would be a high-probability bet that the man driving the Ram was using two bony elbows to do the steering while his hands were doing the *Times* puzzle on the center of the steering wheel, the van's dome light on: a panorama that might momentarily panic a recent arrival from Pensacola or Reno. But the old hands, like Frankie J ("Jumpshot") Sanders, didn't sweat it; they knew that the coach could drive: snow, sleet, whatever.

Phil would crank up the heat to put them to sleep, sending them to their dreams of hitting the fade-away to the delirious roar of 19,000 in the Garden instead of 1,900 in some WPA sandstone edifice in Cincinnati—or 190 in a high school gym in Brockton, Massachusetts, home of the Bombardiers. (They changed into their uniforms in the school's wrestling team's locker room, with broken lockers and broken windows. The first time they entered the wrestlers' enclave, Phil saw a poster on the wall that said, in essence, "To be a superior athlete, you must crush your opponent and humiliate him when he's down." He ripped it off the wall.)

We *can* guess that in the van that night the bluegrass-era Dead were playing on the tape deck. We do know that he was accompanied up front by Charley, his assistant coach, and between the two of them, diminutive Joe Hennessy, the radio guy, sitting in an unanchored metal folding chair straddling the driveshaft hump.

If it was snowing, add this semiterrifying sight: With the right elbow steering and the right hand anchoring the crossword, the left arm is cranking the window down to reach around to wipe the wet snow off the wiper.

We do know that it wasn't the night when Phil was highballing from Lancaster, Pennsylvania, to Albany in a blizzard, on Route 209, doing 50 or 60. The unmistakable scent of weed drifted through the bus, and when Charley asked what the hell was up, as Charley remembers it, Frankie's voice floated up from the back: "If I'm going to die, then I'm going to die stoned."

We do know that it wasn't the night that the luggage rack holding the uniforms, equipment and clothes went flying off the top of the van and the hurricane of detritus scattered its way across the Mass Pike, because the trip from Albany to Brockton was only four hours, max, and on this particular night of which we speak, the game of Who Am I was well into its fifth hour without a resolution.

"We'd pick a character out of history, or a fictional character," Hennessy said. "It wasn't like twenty-one questions, where you had a limited number of questions. You'd go until you got a no. So it could go on forever. When it was my turn, I'd be, you know, King Kong. Charley would pick maybe Eleanor Roosevelt.

"But Phil? He'd pick these people no one knew. So this one time I swear we played for five hours—one game—and we couldn't get an answer. Five hours goes by. I'm not kidding. Finally, we say, 'We've had enough. Who is it?'

"'It's Jim Bridger,' Phil says. I say, 'Who the fuck was Jim fucking Bridger?' So it turns out he was some explorer who hiked his way through the mountains outside Rapid City in, like, the middle of the nineteenth century.

"I say, 'How could you pick Jim Bridger?' And Phil says, 'I thought everyone knew who Jim Bridger was.'"

Well, everyone who'd studied up on obscure trappers from the West who ended up warring with Brigham Young over trading rights in Utah. "That was Phil. He meant it, too: He really *did* think that everyone knew who Jim Bridger was. But, I mean, he knew everything about *everything*. I'm a Civil War guy, and when I first met him in '82, and we started talking about the Civil War, I thought I had a pretty good knowledge. But it paled in comparison.

"And this wasn't just the Civil War—this was every topic. It was a little unnerving at first. But he has this sort of comforting demeanor about him. Even if he was riding or reprimanding you, he would do it in a non-confrontational way. So whenever he knew more than me, he'd find a way to make me feel comfortable in my ignorance."

They wouldn't play Who Am I? when they'd checked into a hotel in Lima or Casper or Tampa and Phil would tell Charley and Jim that they were going to go eat at some place he'd heard about. Then they'd be playing, "Where the fuck *are* we?"

"He was a human GPS," says Hennessy. "He had this innate ability to find a restaurant. We'd check into the hotel in Pensacola, and he'd say, 'We're going to Lenny's Crab-something.' I'd say, 'Do you know where it is?' He'd say, 'No, but I've heard about it. Don't worry.' We'd drive back roads, through woods. Charley'd be asking, 'Phil, where the hell are we?' And I'd say, 'We're going nowhere. Where the hell we going?'

Phil would say, 'I know where we're going.' I'd say, 'How? You've never been here before.' He'd say, 'I was told the directions. It's a left, a right, a right, another left, a right' . . . and all of a sudden, we pull up to Lenny's Crabhouse."

"The thing was," Rosen says now, "the next time we'd go down there, Phil wanted to see if he could find a different way to get to the crab shack."

It's not the destination. It's the journey.

If it wasn't a long drive to a game, Phil and Charley would let the team have the van—they didn't want to even *know* who was driving—and take their own car. Charley recalls one trip, from Massachusetts to Albany, in a snowstorm. "As usual, he had to go off on some weird road, and this time we're, like, in the middle of nowhere."

Then Phil pulled up in front of an old abandoned wooden house. "This is the Jackson house," he said. It was his ancestors' home—legendarily, and no doubt apocryphally, the first wood-frame in New England.

This may or may not have been the trip when Phil pulled the car over next to a field on a back road in a snowstorm.

"What're we doing?" asked Charley.

"It's beautiful," Phil said. "It's quiet. Let's just enjoy the nature for a second."

Charley wandered into the field, then stopped, did some meditation breathing—and felt a Jackson-fastball snowball hit him in the back of the head. Jackson's cackle, Charley remembers, echoed into the falling snow.

Jackson's journey to the armory began with a flight through snow on Christmas night of 1982 in a small plane en route to Lima, Ohio. The passengers: a pilot, three execs of the expansion Patroons—County Executive Jim Coyne, investor Mike Sandman and GM Gary Holle—and a journeyman ballplayer named Sam Worthen. Six weeks into their inaugural season, with a record of 3-14, a player had called Sandman to say that coach Dean Meminger was impossible to play for. That he had a mutiny on his hands.

"I was worried we'd lose the franchise," Sandman says now. He had twenty-five investors who'd paid $4,000 each. It was the best chance for a high profile in a very long time for the state capital—a town, since Al Smith, synonymous with corruption. The arrival of the CBA expansion team meant more than it would have in Albuquerque or Toronto. The CBA, billing itself as "the oldest professional basketball league in the world," wasn't bad basketball. It was as high as minor-league could get.

Jim Coyne was a beloved county executive, a rising star. "He did more for this area than anyone but Nelson Rockefeller," Mike Sandman says now, even after Jim did time in federal prison for being convicted of inappropriately cashing a check from a potential architect; a charge that he insists today was specious. The execs' roots were within their village. They wanted to bring the tribe some pride. And after a conversation with DeBusschere, by now the GM of the Knicks, Coyne knew whom he wanted to coach the fledgling franchise. DeBusschere said it was a no-brainer: his old poker buddy Phil, who was currently in the outback of Montana, spinning his wheels. After the apprenticeships with Fitch, Holzman and Loughery, Dave advised, Jackson should be coaching instead of trying to figure out whether to join the ministry or apply to law school.

"I'd wanted Phil from the start," Coyne says now, in his modest Albany living room. "I wanted us to have a Knick relationship. But the first time we talked, he told me he didn't want to coach. He wanted to be in Montana. Then I tried to get Henry Bibby, but he was only interested in college. So then I got Dean: a character."

"One day Dean actually said, 'Guys, who would you rather have running your ball club?'" recalls Derrick Rowland, a forward. "'Me, like a cat, down low, or Magic Johnson, standing straight up, breaking the rules of his position?' We looked around at each other and thought, *The end is definitely near.*"

The plane made it through the snow and bounced onto the runway as the team was readying for a game against the Ohio Mixers (cement, not cocktails) in the six-seater that a Patroon supporter had provided.

Worthen, a fringe player for the Bulls in previous years, would serve as interim player-coach as the brain trust desperately looked for an answer. They summoned Meminger to give him the ax. Dean took the news remarkably well; he was anxious to get back into the NBA as a player. (On the flight back, with Meminger sitting in Worthen's seat, Coyne recalls that he had headphones on, "bopping to his music, as if nothing had happened.")

The execs gathered at the American Legion Hall to bend an elbow and game-plan. Coyne asked Holle for Jackson's number. Phil picked up, out in Montana.

"I guess basketball started coming back into his head a little bit," Coyne says now. "I said, 'I'm in Ohio. I'm firing Meminger and I'd love to have you come in and finish the season. If you don't like it, we'll call it quits at the end of the year.' He said, 'Give me a call in an hour.'"

Sixty minutes later, Coyne made the call. "Yeah," Phil said. "I'll do it."

Here was the thing: In the law, in the ministry, at the college podium, you might be brilliant—but no one's keeping score. There aren't any standings. No quantifiable competition. No winners, no losers.

"Imagine if I hadn't taken that flight out there," Coyne says now. "If Dean hadn't done so poorly, Phil never would have ended up in Albany. Or Chicago. Or L.A."

One factor: He could live an hour to the south, in Woodstock, Rosen's domain—the town to which, after the Jacksons had their first child down in the city, June had sometimes retreated for some peace and quiet, leaving Phil in the loft. The quiet, post–Woodstock Festival region, enlivened by shops like the Talisman, the Flying Watermelon, the Three of Cups and Books in Flight ("specializing in Arthurian legend and Celtic mythology"—but not the Auerbach kind).

"It was the kind of place that expressed a lot of the values I believed in," Jackson would tell me some years later. "I've always had a sympathy toward pacifism, but I'd never lived in a community that had my values.

They were very conscious people. There were multiracial families, gay couples. My daughter was in a class once where five of the twenty-five kids came from families with married parents.

"It opened up a lot of horizons in my life. I think I needed to live there to complete all the sentiments I'd only been able to intellectualize, but not participate in, during the sixties and seventies. A period of time I'd missed when I was playing with the Knicks."

June Jackson rose to a position as administrative director of an Ulster County hospice service. Both did volunteer work with Family of Woodstock, an all-purpose hotline and counseling group for substance abusers and the homeless.

Not quite as easily at home was the new coach in his new arena. This armory's architect, one Isaac Perry, was famous for designing the New York State Inebriate Asylum. The armory hadn't been maintained too well, having no actual tenants. The onus fell to GM Holle.

"I got a heat bill that's killing us," Holle recalls. "We can't turn the heat up because of expense, but it was so cold that one day Phil calls me and says, 'The ball won't bounce. Seriously.' During some games we turned the heat up too much and there's snow on the roof, which has holes. And it drips water on the floor."

When the crowds went crazy, the vibrations would set off the security alarms, because of all the ammo in the basement. But they couldn't be turned off automatically. Ten minutes later, the games could resume. And then there was the locker room itself: in the basement, next to the public men's rest room . . . which also housed the showers. A fan taking a post-game leak might see Frankie J soaping up.

Intercity travel in the air was even more exhausting—between cities that, as far as the airlines were concerned, barely counted as cities at all. Like Casper: the Friendly Ghost Town. "To save money," Jim Drucker remembers, "we'd have teams play three games in four nights. One year [the defunct airline] People's Express kept the league in business, because they had a $19 fare from Newark to Cincinnati, which was near Lima. Another year, it was [defunct] Eastern. For $49 you could fly unlimited amounts from a single airport a month—but you couldn't go through the same city more than once. So Albany would fly from Albany, change planes in Atlanta, then from Pensacola back to Albany, then back down to Savannah, then to Albany. Then a couple of home games. Then start again—only now, Hartford's been used, so you go through Syracuse. Insane."

This would often mean a very early wake-up call. For the three-legged flight to Billings—the toughest, as Jackson recalled—they would leave Oshkosh at four thirty in the morning to catch a leg to Milwaukee. Then to Atlanta. Wait forever for a flight to Evanston. Quite the journey, for a man once so intent on taking paths of peace.

The road trips? History lessons. In Rapid City, South Dakota, there stood an assortment of young men, inner-city guys, Texas guys, a motley crew, standing at the foot of Mount Rushmore. "Although sometimes when we were in Rapid City, he'd take the team to an Indian reservation," says Hennessy. "They'd all bitch about getting on the bus, but once they got there, they felt good about [the fact that] the team was bonding. Just as important, they'd think, *I'm smarter than I think I am.* He opened up their mind by letting them see that they were bigger than just basketball players.

"Then we'd go stomp the Rapid City Thrillers."

Jefferson Davis's summer home, Beauvoir, over in Biloxi, ninety minutes west of Pensacola, with a gift shop replete with Confederate flags, hadn't seen any large groups of black players since antebellum time. Nothing like visiting a plantation to get you stoked. Maybe that's why the Pats never had trouble with the Pensacola Tornados.

Then, even the most eccentric ex-jocks are still jocks—if the Savannah Spirit's play-by-play guy's memory is accurate. It was a few years later, when Rosen had landed the Spirit head-coaching job.

"We fly into Biloxi to play Pensacola," Craig Kilborn recalls. "Albany had played there the night before. The Patroons were staying an extra day. So after the game, Charley and Phil invite me along for a bite to eat. I say,

'Cool.'" Kilborn was a hoops freak on a scholarship from Montana State (an hour east of Anaconda). In Moscow, he hit all four threes plus eight from the free-throw line and finished with 20. That'd be Moscow, Idaho.

Then he trooped to the media lights, showing signs of happily heading for the less traveled roads of sports journalism. One night, with his father in town, Kilborn interviewed him on the radio but identified him as the son of James Naismith, the inventor of basketball. The local print reporter was impressed.

When he got Phil into the studio for his TV show the first time, Kilborn being Kilborn, his first on-camera question, unrehearsed, was "What's your favorite recipe?"

Jackson didn't miss a beat. Kilborn had no idea that one of Phil's hobbies was gourmet cooking. (Rosen: "He uses, like, fifteen ingredients for dinners; shopping is a trip, great wine, butcher's favorite cut—no expenses spared.")

"It was a chicken dish," Kilborn recalls. "I don't remember what was in it. White wine or garlic, maybe." So he figured dinner that night might be special. But on this night in Pensacola, the crab house wasn't the destination. "Phil or Charley says, 'Someone said there was a strip club somewhere over here . . . we've never been. But do you want to pop in there and get a bite to eat?' They made sure the point was only to eat. Never been there. Not a common thing.

"We walk in. And for whatever reason, most of the strippers are Asian. And they're all waving: 'Uncle Phil! Uncle Phil!'"

Coyne's plane flight changed basketball history. The expansion Patroons, freed of Dean's dictatorship, dying to get the NBA to notice them, played their hearts out for this Phil Jackson guy. "He didn't overcomplicate things," TCU's Ralph McPherson recalls. "He was definitely a player's coach. He'd call a time-out with that whistle—he had such a deep voice, in the midst of a game if he was yelling at you, it would blend in with the crowd noise, and the whistle was the only way he could get your attention—and sit you down, and say, 'Keep it simple! What you're doing isn't working. If you keep doing it, it's not going to work. So just take care of what your responsibility is, and we'll get the job done.'"

"He was the kind of guy you didn't want to let down," Derrick Rowland says, "because he knew that the key for each of us was finding our niche. See, Phil understood the game at a different level. Most people see it as shots, rebounds and scoring. He had an understanding of the big picture, the flow of the game. But I guess your biggest thing was, you wanted to do it for him. He was that kind of guy because of the way he treated you: in practice, in games. You wanted to show him you'd learned . . . to do it for him.

"He never put us on the spot. He would never single you out and embarrass you. He was always up front and honest with you. No games. None of that stuff. He was fair. He respected you during game time. He didn't jump on mistakes, and believe me, that matters to the guy who made the mistake. He kept his own life to himself. He was definitely one of us. To every degree."

Rowland and Jackson both knew that what NBA scouts looked for was not the high numbers, but the guys who would come in and know their roles: role players who had no egos, who had done their time, who knew what the concept of *team* meant. "On a plane," Rowland says, "you don't see your teammate. In a van, you can smell his breath. We had the kind of guys who did it because we were humble."

As on all of his teams, it was a closed circle. Players, trainer, coach, assistant coaches—everyone else was outside the circle. The man who'd carved his media niche as a player now shut the media pretty much out. He had his eye on the big prize.

"A wall had been put up," says Tim Layden, covering the team for the Schenectady paper. "Dean was very chummy with everyone. Social and chatty. Phil immediately took some getting used to. He had a tremendous physical presence. It seemed superhero-esque. His personality and his airspace both filled the room. But he didn't deliver prepackaged quotes. You had to learn how to talk to him. He was as smart as you—at the very least."

The century-old armory provided a true home-court advantage. "There was a mystique," says Holle. Unlike the legislators and the lawyers, the Patroons, all of whom lived in rooms within walking distance of the armory, represented the city. "It was a very, very big deal for Albany," says Layden. "Bringing in a high minor-league team with a big-name coach."

They finished in fourth place, Jackson the rookie head coach unable to unbury himself from the mess Meminger had left. Hennessy was, at first, frustrated by his laid-back ways. But the next year, as the victories added up, the place started to come alive. The major addition? Not a player. Phil knew that Rosen, as outspoken as they come, could teach, as well as draw attention away from Phil to let him learn to do his job without the usual histrionics.

"When he first showed up on the bench," point guard Lowes Moore recalls, "everyone just figured he was Phil's hippie friend from Woodstock." Not quite. As Jackson himself put it the next year, "I see the total picture—and Charley sees it in segments."

"Phil was not always easily understood to some of the players," says Gary Holle. "Charley was sort of a mental translator."

"Charley was Phil's conscience—not his voice," says Layden. "Phil was the mystical philosopher. Charley was the New York troublemaker. Phil would negotiate his way out of a fight; Charley would throw punches. At the end, there was a lot more of Charley."

Layden remembers Phil standing behind writers to see if they were correctly transcribing his words—"although if you challenged him, he'd back down. He didn't invite cozying up to." Charley filtered no words. Thus was an unholy collaboration born, and CBA sideline history made: the neatly bearded head coach next to the man whose ties would be banned in Tijuana, hair flying out like some Gene Wilder with his finger in a socket.

"He was wearing tie-dyed T-shirts and shorts," says David Magley, a shooting forward that year. "He shows up like he's going to the Dead concert, with the Jew-fro going out of a control. We'd look at Phil, like, *What?* But a great guy. A great laugher." (Frankie J's best line to Charley: "Where'd you get the tie? You cut up your curtains?")

As had been the case when Phil apprenticed with Holzman, CBA assistants weren't allowed. So on the road, Charley dressed like a trainer in white. It made him look like an ice-cream-truck driver—"because he thought a trainer would be all white . . . because it would mock the rule," said Layden. "He even had a scissors on his belt. He'd stand up and yell, this balding guy with whitening hair, big beard. I always thought of him like a tall Allen Ginsberg."

When Phil had first asked if he could bring on an assistant, it took Hunter College grad and former teammate Mike Sandman about three seconds to grant Phil's wish. "We were Division III, but he could have played Division I," Sandman says now. "Mostly he was my protector. I played point guard, and in a game against Brooklyn College, I was having an atypically good game. I drove down the lane at one point, and their center stuck out his knee and caught me in the thigh. I couldn't continue. On the next play, as they were lining up for the foul shots I couldn't take, we heard a crack. It was Charley's elbow breaking the guy's nose." The Patroons called him the team psychiatrist. In practice, they'd stay away from his picks, lest he kill them.

The basic scheme, per any Jackson philosophy, was a fluid offense—the flex: designed, as the triangle would be, as Red's offenses were, to get people open. But when the thing was on the line, you put it in the hands of the shooters. For their solos. As former NBA commissioner David Stern described it to me, the best analogy for the game he stewarded for three decades is jazz. "It needs structure, and then it needs a riff."

The early-eighties CBA, mirroring the NBA, was high scoring. Jackson knew that some people could hit the shot; others never will. But all can be taught defense. So if he had his natural scorers and he taught D, he'd win. So he found his riffers.

★

When the phone rang, Rudy Macklin had been on his couch in his Jersey condo. After two years with the Hawks under Loughery, he'd been traded to the Knicks for Sly Williams but lasted just eight games: A rare condition that caused him to lose fluids at an abnormal rate had caused unbearable cramping, and in his second year with the Hawks, in the hospital after one game, he'd been told to find another profession or face a dangerous fate.

But he had to give it a final shot. For a baller, that's a no-brainer. When Macklin took my call in Louisiana, where he's on the Governor's Council on Fitness and Sports, he said to me, "I think about the Robert Frost poem. I took the road less traveled, and it made all the difference. I decide to go to the Albany Patroons, to a city where it's always snowing, playing in a terrible arena, and wonderful things happened. I played for the winningest coach in history and helped him win his first championship."

Moore? Now he's director of the Mount Vernon Boys and Girls Club—the place that Denzel says changed his life. As a kid? The stud of Mount Vernon (*Four Square Miles to Glory*, as Jerald L. Hoover's documentary of Mount Vernon calls it). A veteran of the playground at the projects they called 70—the address of the apartment buildings where former Harlem Globetrotter Goose Tatum taught the kids after getting out there at six in the morning himself—Moore had grown up a Knicks fan: "They were five people together, working as a team, and they had Monroe—the greatest one-on-one player ever—so I knew you could have a team and also have individual expression on the court." He'd have stints with three NBA teams. He knew the ropes.

"I need you to run the team," Phil told him over the phone. "I need you to make these guys around you better. But there are going to be times when I need you to take over the ball game."

"Before long, I get the vibe," Moore says now. "Phil's laid-back. Spiritual, mentally very bright . . . in the moment. There was peace in the craziness, the hype of the game. There was a sense of peace and serenity in those moments for him, and because of that, for me."

Frankie "Jumpshot" Sanders? The man who, on the night in Lima when a balloon popped during a promotion, immediately hit the deck, lest it be a gunshot? ("You can never be too careful," he said to Rosen.) Sixty-nine games for the Spurs, Celtics and Kings. Sanders stories are legion. Like the night a Thriller fan in the Tampa gym riled him at the foul line. "I fucked your mother," Frankie said, loudly, before converting the shot. A six-five shooting guard averse to playing defense or dribbling, he was Jackson's most problematic player.

"You see how Phil handled Dennis Rodman? Frankie was his first Dennis Rodman," says Macklin now. "Frankie would fly off the handle like Dennis, and Phil would sit Frankie down, and Frankie would pout. Then, a few minutes later, Phil, with his arms still folded, would sort of wander down to the end of the bench and say nothing. Then he'd wander away. Then he'd come back and ask, 'Are you ready to play?' And Frankie would say, like a little kid saying he was sorry, 'Yes.' And Phil would put him back in—and he'd light the place up."

It was in the armory where Phil began to coach in a new way, freed of constraint, with nothing to lose. If it wasn't entirely Werner Erhard, it was hardly Red Auerbach.

Before long, Patroon practices weren't just a matter of running the flex. They began or ended or both with meditation/prayer circles, based in part on a passage from Black Elk in his *Black Elk Speaks:* "The sacred hoop of my people was one of many hoops that made one circle." The circle: the only shape in nature. If the brain can't embrace the concept of infinity, it can envision a sphere, if ever-expanding. It's the shape of the sun, the planets and the solar system. It's the shape of a basketball. "We'd gather, hold hands, in a circle, thirty seconds of meditation, or more," says Rowland. "We'd relax, let the energy go through the group. We'd be smiling at each other.

"Hey. We knew there was a method to the madness. We knew what he was doing. After practice, we were a tight-knit group. We all lived in the vicinity, around the armory, we'd walk to practice." Some of them even read the books he'd given them.

"He wouldn't ask for book reports," Hennessy says. "It'd just be something he'd read that he thought would be beneficial to them. Initially some guys would say he was nuts, but then someone would read one and like it, and the next thing you know, another would buy into it, and another."

"I read them," says Macklin. "Because he really made a point of trying to know what was going on inside of us, psychologically. He knew what we'd gone through, wanting to be pros. He wanted to handle us delicately, because he knew we felt our dreams had been shattered, and psychologically we were fragile. He was a coach-slash-psychologist in a stressful situation."

"He could talk to them a different way than anyone else had in their careers," Hennessy says. Practices were not Fitchian. "I'd get frustrated because I thought players were taking advantage of him. Used to aggravate the hell out of me. I'd say, 'Why aren't you more of a disciplinarian with these guys?' He'd say, 'I'm working it out my own way. I got it under control.' I'd say, 'Kick 'em in the ass.' 'We'll see,' he'd say. 'Right now we'll do it my way.' And invariably it was the right way."

The widely held perception was that CBA players had talent but lacked some microchip necessary to notch it up to the grueling, psychologically demanding routine of the NBA. Jackson saw it differently. "That's not the case," Tim Layden remembers him saying. "It's because they're not good enough. They're in denial about that. I have to get them to subvert that shortcoming and play together. They're flawed athletes, but they don't have to be flawed men."

Make no mistake: Jackson wasn't coaching in a monastery. He wasn't going to get to the NBA by mysticism. There were times when his outer Fitch would silence his inner Buddha. Like the night he reamed them all a new one at halftime: "You guys are supposed to be fucking professionals! You're supposed to be aware of the fucking game situation! Dammit! Get your head out of your ass! I know you all want to be in the NBA, but right here is where we are! Dammit!"

Then he threw his clipboard and left the room and lit a cigarette and turned to Rosen: "You think they believed that?"

Nor, when there weren't enough bodies and he suited up, could he help but revert to Phil circa 1975. In one practice in the fall of '83, he kneed David Magley in the thigh—and put him on the IR list. As Magley points out, "Since I was beating him and I was talking, maybe he didn't like the talk."

Or the practice the day before a game in Savannah. It was a full-court drill, and the Patroons didn't have enough players, so Jackson and Rosen paired up on one team. At one point, Jackson broke open and motioned for the pass, whereupon Charley threw it five feet over his head. Jackson was livid. "What the hell, Charley?"

Now it so happened that, the day before, Rosen's ex-wife had driven over from the Gulf Coast to see her ex. According to Rosen, they did some extensive partying.

"So I pass it, like, out of bounds. Then I took him aside and explained the situation, and he nodded and said, 'Oh. OK.' "

That first year, he stuck to his promise to play everyone—so much so that not a single player got a call-up from a championship team. It was the journey, not the destination. Not a single Patroon to whom I talked expressed any regret at not being featured that year. For most, it was the highlight of their lives.

But then, I never did find Frankie Jumpshot.

On game days, Phil and Charley's ritual began with the hour-long drive. He could have easily moved to a more convenient location, a suburb of the capital. But it *was* on the fringe where he belonged, where he wanted to belong: reined in, yes, as anyone running a company must be, but out at the far edges of a very, very big pasture.

"In truth, who I really am," he would tell Rosen many years later, "is a mediator who's sitting at the edge of this culture and looking in."

Woodstock had a good school system. The scent of patchouli flavored the exhilarating mountain air from one end of town to the other. Musicians strumming. Catskill crags and peaks, slathered in powdered-sugar snow. His friends: a dentist, a Rolfer, an environmentalist with a Harvard degree who'd opted for a tie-dyed environment.

Ah, to have been a fly on the wall of Rosen's old Chevy wagon (which once broke down on the Thruway in a snowstorm on the way to a shoot-around; they hitched, coached, hitched back—and the car started right up). You'd have gotten an introduction to historical novels about Native Americans, listened to comparisons of bluegrass pickers and sorted out unfathomable mystics.

"Sooner or later, we'd get around to the team we were playing," says Rosen. But first there was a *real* game to be played. They'd hit the court of the Albany Athletic Club one-on-one full court. This was much more than a casual workout. ("They'd *pound* on each other," says Rowland.) And even if the outcome was a foregone conclusion—of the 250 or so games the two played over the years, Charley won 1, after a flagrant foul—it was huge to both of them.

If the games got close? "I'm done," Rosen says. "I'm reduced to Tommy Heinsohn hooks from the corner." The one Rosen won? He clearly fouled Jackson on a drive for the game-winner—"and he was *pissed*. He ran off by himself and did some yoga exercises. After that he was cool.

"Hey, no matter where or how you play it, it's the game. Like Oscar says: You play it whenever you can and as long as you can.

"One time we were snowbound in Louisville. I taught him this card game, Casino. I knew how to win—you memorize the tens, the aces. So I was winning, maybe, $2.60, and he couldn't beat me. So he took the cards and threw them: 'Screw this game!' "

What kind of guy never lets his friend win just once? The cliché that someone burns with a competitive fire? Phil was a nuclear fuel rod, cooled by the water of his search for spiritual peace. Why the intense need to compete? Perhaps because Pentecostalism had tried to leach all individuality out of him, an empty vessel for the Lord to fill, lest damnation ensue.

So how better to insist as you grow that you have free will than by emerging as an individual? How better to stand up and say, "I *am*," than by pitting yourself forever against other mortal men (after all, you can't fight Jesus) and slapping them down? Fuck turning the other cheek.

On the other hand, by his own admission, Charley was such a dirty player that in later years, maybe Rosen just naturally brought the beast out of Phil's belly. (Wouldn't be the first time. "I *hate* that guy Rosen," Walk says now, with a verbal wink, a veteran of many pickup games.)

After their combat, the ritual would continue. Jackson and Rosen would dine at a place on Swan Street, a quiet pub that favored jazz, the ceremony capped with a cup of coffee and a Bailey's Irish Cream: "To stoke us. Bailey's and coffee. We were ready, man. We were ready."

★

They finished in second place, hungry for the playoffs. Literally. In the CBA, per diem was $15, but a five-game playoff series meant $400 per player—in other words, if you play in all three rounds, more than a cool grand. Not Kobe beef, but a New York strip for sure.

They started inauspiciously. The first round pitted the Pats in a best of five (all rounds were best of five) against the Bay State (Massachusetts) Bombardiers, coached by Jo Jo White, who promptly took two in the armory, in part thanks to a winter storm that held the crowd to 986 in the first game. In the second, a dagger to the heart: One of the CBA's quirkier rules was that the first team to score three in overtime won. A Bombardier hit a bomb within the first few seconds. Game.

The next night in the van going to Brockton, one of the players opined that the trip back that night was going to be a long one if they lost and bowed out in three.

"Knock it off," Staten Island's Andre Gaddy famously said. "We're going to win this one, and after that we're going to win the next one, and the one after that, the next series and the final. We're going to win the whole thing." He should have opened a psychic hotline.

In game three in Brockton, Moore hit an answering three-pointer in OT to win in front of 685. The owner fired coach Johnny Neuman. He was leading the series 2–1. Tough league.

In game four, with the Bombardiers now coached by GM Jim Sleeper, Patroon center Ralph McPherson went to the foul line, with the Pats down one, and seconds to go. Celtic draftee Perry Moss stood directly behind him: "Are you gonna miss, Ralph? Are you gonna miss?"

"And all I did was look at the rim and put the sons of guns in," Ralph says now. In game five back in Albany, in front of a packed house announced as 3,203—which was impossible, because the capacity was 2,413, including the 144 in the balcony and the 350 in the general-admission bleachers rented from a wrestling promoter—they routed the Bombardiers, behind Moore and Macklin, and prepared for the next round against the Coquis. That would be Tree Frogs, to non–Puerto Ricans, who were missing their all-star, a huge journeyman center named Geoff Crompton, called up to Cleveland, best known for sleeping with a half-dozen quarter-pounders under his bed, for a snack every hour.

They finished off Herb Brown's guys in three and headed to Casper the Friendly Ghost Town for the finals, against the Wildcatters, who played in a new arena, in front of huge crowds—5,221 watched the Pats take the first, 129–121. There was a ninety-minute delay because the refs' plane out of Denver to Casper had been canceled. A police escort drove them to Wyoming.

"Afterward, in the bar of the Casper Hilton," Layden recalls, "it was crazy. Late night, bar full of noise and music, and Phil and Charley are down at the end of the bar. Charley's yelling, 'Someone get this man a cigarette!' Because Phil would never buy. He was always bumming. And Phil is just laughing and laughing, his eyes squinting in that way, and I got right then the whole sense of this Charley-Phil thing. It was just another wild adventure for these guys. The whole thing was an adventure."

Wyoming tied it the next night, 128–126, in front of 6,258. Back in Albany, the Patroons prevailed by nine. But in game four, the Wildcatters tied it, and in the decisive fifth, the Patroons were down by 14 at the half, at home. Twenty-four minutes from elimination.

"At halftime, he gave this speech," Macklin said. "I'd never heard anything like it. He said, 'You know, a lot of us, we'll leave here, some of us will go on to different things in life, some to the NBA, but at this particular moment,' he said, 'we have a chance to win a championship. And you're going to have to find a way to do it. Now, if we don't do it, we can go on with our separate lives and say our good-byes tonight.'

"Then he looked at us and said, 'But I'm not ready to do that.'"

Macklin had scored 20 in the first half. "And then Frankie said, 'I ain't touched the ball,'" Rudy recalls. "I said, 'Cool, we go to Frankie.' We come out like gangbusters. Frankie lit it up the second half. We won that one. And it was Phil's speech that turned it around. Best speech I ever heard."

"Phil was cool when the final buzzer went off," Rosen recalls. "He stayed to the side and let everybody celebrate. But when the fans emptied, we poured beer on each other. It had been a long grind. It was beautiful. He had won championships before, but he hadn't coached one.

"Then afterward we went to this bar where there were free chicken wings."

Make no mistake about the stature of the achievement of that title. Winning a championship in a league where every player is trying to put up 32 points for the scout from Milwaukee after an eight-hour bus ride is arguably a lot harder than winning one in a league where your players are already among the elite riding a chartered 757 between cities. Molding a team out of fringe rogues playing in the Dome Arena of the Rochester Zeniths, with its carpeted court, might be the greatest coaching feat of

Jackson's career—although once he made it up the next level, as he described in later autobiographies, Albany faded quickly into his rearview mirror.

Drucker was quoted later in the paper as saying that an NBA team had expressed interest in Phil. Jackson vowed that he and June were committed for at least a few more years in town. He wasn't through serving his apprenticeship.

Meantime, his next parish would be in a warmer clime. Mentor Holzman had done his time in the summer Liga de Baloncesto Superior Nacional, as would P. J. Carlesimo and Doug Moe. It looked good on the résumé. And now that he was a made man, a ring winner his first time out, he was inevitably growing more interested in the real bucks that an NBA job could bring. But cracking the old-boy network of the NBA was hard enough, harder still when you've published a book dissing teammates and revealing your pharmaceutical past.

On his playoff visit to San Juan, a businessman who owned the Quebradillas team had offered him the summer gig. He didn't have to think twice. It didn't pay much, but you couldn't beat the Puerto Rican beaches.

TEN

Pick up your sharpened No. 2 pencil. Stay within the lines. Question 1: Which two items do *not* belong in the series below?

1. a quenepa fruit
2. a kid's shoe
3. a C battery
4. a recently beheaded, but still highly mobile, chicken
5. a plastic cup of Medalla beer
6. a bullet fired by the mayor of Quebradillas

Answer: 4 and 6. All of the objects were thrown at one time or another at Puerto Rican League referees in the 1980s, but 4 and 6 missed their targets: The chicken didn't hit anyone, and the bullet fired by the mayor missed its mark, wounding a vendor. All other missiles, and several others not named in the list, regularly met their mark, although no one ever recalls getting nailed by a piece of dog meat on a stick, one of the vendors' delicacies.

The quenepas were the bitch. Only the outer quarter inch of the tasty green tree fruit is pulp; the rest is a rock-hard pit the size of a golf ball. You haven't earned your referee stripes until you've been skulled by a well-aimed quenepa pit.

Jack Nies did. "And my wife used to get hit with piña coladas," Nies recalls, retired after thirty-one years in the NBA—and twenty-nine on the island: a paid vacation—even if, because each officiating team comprised one NBA guy and one local, Nies would have to call the hard fouls and risk the pelting. "The other guy had to live there all year. I had to protect him. We'd take one for the team."

A local official's health would be at risk should the home team lose. Hence it seldom did. "If it did, referees in one arena would enter a trap-door at midcourt at the end of the game," Rosen recalls, after writing a few pieces about the *liga*, "and wait for the police to knock and let them know it was safe." (Although there was no guarantee that their car would still be in the parking lot in one piece.)

Founded in 1930, the *liga* took its sport seriously. Carmelite nuns sacrific-ing chickens to spread blood on the visiting-team bench? A tad more intimidating than waving white towels at opposing free-throw shooters.

A pleasant city on the beach known for its great surfing (and pirates' caves), Quebradillas was the home of a charter team. The Pirates hadn't won a title in five years, but employed the immortal Raymond Dalmau—thirty-six but still the Big O of the league. In a league where the sacred lifetime level of scoring was 5,000 points, Dalmau retired with more than 11,000. He'd been courted by Utah but declined in order to keep his ama-teur status and play in three Olympics.

Before he coached a single game, Jackson set pen to paper on the offi-cial stationery of his residence, the Parador Vistamar—a first-class hotel back then, with a lovely view of the sea. "Dear Jim," Phil wrote in measured longhand spotted by the occasional inexplicable capital letter, "Arrived here on Monday and went right to work. The Town of Quebradillas is ex-tremely picturesque. Vistamar sits high above the ocean facing north northeast and the coastal breeze is very refreshing."

Prelims out of the way, Jackson then informs Coyne that he has re-ceived a tentative job offer from Wayne Ellis, wealthy Patroon board member, which would be available while he coached, and while he wasn't sure the offer was firm, he had to consider it.

"I remain sincere in wanting $30,000 as a salary due to the potential loss of outside revenue. I don't believe I'm asking too much to be paid at the current level many of my contemporaries will make. I would take a poll of salaries and bet odds on Dave Cowens, Cazzie Russell and others making as much if not more than that.

"However," he adds, "you know I will never put a team in monetary stress for a few more bucks. But I do think you know that I am worth that much."

He then asks for Charley to get $250 a week, because his wife feels he's working for less than travel expenses. He also asks that the team reimburse him for technicals: "It should not cost me $ to make that tool [T] a useful wedge. I don't abuse them!" Finally, he asks his per diem to go from the players' $15 to $25 for him.

"I am looking forward to an enjoyable, educational summer here in P.R.," he finishes. "Please respond if necessary at the address located on this letterhead. Thanks Jim, Good wishes, Phil Jackson." Hardly the demands of a megalomaniac.

Coyne's response reached Jackson a month later: $30,000 is good. Bad news: The league had ruled that while a team *could* have an assistant, it couldn't pay him. The techs? Negotiable. On the third point? "We may be able to arrange for something in the $20 area."

Coyne closes by wishing Phil success with his tennis game and his basketball team, in that order, and invites Phil to Saratoga to see some of Coyne's horses in August.

The reason it might have taken the missive a full month to get to Phil was that Phil was no longer coaching the Pirates. Scoffing at the "flex" offense that Jackson had used to win their title back in the snow, Dalmau convinced the owner to fire Jackson seven games into the season. But as the hoop fates would have it, just down the road in Isabela, Los Gallitos were off to a horrid start, coached by a man named Tom Sullivan of the University of New Hampshire.

"Me and Sullivan almost got into fisticuffs one time," Edwin Pellot-Rosa recalls. Edwin, of half Puerto Rican and half Texan blood, was judged one of the top fifty LBN players of all time. "I said to him, 'This is a pro league. This is not high school. This is not college. No, bro, we are men. We are not trying to earn a scholarship back to wherever you come from.'"

After Sullivan benched Alex Vega, a local hero, Sullivan's car was trashed. And soon thereafter was his job. Three days later, Phil was in charge in Ciudad de los Gallitos (City of the Roosters, i.e., fighting cocks) on an island where the legal matches featured blood spattering the first few rows and the losing cock was smashed against a wall by an investor, whereupon local kids would fight for the carcass.

Blood sport? That was blood sport.

The Gallitos? With Rosen tutoring seven-one Frankie Torruella of Seton Hall and Pellot-Rosa going from penetrator to all-around player, Isabela made the finals, only to lose to the Indios de Canóvanas in seven. Pellot-Rosa recalls, "I was Phil's first Michael Jordan. And I was his first Dennis Rodman. And I knew he'd be a good coach immediately. Practices covered every game situation. And when other teams had to call time-outs, we didn't. He'd just whistle, and it automatically clicked, and every opportunity and every situation, he had us trained to react. He had a complete game plan.

"But mostly, he had tremendous respect for a lot of different kinds of people and cultures. He knew you gotta learn something about your players off the court so you can get the most on the court. Had a lot of hippie in him, too. I can imagine a few mushrooms in there sometime, you know? Many times, we'd sit at the bar, smoke—Marlboros—and a lot of the time, it wasn't basketball we were talking. Philosophy. Life. We became friends." Jackson was a regular visitor to the Pellot-Rosa home, where his star's mother regularly cooked him San Antonio soul food, from collards to cornbread.

By Jackson's own admission, his inability to speak the language proved to add a useful tool to his coaching toolbox. It taught him that body language, an arched eyebrow, could speak words. Oddly, as in the case of the mysterious vanishing Albany ring, as he wrote in subsequent books, Jackson's brief account of coaching three summers in Isabela in *More Than a Game* dwells mostly on pedantic coachspeak: Puerto Rican rules that could help the NBA. As if he were already disowning *Maverick*.

(On the other hand, why would Jackson celebrate his only stint without a ring? After failing to make the playoffs in 1986, the owner cut him loose.)

ELEVEN

Jackson was right in thinking that an NBA old-boy network would never have him as a member. But Jerry Krause was never a member of a network. After Jackson's second year in Isabela, the call came from the little guy, who'd made a point of staying in touch, asking for CBA player dossiers, which had impressed him with their thoroughness. His new coach, Stan Albeck, was hiring. Krause invited him out.

But as eager as Jackson was to coach in the NBA, there was enough vestigial loft in him to show up with a "long beard," in Krause's memory, wearing one of his favorite straw hats, with a macaw feather in the hatband. He tried to explain to Albeck the significance of the feather (for the record, in some Latin cultures, macaw energy is said to enhance our understanding of our inner selves, heighten our perceptions and bring about a sense of balance). This was a little akin to Lady Gaga explaining the symbolism of her *Bad Romance* video to Yo-Yo Ma. By Jackson's own admission, Stan's eyes glazed over (much as yours just did).

"They asked, 'Who is this guy?' " Rosen says now. "Well, he is who he is. Take him or leave him the way he is."

They left him. No job. Jackson never spoke of it as a tipping point, but to the adolescent rebel willing to risk his chosen vocation to make the interview about him, this was a shot across the bow. It may not have been like lighting a joint during your Smith-Barney interview, but it was close. There would be no more rebel without a cause in this story. From here on in, he'd pick his battles to win his war.

He was the model coach in 1984–85, according to Coyne, honoring every public-appearance request. According to Commissioner Drucker, "In my twelve years, I must have seen a hundred twenty coaches, and Phil was one of the five who stood out far above all the others.

"No other coach had such a mature methodology in working with the league office. He wanted nothing but the best equation for the team. I've always said, if I were part of a group of people doing something, going for the Nobel Prize, as a group, I would want Phil on my team."

And then, at season's end, the phone rang again. It was Jimmy Rodgers, an assistant on the staff of K. C. Jones's Celtics—who had just won the NBA title, while the Knicks, under Hubie Brown, had gone 24-58. "Would you be interested," he asked, "in being my assistant in Madison Square Garden next year?"

Did North Dakota Route 2 attract snowdrifts?

"I was an item at the time," Rodgers says now. "Phil and I had talked along the way. I sensed that, obviously, he would be a very good choice. Smart, competitive, high character. The people in New York would understand his being there, and he'd know his role a coach just as he'd known his role as a player.

The perfect circle: the Knicks, the Garden and a boss against whom he had played in college and who had been his coach in the field house. But it was not to be. Maybe the ensuing episode and confusion were simply a matter of Red being awoken during an afternoon nap in his office (according to Fitch, he'd fall asleep to episodes of *Hawaii Five-O*), and groggily answering, "Sure, go ahead," when Rodgers asked if Auerbach minded if he talked to the Knicks. More likely it was Red playing with the Knicks and using Rodgers as a pawn. Rodgers flew down for a physical. All seemed ready—until Auerbach said, "By the way, I'll need a number-one draft pick in return."

No one had ever asked for a draft pick in return for losing a coach. Stern was at a loss. In the end, Jimmy stayed with the Celts and the Knicks kept Hubie. Red promised Jimmy the head job, which he soon got—with an aging, doomed team. He'd last two seasons. But he'd get his rings working for Phil.

By the 1985–86 season, Jackson sensed the time had come. "We never talked about where his next job might be or what it would be. I think that's the way he wanted it," Hennessy says. "He was never outwardly ambitious, but inside I think he had a burning desire."

He'd been beating the bushes. He'd called Hubie; dead end. When the University of Minnesota job opened up in midseason, Paul Presthus got a call: "Got any contacts for me?" Paul told him word was the job had been offered to Jimmy Williams, who took it.

Unlike in the NBA, once you win a CBA title, why stick around? Who counts CBA rings? One is the same as a dozen. On top of which, Charley'd taken the Savannah Spirit head job. There'd be no more of the complaints from the two wives about their husbands spending more time with each other than their spouses. (Rosen would then coach in Rockford and Oklahoma City and Albany. Never with any titles. But the guy can type pretty well.)

Where, at this point, to find psychic salvation? On the court, of course. In the summer before Jackson's last year in Albany, another gym-rat slot opened up, a place for the big man to satisfy his biggest jones: Big Man Camp. Where meditation went out the window. Where, despite the location of the court in a Catholic school gym, spirituality and deep thoughts weren't flying around. Just elbows.

A few years earlier, Mast and his buddy Bobby Greacen realized that no one teaches the fundamentals to the big kids. Not the NBA-bound Waltons and Shaqs who flocked to Pete Newell's camp, the high schoolers from Allentown, the D-IIs from Lehigh and Lafayette—big kids who might learn enough to add a few more points, a few more rebounds or a few more blocks to get the scholarship or the assistant coaching job at the community college.

Greacen was big, too, a Jersey guy who helped lead Rutgers into the NIT in 1967, where they were knocked out by the Salukis and that kid Frazier, although a lot of the credit should probably go to his teammate

Jimmy Valvano. Two years later, Mast and Greacen were in the NIT, the year that Eddie's Owls won. They'd first met at a camp in the Poconos, both as freshmen, because that's what college coaches did with their new signees out of high school—sent them to coach at the camps. Each was six foot nine. Each loved the game. And by the early eighties, each was out of it. Greacen had a ring off the bench for the Bucks. Mast had an Eastern League MVP.

"Since Eddie had friends all over the place," Greacen says, "he'd rig up these games all over South Jersey. Brooklyn. Woodstock. He'd pick the guys he wanted. We'd go play hoops for a few hours, anywhere, then drink a lot of beer." In other words, time for the Philly street kid to minister to the next generation.

No little guys allowed. No fancy-dribbling ball hawks, no skydunkers from the free-throw line. No Philly flashes, no White Jesus from the Rucker Tournament. Just kids whose dads maybe worked at the Bethle-hem mill.

And the big kids flocked. Eddie and Bobby accentuated the basics: Drop, step, layup. Jump hook. Moving. Not moving. When to come out. When to stay in. The satisfaction was knowing that they could help a few get a leg up in life. A half-dozen of them would become high school coaches, ADs.

Then Eddie and Bobby figured, why not get Charley in? To teach them how to back in and throw an elbow into a guy's esophagus? Or set an im-movable pick? Wait: Why not also get the biggest of the Big Men? The guy with the rings? Phil was instantly on board.

Big Man Camp was now Newell East, without the neon: Mast from the Eastern League, a minor circuit where the only thing that counted was toughness; Rosen the Renaissance man; Greacen, who'd guarded Alcindor in practice (and had scored 20 his first night on an NBA floor); and Jack-son. Three rings—including one coaching minor-league head cases.

For the kids? A hoop PhD. For the Big Men? Hoop heaven, starting with the lunchtime game. The kids were given an hour off, during which the Big Men would hit the court for three on three. The other two? Maybe the best big kid in the camp. Maybe a former Allentown Jet. Or Woodstock Jones-er.

"They were the most intense games I've ever played in," says Greacen, who guarded Chamberlain, Unseld, Nate Thurmond and Reed. "Eddie? Six–nine, and Charley would toss him around like a rag doll. And Phil? When he has his hand on your hip? It doesn't get more physical than that."

I asked Bobby if he thought that, beneath all of the cerebralness, the aura of spirituality, what's always driven Jackson more than anything else is simply . . . competition?

He laughed. "Bull's-eye. He and Charley, they both had that extra thing. They were *way* into it. More than the average hooper. Me, I'm sixty-five, and I still play, but it's not spiritual. I just like to run up and down the court. But for Phil and Charley, it was spiritual. Charley ramming an elbow into your chest . . . I don't know where the spirituality is in that.

"But the game itself is spiritual. I mean, you're not going for a two-minute run. There has to be a connection and a trust with the teammates. Which I think is where the spirituality is."

The undisputed highlight for the men? Saturday night up at Eddie and Diane's house, talking basketball and listening to Magic Sam, Buddy Guy. Phil was in his wheelhouse. How else to explain that he came back for Big Man Camp—for $100? Well, for the friendships, because once you put on that suit, and you're coaching millionaires for a national TV audience, wherein the spectacle outweighs the sport, and fans shove your wife aside to get your autograph, and everyone wants to be your friend, you've entered that sporting limbo: Is this a potential friend or a parasite? That virtually every friend of Phil's from the day speaks of his eternal loyalty says a lot about the people you meet once you're at the top; the ones who knew you best at first will always know you best.

"They'd break camp and come up to the house ready for a shower and cold beer," Diane Mast says now, at that same kitchen table. "The kitchen would fill up with the big guys and some of the younger guys who'd listen to Greek [Greacen] and Eddie and Phil and Charley talk shop: 'Is it anticipation or reaction to the ball on the court?' Stuff like that. Then there would be discussion of plays and the breakdown of their execution.

"I'd have the wok ready to go: stir-fried beef and snow peas, maybe hot and spicy shrimp, brown rice. But I never thought they noticed what they were eating because the serious game chatter was going on—and of course, music, music, music. And it was in late April–early May, so there'd be games on the TV, late-seasoners.

"One year I was expecting, and I was stirring up the boil in the wok, and Phil came around behind me to look over the cooking and put both hands on my big stomach, and we connected—a sort of knowing respect for exactly how I was feeling: big. I had to smile at him for just the acknowledgment of my pregnancy and felt that belly full of a baby. He didn't say anything. He didn't have to.

"Then on Sunday, Phil would have them say the Lord's Prayer before they got going on the breakdown of drills. It would be over Sunday, and off they'd go filled up with their full share of hoops—kids and men. It was all good."

This would be the swan song, he told me in March 1987, sitting in the armory bleachers after practice. He was upbeat about it, knowing he'd run this course. And a look back was in order. In triumph. He hadn't won it since 1984, but twice in a row in the CBA was tough, especially against the likes of Bill Musselman, who'd simply hire ex-NBA guys from his giant notebook, week in, week out, whenever he needed a win.

No, what Jackson was leaving behind was a tradition. "When I first got here, we used to have one of those little electric signs on wheels you see in strip malls," he told me. "We'd wheel it out and it'd say, 'Patroon Game Tonight.' Now everyone knows where we play."

The morning walk-through for that night's game against the Tampa Bay Thrillers had ended, and Phil was waiting for the last of his players to shower and leave, because he possessed the master key for the armory.

Phil Jackson in charge of artillery. Cool. He was munching Freihofer's chocolate-chip cookies from a box that was left over from a promotion where, apparently, the lucky-number winner had missed his chance.

But this was what was weighing most heavily on him: The Knicks were at a nadir. They were a laughingstock. Hubie had been fired, interim Bob Hill was in the middle of a 20-46 run. Their general manager, Scotty Stirling, was a house man from the league offices uptown. Patrick Ewing, in his second year, had not proved a savior despite being surrounded by legitimate talent, from Bill Cartwright to Gerald Wilkins to the remarkable, if enigmatic and hardly team-oriented, Bernard King. In other words: bad coaching.

But 170 miles to the north, the man with a title hadn't gotten a call.

Why not? He shrugged. "I always thought I was the right guy for the job," he told me. And then he added some coaching philosophy, advice that, perhaps if the quote made the wires, could enhance his dwindling chances.

"I think a team in New York has to rise to the challenge, and I don't think the kids they have now are ready to do that. There are two plateaus you have to reach as a Knick. They've reached the first, which is to get the contract: to be in the league. But now they have to come and face the fans. They have to live in the city, and drink with the fans and make themselves visible. You have to be seen on the street. New Yorkers want to see a team that's going to represent them."

He pulled a gray wool button-down sweater over his shoulders as we stepped into the spring wind. He was pretty resigned by now to the reality of that old-boy network.

"I should probably be more political," he said. As if. "But I've always had a tendency to believe that when it happens, it'll all fall into place. Want a cookie?"

I thought for a sec. *They're in a box. They look manufactured. What are the chances they've been, say, enhanced? Nah.* I bit.

He quit after the season and headed back home.

And the phone rang again. "This time," Krause said, "don't come in with a beard. Wear a suit." At which point, Jackson told an interviewer, "it was time to conform."

With Albeck fired, Doug Collins was in, and he took to Jackson (at the beginning, anyway). Owner Jerry Reinsdorf of Brooklyn, a Knicks fan in the glory years, liked him. Krause, of course, loved him. You can teach the technical stuff—and with coaches like Tex Winter and Johnny Bach on board, there were several decades by his side—but you can't teach what Phil had: the way to reach anyone and everyone. Or as Neal Walk puts it now, "He can talk with politicians. He can talk with poverty-stricken people. He can ride limos, motorcycles, bicycles. He doesn't need suits, all that crapola."

"The main thing about him is he's comfortable wherever he is, in every situation he finds himself in," says Rosen. "To me, that's just amazing. He treats waiters and car parkers the way he'd treat a CEO."

Not incidentally, he also had a ring. To men who labor a lifetime for that piece of jewelry, this adornment meant a whole lot more than a glimmering résumé.

And now he was in. He'd sidestepped the old boys and could now get down to the business of beating them. All of them.

TWELVE

Things happen in threes, right? He'd gather titles in three cities. He would have three wives and three overlapping branches of faith: Christian, Zen, Native American. He'd teach the triangle.

And the third camp had Jackson written all over it. Stephan Rechtschaffen, a mystic and hoop junkie whom he'd met playing in local games, had founded the Omega Institute for Holistic Studies with his wife, the *Oprah* regular and women-empowerment author Elizabeth Lesser, eventually settling on a two-hundred-acre campus on the other side of the Hudson. The pat version would be to call Omega a New Age institute. The realer version would say that it is a more serious endeavor for serious explorers signing up for expensive but intriguing workshops: "All the enlightenment," Charley says now, "that money can buy." (Leader of a three-day workshop on sustainability in early October 2013? William Clinton.)

Rechtschaffen knew that Phil the seeker needed more than a nexus where basketball met spirituality. He needed money. So why not offer a clinic about basketball, only sort of beyond basketball? Hence in 1984, a new offering appeared in the catalogue: Exercise Your Basketball Jones. On a cracked and way-too-small blacktop court for three days each year, Jackson, with Charley by his side, taught groups of well-educated men who'd had to relinquish the bliss of hit-the-wall hoop exhaustion they'd once known on a schoolboy court in order to make it in Manhattan.

Like the rabbi Jonathan Kligler, who enrolled to see if he was as good as he thought he'd been back in White Plains, when his coaches didn't think so. But then, he didn't think they could coach. This time, the coach would be one degree of separation from Red Holzman.

Before long, Jackson's workshop was ruffling some New Age feathers. "A lot of other Omega participants in the workshops got pissed because all of this competitive male energy was in the middle of their campus," says Kligler now. "It was really funny."

At a retreat founded on the principles of Sufi mystic Pir Vilayat Inayat Khan, Phil would open the weekend with a Lakota Sioux prayer (nearby Overlook Mountain was said to have been sacred to the local Wappinger tribe). Then there'd be a walking meditation in the labyrinth, the idea being to journey to your essence before releasing yourself back into the world a changed person—a metaphoric sweat-lodge ceremony.

For Kligler, the lunchtime conversations were equally intriguing. "He was much more interested in religion, politics of the Middle East and philosophy. That was cool: Me, a rabbi, talking about the Middle East situation, Israel and Palestine, and debating the merits of organized religion, with Phil Jackson. Often it was a conversation about spiritual life, really. He wasn't coming with a sense of need. Just interest. He was curious. He always wanted to learn."

So did his disciples—about him. What it was like to grow up in the intense fundamentalist background. Kligler sensed an innate respect for his folks—and his own beliefs, when other campers were less pro-Israel. "I never sensed he was trying to show me I was wrong to be a rabbi."

Then, a few years after the first workshop, with a single, second phone call from Jerry Krause, Omega changed. Jackson was now an assistant coach with the Bulls. And on Labor Day weekend of 1988, being in Phil Jackson's Woodstock-infused workshop took on a whole different meaning.

"The annual players in the workshop all agreed," says the rabbi now, "we would call the Omega registration line the moment it opened on

March first to make sure we could get in. The workshop filled in instantly."
And now the hillside filled with spectators to watch the NBA coach play—
three on two, with Jackson and Rosen on defense, daring the campers to
get through, Jackson teaching an elementary triangle. ("No one knew
what the fuck he was talking about at first," laughs Rosen.) Soon the name
had changed to Beyond Basketball.

"So then what happened was it became this annual kind of . . . not
men's group, exactly, but just rendezvousing with all these new friends,"
the rabbi recalls. "And it started to feel like for Phil it was something
he looked forward to. A chance to let his hair down with a bunch of guys
who knew him. And then he started to reserve a part of the schedule to
tell us what the season had been like. I couldn't believe it. One year a few
years later we're sitting there one Labor Day, and he's telling us about how
he'd persuaded Michael to come out of retirement . . . and why he got Rodman, and what Pippen was like . . . and we're all getting this firsthand
schmooze."

When Phil finally gave it up, Rosen took over Omega, with Mast by his
side. The tradition lived on. Eddie would arrive with a cooler full of beer, a
few joints, and in spirit Beyond Basketball lived on. They'd do two a year.
This past summer was his thirty-fifth year, although the surroundings
have changed. The Institute seems to be doing quite well. There's the new
Ram Dass Library, the new dining hall, some new cabins. The new Sanctuary ("May this sacred space be fed by your spiritual aspirations").

At some point in there, Phil brought Kligler out to Chicago, where they
could talk Middle East politics a few feet away from Michael Jordan. And
the rabbi asked Phil for a copy of the Lakota prayer. It arrived in the mail,
typed out in capital letters by Jackson:

SIOUX PRAYER BY YELLOW LARK

O great spirit, whose voice I hear in the winds
And whose breath gives life to all the world, hear me:
I come before you one of your many children.

I am small and weak. I need your strength and wisdom.

Let me walk in beauty, and make my eyes

Ever behold the red and purple sunset.

Make my hands respect the things you have made

And my ears sharp to hear your voice.

Make me wise so that I may know the things

You have taught my people,

The lessons you have hidden in every leaf and rock.

I seek strength not to be superior to my brothers

But to fight my greatest enemy—myself.

Make me ever ready to come to you

With clean hands and straight eyes

So that when life fades as a fading sunset

My spirit may come to you without shame.

A few Patroons extended their basketball careers. The next year, Bill Musselman won a championship for Albany before going on to coach the Timberwolves. Three years later, George Karl's Patroon team went 50-6, led by Mario Elie, but didn't win the title.

The franchise disappeared for a decade. Then, in a reincarnation, Micheal Ray Richardson had them in the finals in 2006–07 against the Yakima Sun Kings. (Unfortunately for Richardson, he didn't make it through the series, after uttering a few tone-deaf remarks in a conversation about his contract extension: "I've got big-time Jew lawyers.") The Sun Kings went on to win anyway. The league was bought by Isiah Thomas, and, like everything Isiah touches, it failed.

Lowes Moore? Presiding over the Boys and Girls Club where Denzel funded their century celebration. Happy as hell. Derrick Rowland? Running that storied athletic club in Albany. Happy as hell. Hennessy? Passed away suddenly in September 2013 at fifty-eight, far too early. Frankie J? Your guess is as good as mine.

Charley? Eighteen books so far.

Eddie Mast died at forty-six, on the court, over in the Lehigh Gym during the Tuesday night run. "He was on the sidelines," Diane says now. "He sat out that second game. They won the first, and I think he chose to sit it out. It wasn't like this clamp on his heart . . . he just kind of faded. He sat down, he didn't feel good, and he just kind of faded. If you could pick it off the menu, that's the one he'd have circled."

At the memorial service, Charley threw a couple of tapes into the casket: Stevie Ray Vaughan and Johnny Winter.

The following Labor Day, Phil returned and ran the Eddie Mast Memorial Beyond Basketball workshop. Today, inside the Sanctuary, a space empty save for a sculpture of stone, hangs a plaque that reads, "The Sanctuary skylight is dedicated in memory of Eddie Mast—friend, colleague, co-teacher of the Beyond Basketball Workshops. May Your Light Shine On. Dedicated by June and Phil Jackson."

Phil Jackson? Embarking on another journey—this time, heading to the heartland Oz that had beckoned to so many Westerners as he was growing up: the big-shouldered town for the big-shouldered guy.

And all the wondering about the ministry or law school or teaching or whatever? Was there deliberation?

Diane Mast laughs. "He was packed, and he was ready."

THIRTEEN

lean-shaven and suited on the sideline in those first few days in Chicago, he tried to look as straight as possible, hair trimmed, as if he really did belong alongside triangle genius Tex Winter, in his brown polyester, and the impeccably groomed defensive coach, Johnny Bach, who liked to kid Jackson about wearing jeans on the plane. ("A typical lefty, a free spirit," Collins would say of his new guy, with a smile—at first.)

He'd reside in Woodstock-through-the-looking-glass: upscale Bannockburn, in one of the more unassuming homes in the village. It looked like a middle-management guy's place, the place he'd return to each night after spending the day working on Marshmallow Fluff spreadsheets. It was as close to Woodstock as *Archie* was to *Zap Comix*.

His new owner? Unlike Coyne, and Ned Irish of the Knicks, the lovable grad of Erasmus Hall High in Brooklyn, hardly beloved. Jerry Reinsdorf (also out of Erasmus Hall) seemed to have the same emotional commitment to Chicago's sports ethos that Mitt Romney's Bain Capital had to the family handkerchief-manufacturing plant in Ames, Iowa.

A native Brooklynite and a former IRS lawyer who became a real-estate magnate, Reinsdorf, with a group of minority investors, had bought the White Sox in 1981 from one of the most beloved owners in sports history. Peg-legged Bill Veeck was keeping the Sox alive in Comiskey with rubber bands and duct tape, but he was keeping them alive because he understood the love of blue-collar Chicagoland for its South Side ugly sister.

When he gave them up to the Reinsdorf consortium, it was with the naive hope that they understood that towns and teams have an inexorable bond. It was quickly obvious that Reinsdorf's idea of city-sports bonds was highly exorable (if that's a word).

His first utterance was about how he would "restore class" to the South Side. Reinsdorf's "restoration"? Industrial revenue bond sales to add sky-boxes to a park he was already committed to demolishing. "I have no sympathy for preserving buildings that are unprofitable," he told me in 1990. "There was so much deterioration, the engineers told us that the upper deck would have collapsed within a year or two."

(A minority partner told me, "That wasn't true. They just didn't want to keep it up.")

He'd told Tampa–St. Pete he'd move to their town, which had already built the Mold Dome (aka the Florida Suncoast Dome), unless the Illinois state legislature passed a bill to finance the new Comiskey. As of midnight on the last night of the session in 1988, the legislature hadn't passed the bill. So after midnight, Governor James Thompson managed to twist a few arms, get the right votes and pass the tax to build the thing, at which point, someone, somehow, turned the chamber's clock back to midnight to make it legal—bizarre even by Chicago political maneuverings.

In other words, between midnight and twelve fifteen that night, the Sox belonged to Florida . . . until, fifteen minutes later, they didn't.

In 1984, after selling his real-estate company to Amex for $53 million, Reinsdorf bought more than half the shares of the Bulls, a team that, since its founding in 1966, had been the lowest pro franchise in town. Then general manager Rod Thorn drafted Michael Jordan.

Thankfully, Chicago Stadium still stood on the near West Side. If not as funky as Washington Street Armory or Phil's first Garden, it was as intimate in its own way: cigar-and-beer-and-popcorn-fragrant hallways. Built in 1929, the place was so sticky, literally and otherwise, that Bill Bradley used to change shoes after he played there, because the hallways were so dirty, and he was robbed once walking to a friend's car in the parking lot.

It was a stockyard town's arena. "The graceful barn," as writer David Remnick once termed it, was "four walls in search of the wrecking ball."

The walls choked beneath six decades of pungent, thick paint. A leaden, steam-radiator smell caught in your nostrils. A first-time visitor to the locker rooms one Dantean level below would find himself glancing over his shoulder, half expecting some Lovecraftian terror to leap out from behind the next bend in the brick maze.

At first Jackson wondered whether the stadium was just a way station. Before an exhibition game in Columbus, he gave a call to his old hospital-ward colleague, Hosket, leaving tickets for Bill and his kids. "I'll never forget: He was wearing a burgundy polyester jacket and khakis. After the game, he immediately asked me what I was up to, and I told him I was in the paper business. He says, 'Do you like it?' He was really curious. I asked why. He said, 'This could be a one-year deal. I think the only reason they selected me is that I had a championship ring.' He was quizzing all his former teammates and people he knew about what do you do after basketball."

Before their first game in Sacramento, he invited his old teammate John Gianelli to the game. Afterward they had a few beers. "'It was kind of a fluke,' he said," Gianelli says now. "He was living in Woodstock and said he didn't see much of a future in coaching. He said he wanted to come back east and do some teaching, maybe in college."

But how long would he last? How long would any of them last? With enviable talent, an energetic and charismatic coach and two world-class assistants, the Bulls had gone 40-42 in '87, to be swept 3–0 by the Celtics for the second year in a row. (Covering the second game from under the basket, I'd watched Jordan score 63 points and been splattered by his sweat—in a Bull loss to a Boston team that played like a team.)

On the other hand, Krause had chosen future all-star Horace Grant out of Clemson and hoodwinked Seattle out of its own pick by trading the Bulls' pick, Olden Polynice, for the Seattle pick, which he used on a man named Maurice Pippen out of Arkansas State. O.P. was a very likable big man beginning a mediocre career. Pippen would be the constant that held the bricks of six championship teams together.

"Pip had a more all-around game [than Michael]," Ron Harper, Jackson's ever-reliable on-court quarterback, told me. Twenty years later, in a post-Lakers interview with HBO, Jackson would go out of his way to mention one player: "Scottie Pippen," Jackson said, "is a person I want to see get back into coaching in basketball. He's got a lot to offer."

He'd had a lot to offer Phil, thanks to Krause: a point guard who became a forward who could intuit the whole floor's flow in a second.

Hamburg, Arkansas, is tucked into the numbingly flat and rural southeast corner of the state, two hundred miles southeast of West Memphis. Pippen was the youngest of twelve children, raised poor but not destitute, although having to wear hand-me-down underwear is tough for any kid. He was "a rural version of a street kid," Sam Smith wrote in *The Jordan Rules,* "wild, somewhat irresponsible and subject to running with people of questionable character." In his senior year at Central Arkansas, Pippen's negotiations with Chicago were quick: Two other brothers had gone through serious injuries, his dad had had a stroke, and from now on in life, all Pippen wanted was security for his family. Reinsdorf wanted to hoodwink him. Six years for $5.1 million. Still, his annual income would be, after taxes, a half mil when the per capita income in Arkansas was under $8,000.

Doug Collins? He'd been a native-son hero, an Illinois State stud, and the first pick of the 9-73 Sixers in 1973. Three years later, his shooting (and Darryl Dawkins's Lovetron vibe) had them in the finals. Replacing Albeck, he'd jump-started the somnolent Bulls, but his hysterical style was befuddling a young roster, which needed Steven Wright, not Sam Kinison. "The guy just wore you down," says Brad Sellers now, the top Bulls pick in '86.

And despite a reported promise to Krause to use Tex's triangle, he didn't. Winter silently simmered. "We'd have won it all before Phil if Collins had used Tex's triangle," Craig Hodges, who would come on board the next year, says now. "He refused."

To Sellers, Jackson's arrival was a gift from the gods. He was a seven-foot shooting forward out of Ohio State, but Collins had tried to turn him into a center. On top of which, Jordan would put Sellers down for his soft play, and Sellers wasn't the kind of guy to fight back. He needed a big-man forward as a mentor. Winter? Being conspicuously marginalized by Collins. Bach? Purely a defensive coach, nor the kind of guy who would tolerate passivity; to inspire his defense, he once played a clip from Kubrick's *Full Metal Jacket* of a soldier blowing his brains out all over the wall of a latrine.

In Phil, Sellers had a "head" coach. "I see instantly that Phil sees something in me that Collins can't see. One day after practice, I'm shooting. I'm walking off, and Phil comes over and says, 'I gotta talk to you.' He says, 'I see what you bring to the table here, and you gotta shoot every ball you can get. Put all the other stuff out of your mind.' I say, 'But I'm trying to stay on the floor, not come off it.' 'Just do it,' he says. 'That's your role. That's how you can help this team.'

"Some guys look for negativity. Phil looked at the positive: 'What can this guy do that can help both the team and the player? We should be putting a player out there to do what he does, along with people who can compensate for his deficiencies.'"

Sellers is now the mayor of Warrensville Heights, Ohio, a Cleveland suburb of fourteen thousand people. A thoughtful guy. I asked him to sum the man up.

"His thinking was always a cut above. But it was strange . . . he just seemed like a very . . . *powerful* guy. Light-years ahead. He'd just say, 'This is what I need you to do,' clear and concise, in a way that just makes you say, 'OK, I can do that for you.' And you did. Even if you did have to look some of his words up to see what they meant." Sellers averaged 10 points a game that year.

Center Dave Corzine saw him "in an observation mode, a little hesitant, hanging back, kind of quiet," but point guard Sam Vincent welcomed the "calming effect," since Vincent, a friend of Jordan's since McDonald's camp, was caught between a rock and a hard place: what his friend wanted and what his coach wanted.

To those who wanted to listen to an assistant off the court, Phil continued to teach the power of aggression when it's redirected. "For Lakota warriors," Jackson would write, "life was a fascinating game." (Their war cry was *Hanta yo,* "The Spirit goes ahead of us.") "They would trek across half of Montana, enduring untold hardships, for the thrill of sneaking into an enemy camp and making off with a string of ponies. It wasn't the ponies per se that mattered so much, but the experience of pulling something off difficult together as a team."

They were peaceful warriors.

In Jackson's first year on the bench, the Bulls gained ten wins over the previous year, thanks to enhanced bench contributions, even with Pippen's back hurting—before being mauled by Rick Mahorn and Bill Laimbeer, outmaneuvered by Isiah, and unable to defend against the likes of John Salley and Dennis Rodman off the bench. The Pistons won in five; they'd lose in a seven-game final to the Showtime Lakers.

That summer, Rosen, now head coach of the CBA team in Rockford, Illinois, with whom the Bulls had a player-development agreement, was in Los Angeles for the summer leagues with Jackson and Winter, with whom he struck up a relationship. Charley wanted to tap Winter's brain ("He's honest, outspoken, forgiving, knowledgeable, sincere, real"), but to his surprise, discovered a man who'd lost his spirit.

"Collins wouldn't even let him talk to the players. Tex says to me, 'I'm going to quit. Collins won't let me do anything. I'm useless. He won't talk to me, listen to me, be around me. Makes me sit back of the bench. I'm a fifth wheel. I'm wasting whatever time I have left. I'm going to quit.'

"I said, 'Tex, don't quit. Sooner or later, Phil is gonna be the coach. He loves the triangle. It's the offense he's been looking for. You'll be right there.'"

One tipping point in the Jordan-Collins relationship occurred in a practice Rosen attended. The problem with Jordan was that he destroyed practices. If it was a defensive drill, his offense would shred the D. So to try to keep it a little more competitive, Collins would fudge about the score: "It's 10–9," Collins'd say. "No, no," Jordan would say, "It's 10–7."

"Jordan went ballistic," Rosen recalls. "You don't mess around with things like that. The game is the game. It's sacred. After that, Jordan just thought, *How can we ever trust this guy?*"

Collins was about to hit his career-defining wall: getting in sight of the finish line but coming up short. In twenty-seven years, Collins has never coached a team for more than three years. He's the Billy Martin of basketball: He gets 'em off the ground, then burns himself out.

But by 1988–89, Krause had assembled a pretty stellar roster. "I always thought that Jerry had a bad rap in town," Corzine says now. "I never got it. He was putting together a dynasty of a team. We were getting better and better. We were on the right track. Yes, we had Michael, and he was obviously great from day one. And his competitiveness was one of the main things [that] allowed him to be at the level he was at. There was no resentment, either, because of the way he approached the game, the practice situations, the day-to-day; he never backed down or made an excuse or took a day off. He had expectations for what he wanted and his idea of success. It wasn't an individual goal.

"But the media picks up on it. 'It's all about Michael' because that's what interests the fans. They don't see the chemistry, and they certainly aren't anxious to give the GM the credit he deserves. Behind the scenes, Krause had a reputation for working harder than anyone in the league. He had a good relationship with the front office. He assembled a hell of a team."

★

Hoopswise, Jackson's addition made sense. Collins's 76ers teams were led by the caped superhero, Dr. J; his first Bulls team comprised Jordan, enforcer Charles Oakley and a lot of supporters, like Corzine. Phil had big-man experience, and after 250 games of one-on-one wrestling matches with Rosen, he knew how to play in the paint. And as long as Collins refused to run Tex's triangle, they needed a big man.

So Krause, with a new big-man coach, got him a big man. Bill Cartwright, one of the least-heralded post men in the league, came over in exchange for Oakley. Krause had fleeced yet another team. Oakley, like Polynice, would never earn a ring. Cartwright became Phil's captain and his channel to the team. As Charley put it, "He was barking at his squad for their carelessness and lack of hustle ten minutes into day one."

Collins was entering his fabled third-year meltdown. With the Bulls at 10-10, Krause traded for Buck guard Hodges, a Chicago street kid who'd played for Tex at Long Beach State. If Collins refused to go triangle, then he'd have to be coaching a guard who was a master of it, who'd learned it not only on the court, but also in classrooms.

"It's so simple," Hodges says now. "You play pickup? You're playing the triangle. It's all predicated on ball movement and player spacing. It's just all about how you make your reads and counters, based on where the ball moves to. If it's on a certain part of the court, I know where to go to get space and balance for the shot. And if it doesn't work, it's a system that fails—not an individual missing a shot.

"But you can't teach what you don't know. You can't teach the system by looking at it on tape. You have to live it."

As former Laker and Timberwolf Mark Madsen, a Stanford business-degree guy, describes it, "Imagine a decision tree, OK? The triangle is a decision tree with a thousand different possibilities. Literally a thousand different things could happen on any one trip down the court. Now, a lot of those things are natural basketball reactions, but once you have those sequences down, there are literally times when I could have my eyes closed and know where to throw the ball. In fact, you could have three or four guys with their eyes closed."

And then, on the night of December 17, 1988, the die was almost inadvertently cast. From that night on, all thoughts of the ministry and professorship began to recede. On that night, hoops took hold and never let go.

The 11-10 Bulls bused up the interstate to play the 11-9 Bucks. The Bulls were down by double figures when Collins was ejected. He handed the mantle to Jackson. In the second half, the Bulls scored 66, held the Bucks to 38 and humiliated Del Harris's guys. Hodges came off the bench to score 14. How'd Jackson do it? He told the players to press on defense—and make up their offense as they went along.

"It was like we were let out of a cage," Horace Grant would say. As fate would have it, that night June Jackson was in the crowd, the guest of Jerry and Thelma Krause. Television cameras found the trio, and Bulls fans at home got the idea that the future was already ordained. Collins was not too pleased. An angry meeting between Krause and the two coaches solved nothing.

With Hodges's arrival, the team won 12 of its next 16. In his second game, he came off the bench to score 18. Collins wasn't using a triangle, but Hodges was, and Phil saw it. And as he'd advised Sellers, he told Hodges, "Do what you do."

In the final months of the season, Collins was reportedly coming apart, breaking down in his office, asking associates to find out to whom Jackson was talking, barring Winter from practices, reportedly trying to take over Krause's job. His obscenities directed at players were audible to fans. And according to a *Chicago Tribune* story, he was "given to excess in his lifestyle off the floor."

He'd thrown Jordan in as a point guard starting in March, against MJ's wishes; the move bore early fruit. His Bulls stomped Lenny Wilkens's impressive Cavaliers in the first round and had no trouble with Rick Pitino's Knicks, who'd won five more in the regular season. They even won two of the first three against those Bad Boys before the Pistons clamped down on Jordan, holding him to 23 and 18. Pippen bowed out with a concussion, thanks to a Laimbeer elbow, and the Pistons won in six.

Detroit swept the Lakers for the title, whereupon Reinsdorf and Krause decided to sweep clean.

★

The call came in Montana, but with Phil's phone on a party line, the elfin GM insisted that Jackson find a secure phone. Phil biked into Lakeside, called back on a pay phone, agreed to terms and got back on his bike.

The young searcher who had loved the crystalline ice forms on the Catskills back in the minor-league days had, in the space of a few minutes, turned his back and plunged, for better or worse, headlong into the ever-polluted big-time pool.

He found himself backing off the accelerator on winding Route 93, wondering whether he had to change his ways. Then, he would recount, he gunned the bike as fast as ever. He'd be himself, no matter what the trappings. They would not be at a Montana college teaching spirituality and faith and sport. They'd be bespoke.

"Can I do this?" is the question Rosen recalls his friend asking back in Woodstock, before he headed for camp.

"It was the only time I ever saw him showing any qualms about what he could or could not do. I told him he'd win five championships in Chicago. I was off by one."

★

The new coach appeared at the press conference with short hair, shirt and tie, bushy mustache. His look was going to facially shape-shift through the rest of his career—a physical manifestation of his determination to never really be pin-down-able. To keep moving.

He was flanked by Krause and Reinsdorf, each looking distinctly peeved. Not because they didn't like their new coaching team: the head with the Dead in his tape deck, Winter and Bach, and a new coach in Jim Cleamons, his quiet, self-assured old teammate. No, because the press wanted to know what in the hell had happened to Collins—a proven winner. "We don't care so much about our public image," said Reinsdorf. "We care about . . . everyone connected with our franchise"—which sounded as if they thought Collins had been about to crack up. Now, *that* would have been embarrassing.

Phil paid homage to Holzman as he offered this philosophy: "Hit the open man, see the ball, and get back on defense. You'll see a team using speed and quickness in an up-tempo game. . . . We want to see a rotation where we play nine and ten deep, where everyone feels a part of this winning thing we're trying to develop." It sounded like coachspeak. It turned out to be the gospel truth.

Michael? "Less work to accomplish more on the floor. We want him to be strong for the end of the year when we need him."

And his theories about discipline? "I like discipline—not as a weapon, but to put harmony in people's lives." Bill Fitch meets Black Elk. "We'd like to have a stable environment."

"The thing I realized as an assistant," he said a few months later, "[was that] we needed a real even-tempered team, not a roller-coaster ride. I could pretend to be someone else, a screamer, but I'm not good at playacting. You have to be who you are, or the guys will see right through you."

JACKSON SPIRITUAL, INTELLECTUAL TYPE, headlined the *Chicago Tribune*. He read philosophy and religion on the road! He was nine credits short of his master's! He joined Athletes for George McGovern! As a player, he had a beard! (No mention of the recreations of the loft years; apparently Sam Smith hadn't read *Maverick*.) "The 43-year-old is being placed, in a sense, in the spiritual role he once considered. He hopes to take his congregation to the holy land, even if it's merely the NBA championship."

★

The two most competitive men in Chicago had their first meeting as head coach and superstar after Labor Day. "You've got to share the spotlight with your teammates, because if you don't, they won't grow," he told number 23.

"Does that mean we're going to use Tex's equal-opportunity offense?" Jordan asked. Jackson said it did. Everyone would touch the ball. They'd be a team, and the less-used players would feel as if they were part of it. If Jordan were constantly moving, other defenders would always be watching him and would take their eyes off the guy they were covering—a point proven again and again in the championship series to come.

It's not that Phil didn't know that, as he once put it, he had a "one-man wrecking crew, the greatest luxury a coach could ever have." It's that he had an offensive system of ever-shifting passing lanes, which, when executed perfectly, he would say a few years later, was nothing less than "a work of art."

While it would take a good couple of years for Jordan to see the truth in that, Michael said the right things from the start: "If Phil feels I'm out of line, he'll let me know," Jordan said in a newspaper interview. "I really respect him for that. A lot of coaches have been afraid to do that with me. They were afraid it would ruin their relationship with me, which it wouldn't have, of course. But Phil is honest and trustworthy. He's been around basketball a lot longer than me, and there's a lot I can learn from him."

Before 1987–88, Jackson's greatest inspiration from George Orwell would have been the message of *1984:* Getting out from under Big Brother is the path to enlightenment. What he saw under Collins owed more to Orwell's *Animal Farm*: "All animals are equal, but some animals are more equal than others." The Jordan Rules, as chronicled by Smith in the book of that title, did exist: If he was sick, they called practice. They sent a therapeutic machine to his home. He forced Collins to call off a Christmas Eve practice so he wouldn't have to fly back to Chicago. He basically did whatever he wanted.

Soon, wrote Smith, Jackson pretty much erased that code. From here on in, it was the Jackson Rules. "The one thing that was consistent, from day one in Chicago, was that you knew who ran the show," Hodges told me, of the first few days under Phil. "*Everybody* knew who ran the show, whether it was Michael or Scottie—or later, Kobe. There was never a situation where that was in question.

"I look at it like this: In a corporate environment where you have limited numbers, you can have a cruel dictatorship or have a philanthropic dictatorship. We had the second one."

In training camp, practices stressed what Holzman had stressed: defense. It didn't hurt that Jackson's two best offensive players were also his two best defensive players. Mike Dunleavy once told David Halberstam that he thought Jordan, tutored by Dean Smith, was the best defensive shooting guard in history. Pippen was even better at defense—because they'd guard each other in practice.

And the triangle was out from under the tarp. The author of *The Triple Post Offense* (Prentice-Hall, 1962, dedicated "To the young men who have played for me" before his family), Winter was now in charge of the system that, as Hodges notes, was virtually the sole reason for the championships—not the players.

The man behind it? Possessed of a personality that had always been overlooked. "Great sense of humor," Rosen says. "He remembered everything. Tex was a lot older, so there was a certain degree of respect and separation on Phil's part. He couldn't say, 'Tex, what the fuck, let's get some fucking beers and hear some blues!' But he would tease Tex. Tex was such an easy mark.

"They used Tex's terminology. One play where a guy comes in from power forward to the weak side was called Blind Pig. One day in practice

Phil says to him, 'Did you know that's what they used to call marijuana cigarettes in the thirties?' Tex was flummoxed." (The actual term was "pigfoot.")

"And he and Nancy were always buying houses. I went to his house once, doing a story on Pippen. He shows me his new houses. That was his thing. The famous line was that Nancy calls and asks, 'What are you doing?' and Tex says, 'Watching film,' and Nancy says, 'I'm going to buy a house,' and then she went and bought a house."

They opened at home with an OT win over Cleveland—with Jordan scoring 54. He would not embrace the triangle without a fight. They were 4-2 when they took off for their first Western road trip (no curfews, the old John Madden style) and received the first round of books. Some were well suited to their targets; some were more reflective of Jackson's attempt to stamp them with his ideologies. John Paxson, future GM, found some speed bumps in *Zen and the Art of Motorcycle Maintenance*.

"Pax was an intelligent guy," Will Perdue says now. "He says, 'This is wack. This is weird.' Somewhere in California, Pax wanted to go to a bookstore to figure this out. The guy at the bookstore says, 'Read this book about that book.' Pax says, 'Why would this jackass give me this book that I have to read another book to explain it?'"

But Hodges immediately immersed himself in Dan Millman's *Way of the Peaceful Warrior*. "We read them because I knew PJ would ask us, 'What did you think about this part?' So you go ahead and read the shit. That book, man, that was an eye-opener. It hit home. I was an urbanized cat. The idea seemed to be oxymoronic . . . but it wasn't. It was just about the possibilities within one's own self.

"You know, we're athletes, but you never stop being a student, so we were student athletes, and he knew that. The books, the life lessons, some didn't take it for what it was worth, but it kept us on point." That season Hodges hit eighty-seven three-pointers and won the all-star three-point competition. In one round, he hit nineteen straight. Credit Winter for triangle teaching: If while you're moving you find a place where you can get a pass, be balanced and be set, then take the shot. Credit Millman, too, if you're so inclined.

And Phil. "Being around Phil there's just a certain . . . aura," Hodges says now. "His aura precedes him. His energy precedes him. You walk in and there's just a certain kind of charismatic presence. He's not *trying* to be charismatic, or knowledgeable, or a leader. He just is."

Perdue once got *On the Road,* which was Jackson's anarchic doppelganger manifesto with a few differences. Phil would come to relish getting on the bike at the end of each season for his solo road trips—but he knew that six months hence, he'd be back in a suit earning seven figures. Phil tried to not care about tomorrow; Kerouac was actually *living* moment to moment, and completely for the journey: a bottle of Tokay to start the day in the Tenderloin, hooking up with a teenage Mexican migrant worker, helping cover up a murder a friend had committed—at the age that Jackson was hanging with Eddie Mast. Dead at forty-seven of cirrhosis.

Pippen and Jordan never read the books.

They won 21 of their first 30, including a 93–83 defeat of Showtime when they held the Lakers to 14 in that all-important third. (After a loss in Atlanta, the night after a speech by George H. W. Bush, Jackson jokingly blamed it on Bush's defense policies—the first distinctly Jacksonian quip in an upcoming two decades of them: Well, he had a national platform. Why not market it? Who says Abbie Hoffman didn't rake it in when he wrote *Steal This Book*?)

On a trip to Washington, Phil asked Bill Bradley if he could visit the Hill with his gang. And thus did the likes of Scottie Pippen of Hamburg, Arkansas, and Ed Nealy of Pittsburg, Kansas, find themselves riding on the underground subway that shuttles the legislators from offices to the Capitol floor.

Chemistry was improving, with a few exceptions. One cerebral big guy didn't get the Big Man's signals. The Bulls had traded up to get Will Perdue in the first round of the 1988 draft, as part of the Cartwright trade. The idea was to bring him on slowly as Cartwright's eventual successor. He had the résumé. As a junior, his Commodores had beaten Bobby Knight. As a senior, he'd been the Southeastern Conference Player of the Year for Vandy.

In an early practice, preparing for an opponent that favored a screen-roll pick to slow Jordan down and tire him out, Perdue—whom Jordan liked to call Will Vanderbilt—kept slamming into Jordan. After one particularly hard hit, Jordan said, "Do that again, I'll hit you." Of course, Phil and Bach called the play again. Perdue put MJ on the floor again. Jordan hopped up and swung. Perdue began to fight back . . . until he realized with whom he was tangling: his meal ticket.

He'd spent virtually the entire season on the bench his first year under Collins, but under Jackson, everything immediately doubled: minutes, points and rebounds. He would go on to win three rings with the man. Coach-to-player-wise, it was not a good fit. Phil's idea of a center, Perdue soon discovered, wasn't the big, heavy guy; it was the gutsy, small, super-strong, mobile Bullet center who used to befuddle him. "He used to always talk about Wes Unseld," Perdue says now. "Phil told me Wes could throw the ball off the backboard, catch it and had the strength to throw it and hit the other backboard. I said, 'I can try it all I want, and I'm not ever going to be Wes Unseld.'"

Nor was Perdue at all pleased with Jackson's legendary habit of not explaining to a player he's just pulled why he's pulled him. Vanderbilt grads who've once majored in civil engineering aren't big on mind games. In the case of these two big men, the signals were weak.

"Maybe he thought he was trying to build me into more than I could do . . . overlooking my talents. Disrespecting me. 'What about my body of work? Why are you always bringing in someone to replace me? What is it about my game you don't like?' But there's that sense of entitlement that athletes have . . . every guy thinks he can do more.

"Have you talked to a player who's said, 'I love that man that made me who I was today'? No. He understood me. That's the best way to put it. Let me put it this way. I don't think there's anybody that hates the guy . . . that's a strong word. You'll maybe come across a few guys who didn't like him . . . because of what he did to make them play: 'I'm going to poke you with this stick, and unfortunately, it's what I have to do, but when it's all said and done, you have to respect me for it.'

"He had discovered or concocted ways to get guys to perform. I would say that it wasn't always ways that guys liked . . . or appreciated . . . but yet they still responded. You could say maybe he even tricked guys . . . for a lack of a better word.

"At times, I don't think Phil really wanted people to know exactly who he was. I think he actually got a little thrill of keeping players off balance. The first thing they'll say about him is 'eleven championships.' The next is 'unorthodox.' And while he should get plenty of credit, he would occasionally tweak the media, not necessarily give them what they desired, and he will never get the full credit. There's always going to be people trying to understand who is Phil Jackson. Who is he? The mastermind of keeping us off balance."

"Phil did pick on Will," Steve Kerr told me. "There were times when Phil would yank him out quickly. Will had a broken nose one time, wearing a mask. He'd fire that mask across the floor. They never hit it off. Phil definitely pushed his buttons.

"Phil picked on big guys an awful lot. We used to do this one practice in training camp, Fairies Versus Goons, and the guards, the fairies, would play a scrimmage against the goons. You had to figure out how to play the other position. Guards learned how to get rebounds; big guys learned how to handle the ball. One of those, Will broke his thumb." (No mention of what guys thought of the names of the teams, but a decade after AIDS had decimated the town in which Phil earned his ring, a tad un-PC.)

★

But he had a lighter way of pushing buttons: film splicing. Like a shot of B. J. Armstrong penetrating, out of control, getting slapped to the floor as he turns the ball over. The next shot? Dorothy saying, "Toto, I've got a feeling we're not in Kansas anymore." Or the Tin Man looking to gain courage against the monster Laimbeer.

"There was one story," John Salley remembers, "about everyone in this German town looking for gold that's hidden somewhere . . . and it's right in the middle of the town. This is what the idea is: 'What you're looking for is right in front of you.'"

In January of that rookie year, at the all-star weekend in Miami, Jackson was eating oatmeal in a sunny hotel, dressed in creased slacks and a button-down shirt. He looked weary. He was 27-19, but he'd just come off a four-game losing streak on a disastrous road trip in which the Bulls had melted in the glare of the Forum's Showtime spotlight. Crow's-feet had appeared at the corners of his eyes at forty-five. But I also noticed that when he smiled, they slanted upward, like the rivulets of a river delta heading north.

Four years after I'd seen him in Albany, I wanted to know how in hell he'd passed through the *Maverick* ceiling. The answer intimated that he was now, in fact, quite conscious of the boundaries of the NBA's executive arena. "Some people think that because I was off-center, I'd tend to be wild, unpredictable," he said. "I do unusual things, yes, but I'm very, very sane.

"I have a sympathy for a certain group of people called pacifist, but I'm a very centered person. I feel very much in control. I guess I'll know how much I'm really in control after I've done it for a while. That's when I'll know whether you can be successful without having to jump into a mold that's been prepared for you."

He'd certainly acted outside the usual mold for a coach a few weeks earlier in his first revisit to the Garden. With one-tenth of one second on the shot clock, a Knick inbounded the ball to Trent Tucker, who then got off a shot and hit it for the game-winner. In Albany, he'd have thrown a chair. Jackson just walked off.

"I'd had a confrontational half with that refereeing crew. I'd confronted them in the hallway. Right before the second half, Ronnie Nunn came over to me and actually said, 'Phil, are you ready to start the second half now?' Like he was saying, 'Settle down and give us a chance to call the game.'

"So at that point I said to myself, *If there's anything I'm going to do on this day, I'm going to walk out of here and stay real poised and calm. This is my home floor.* When the game ended so suddenly, I said to myself, *If he deserved to make that shot and we couldn't stop it, then they deserved that ball game.* But that night I felt, maybe I didn't stand up for my team enough. It was definitely a mistake. I'm learning. I have good games. I have bad games. Just like playing."

"What we liked about Phil was, he would never complain to the junior guys, only to the crew chief, even if the junior guy'd made the call," says ref Jack Nies. "It was appreciated. And Phil was so cagey and so smart that when he got on an official, on the court, for everyone to see, he had a reason."

In one game in Phil's first year in the stadium, right after the halftime-ending buzzer, Nies had T'ed Phil after he "had gone a little crazy on the court." Now, keep in mind that the refs and both teams had to walk down the same set of stairs to get to the sublevel down in steerage. "So I'm going down the stairs, and there's Phil and a couple of his coaches, waiting for me." Johnny Bach and Tex Winter were hardly Bloods or Crips, "but they all let me have it. Phil especially. I listened. Said nothing. Then I just said to Phil, 'By the way, don't bother coming up the stairs for the second half. I'm giving you another T.'

"One of my crew says, 'How do you stay so calm?' I say, 'What's the sense of two screaming maniacs instead of just one? Plus, we don't have to worry about him anymore tonight.' And here's the ending: There was no wives' waiting room. They waited by the Zamboni. Now, keep in mind this isn't the first game I've worked with him. I mean, I like Phil. So Phil comes out of his locker room before I do. And he goes over and gives my wife a kiss on the cheek. And after that, he was always like that, when she was on the road with me, and he was on the road. We'd be waiting for the tickets to come down for our wives, and Phil would walk by and give her a kiss."

There was a clear method to another form of Jackson madness. As in Albany, he would occasionally get himself thrown out to let an assistant take over. "In one of his early years with the Bulls, in the Garden," Neal Walk recalls, "he'd gotten himself thrown out, and he had this grin on his face like Nicholson in *The Shining* and gave Jimmy Cleamons the helm."

In mid-February, the team hit its nadir. They went into Orlando at 29-19, having lost 4 of 5, blew a 17-point lead, and lost in double overtime. (Jordan had tried to take the game over, scored 49 and skewed the game plan.) Jackson walked into the locker room and kicked a soda can into the wall. They won their next nine. Somewhere Buddha was laughing.

FOURTEEN

The barn was packed to the rafters for a Saturday night showdown. The cocky, first-place Sixers were in town, coached by Whinin' Jimmy Lynam, led by Charles Barkley, en route to league MVP that year. He was being fed by point guard Johnny Dawkins, the man who, had Krause listened to Jordan a few drafts back, would have been point-guarding for the Bulls by now (so perhaps Collins would have *beaten* the Pistons and Phil would have still been an assistant—sliding doors, as in the Gwyneth Paltrow film about alternate lifetimes).

On this night, Phil's Bulls had the fifth-best record in the league. With suit jacket on, suspenders winking out against white dress shirt, Jackson looked every bit the coach, using the look and the whistle instead of the voice. When Pippen jammed home an offensive rebound, and found Jackson's eyes from ninety feet away, their eyes locked, Pippen grinning like a madman, Jackson smiling back.

The Bulls opened up a 13-point lead, but the second team gave it all back. Jackson left the unit in: Work it out yourself, dudes. Barkley was everywhere: hitting jumpers, blocking shots. The Bulls were leading by 7 after three; the Sixers pulled within 3 in the fourth. With the barn rocking off its century-old moorings, the Bulls held on to win by 5.

Jackson gave some peremptory answers to the press in the hallway, in full suit, before waiting for them to dissipate. "Come on," he said to me. "Step into my office"—a spot behind a concrete column, in a sort of Minoan labyrinth where he could sip the beer he'd hidden from the press.

The tails of the mustache had been eliminated, the only hair askew a little flip over his back collar, like a wave about to break and try to become a mullet.

He splayed his skeleton into a folding chair, fished a cigarette out of a jacket pocket, lit it and took a drag, then took a long sip from the plastic cup. I was with Albany Phil again—his improbably huge big-man body settling into a comfort zone like a very large dog that has circled six or seven times.

I commented on how comfortably he seemed to have eased into the big time, in front of fifteen thousand people growing impatient with Krause's coaching wheel, now watching their team led by an unusual guy who that season would protest the closing of a factory in Deerfield and decry the living conditions of the neighborhood around the barn. Who had once asked Bradley to change his vote on giving aid to the Contras trying to overthrow Daniel Ortega's Sandinistas.

Will it change him? I ask. He drags on the cigarette. "I just hope it doesn't affect me," he says. "Of course it'll affect me. I just hope it doesn't make me affected. What did Kipling say? 'If you can . . . walk with Kings—nor lose the common touch'?"

Before we fold up the chairs, he asks a clubhouse kid for a cigarette for the road. Still bummin' 'em. (This is way before the routine years later, after many rings, when his car would be pre–warmed up by a Bulls staffer, and a six-pack of beer, I was told by an anonymous source, would be secreted in the Caddy he endorsed.)

I compliment him on the cut of the suit. He laughs. "I like it because it hides that I'm getting a little broad in the beam." Literally, he means his butt is getting wider. Figuratively, I see it this way: He's beginning to savor the taste of the big time. And his next challenge isn't just to win a title. It's how to reconcile all of the tugs, from Plains parents to Michigan Avenue shops. Because this time, when he spoke of meditating during a recent winning streak, his face then grew less animated. "That's a joke."

Sure it was.

★

"It was an easy choice," Reinsdorf told me the next day. "I knew how well he was respected by our players. I was only thinking of him as an assistant, but as I got to know him it became obvious to me he'd be a head coach. It didn't take a genius to see that he related to players, gets along with them, understands them."

Phil was Krause's pride and joy—for now. "I don't think I took a chance with Phil," he told me at the time, "even though the city acted like I killed Christ. The beard and all that? I was used to people like that. Plus, Phil does not have a huge ego. If your ego gets too big, it gets in the way of your brain," he said. He was predicting the future. His own. "Phil just doesn't have that ego."

Last stop was a revisit with Jackson in his office in the health club north of Chicago (these were pre–Berto Center days) for a few more minutes for the piece I was writing. I reminded him that three years ago he had told me that he and the NBA were probably never destined to be together, but now he'd become The Man.

"Well, I look at my Knick team, and I think, 'Yes, I'm the most logical one to be coaching. For a lot of people the appeal of the Knick teams I played on was watching Walt Frazier or Bill Bradley, or Willis Reed or Dave DeBusschere or Earl Monroe. But of all the people who would coach, I'm the most legitimate person who should be coaching from that club."

History would bear him out. DeBusschere was a terrible GM. Willis was no coach. Clyde's ego was as big as the brim of those seventies hats. Pearl was en route to a Grammy for a documentary. Bradley never came close in his run for the White House.

"The thing that is somewhat surprising," he said, rising and unfolding in layers for a workout in the weight room, "is that someone would choose me." Now he was smiling. "But I think there's a lot of room to operate out on the fringe."

Later, transcribing the tape, I realized he hadn't said, "Bill, Clyde, Willis, Dave or Pearl." He'd used their formal full names. It had been our fourth interview in three years, but the first one in which I'd felt that I no longer was in the presence of just the old Knick, the old Patroon, the old Woodstockian. I had been in the presence of an NBA coach.

"All I know is that he's unlike any other coach I've played for," Pippen told me down on the practice court. "He lets his players play."

"He wants us to be of one mind," said the humble Cartwright, the ultimate team man, now freed to win a ring because of so little pressure. "He's given us focus and maturity."

Jordan was the last one to finish working out. He was willing to talk, although not at first willing to much look me in the eye. "I *like* Phil," he said. "He's given Scottie and Horace maturity. . . . Phil's led a strange life," Jordan then said, clutching a ball to his chest, and catching my glance. "But it's not as if it's all wildflowers and peace anymore. This is serious." Clearly this was to be the most intriguing dynamic in professional basketball history: two of the most competitive men in the game, one single-minded, the other of many minds. The task now lay on the wide coat-hanger shoulders: How to convince a man who wants to be a god that to get there he has to become a member of a parish?

Back in Woodstock, I lunched with an old friend of Phil's named Susan Goldman, a former PBS producer, over broccoli tofu. (She'd left her old Patroon cap in the car.) "I always felt he cared about his players themselves, more than how they played for him," she said. "With both friends and players, he makes a heart-to-heart spiritual connection. With the Bulls, even as a layperson, I can see the freedom the team is playing with, and the growth and flexibility."

They lost eight games after the All-Star break, and finished on a 17-3 run, during which he was tentative in answering a reporter's question about pinpointing the reason for the successful run: "I sometimes fear that if you talk about it, it becomes something in the past or future, not the present." The Buddha was speaking.

After beating the Bucks in the opening round of the playoffs (with something-to-prove Perdue scoring 15 in sixteen minutes and adding 5 rebounds in the clincher), in the pivotal fourth game at the Spectrum against the Sixers in a five-game series, the triangle became, for one night, the Jordan: 45 points.

Now loomed inevitably for the third time in a row, the Pistons. It was Chuck Daly who did the better coaching, challenging Jordan to beat them by himself, a challenge Jordan couldn't refuse. It went to seven, in Detroit—where Pippen suffered the onset of a migraine before the game.

"Can you play?" asked trainer Mark Pfeil. "Hell, yes, he can play," said Jordan, whose berating of his team for their lack of intensity at halftime of the second game and at practice the next day—and the Bulls' subsequent bounce-back—had at least made the series close.

Pippen played and shot one of ten. Salley, off the Piston bench, scored 14 and blocked *five shots:* a nice spare arrow to pack in your quiver. The Pistons cruised, 93–74.

Krause came into the locker room and yelled at the team. This would be the first chink in the relationship between the coach and GM, the thin edge of the wedge that, six rings later, would end Phil's Bulls career.

Jordan sat in the back of the bus, with his father, and cried. According to the late David Halberstam's book on Jordan, *Playing for Keeps,* he was particularly disappointed in Pippen.

Halberstam didn't mention that Pippen's father had died earlier in the playoffs.

The final season stats? Five more regular-season victories than the season before. Twenty thousand more fans. Unfortunately, Michael had scored one more point per game. They'd crawled. Now they could walk. Remember: the journey, not the destination.

Phil's first draft via Krause not only brought him no players; it widened the rift between Krause and his two stars. With the twenty-ninth pick, he chose Toni Kukoč of Croatia, considered the best player in Europe. Even though he wouldn't be able to play for another two years. If ever. Obviously, Jordan and Pippen were less than pleased.

Leon Douglas, a former fringe NBA guy playing for Maltinti/Kleenex Pistoia, had sidled up to Krause at an NBA playoff game. "He told me, 'I saw this guy playing in Yugoslavia. He's like a white ghetto rat. He plays like a brother,'" Krause would later tell me. "I'm thinking, *Shit, a black guy sees something in this white guy?* In '90, he blocks a dunk by [Alonzo] Mourning—just smacks it back in his face. And he dunks on Mourning. Mourning was totally shocked. I don't think a white guy had ever dunked on him.

"Plus, he doesn't know how to lie," Krause told me. "Toni's ass hasn't been kissed since he was seventeen, like some of the kids here."

Pippen missed the beginning of training camp, driving his $80,000 Mercedes to Memphis and hiding out to let Krause squirm, although he ultimately showed; his agent pointed out that he could be endangering his shoe contract.

Three new faces graced the roster. Dennis Hopson, the third pick in the first round of the draft three years earlier by Bill Fitch's Nets, had not found the right chemistry. Krause had also signed big-man banger Cliff Levingston, a former first-round pick for Detroit. That the Bulls promptly nicknamed him Good News spoke of the eternal smile on his face. The triangle confused him, but his energy would come to catalyze the team.

The only rookie to make the team was a solid six-ten center forward out of UNC named Scott Williams, who had been told by Dean Smith on October 15, 1987, when he was nineteen, that his father had shot himself after killing his mother the night before. Williams was a Phil Jackson fit from the start. He would help to win three championships in the next three years using constant mobility, fluidity and brains.

He'd heard that his new coach was a different kind of cat. But that's not what he saw upon arrival. Yet another Piston knockout had back-burnered some of the Buddha. "It was surreal," Williams says now. "He was completely hell-bent on getting by the Pistons. It was the same with Phil as it was with Michael. I walked into this war until the final buzzer of the season. Getting a championship is all that counted from the first day to the last."

Not that he didn't enjoy some of the behind-the-scene arcana. The smudging of the locker room with sage plants? The books? "A great way to keep everything fresh as he tried to figure out how much of his knowledge belonged on a court without freaking everyone out. Closing your eyes in a dark room? Clear your head of all thought? It just seemed to take off some of the pressure."

None of his teammates ever heard him refer to the tragedy at home, but they saw a mean streak in Scott Williams. "He took no shit," said one. They called him Tank.

They won 11 of the first 15. In December and January, a 14-2 streak was marred by a mauling in Detroit in which Pippen missed 16 of 18 shots. Statistically, it was Jordan and Pippen's team backed by an emerging Horace Grant and the Notre Dame vet Paxson, drafted by Rod Thorn in 1983, who had now, following Craig Hodges, become the best three-point shooter in the Central Division.

"By then," says Hodges, "we had a complement of players who knew the nuances, knew that Phil knew what we were capable of. Everybody did what they had to do." He laughs. "And with ten minutes left in a game, with Michael, we always knew we could get back in it."

But Pippen? Hardly growing, psychologically, in leaps and bounds.

That first contract was eating away at him. In February, the 40-14 Celtics visited the 40-13 Bulls, won and took first. Pippen missed practice the next day. Said he had a bad stomach. But "sources close to Pippen," according to *Jet* magazine, said he was unhappy with the pace of contract negotiations. One of the troubles with teaching Zen/Lakota mindfulness was that the students had to want to listen to the lessons.

They went 18-1 after the break, but the twelve-man rotation was shrinking, with only Perdue and B.J. getting a lot of time off the bench; Cartwright was tiring. In a 10-game stretch ending April 12, they went 5-5. It should have been a happy time; they'd clinched the team's second division title in twenty-five years. But Jackson, still learning, was increasingly allowing the offense to operate with Jordan standing at the top of the key.

Meantime, Pippen had given an interview to the *Sun-Times* decrying Krause's trip to Europe to negotiate with Kukoč, in which he'd implied . . . that he wouldn't play as hard as he could the rest of the way. Silver-haired Gilberto Benetton wanted Kukoč, too; he'd offered Toni $4.25 million a year for six years. "Toni is paid more than any player in Europe," he told me one day in his seventeenth-century "villa" headquarters in the Italian countryside. "He is not in prison here. I would like to win more games with him."

Back home, they won the last 4 and finished with 61 wins, 2 behind the Western champ Blazers. First up: the Knicks in the "gamy old basketball palace," wrote one New York columnist. The Bulls took the first two; in the second, a Cartwright elbow opened a seven-stitch gash above Mark Jackson's eye. Chicago coasted in five—and Ewing asked for a trade out of New York.

Then it was the tenacious 76ers. With balanced scoring (Armstrong and Hodges contributing 14 off the bench), the Bulls won by 12. The second was a squeaker: 112–110, with Perdue adding 8. Game three was all Jordan (46) and a 76er victory. Now a victory by the 76ers in the Spectrum would even the thing. Jordan took 27 shots and made 11, but Perdue, Armstrong and Hodges made up for it with 17 off the bench, and the Bulls coasted.

Back in Chicago, Michael had to take over again, hoisting 31 shots, but he scored 38; the Bulls won by 5. They took the next two with ease. Then they took a deep breath and readied for the enemy. Detroit had been less effective in the regular season, finishing eleven behind Chicago, but were still the defenders and had just whipped the Celts in six.

In the first game, Holzman defense prevailed: The Pistons scored 13 in the first quarter, 18 in the fourth. Isiah, Dumars and Laimbeer were 7 of 26 from the field, while the Bulls' scoring stats reflected the optimum effect of the triangle: Jordan, 22; Pippen, 18; Cartwright, 16. There was more good news. While former Piston Levingston's woeful regular-season second half had caused criticism of Krause (what didn't?), in this game he took more shots—six—than he'd taken in any game in more than two months. He made four. At one point the Pistons had closed to 72–70. Jackson went to his second team. Levingston hit a short jumper, then tipped in a missed Hodges shot. Perdue hit a turnaround, Hodges hit a three, and it was over.

Then a surprisingly easy repeat. It was 74–61 after three. The Bulls coasted, as this time Perdue stepped up, releasing pent-up frustration at Jackson's prods and Jordan's hard-edged "Will Vanderbilt."

Both the baby-faced Perdue and Death-Star Laimbeer, wearing a Hannibal Lecter broken-nose mask, went up for a rebound. Perdue had the ball until Laimbeer wrested it away in ungainly fashion. They wrestled. It grew ugly. Perdue had to be pulled away. It had taken a bench guy to keep the spark alive with a defiant move that would have made Unseld proud— especially when Rodman, of all people, approached Perdue afterward, calmly, and the two nodded before shaking hands.

("Even Will Perdue, who some think is an overgrown Gomer Pyle," said the tin-eared *Sports Illustrated* reporter, "is banging with the big boys inside the lane.")

By the third game in the luxury-box-spackled Palace, the home team's frustration was palpable. Detroit simply couldn't be as bad as they wanted to be unless they could keep up with Tex's fluid offense. On one play in game three, Pippen, guarded by Rodman on the perimeter, blew past his man, took Cartwright's no-look behind-the-back pass and went in for the dunk. Rodman, unable to block it from behind, shoved Pippen hard, sending him flying to the ground: a flagrant foul that summed up the Pistons' collective frustration—but not nearly as ugly as at the end of game four, a Bulls rout, when, with 7.9 seconds left, the entire Piston team, led by the baby-faced, petulant Isiah, walked off the court.

Two Pistons stayed to shake hands: Joe Dumars, who would become the president of the Pistons and an NBA Executive of the Year, and Brooklyn kid John Salley.

Oh, wait. The finals remained, against the Lakers, led by a man not without some Jackson in him. Rookie coach Mike Dunleavy, Brooklyn-born, a journeyman in his four-team playing career, had followed tough-guy Pat Riley, who'd won 63 the year before but lost in the Western semis; that marriage had run its course.

Dunleavy, no Showtime kind of guy, had started the season 2-5, and at that point said to his locker room, in effect, "No sweat. We'll work out of this." The team loved him, and finished at 58-24. In the playoffs, they knocked off the Nuggets and Warriors, and then, after Magic dished out 21 assists in the first game of the Western finals, upset the favored Blazers, 4–2. The Lakers were making their eighth trip in the last ten finals. Phil was making his first. He'd gotten the Pistons off Chicago's back, but so what? Without a title, that would be a hollow victory.

In the first game in the barn, Dunleavy's defense prevailed. Jordan shot 14 of 24, but the other four Bull starters made 16 of 45. With Magic doing his magic (19-11-10) the Lakers won, 93–91. If the team that had defined basketball for a decade could take a 2–0 lead in the Bulls' home barn, it was effectively over.

The box score would say that Michael scored 33, Scottie and Horace 20 each, Paxson 16 and Cartwright 12. But the stat that mattered? Assists: Jordan, 13. Five fewer than the entire starting five of the Lakers. He was buying into the fluid flow of Tex's scheme. The final was 107–86. A counterpunch that counted.

Now on to Los Angeles. Jordan, no doubt wanting to out-showtime

Showtime, went an ugly 11 for 28—but hit a jump shot to tie it with seconds remaining in regulation. And 6 more in a 12–4 OT. The final was 104–96. The Forum was silenced; the tide had been turned. In game four, defense and balanced scoring (Michael took just 20 shots) led to an embarrassing (for the Lakers) rout, 97–82.

Anticipating headlines like JORDAN WINS FIRST TITLE, Michael took virtually every Bull shot at the beginning, many errant. During one early time-out, Jackson subtly shifted to a different course. "Who's open?" he asked the other four. The message got through: With the game on the line, Jordan passed to Paxson, who made four jump shots in the fourth quarter. The final: 108–101.

Twenty-five years after playing their first game in the International Amphitheater adjacent to the Union Stockyards, the Chicago Bulls had their ring.

After a group prayer from Hodges, the kid who'd grown up on the south side ("I'm humbled just to know that God accepted us. . . . Hopefully, we'll handle it properly"), Magic walked into the Bulls' locker room to congratulate the victors, as only champions with champion egos know how to do: reaching out graciously, while also reducing the sport to the saga of two men.

Occam's razor is the principle that, if there are different theories about why something happened, the likeliest is the one that has to make the fewest assumptions. So why did they win where they hadn't before? Because they had a new kind of head coach: "A guy who saw the importance of people as people," Hodges says now.

Back in Chicago, abandoning any pretense of objectivity, Sam Smith's *Tribune* story read, from the start: "INGLEWOOD, Calif.—Champions!" Followed by a Jordan quote: "I'm so happy for my family and the team and this franchise. It's something I've worked seven years for, and I thank God for the talent and the opportunity I've had."

The third graph, in its entirety: "Champions!" Then a Paxson quote praising the city. Then the fifth graph, in its entirety: "Champions!" Then the eighth graph, in its entirety: "Champions!"

Sam wasn't the only one to overreact. Moments after the game, celebratory gunfire symphonized the streets. Looting at the Shell Food Mart on Pulaski Road enabled some one hundred celebrants to help themselves to Marlboro Lights and pork rinds. Over on Ridgeway, at Sunrise Food and Liquors, looters supplemented their beef jerky with all the Old Style they could carry. Between State and Dearborn, the patrons spilling out from Mother's and the Alumni Club and Shenanigans soon swelled to an estimated ten thousand. Police on horseback did their best to keep folks from selling beer on the street. They were not successful. On this night, the Big Shoulders were allowed to get nuts.

Within a couple of days, Phil quietly slipped back into the Beemer and, presumably diverting to his favorite road, the historic but obscure Lincoln Highway, drove off to Flathead for the summer—much to the befuddlement of the press, which couldn't quite fathom why Phil Jackson wouldn't want to celebrate himself. This wasn't how it was done.

"You didn't see or hear *anything* from the coach," wrote Bob Ryan of the *Boston Globe*. "He simply took off, to Montana, where he maintains an off-season residence you couldn't find with a Sherpa guide and a compass." Actually, his spread lies just west of tourist mecca Glacier National Park, a few miles south of the town of Lakeside, on a well-traveled highway, and on any given night you might find him having a beer in Del's, up the road in Somers. ("Congratulations, Lynn! Bartender of the Year!")

Winning cures a lot of ills. Like a rocky off-season. Like Jordan skipping the White House after telling Grant he was going to play golf, then telling the press he wanted to be with his family. "I'm not disrespecting the President. He has a family so he understands that." (Grant publicly scoffed: "It's a double standard, and it's been a double standard for the four years that I've played here." Jordan wasn't happy. Horace lasted one more year in Chicago.)

Like the publication of Sam Smith's book, which spilled a cornucopia of in-family stuff, critical of Jordan. Journalist Michael Crowley, then with the *Providence Phoenix,* described its characterization of Jordan as "selfish, arrogant, obsessed with statistics, and disparaging to his teammates." Phil said he didn't read past the first hundred pages of a book that depicted Jordan and Pippen openly making fun of Krause.

"Sam Smith wrote a book that was total bullshit," Krause told me. "I went to the best libel lawyer. Sam got away with it."

FIFTEEN

There was no reason to mess with success. Only one man disappeared: Two games into the season, Hopson was traded to the Kings for their second-round pick and a guard named Bobby Hansen, who'd played in Sacramento the year before after seven years with the Jazz. (Hopson, once the third pick in the draft, finished out his career with every international team from Purefoods Carne Norte to Maccabi Kiryat Motzkin. He is currently an assistant at Bowling Green, where presumably he also teaches world geography.)

Hansen was the prototypical Krause-Jackson bench man out of University of Iowa. He knew his role: tough defensive guy, in your face. He never averaged more than 9 points a season over eleven years. He was known for his feistiness on and off the court, as in a particular New Year's Eve party after a three-game Jazz winning streak in which Hansen had averaged 10 a night. He squared off with teammate Bart Kofoed, a draftee out of rival Nebraska. Hansen's cheekbone was broken. Kofoed was waived.

But Hansen immediately found a comfort zone playing for the new guy. Rich Kelley, Jackson's lifelong friend, had told Hansen they'd hit it off, and he wasn't wrong. Hansen delighted in the trappings of his strange new world.

"First thing I remember at that health club film room," says Hansen, "was a picture of a white buffalo, and a big old painting of a Native American chief. And the first time he burnt the sage, guys are saying, 'Typical Phil, smoking pot again.' Then he explains that this is what you burn in the sweat lodges, and immediately I know I'm supposed to be thinking beyond traditional boundaries.

"Stuff like that, other people couldn't pull it off, but he could, because he obviously believed in it. It was ingrained in him, that respect for Native Americans. I mean, he'd splice Indians routing cowboys from movies into the films.

"But there were all these other things. We'd read from L. Ron Hubbard, the Bible . . . It was such a fascinating way to start the day. To talk about gun control. General Pulaski. A pamphlet about not being promiscuous. Drunk driving. 'Get a cab,' he'd say. I remember someone saying, 'But what if the cabbie is drunker than you are?'

"Phil had something different that made going to class interesting. He was a teacher that kept it fresh, not just at game time, but every day: he'd stimulate, he'd motivate. I swear: Phil could lead a team of genius children in an honors class. He didn't say a lot. It wasn't a nonstop talking thing, but whatever he said was always insightful to me. And I liked how he had his family around a lot. The boys were ball boys, and there was a sense of family and team all the time. It was all about team.

"Yes, we had the greatest players, but it wasn't going to work for everybody without everybody buying in. So he found ways to pump up everybody. For me, he could always tell when I was down. He had that weird ability to read you pretty good. He lifted you up. Put his arm around you. He made you feel as if he was always aware of you, even if you weren't a star. One time, when things weren't going well, he came up to Hodgie and said, 'Hey, be ready,' and Hodgie would have a great game off the bench. Or Jordan would come up to me and say, 'Chief says get some sleep tonight,' which was his way of letting me know Phil was going to use me tomorrow."

One of the unforgettable nonbook discussions was his late-January talk on Martin Luther King Day. "Whites are dealing, by and large, with more blacks than we've ever dealt with in our lives," Jackson would explain to a writer. "And blacks are dealing with more whites than they ever would, and there has to be a give and take. And if not in our world, if not in the NBA, then where else is it going to happen in society? Not in the business place, where people work for eight hours with 2.6 percent minorities."

Other Jacksonian motivational techniques hardly broke the mold. He cleaved to military freak Al Davis's "us against them" philosophy. Nothing instills tiger blood in a player like the feeling that he is up against an enemy tribe. Phil's world comprised two tribes: the team in the room, and everyone else. The team? The coaches, the players and the trainer. Everyone else? The front office. The writers. The leeches. Jesse Jackson, on his way into the locker room that first season? Barred.

No, this was about Black Elk's circle. This was about whomever had been allowed into the sweat lodge.

By now, the Native American theme was prevalent in the Bulls' lifeblood, raising an interesting question about a man who describes himself as Zen/Christian. Why not bedeck the halls with boughs of Buddha? Whence the insistence that Native America be the motivational theme of what was becoming one of the greatest sports teams in history?

Because the Sioux respect the tribe before the individual.

"His Native American attachment keeps his focus," Diane Mast told me. "I honestly think this is an equally substantive spiritual dwelling for him as much as his Zenishness. It's way easier for the press to hold on to the Zen because all they have to do is say that he is this or that . . . there is no 'incorrect' Zen.

"But Native Americans? Phil is truly in line with their thinking. That way of seeing with your third eye, or listening to nature, protecting it, for it provides as mother. And then, the warrior is also Native American. And Phil's very much tied to that motif. His roots rock with Native American culture. Then he goes off to college and finds Buddhism, which isn't such a leap of faith. When the Buddha realized Enlightenment, how did he know it? Legend tells us that this question was asked of him and he answered by pointing to the earth upon which he sat: total reverence for the earth as mother."

★

It's supposed to be a given that staying on top is harder than getting on top. A canard. In the previous four years, both the Lakers and Pistons had won back-to-backs. The Bulls started at 17-3, partly because Jackson, knowing the older guys had just been through seasons of 106 and 107 games, held a lot of one-day camps. They went 36-5 in the first half.

The triangle was becoming systemic and instinctive. It was allowing kids who'd started on playgrounds playing games where the only way to win was to find the open man to revert to mental and muscle memory. "It's so logical, it's elementary. It's junior high school," says Hodges.

"The beauty is how it's not regimented," says Neal Walk. "It's full of freedom. Because there's no play-calling: Get downcourt, set up, and as soon as the defense tries to establish itself, move to a spot dictated by where the last pass had been. And keep moving off that cue."

It never stops. "Unceasing change turns the wheel of life so we may experience life in all its many forms," the Buddha said. In fact, to true Zen believers, the triangle is a more perfect shape than the circle, as the definitive Zen magazine *Tricycle* attests. "A three-wheeled vehicle aptly evokes the fundamental components of Buddhist philosophy," *Tricycle's* Alex Caring-Lobel told me. "Buddhism itself is often referred to as the 'vehicle to enlightenment,' and the tricycle's three wheels allude to the three treasures: the Buddha, dharma and sangha, or the enlightened teacher, the teachings and the community. The wheels also relate to the turning of the wheel of dharma, or skillfully using the teachings of the Buddha to face the challenges that the circle of life presents."

The offense reveals an infinite number of possibilities every moment. Players will always improvise—it will always be the city game—so any offense has to allow for a mutable structure that doesn't deny stardom but simply incorporates it.

Western civilization has embraced the triangle, too. Father, Son, Holy Ghost. Gilded triptychs. The Three Musketeers. The Three Amigos. And of course, the Three Stooges.

In the man, there'd been a subtle shift—at least, as far as his wife was concerned. He was now a made man in the corporation. All the head-butting with convention was predicated on fighting the system; now, with the ring, he *was* the system . . . and, "He's become more conservative," June Jackson told a writer. "And it scares me. When people have nicer cars and live in nicer houses and neighborhoods, conservatism naturally comes along with it."

"We all change as we grow older," Bill Bradley said at the time. "I don't think Phil's maturing process is that much different than anyone else who's committed to personal growth."

Jackson was now forty-six. To quote from *Maverick,* "Any man who is not a communist at 21 is a fool, and any man who is a communist at 31 is also a fool."

The only semi-slump of the season was a patch in January when they lost four of five and endured a practice wherein, under the watchful eye of Winter, they practiced chest-to-chest passes . . . for ninety minutes. Practices were always intense, especially when Bach would release the "Dobermans"—Michael and Scottie—on second-team forwards. "They'd double you," Hansen says, "and you'd be dead. They'd play the entire scrimmage. And never seem to tire—despite having started the day in the weight room."

But the enforcer? That was Cartwright. One day Jordan was late for practice, and knocking on the door from the outside. Hansen went to open it. Cartwright stopped him. "Let the fucker go around like the rest of us."

They finished 67-15 and swept Miami in the first round of the second season. But now loomed the Knicks in their first year under Pat Riley:

Oakley, Xavier McDaniel ("X"), Anthony Mason, howling and fouling (sorry, Clyde). The idea was to slam Jordan and Pippen into the next dimension. And it almost worked. In the sixth game in the Garden, John Starks came off the bench to score 27 and send it back to Chicago—where Pippen's triple-double complemented Jordan's 42, and the Bulls coasted home. Then Lenny Wilkens and Larry Nance's Cavs took the Bulls to six, but in Richfield Coliseum, the Bulls closed it out with Jordan playing defense (he scored only 24).

The Blazers, though, would be a bitch. Clyde "the Glide" Drexler and company, coached by Rick Adelman, a former bench player whose whole bench adored his philosophy: "Get the right people together so they understand, and more importantly, accept their roles."

The Bulls won the first at home. In the second, Jordan took the last shot in a tie game at the buzzer—and missed. The Blazers won in OT. Back in Portland, the Bulls took two of three. In game six, after three, the Blazers had clamped down on Pippen and Jordan, who were both off. After three quarters, with the Blazers' up-tempo offense perfectly balanced, it was 79-64, Portland.

And *no* one wants to play a seventh game coming off a loss, even if it's at home. At which point, Phil could have said, "I'm going to do a Riley, a Daly: dance with the one who brung me, say, 'The shots didn't fall, and we'll be ready tomorrow,' and start plotting a D that would snuff the enemy."

Instead, a few minutes into the fourth, trailing by 15 (and no one had ever come back from 15 in a final), he called a time-out. Now, Hansen had averaged eleven minutes and 2 points per game in the season. Not that he hadn't seen action: he, Jordan and Pippen held three-man shooting drills after practices. But this was a tad different.

"You could see the coaches looking at their watches," Hansen recalls. "'OK, game seven coming up. Better get ready to go to work [after the game.]' But Stacey King and B. J. Armstrong are saying, 'Come on, Phil. Do something.'"

Phil looked over at Hansen. "Bobby, get in there."

Hansen said, "For who?"

"For Michael," Phil said, and walked away, as if it were a substitution in January against the 14-32 Hornets. Hansen hadn't played. He hadn't taken a shot in three hours.

Drawing on the first day that Paxson had taught him the triangle, he worked his way open to a corner—and B.J. whipped him the ball. And he shot it. Three. All net.

"Thank God it went in," he says. "It took everything I had to get it up there." A second later, he stole a pass to Jerome Kersey, got it up to Pippen for two more. Adelman called a time-out. Hansen was hyperventilating. " 'Get in,' I said to Jordan. 'No, no,' he says. 'Keep doing it.' I look over at Phil. He looks me in the eye. Then he says, 'You did a good job. Don't fuck it up.'

"Then, a few minutes later, Adelman calls another time-out. I come off and look at Michael. 'Get back in,' he says. 'Take us home.' "

The run, with Scott Williams in and Stacey King scoring 5 of his own, was 14–2. With six minutes to go, Jackson called a time-out. "OK," Michael said to Bobby, "I'll take it from here." He scored 12, and they won 97–93.

At the end, Paxson threw the ball in the air. Bobby Hansen caught it.

Back to back.

Down in the locker room, they didn't say the Lord's Prayer—they shouted it, in unison, at the top of their lungs. Then Jackson said the crowd wanted them back upstairs and asked if they wanted to do it. He hadn't had to. Soon they were dancing on the scorer's table.

Hansen found Jordan down outside the locker room having a moment with his father. Hansen offered him the ball, hoping Michael would say, "Keep it," but he didn't. Jordan grabbed it.

"They were the five minutes that changed my life," Hansen says now. "My kids' lives. Just five minutes, that's all it took. I still can't describe it. It means more now than it ever did. I owe it all to Phil." And Michael.

It was the last game Hansen played. He promptly retired. Unlike Barkley, Ewing, John Stockton, Karl Malone and dozens of other superstars, Hansen had his ring.

★

This year things were decidedly even more festive outside the barn. Roving bands of children were purse-snatching through the surrounding streets. Shots rang out from the nearby Henry Horner Homes. Once again, Pulaski Road got woolly. A policeman was shot, but only in the foot. A fast-food chicken place stood lit but empty, windows shattered, thighs and drumsticks looted. People jumped on cabs. Cops taped their cruiser windows to keep them from shattering as they tried to disperse the bottle throwers. Cops reported several smash-and-grabs. When it was over, 107 police officers were hurt. The monetary cost was incalculable, including a quarter million in damage at one shopping center. Mayor Richard Daley was ecstatic about the victory, less so about the celebration. He stated that he wished they'd just win somewhere else.

No wonder Phil wanted to get back out of town to the lake.

★

That spring, I'd gone to Europe to watch Kukoč in Treviso, north of Venice, across the Adriatic from his home in the ancient Roman Empire city of Split, Croatia. He doled out 16 assists in a game against Hyundai Desio. On one of them, he had not yet reached the half-court line when, with his arms down at his waist, he wrist-flicked an arc toward the basket, where Cadillac Anderson caught it and dunked it. It remains to this day the best pass I've ever seen.

On every play, the ball moved through him, but he was not a Jordan soarer. He was a guard. On the other hand, on the occasion when he did choose to drive, he generally enjoyed success, given that, in this league, "matador defense" was the style of the time.

The next night, over dinner in his Italian apartment, he told me he'd decided to come to Chicago because no one in his league took the game seriously enough—although he admitted he was worried about the NBA obsession with stats: "Here, we don't care about how many baskets someone scores."

Then he shoved a Pat Riley inspirational tape into the VCR. (His tape library also included Prince and Dire Straits.) "It doesn't happen by chance," Riley told the camera. "You don't ever get here because of your talent. Hard work and dedication and concentration is not going to guarantee you anything—but without them, you don't stand a chance."

"That is the part I like very much," Kukoč said.

★

In the second game of the 1992 Olympics, Pippen and Jordan reduced Kukoč to a gelatinous mass. Krause always maintained thereafter that Piston nemesis Daly goaded Pippen into making Kukoč look bad. But Pippen needed no incentive. Krause had signed Kukoč but still hadn't resigned Pippen, who had yet to get a renegotiation of his paltry contract.

"It was Krause who actually got it started," Jordan told Melissa Isaacson of the *Tribune*. "Because it was he who said the kid was so great." Reportedly, during the game, Jordan said to Pippen: "Let's test him and see how fucking good he is. If you get tired, call me and we'll switch."

"I have never seen defense like that," Kukoč said afterward.

"See you in Chicago," Jordan said.

★

Back in Chicago, I asked Krause why'd he'd taken the chance on the guy three years earlier. "Personally," he said, "I want to win one without Michael Jordan. I want to win a championship without Michael."

What kind of GM would admit such a thing? A really small man with a really big burgundy Cadillac who was a good scout but not a manager of men. A man who could divine the ore but not admit that the coaches were doing the alchemy.

In Jackson's office, I asked about Toni, whom he'd never seen play in person. "The team is getting older," he said. "That's what Toni fills in our plans. To rejuvenate us, hopefully. Bring youth and talent to the team."

But, I pointed out, Michael Jordan wasn't exactly Methuselah. Pippen was only twenty-eight. "Everybody will have to slide over a space . . . there's no doubt about it." Jackson was not smiling. But he *was* wearing sandals. "Toni has every right to expect a good career in the NBA. And everyone has to move over and allow him to realize that potential."

Everyone? Allowances have to be made. After the Olympics, Michael said to me, "He'll fit in. I have no doubt he'll do what's necessary."

This White House visit wasn't without controversy, either. Having grown up in neighborhoods that were "shooting ranges with live ammo," and having ripped Jordan in the press during the season about his lack of involvement with the black community, Hodges showed up in a dashiki to protest Bush's "militarism, economic exploitation and racism." He delivered to Bush a handwritten letter pleading for more social responsibility.

Hodges was a free agent. After that episode, he didn't get a call, let alone a tryout. He never played again. Jackson would later admit to being stunned. "I found it strange that not a single team called to inquire about him. Usually, I get at least one call about a player we've decided not to sign. And yes, he couldn't play much defense, but a lot of guys in the league can't, but not many can shoot from his range, either."

Hodges's support of Louis Farrakhan apparently didn't light up his résumé. He was clearly being blacklisted—until, twelve years later, Phil hired Hodges as his shooting coach in Los Angeles. Three more championships ensued.

SIXTEEN

In his first appearance in the film room at the start of the 1992–93 season, after wondering why the place smelled like weed, second-round pick Corey Williams out of Oklahoma State noticed one little kid's chair amid the regular ones. "Who's that for?" he asked Phil. "You," said Phil. From thereafter, he'd be Pee Wee.

Now in his first year as head coach at Stetson University after six as an assistant at Florida State, Williams says, "His message was 'This is your starting position. You see where those other guys are sitting? That's what you're aiming for.'

"Golly, he was always trying to teach me about life," he says now, because that's the way he really talks. "And now I feel like I have a Phil Jackson in me, as a coach. He was always calm, and he'd talk to you in a tone that was nonthreatening. You never had to brace yourself or be combative, because he talked in a manner you respected. Now as I coach these young men, I talk to them in tones they understand."

Like those who came before him—and those who would follow—Williams was stunned at Jordan's commitment in practice. "He knew he was the best, and he didn't want anyone to take that away from him. You come to practice and see the best basketball player working his tail off, you have to work hard! And that trickled all the way down."

Pippen befriended Corey immediately: The star from Hamburg, Arkansas, bonded with the kid from Twiggs County, Georgia. But it was Phil who always went out of his way, Williams said, to include his number 12.

Like the day he gave Williams tape on an opponent in tomorrow's game. "Watch this guy, and watch him carefully." The next night, Williams never got in. Jackson apologized. "I didn't care. It was his way of making me feel as if I was one of the team . . .

"Then, finally, in my first game, about five seconds left, he says, 'Get in for Michael.' I make one pass, the game is over. I say, 'Phil, those were the best five seconds of my life.' 'Don't worry, Pee Wee,' he said to me. 'You're going to see a lot of good moments in your life.'"

Six months later, Jackson called Williams in to release him. "He said, 'Pee Wee, we thank you for your services.' I said, 'Thank you for the opportunity of a lifetime.' It was one of the highlights of my life. I can tell my kids, 'I got a chance to stop Michael Jordan in practices.' It was truly a blessing for me."

To replace Hodges, another three-point specialist was in town: Trent "Tenth of a Second" Tucker. He was quickly indoctrinated into the ways of the new world. In one of the first exhibition games, he missed two jumpers in a row. He was walking off when Jordan grabbed him and said, "You can miss two open shots in a row. You can't miss three. The next one must go in."

The next series, Jordan passed to Tucker. It rattled, but it went in.

They were practicing in a new facility now—the Berto Center. The high profile of the team had made practicing in the old health club impractical. The decor quickly took on the Lakota vibe, right down to the bull horns with the bull's balls in a pouch between them, a Bach gift.

★

By now, says Scott Williams, who was spelling Cartwright for twenty minutes a game, the intensity in the regular season had lessened, with marketers and media, the outer ring of people, looking for a way in, moneywise. They would finish in second place to Riley's rejuvenated Knicks, having won only 57.

In mid-March, Phil had a chance to hook up with an old Knicks pal at Riordan's Saloon in Annapolis, where the Bulls were practicing for a game with the Bullets (prior to Mike's gentleman farmer days). And how the tables had turned.

"He stops in with some players and coaches to get a bite," Riordan recalls. "Lunch is chaos. I got an apron, sweaty T-shirt, hairnet, working between cooks and waitresses. I come out. He's in a three-thousand-dollar Armani, Bruno Magli shoes. I say, 'Hey, Phil, isn't this something. I'm dirt-baggin' in a kitchen, sweating my ass off to make a living; you're out here in an Armani when it used to be a fatigue jacket.'

"He said, 'You gotta do what you gotta do.' I say, 'I understand that. To coach in the NBA, you gotta look the part. I'm not judging you. Just a change of events.'

"After he left, I started thinking. I was the guy addicted to basketball. Now his whole life is centered around the game."

Jackson had the Bulls honed; they won 22 of their last 28, and in their first two playoff series, they won 7 straight, allowing the Hawks and Cavs not a single victory.

The Knicks series? A predictable Texas death match: Two go in, one comes out. "Oakley, Mason?" Scott Williams recalls. "Guys would be taking Scottie's and MJ's heads off. Body blows. I mean, you could be thirty-five feet away from a play and you had to watch your chin."

With Doc Rivers at point guard, Riley's guys won both in the Garden, the second setting an ominous tone when Starks dunked dramatically over Jordan. On the flight back to Chicago, Zen Jackson showed Pink Floyd videos. "Phil," Jordan reportedly said, "you must have smoked some crazy shit in your day."

The Bulls took the next two at home. After going 3 for 18 in the first one—an easy win, 103–83, because a clampdown defense held the Knicks to 30 field goals on 69 attempts—Jordan scored 54 in the next one, including 14 from the line. ("The way the game is officiated is basically a caste system," Steve Kerr said in 1995. "If this were India, guys like Michael . . . would be members of the Gandhi family and guys like me would be peasants."

Game five, back in the Garden, promised to be a simple question of who's tougher. Power forward Charles Smith wasn't. He'd come into town to help fill the void left by Xavier McDaniel. He didn't. With seconds left, the Knicks trailing, 95–94, Smith went up for the game-winning layup. Horace Grant blocked it. Smith got it back, Jordan stripped it, Smith got it back, went up, Pippen blocked it from behind. At which point every Knick fan from here to the Betelgeuse system is screaming, "Dunk it!" Instead, he tried to lay it in again, and Pippen blocked it again. Bulls win. And win the next. And go to New York, and eliminate the mixed-martial-arts Knicks.

The finals presented the third opponent in three years. Charles Barkley, Dan Majerle and Kevin Johnson had taken the Suns to their best regular-season record in years, to the delight of fans in a new arena, which was extraordinarily loud. They'd beaten the eighth-seeded Lakers in five, the Spurs in six, the Sonics in an exhausting seven.

But they were coached by a rookie who'd be haunted by the old axiom that great players make mediocre coaches. After making five all-star teams for the Celtics, including a 1974 championship ring, Paul Westphal replaced Fitzsimmons, who'd been jettisoned despite a 59-victory season for losing to the Blazers in the Western semis the year before. If Cotton, a triangle scholar, had stayed, he'd have been able to counter the triangle, and they might have stopped the dramatic final shot of the series.

The Suns dug themselves a huge hole, letting the Bulls win both games in Phoenix. But they recovered for a dramatic triple-overtime win in the next game, in Chicago.

According to a blog posting written by a neutral observer who happened to have dinner with Johnny Bach one night a few years ago and posted his recollections of Bach's conversation, Bach told his fellow diners that the day before the fourth game of that series, Michael and Charles played forty-eight holes of golf and Michael bought Barkley a $20,000 earring in the hopes that he'd soften his opponent.

The next day Jordan scored 55 points, and the Bulls had a 3–1 lead. In game five, eager for a home celebration, Michael took 29 shots, Scottie 20, and maybe someone else took 1 or 2 . . . and the Suns won it by 10. The Suns had broken to an angry-defense 33–21 lead after the first and held on to force the series back to Phoenix.

It was 87–79 at the start of the fourth quarter in game six—at which point the Sun defense notched it up, and it was 98–96 Suns with 14.4 seconds left when Jackson took his final time-out. The Bullets had scored nine in the entire quarter. All nine had been scored by Jordan.

Tex is probably still smiling over the last seconds: Jordan took the ball to midcourt, whipped it to Pippen at the top of the key. Scottie drove. Barkley stepped up—and Pippen whipped a pass to Grant, who was getting open in the corner. He began to drive, and then whipped the ball out to the three-point line, where John Paxson was standing with no one within thirty feet of him. The Notre Dame guy could have recited the Twenty-Third Psalm before shooting.

Swish. Title. In the triangle, every good boy deserves favor.

The White House ceremony went well. But the summer did not.

On August 3, a fisherman found a body in a South Carolina swamp sixty miles from Fayetteville, in Lumberton County, an area of North Carolina where "cocaine trafficking involves tens of millions of dollars," Assistant U.S. Attorney William Webb was quoted as saying in 1987. The corpse had been dead for one to three weeks, of a gunshot wound to the chest. James Jordan had not been reported missing, although no one had talked to him in the prior three weeks, which included his birthday. It was not unusual for him to go without communication. On August 4, he was listed as a John Doe.

On August 5, authorities discovered a damaged Lexus 400 two hundred yards from the parking lot of the Quality Inn off I-95. On August 12, the Jordan family filed a missing-person report. With no refrigeration equipment at hand, the coroner had cremated the body but kept the man's teeth, which confirmed that the body was that of James Jordan. The sheriff of Lumberton County, where the car was discovered, said that there had been "no signs of struggle in the car. . . . We don't think it happened in this car."

A few days after the identification of the corpse, Larry Demery, a Lumbee Indian, and Daniel Green, an African American, were arrested and charged with the crime. The sheriff contended that the two were looking to rob a tourist, discovered Jones, shot him with one .38-caliber bullet that severed his aorta, and dumped the body in the swamp. They then drove the car for a few days, using Jordan's video camera to film the championship ring and watch his son had given him.

According to the police reports, James Jordan had been dead since July 23, which was the day he was last seen, leaving a friend's house in Wilmington. But according to news reports, James Jordan's wife talked to him on July 26. On July 26 or 27, a convenience store clerk and bread delivery driver told police that Demery, Green and James Jordan had entered the store, and the clerk chatted with Jordan. She remembered the gold trim on the Lexus.

Questions surfaced immediately about the possibility of the death being other than a random killing. On August 19, Michael Jordan issued a statement. "Throughout this painful ordeal I never wavered from my conviction that Dad's death was a random act of violence. Thus, I was deeply disturbed by the early reports speculating that there was a sinister connection [between Michael's gambling activities and] Dad's death. I was outraged when this speculation continued even after the arrest of the alleged murderers. These totally unsubstantiated reports reflect a complete lack of sensitivity to basic human decency."

In the first week of October, one month before the season began, Jordan announced his retirement, explaining that now at the age of thirty, he didn't want to go out like Dr. J., with people whispering that he wasn't as good as he had been. With the way Phil coached—the right way, he said, no question—subsequent years would see less of Mike shooting and more passing.

Jordan had first confided in Jackson a month earlier about the possibility. Phil, who'd always seen Jordan's basketball commitment as the thing that held his life together, figured that his father's death would make it harder for him to continue at a high level. By Jordan's own account, on the day he made it official to Krause, the GM told him to go talk to Phil. Jordan knew that Phil, psych/philosophy major, would want to mindmeld with his superstar and talk him out of it. When Phil said, "Take a year to think about it," Michael said no: What's done is done. As Jordan recounted it, Phil cried.

The truth is, off court, waters had hardly been calm in the Jordan world. Flash back to the locker-room discussion of a pamphlet offering a modern interpretation of the Ten Commandments, especially the sixth, as interpreted in both Exodus and Deuteronomy: Don't kill anyone. Phil had long thought of this particular commandment ever since the night in the seventies when he'd been on the court screaming at a ref as usual, ready to punch him, and trainer Danny Whelan had said, "So if you had a gun right now, you'd shoot him, right?" Jackson had thought about those words that night.

"What you think, happens," Jackson said in 1994. "As you think, so you are. Which is tough to buy for these kids, because they don't see thought becoming reality . . . I got the feeling there were more and more guns; I could hear chatter, and I worried about it."

"MJ was always going to the shooting range. He had guns with scopes and shit," Hodges says now. "When that happened to his old man, that's so sad . . . [but] the spirit of the weapon is to maim and kill. We don't need to know how it's made, know its metallurgy, whatever. Its components are irrelevant. The spirit is to maim and kill, once you pick up that spirit in your league, in your circle, that doesn't maybe come to affect you personally, but it's the effect on the team."

In February 1992 Jordan-issued cashier's checks totaling more than $100,000 had been discovered in the briefcase of a man named Eddie Dow, a Charlotte bail bondsman and, according to later court testimony, a cocaine dealer.

The defendant himself had been murdered a month earlier.

David Stern asked that Michael come to New York, where he reportedly told Michael that he should be more careful about his business associates.

Then, the following October, the season of three-peat, Jordan was subpoenaed to testify at the trial of one James Bouler for conspiracy to distribute coke and launder coke money. Jordan testified that the $57,000 cashier's check he'd given to Bouler was restitution for a weekend of cards and links. Asked how often he'd go on such outings with these guys, Michael conceded that it might be two or three times a month.

From the start, Stern, the son of a deli owner on the Lower West Side, had a Marshall Plan for saving the league—restore the public's faith in the NBA's early-eighties outlaw vibe. It's one thing to have a bench guy hanging with high rollers. It's another to have your league's emblem reportedly lose $1.25 million on a golf course in ten days, hit Atlantic City the night before a Knicks playoff game (he was rumored to sometimes play four blackjack tables simultaneously), and have to face Ed Bradley's question on *60 Minutes:* "Has your gambling jeopardized or endangered your family?" The answer was, of course, "No." (The figures did not seem unreal. Bach had reportedly said to the previously referred-to dinner-party blogger that he'd seen Jordan being given $3 million in chips in casino VIP rooms and that he had seen Michael lose and win $3 million in a single evening.)

"I wanted to astonish the spectators by taking senseless chances," says the narrator of Dostoevsky's *The Gambler,* "and—a strange sensation—I clearly remember that even without any prompting of vanity, I really was suddenly overcome by a terrible craving for risk." The chronic gambler is unbalanced. He has never been able to find peace and self-satisfaction in the now.

"My son doesn't have a gambling problem," James Jordan had said. "He has a competition problem"—implying that the likeliest reason he quit was the trait he shared with his coach: ultracompetitiveness. But whereas Jackson had always known when to stay inside the fence, Michael hadn't.

On October 5, the Lumberton County DA sought the death penalty for Demery and Green, although questions remain as to whether they were guilty of the crime. The next day, Jordan announced his retirement.

Jordan's sabbatical would last fewer than two years. In his one year as a baseball player, he hit .202. *Sports Illustrated* advised, "Bag it, Michael! Jordan and the White Sox Are Embarrassing Baseball." Jordan called the story "un-American" and basically never spoke to the mag again. Soon after Jordan's retirement, the NBA dropped its second investigation. There were already rumors that the league had advised him to take a sabbatical and lie low.

I didn't put a lot of credence in them until the day I was interviewing the famously reclusive Hollywood producer Bert Schneider (*Five Easy Pieces*) at the Beverly Hilton one day when he told me that there was no story to be told about him, but why didn't I find the girl who used to work at his BMW dealership in Beverly Hills who'd told him that she was a hostess on the private plane of a league owner the night he called Jordan to tell him that the league was giving him the choice: Take some time off, or be told to take some time off.

I couldn't find the woman. Schneider passed away. Trail went cold.

Jackson now had the chance to prove that he didn't need one of the best players in the game's history. And he didn't. He won 55 games—"the greatest coaching season of his life," says Rosen now, and not only because of Jordan's absence; the season would be mottled with mistakes of all kinds by Pippen, the one head that Jackson couldn't quite corral.

★

In the meantime, along with Kukoč, a couple of new guys arrived to help heft the load. If Google were perfect, you could look up "Phil Jackson bench guy basketball savant high-IQ intellectual compatriot" and there'd be a picture of Steve Kerr. He was born in . . . Beirut. His dad was a scholar of Middle Eastern affairs, born and raised in Beirut, where his parents had taught for four decades at the American University of Beirut. After Deerfield and Princeton, Malcolm Kerr, author of *The Arab Cold War* and *Islamic Reform*, returned and took on the presidency of the American University. It was a prestigious and dicey job. His predecessor had been kidnapped and was still being held hostage. Steve Kerr was beginning his sophomore year in Arizona when the phone in his dorm rang at three A.M. His father had been assassinated. Islamic Jihad claimed responsibility. No one was ever arrested. Two nights later, Kerr scored 15 in a blowout of Arizona State, Lute Olson's first Pac-10 victory.

"Opie" was the archetypal scrapper and loose-ball diver. "Steve is one of the smartest players I've ever seen," Olson would say. "He's the glue that holds the team together. There is never confusion when he's out there. It doesn't matter if he scores a point or not."

As if Kerr needed further experience of evil, in warm-ups before an away game against Arizona State in his senior year, the chants started to come out of the stands: "PLO . . . PLO . . ." and "Your father's history." Three hours later, he'd hit all six of his threes and scored 22 in a 101–73 Arizona victory. Inspired by his tale, *People* magazine interviewed him. The writer conceded, though, that "it's unlikely he'll ever play in the pros."

Mindful that they'd finished eighteenth in attendance in a twenty-three-team league the year before, the Suns took Kerr with the fiftieth pick. Every now and then, Fitzsimmons let him play. He averaged 2 points. He moved on for three years to Cleveland, backing up Mark Price. Under Lenny Wilkens, the '91–'92 Cavs made it to the Eastern finals with a balanced offense that included Ron Harper, Kerr's future teammate. They took the Bulls to six games. Kerr scored in one game—five points, in garbage time. On signing with the Bulls in 1993, Kerr had found his basketball home for the next five years. He had some triangle training. He had some leadership skills. Now he had a coach he admired from the first day.

"I'd never met anybody like Phil," Kerr says now. "Most coaches are cut of the same cloth. But from the beginning, you could just sense there was a huge difference in the way he approached coaching and leading. When players first got to Chicago, they were always looking around: Is the joke on me? When we were meditating, the new guy would have one eye open waiting for everyone to laugh at him—but then you realize it's real."

His first book? "A Tony Hillerman novel—based on my interest in the Southwest. And then one of his favorite Wallace Stegner novels. Even the players who didn't read them understood that reaching out meant that he wanted to get to know you, the individual. The gesture counted. He cared."

Did the spiritual searching that he interwove through every day strike him as authentic? "You can't make up that kind of interest in everything," Kerr says. "The best thing about it was that it kept it all real, every day. Something new. The biggest challenge in an eighty-two-game season is keeping the players interested, over and over. And with Phil, he never stopped being curious, and that kept us on our toes."

In his first season, playing all eighty-two and starting none, Kerr averaged 9 points, 3 assists and twenty-five minutes a game.

The other walk-on? A sixty-day fill-in who stayed six years. Bill Cartwright was thirty-six and hurting in the summer of 1993. His backups were Perdue, Stacey King and Scott Williams. If Cartwright couldn't make it, Perdue had the physical strength to endure a matchup down the line with Shaq or Ewing, but he wasn't a huge triangle guy (just a huge guy). Cartwright was going to sit out training camp. Cannon fodder was needed. Krause's Italian eyes had found a St. John's grad in Bologna. They were bringing him in to play tackling dummy.

"Phil wasn't counting on me for a whole lot; they made it clear from the start," Bill Wennington says now. "Phil's always very aware of how much anyone can take at any given point, and Cartwright's health was important. 'We'll keep you for training camp, and after a month of the season, you have to plan on us releasing you,' he said. So I had a month to impress somebody."

★

They lost the first home game of the season embarrassingly to Miami 95–71, shooting less than 20 percent in the first half with Jordan watching from courtside. They were 4-5 when they took the court against the 9-0 Rockets, led by a man named Hakeem Olajuwon. Perdue started at center. They were getting blown out in the middle of the second quarter when Phil approached Wennington, who was making the league minimum, $150,000.

"Sorry to do this to you," he said, "because I didn't prepare you. But get in there." Wennington scored 19 on 9 of 15 from the field and pulled down 8 rebounds. They won 25 of their next 30. Wennington was in for the duration.

But Pippen, the new leader, wasn't winning the fans over. One night he gave the home crowd the finger because they were booing him. Pippen subsequently said they were booing because he was black. In Chicago?

If Rosen was right that this season represented Phil's finest hour, it wasn't enough to get past the Knicks. Sensing that a non-Jordan Bull team could be taken, for once, New York made its de rigueur physical statement. Jackson's statement? He was livid about home-team reffing in a 92–86 opening-game loss in which Pippen was assessed five fouls—and even Kerr got four.

"They blew a fifteen-point lead with fourteen minutes left," Riley countered. "It's got nothing to do with officiating. If he wants to make excuses, he should take a good, hard look at his team."

The next day, Jackson needed to pull some Zen out of his hat. So while reporters waited at a deserted practice gym at the exclusive (and white) Downtown Athletic Club, the bus driver headed for the Staten Island Ferry wharf for a day of sightseeing. They took in the harbor. They took in Wall Street. Horace Grant learned that the Statue of Liberty was a woman.

"We had much more to learn about, being together in the fresh air, and the ocean," Jackson would later say, "than being on the basketball court. Living life is living it in the moment."

(He believed that, says Diane Mast. "Time is not to waste away—that's definitely a Phil message. I never saw the guy when he wasn't working at something, even if it was chasing a photo down on the rocks. He is always tinkering, reading, driving, lecturing, thinking, writing, walking around.")

They lost anyway. Pippen used the travel day to suggest, with lousy timing, that he should be the highest-paid Bull. He was making $3 million a year for two more years, but Kukoč had a clause that might allow him to go above that the following season.

Game three was a war. Stern had a good view from about the tenth row to see Pippen and Charles Smith drawing technicals—before the game had started. And then disaster.

Krause had called up CBA guard Jo Jo English during a November slump. He'd averaged eleven minutes a game. On this night, he was determined to make the most of them. In the second quarter, with the Bulls up by ten, English elbowed Derek Harper. When Grant subsequently fouled Oakley, English and Harper shoved each other and started a rumble. Harper threw the only punch, but just about everyone got into a little shoving. As Cartwright was trying to separate the two, Starks got set to throw a punch—but Jackson blocked him from behind.

Stern's worst nightmare became an historic footnote because of what happened about ninety minutes later. It was 102–102. Ewing had just flipped in a baby hook, and 1.8 seconds remained. In a time-out, Jackson called a play for Kukoč, top of the key, off an inbounds pass from Pippen. Kukoč had already won a remarkable five games that season at the buzzer. In the final quarter, Pippen had converted 1 field goal in four attempts.

"Scottie wasn't real happy," Kerr recalls. "He snapped. He said, 'I'm not going in.' Then he sat down. It was really weird." (Earlier reports had it along the lines of, "Fuck. I'm tired of this. Fuck.") He and Jackson exchanged words, and Pippen sat down. Teammates implored him to get up. He ignored them.

"So Phil says, 'Fuck him. We'll play without him,'" Kerr recalls.

Four players took the court. Jackson had to call another time-out. Then Pete Myers threw the inbound pass to Kukoč. He and Anthony Mason bumped, and Kukoč nailed the twenty-two-footer.

"Scottie had had that tremendous year," Kerr says. "I feel bad for him that that moment lives on. People don't know him. People think in those terms, of that night, but that was completely against what he was really about.

"So we go down to the old locker room, everyone expecting Phil to light into him, but in typical Phil fashion, he says, 'I gotta talk to the media. I'll do the best I can to lighten it up. Oh, and Bill has something to say.'

"Then Cartwright stands up, tears streaming down his face. 'I can't believe you'd do this to us after everything we've been through together, all of the effort we've put in as a team.' But he does it without yelling at him. The way he said it was one of the coolest moments of my entire career. That kind of emotion, coming from a sixteen-year vet?"

Pippen, humiliated, was silent.

Out in the corridor, Jackson said to reporters, "Scottie was not in the play. He asked out of the play. That's all I'm going to say about it."

The next day, Jackson said, "We have healed our wounds. We are together as a basketball team again." A few days later, needing a victory to stay alive at home, Grant, Pippen, Paxson and B.J. clamped down on Ewing et al and won easily, holding the Knicks to 79. As usual, the home-team madhouse was shaking in delight. As usual, the fans poured out into the streets in thunderous celebration. For the very last time.

They lost the seventh in New York, 87–77; Pippen missed 14 of his 22 shots; he was 1 for 6 from the three-point line. Armstrong and Cartwright were a collective 5 for 15, and the Knick defense, led by Mason off the bench, held the Bulls under 20 in three of the four quarters—including 14 in the fourth.

★

Phil Jackson had left the building. The next one, the United Center, built in a city that could serve as one collective museum of great American architecture, had all the appeal of a convention center designed by a first-year architecture student from a software program. Once again, Reinsdorf the Wrecker had effected his dictum "I have no sympathy for preserving buildings that are unprofitable"—although this one had been. Statistically, should that matter to historians, the Bulls would never shoot as accurately as they had in the Stadium. United, Jackson once put it, was just "too vast."

He would also soon give an interview in which he said, "I don't see myself in the game very long at all as far as coaching, and I don't see myself as a general manager"—maybe because after the season, he'd had to fire Johnny Bach, the coach with whom, back in his rookie season, he was said to have gotten along famously.

It had long been rumored that Krause was down on Bach for leaking information to the press and that he'd never forgiven him for what he believed were Bach's leaks to Sam Smith for a three-year-old book. But a source with knowledge of the situation says that Bach would sometimes tell Michael to ignore the triangle, subtly undermining Jackson's adherence to Tex's thirty-year-old blueprint.

Why? Maybe because at the first introduction of Phil as head, Krause referred to him as "the designer of the defense." And by now, says a source, Bach was not paying as much attention to the details of his job as he should have.

With Bach gone, the Rockford paper had reported that Phil was going to hire Rosen. But when the phone rang in Charley's office, it was Krause. "Sorry," he said, "we want one of our own guys."

"I was pissed," Rosen says now. "He didn't have the balls to tell me? Krause calls me? Hey, we both used to denigrate Krause. And he had Krause call me and tell me some bullshit story? He didn't have the balls to say, 'Hey, it's not going to happen'?"

"There was a glimmer of a chance for Charley to join my staff," Jackson would write (not with Rosen) in *More Than a Game*. "I respected Charley's eye for the game almost more than anyone else's, and I wanted him there with me. But I also knew that bringing such a close friend on board . . . might be seen as compromising my integrity. Charley had a tough time accepting it, and I could understand his anguish."

Why his reluctance to call his oldest friend himself and explain, if that was his rationale? Years later, in a book also not coauthored by Charley, Phil would say, "I hated discord of any kind. My father used to discipline my brothers with his belt, and I remember sitting at the top of the cellar stairs bursting into tears listening to them get their whippings." But that was forty years earlier. Was the expert communicator, whose words always led to the strength of the family, losing his expertise?

It was years before Charley and Phil fully reconciled, at Eddie Mast's funeral, where they hugged. "In that one moment," Rosen says now, "it gave us an instant message to what was important in life." It was the only speed bump in a relationship that endures to this day.

The hire? An old friend. An old mentor. An old coach. Now Jimmy Rodgers was working for the kid he'd coached in the field house. The Fighting Sioux reunion would prove fortuitous.

SEVENTEEN

Sliding-doors time again: The drumbeats of a major-trade rumor were being passed from hillside to hillside from Chicago to Seattle. The Sonics said they'd heard Pippen was available. Krause insisted he was not shopping Pippen, just listening to offers. Jerry's fill-in leader, Scottie simply hadn't grown into the role Krause had expected him to. As Krause saw it, he was still carrying too much baggage.

As the draft approached, a swap of Pippen for Shawn Kemp seemed so inevitable that a hot-dog place out in Niles featured a "See ya, Scottie" meal. The Bulls were said to also want the Sonics' first-round pick (eleventh) for theirs (twenty-first).

"We had to be overwhelmed to make a deal. We were not overwhelmed," said Krause. The Sonics pulled out right before the draft. Krause came out on top by a country mile. The Sonics pick was Carlos Rogers, a five-team journeyman. The Bulls pick was Dickey Simpkins, who, albeit in a fringe capacity, would earn three Bulls rings, thanks to the fact that Pippen stuck around . . . and grew.

Had the trade been consummated? Jordan would later say he "probably" would not have returned. But of course, Michael the competitor being Michael, he would have—and would've played opposite Kemp, a guy with bad knees and a drug situation. There would not have been three more rings.

But they still needed a leader. So they took Ron Harper to dinner, and act two was ready to begin.

Eight years into his career, Harper, now a free agent, had just come off a steady five years with the Clippers, marked by a disastrous knee injury that had turned him from an airborne scorer into a more earthbound captain.

"Have you seen our offense?" Phil asked. "Do you know about the triangle?" Whereupon Harper answered, "I can tell you everything that offense can do," and he could, because he'd been a Bulls fan ever since his old buddy Brad Sellers had joined Chicago. At the dinner, Harper spent several minutes outlining variations on napkins.

He'd just jumped off a carousel of coaches, including Larry Brown, the man who, Harper says now, "was never happy unless he was unhappy. He was a pisser. He would *wear . . . you . . . down.*" (Sound familiar? As in Doug Collins?) Harper was ready for some love. Yes, he could have stayed with the Clippers, gone on to score 25,000 points for a perennial loser and retired without a ring.

Or he could find a way to win—the way he had as a kid, when he'd dribble a ball to downtown Dayton to hang with his friends, then dribble back—six miles round-trip. Then when he got a bike, he'd do the same thing—dribbling as he biked.

In the meantime, Pippen couldn't have been happy about headlines that he was being shopped, not after enduring the rapids of the previous season. But he took the high road. As camp began, all questions were immediately about his playoff pout.

"It's over," he said, and the words proved to be true.

"He apologized to us, and we've accepted the apology," Perdue said. "It's a new year. Unfortunately, when Scottie's name is mentioned, there's always going to be an asterisk . . . The moment . . . is something he's always going to be remembered for."

Phil took a slightly higher road: "He had a great year, and I'll take another one like it." He'd get it: great effort, but no ring.

Another new face showed up, hardly as high-profile as Harper's, though as Harper calls him now, "Phil's guy." Jud Buechler unofficially leads the league in trillions: the twelve zeros that follow your name if you played in a game but recorded not a single stat. What was he doing there, after bounding through three teams? Having once played for Fitch, he knew what Jackson wanted to see in free-agent tryouts: mania. He made the final cut.

"So he called me in for our first meeting," Buechler says now. "I'm scared to death. The guy already has three rings. I was ready for him to criticize my foot speed or my jumping ability. And his first question was: 'How's [Jud's wife] Lindsey? Settling in?'

"I thought to myself, *Excuse me?* Then he says, 'Have you found a place? Is she making friends?' I was blown away. None of the coaches I'd ever played for even knew I was married, or cared. The other four years, not a single coach had asked about my personal life. But he knew we'd bounced around, how tough that can be on a wife. This was a guy who knew that if you were happy on the court you'd be a better professional at your sport. We spoke for half an hour, none of it about basketball.

"I love the man. Did then, still do."

But the new Bulls were a mess. Simpkins wasn't very good. With the addition of center Luc Longley, they now had more big white centers than any other three teams combined. "Reality was setting in," says Kerr. "Cartwright gone. Paxson retired. The talent level wasn't quite good enough. The previous season, we had lived off the remnants of championship-years toughness and confidence. But the lack thereof became apparent. Phil the competitor was frustrated, but he never panicked."

In the new arena, no one could hit shots. The team was hanging on by fingernails.

Then Michael Jordan started hanging around. And he could hit shots.

By all accounts, Phil hadn't tried to lure him back. Major League Baseball was facing a lockout. Jordan wanted no part of being a scab, and by the end of the spring, he was being drawn back to a place where he knew he'd always be welcome. When he showed up in Jackson's office, Phil said, "I think we've got a jersey for you."

"It was very different than the year before, when he practiced a few times," Wennington says, referring to the previous years he'd show up and practice, for fun. "Now he was *playing*. After the second day, I looked at Steve and said, 'Something's going on.'

"He was there every day for two weeks. At this point, no one knows anything, and no one wants to ask, because if he wasn't coming back, it would be disappointing. But either way it helped, because Michael practiced harder than everyone else. He challenged you, and if you had half a brain, you'd work as hard as he did."

Because if you didn't, you'd risk ridicule. "Michael had a way of making fun of you that was also motivating you," says Sellers. "It wasn't direct." If making fun borders on the cruel, that was Jordan. Was he the best practice player in the modern sport's history? Without a doubt. Did having to guard him every day in practice make the likes of Pippen and Ron Harper better defenders? Absolutely. Was he arrogant enough to think that his disses would be taken by different psyches in all the right ways? When they wouldn't be? Letting his rage spill onto others? Why not? He had his own rules. Other stars shove. Michael punched.

"He had a reputation of being vicious," says Buechler. "He'd test guys' toughness any way he could. There were guys who couldn't handle it, who had to be shipped off—really. But his whole point was a good one: He wanted to know who he could go to battle with when it got down to crunch time. He didn't want to go to battle with guys who couldn't handle it."

But for Buechler, those Jordan-dominated practices told a different story: It was instantly obvious—and surprising—that Michael wasn't in charge. The head coach definitely was. "When Phil said it was time to line up on baseline at the start of practice, Jordan would run to be the first one there—and not with his feet over the line: *on the line*. So you'd try and beat him to the line. Then when you see him standing there, looking eye to eye with the coach, hands behind his back, giving Phil total respect . . . I mean, if the star is showing that much respect, are you kidding?"

On March 18, Jordan made it official: "I'm back," said the release. The Bulls won 13 of their last 17, including a 55-point diva display in the Garden. They beat the Hornets in the first round, but at the end of their first game with Orlando, Nick Anderson stripped Jordan and scored the winning basket. Led by Horace Grant, the disaffected Bull who'd found a new home in Disneyplanet, and a large center named O'Neal, Orlando took the series in six.

A week later, Pippen was hit with a domestic-battery charge against his fiancée. Police records said it was the third such accusation. He was convicted of none . . . but maybe he should have read some of the books Phil was shoving his way each year anyway.

The off-season in Montana was a time of anticipation: Michael, Pippen, Harper, Kukoč? A fairly impressive foursome. The only glaring gap: They'd finished twelfth in the league in rebounding. When Jackson uttered the phonetic syllables ROD-man to his GM, we can be forgiven for imagining Jerry's response to Phil as being something akin to Alvy Singer speaking to Annie Hall's weird brother: "I have to go now, Duane, because I, I'm due back on the planet Earth."

But they needed a force. Orlando had proven it: Shaq's 900 rebounds were more than half of Pippen, Kukoč and Perdue's collective 1,600. And with Kukoč not exactly a WWE specimen, they needed Rodman's credo: Don't swat the ball away. Swat the *man* away.

In Detroit, he'd become a player. And, he'd become a loose cannon; his hair changed color, and tattoos blossomed like heavy-metal kudzu. Nothing wrong with the heart, though: One night he'd sported white hair emblazoned with a red bow for breast-cancer awareness. He was the only Piston to ever visit Chuck Daly's house every Christmas with presents.

"He's probably the most real person in the NBA," John Salley once said. What you saw was what you got: a kid whose father took off when he was three. At age twenty-two, he was fired from his job as a janitor at Dallas–Fort Worth Airport for stealing watches to help his mother, who at times held down four jobs. She threw him out of the house.

"The Demolition Man is no gangsta, never was, just a raw wound," wrote *GQ*'s Scott Raab a few days after they'd each gotten blasted and absorbed a couple of new tats at Trilogy Tattoo in Dallas (Dennis balked when Raab suggested they each get penis tattoos). "Just a sensitive, needy kid."

Krause didn't want him. Not after that *SI* story in the previous playoffs, after Rodman had spent the season in San Antonio. The cover looked like *Dominatrix Monthly:* Dennis posed in a leopard-skin chair with a rhinestone-studded dog collar. Perched on his arm? A macaw. His other sixteen exotic birds hadn't made the cut.

His seven years in Detroit had been terrific, but when the windshield magnate who owned the team fired Daly, "It was like God leaving his people," Rodman said soon after. "It really hurt me." His year in San Antonio was miserable. Hence the tone of the most nihilistic quote in the *SI* piece: "I don't give a fuck about basketball anymore. . . . I'm already out of life in the NBA. . . . I'm not an athlete anymore. I'm an entertainer."

And thus did Dennis Rodman fly in for an overnight at Krause's house, even though Rodman said to Krause, "I don't like general managers. The last three have lied to me." Krause promised nothing, so he wouldn't be in a position to lie.

On the other hand, he liked macaws and motorcycles. So at Krause's house, Phil walked over to greet Rodman, who was sitting on the couch in sunglasses and hat. He stuck out his hand. Phil pulled him to his feet. Jackson asked him why the Spurs hadn't been able to succeed.

"Half the Spurs had their balls locked up in the freezer by the time they left the house," he answered. Then he told Phil he could fit into the triangle and find Jordan when Jordan needed to be found. "You won't have any problem with me, and you'll win an NBA championship." Phil had acquired his *heyoka:* a Native American trickster-spirit who walks backward and rides horses backward—the comic relief of the tribe, intentionally so.

"We believed he could come in and help us if he did what he was capable of doing on the basketball court. Obviously, that is what happened," Pippen would later write—in his plea to the Hall of Fame to induct Dennis Rodman. It did. At the induction, he wore a red-trimmed black tux, a scarf with tassels and an eight-foot-long blue feather boa. The ensemble is encased in Springfield.

Jordan's summer? Filming *Space Jam*—with a practice court on the set. "He came into camp in incredible shape," says Kerr, who was about to discover that up close and personally. To the new faces, Michael felt he had to prove himself all over again. One day, Kerr decided to take a stand and let him know: You're not a god to me.

"We had played the previous season the last seventeen games, but no one really knew him very well," Kerr says. "It was a little strange. I'm sure he'd thought he'd come back and lead us to a championship. But none of us really knew him. He didn't feel like we knew him.

"So one day, well, we got into it." Kerr, as players' rep, had the respect of the team, and with Jordan yapping at him, putting him down, Kerr snapped. Shoves led to punches. "Our teammates pulled us apart. I was glad I stood up to him. Maybe we needed to have that confrontation. He challenges everybody to stand up to him. Literally the next day, I felt a different sense of respect from him."

EIGHTEEN

The 1995–96 season began with Second City media suggesting a 70-win season. They started 23-2. Then they lost a game. Then they won their next 18: 41-3. It was now obvious: They were all part of an unfolding piece of athletic history.

"You had a bunch of guys who had been on horrible teams," Buechler says. "Now? When it was all coming together, I'm sitting in Cleveland next to Steve and Wennington. We're going, 'Are you kidding me? How incredible is this?' I mean, it's one of the most amazing things . . . you could just feel it. We were in the moment, and enjoying it.

"But really, that season? It was all because of the practices. When it was the first unit against the second, the second bonded, and we'd push those guys. But then, when he split up, and it was Michael on one team and Scottie on the other? Those were *way* more intense than the games. And that was all Phil: to put the two of them together. You create that environment in practice, then you go to a game, it's way less intense than practices. And remember: You practice a lot more than you play. I mean, it was nasty."

On the court, the wins were like practices—with Jackson now toning down the volume, as he'd promised himself he would; if he settled down more on the sideline, maybe Rodman would pick up on the vibe out on the court. As the victories piled up, he had the luxury of coaching the way he'd always wanted to: by letting the tribe find its own collective way. To the fans, watching a lead turn from 19 to 9 in a minute, it's a no-brainer:

Stanch the bleeping bleeding, Phil! But he wouldn't call the T. Jimmy Rodgers remembers a classic example: "Worrywart Tex is by his side, going 'Time-out, time-out, time-out!' So Phil crosses his legs, pulls out his fingernail clipper, starts clipping his fingernails.

"The players knew what they were doing wrong. He didn't have to tell them." As in: You're organisms that can self-correct, because you're men. Tonight me and Tex and Johnny and Jimmy, we're just over here pretending to influence your game.

The season had become an endless series of spars with different tomato cans every few nights. But the playoffs were going to be heavyweight matches against teams with seven games to figure out where to exploit their weaknesses. Any smart fighter can pull off an upset with enough time to study his opponent.

On top of which, they were going to face Shaq again. Phil wanted one more big guy—and not just a body. A mind. What had the Buddha said about the unceasing change of the wheel of life? Five years earlier, in the Pistons' 4–3 playoff victory, John Salley had shot 53 percent from the field and scored 9 a game. Two years later, in the heartbreaking seventh-game rout in Detroit, Phil had watched Spider come off the bench to score 14, gather 3 rebounds and block *five* shots—in thirty-two minutes.

Salley started the season in the league, if the Toronto Raptors counted as part of the league, but he already had his eye on Hollywood, media, other horizons. The biteless Raptors were 6-19 when John got his lawyer to get him out of the contract, forfeiting three quarters of a million dollars. A month later, he was in a meeting with a Sony Pictures exec, discussing plans for a late-night show. His pager went off: "Jerry Krause of the Bulls: Call me immediately."

Salley stepped into the hall. "Long-tall," said Krause, "you want to play with us?"

His agent came out: "Good news: We've got him on the hook."

"Um . . . I just joined the Bulls," Salley said.

Why would Salley pass up a hosting gig for a few months back in the league with a bad knee? Well, start with the days when Salley was four, and his cousin was Jackson's housekeeper in Brooklyn, and would brag about the books he'd give her and the religious talks they'd have. Like Jackson, he was into all things spiritual.

Why would Phil want him? Possibly, he surmises now, because he'd stuck around to shake the Bulls' hands five years earlier.

And now found himself in heaven. "Massage tables. A pool, with Jordan running in the water. Him and Scottie doing ninety-five-pound dumbbells. No way. Then they got me doing it too.

"A track. Billiards. Everything you could possibly do to take care of a human being's body and mind. Any other team, you're hurting, the trainer says, 'Put some spit on it. I'm watching the soap opera.' But Phil Jackson treats you like a fine-tuned race car . . . Formula 1, and you're on the Ferrari team out of fuckin' Italy. He doesn't treat you like a NASCAR Busch race car owned by twelve guys who put up enough money to own a team. That's not what he does. That's how he prepares you. Phil *taught* us.

"You know how you go to a Broadway show, and it's dark, then a light comes up, and someone sings, and you listen, you can't help but listen? That was Phil, when he'd say something. I'd pay attention to every word. It was the best experience of all time. How can you play with the best player of all time and not have it be great? Jordan? I played golf with Jordan." (What was that like? "He's a psycho!")

Salley asked his new coach, "Why did it take you this long to get here?" *"Maverick,"* Jackson answered.

Over breakfast, Salley asked me, "Have you read it?"

"Three times, total," I said.

"I guess I really gotta read that book."

★

After a late March loss to *Toronto,* despite 17 for Kerr, Jackson told the team they were falling out of rhythm, no longer playing like the Dead, the band that could jam for four hours and never lose the beat. So the next day's practice was going to be war. "Wrap the tape tightly," he said: no time-outs for equipment repair. For anything.

"Going to be a *scrimmage,*" Salley remembers. "War. It was going to be physical. But first, it was upstairs to the film room for some breathing and meditation for forty-five minutes. Then Jackson walked in."

It was time for the peaceful warriors to leave a little blood on the tracks.

"'OK,' Jackson said, 'practice over. Go home.'

"We got dressed for war. To him it was always 'This is war. You're a warrior, you got to defend your property.' That day? Peaceful war. End of practice. No workout. Pure Phil."

The next game was against Lenny Wilkens's Hawks, who would knock Larry Brown's 52-30 Pacers out of the first round of the playoffs. Kukoč went 10 of 12 from the field; Harper, 6 of 11. Scottie's line: 16-11-8. Jordan? He took all of 12 shots.

The Bulls won by 31. They were 61-8.

Three weeks later, they drove up to Milwaukee en route to the 70th victory. It wasn't Route 2 in North Dakota. It was I-94, overpasses draped in banners, TV helicopters above them. And after the win, Salley and Jordan handing out cigars. Then cars following them home. Flashing lights and honking.

Back at the United Center, June Jackson said to her husband, "See you after the playoffs."

They lost to the Pacers, then romped over Washington to finish at . . . 72-10.

★

Now, though, it was back to square one: Alonzo Mourning in Miami. To prepare, Jackson spliced in a scene from *Friday,* a comedy starring Ice Cube and Chris Tucker as stoners trying to rip off a dealer and surviving a drive-by shooting. The scene? Tucker's dad knocks out the huge bully, Deebo (Tom Lister, Jr.).

Next frame: Mourning. The message: Mourning's a bully. Don't be intimidated.

There was a subtext to this series. At the end of the previous season, in a spat that consumed the New York tabs, Riley had fled town to coach the Heat, claiming that Dave Checketts had reneged on a handshake deal for a contract extension. (Note: I interviewed both at length at the time, and I sensed that Riley, the pugilistic Schenectady street kid, was within his rights. I say so because I would never want to be on Pat Riley's bad side.)

Jackson gave Ron Harper the starting point-guard slot, because of his physical style of defense. His offense waning with that bad knee, he'd perfected his defense. In a three-game sweep, the Bulls outscored the Heat by an average of 23 points.

Don Nelson had led the Knicks to a 35-27 record before being fired because his team had stopped playing for him. Of his short time in the Garden? "I liked everything about it but the team." Seven-year assistant Jeff Van Gundy (five under Riley) lit a fire. Jackson, knowing that Van Gundy had talked to Riley, adjusted. Rodman replaced Kukoč in the starting lineup, anticipating some physicality.

In game one, six of ten starters earned four or more personal fouls. Jordan, ever the ego, hoping to reprise his 55-pointer in his first game against the Knicks a year earlier, took 35 shots. Fortunately, he made 17, to make up for Scottie's 4 of 15. Kerr added 8 in 15 minutes. Chicago, 91–84.

Game two? *Seven* of ten starters earned four or more fouls. The difference? Harper's 15 points and 9 rebounds, and Rodman's 19 rebounds—14 off the defensive glass. A 91–80 victory.

In New York, Phil was unable to keep MJ and Pippen's egos in check; their collective 27 of 64 resulted in a 3-point loss. But the next night, Rodman made sure that the superstar shots were going to go in: of his 19 rebounds, 14 were offensive, which meant fourteen second chances. Bulls, 93–91. Jordan made 7 of 24—the Garden always did that to him; he had to be the star—but the bench all contributed, including three key shots by Phil's guy Buechler.

Up 3–1, back in Chicago, the Bulls' defense smothered the Knicks. Jordan was on target, and the final was 91–84.

On to the Magic, who'd won 60 behind Shaq, Penny Hardaway and Grant. This one would be won with defense. In the first game, Penny and

Shaq combined for 65—and the other ten players for 18. (It didn't hurt the Bulls that in game one, Grant collided with Shaq going for an offensive rebound and messed up his elbow. For the rest of the series, he would not be 100 percent.) The Bulls all scored at will, thanks to Rodman's 21 rebounds. Kerr and Kukoč combined for 26 off the bench, and the final was a humiliating Magic loss: 121–83, an emphatic avenging of the previous year's elimination.

Game two was closer: The Magic was up 53–38 at the half before a patented Jackson third-quarter clampdown held Orlando to 16. In the next game, in Orlando, the Magic were held to *10* in the fourth, and the Bulls coasted, 86–67; Pippen hit 11 of 13.

The next night, savoring the scent of a sweep, Michael decided to show Disney what he could do off the movie screen. He scored 45, and the Bulls won by 5. The Magic held a 75–73 lead in the third quarter, until Jordan took over, and Kerr hit a game-tying three. In the fourth, they held Shaq to . . . 1 shot. Pippen had 17 . . . assists.

The final was 106–101. A team that scored 103 per game in the regular season averaged 84 facing Red Holzman's—that is, Phil's—defense.

"It's sickening," was Claymation Hardaway's locker-room pronouncement.

Seattle's coach was George Karl—the guy who'd won 50 of 56 in Albany a few years after Phil's departure. After unsuccessful stints in Cleveland and Golden State, he'd turned the Sonics around. In the future, he would be dismissive of Jackson's success because of the prevalence of superstar studs on Phil's teams, but he had some talent too: Gary Payton, Kemp, Hersey Hawkins, Sam Perkins off the bench. They'd finished at a hardly shoddy 64-18. They'd gone 7-1 in their first two playoff rounds before the Jazz, second best in the West, took them to seven.

This time, facing the best team in NBA history, they managed to take the Bulls to six, if only because, up by three games after holding the Sonics to an average of 88 points in the first three games, Chicago got sloppy, and Kemp and Payton got professional. In game five, Pippen and Jordan went 10 for 36. Pippen was 5 for 20. They were poised to throw 72-10 away.

(Phil always had trouble with his studs in the playoffs. "I remember one situation," says radio color guy Harvey Catchings of that series. "Phil called a time-out, and he was mapping something out—'Scottie, you go over here; Michael, you come off here . . .' Then on the way out to the court, Michael pulled the guys together and said, 'Just gimme the damn ball.'")

But back in Chicago, with Harper starting again and Rodman wrestling for 19 rebounds and Jackson's defense pressing, they held the Sonics to 75 points. They shot 42 percent while holding Kemp and Perkins to 11 for 31. The final was 83–75. The Jackson scorecard: seven years, four rings.

Jordan was named the series MVP, but it should have been Rodman. Sportswriters, about as tolerant of idiosyncrasy as the pope, tend to regard flamboyant hair color, piercings and tattoos as symptoms of the plague.

"Just five different human beings on a basketball floor, with five different views, but all on the same highway, all going down the same road," Rodman said in the locker room, sucking on a tequila-flavored worm lollipop with his likeness on it.

They'd won 87 of 100. No team had ever lost so few games in a season and playoffs. "[It's] a new level for teams to play toward, a new standard for teams to chase," Jackson said.

In other words, he was now atop the heap of history in one stat. One more remained. It belonged to the Bad Red.

In the long run, how good was this team? As anyone who ever took Statistics 101 can tell you, there exists a statistical measure to prove any point. You just have to find the right test. So let's veer away from pure numbers and turn to the expert, eternal NBA chronicler Bill Simmons. (On Simmons's list of top teams of all time, Phil coached four. No other coach was named more than once.)

And he calls this one the best ever. OK, no, technically he doesn't. Simmons, a man who bleeds the Charles River, questionably ranks K. C. Jones's 67-15 Celtics of 1986 (Larry Bird, Kevin McHale, Robert Parish, Dennis Johnson and Danny Ainge) as the best team ever. They'd won the East by 10 games. But in the finals, that team, leading 3–1, failed to clinch after being routed by a Rocket team starting Ralph Sampson, Rodney Mc-Cray, Robert Reid, Lewis Lloyd and Hakeem Olajuwon.

So distilling out the muddy-water bias, yes, the 1996 Bulls were the best that ever was.

And Phil was at *his* best, because the truth is, he was coaching some very old guys. The average age of Rodman, Jordan, Pippen and Harper was thirty-two.

NINETEEN

odman and Jordan would be free agents for the 1996–97 season, and Jackson himself was due for a new contract. As usual, Krause's negotiations did not help relations between the small GM and the large coach. In addition, another Pippen trade rumor surfaced: to the Celtics, for draft picks numbers three and six. Rebuilding time? Jordan, it was suggested, vetoed this one. As went Scottie, obviously, so went Michael.

The only major change? A new coach named Frank Hamblen, "a man's man," as Jackson would later describe him. All hoop, all the time. The connection? He'd been an assistant to Tex when Winter had been the head coach of the Houston Rockets (not very successfully) in the early seventies. Thereafter he was either scouting or assisting in Denver, Kansas City, Sacramento and Milwaukee, where he did a short interim-head stint.

In Jackson's words, Frank knew "everyone remotely connected with the NBA." He also had a knack for calling the right play at critical times, which he must have done frequently, as once again the team cruised through the league, finishing 69-13. The reason for the slight slip? Dennis was losing a little of the hunger. Rodman missed a third of the season, including thirteen near the end with an injury and eleven on a suspension for kicking a photographer in the balls.

They swept the Bullets and took four of five from the Hawks, allowing a team that had averaged 94 points in the regular season 80 points. Once again, it was the defense of Jordan and Pippen that held sway, not their shooting.

This season, Riley's 61-21 Heat were deeper, more talented and winners of their division . . . but against Phil's defense, in the Eastern finals they scored 77 in game one, 68 in game two, 74 in game three, 87 in their one victory, and 87 in their elimination—78.6 points a game. They might as well have eliminated the twenty-four-second clock. Somewhere above Brooklyn, Red Holzman was enjoying his scotch each and every night.

★

How do you make the fifth time even remotely intriguing? With a fifth different opponent, a nonrival from a town of Mormons whose team was named for African-American roots music.

The intrigue started with the coach, an easy-to-root-for, low-profile Illinois homeboy. Fewer than ten coaches have put together five consecutive winning-record seasons: Virtually all are sports-household names. Then there's Jerry Sloan, "the Original Chicago Bull." He was born in Gobbler's Knob, Illinois, the youngest of ten children, fatherless since age four, and yes, he really had to get up at four thirty to do chores, then walk the two miles to school. After five weeks at the University of Illinois, he grew homesick and transferred to Evansville, where he led the Purple Aces to two championships. In his senior year, they went 29-0.

The expansion 1966 Bulls used their first pick on him. Eight years later, they won their first division title. In the fall of 1977, Sloan reportedly took the head job at the University of Evansville but retired within a week for reasons unknown. Two months later, an airplane carrying the team and all the coaches crashed on takeoff en route to a game against Middle Tennessee. The only survivor died two weeks later in an automobile accident.

Sloan took the head job of the expansion CBA Evansville Thunder, who played against Jackson's Patroons. The Jazz brought him on as an assistant, and in mid-1988, he came on as a head. Since then he'd basically won consistently and impressively, no matter what the personnel. Year in and year out, he was always close, often losing out to the Western champ. This year, the Jazz had won 64 behind the Malone-Stockton duet, Bryon Russell, Jeff Hornacek and everyone's favorite slow, clumsy, big white man, Greg Ostertag.

Game one was a classic. They were tied at 82 when Rodman fouled Malone. "The Mailman doesn't deliver on Sundays, Karl," Scottie is said to have legendarily muttered to the big man . . . whereupon Karl missed both shots. Jordan won it at the buzzer. Game two wasn't as close, as the Mailman failed to deliver again.

Back at the Delta Center, which turned out to be the loudest arena the Bulls had played in all year, Scottie decided to try to win it himself, nailed seven three-pointers . . . and the Jazz coasted.

In game four, with Jackson wearing earplugs, the Jazz broke open a close game with a 12–2 run at the end. Scottie and Michael shot 18 of 43. Rodman went 0 for 1 from the field, with 3 rebounds . . . to Ostertag's 7. Rodman said afterward, "It's difficult to think with all these fucking Mormons out here."

The triangle—well, ball movement and player movement—won the series over the next two riveting games: the Flu Game and the Kerr Shot.

The night before the Flu Game, Jordan had ordered a pizza. He was soon reportedly curled in fetal position with acute stomach pain. Years later, his personal trainer claimed that a rogue deliveryman had poisoned him. According to David Halberstam, Michael was "deathly ill," which makes it all the more remarkable that he not only survived to live another day without checking into an emergency room, but also played extraordinarily well, scoring 15 in the final quarter of the Bulls' dramatic 90–88 victory.

At the line, with the Bulls down by one and the game on the line, he missed his second shot, but Kukoč soared into the lane and tapped it back to Jordan. Michael gave it to Pippen, who drew a double team while Jordan weaved his way to an open spot, took the Pippen pass and hit a three. Pure resurrection.

★

It was back to the United Center now, where, two hours before game-time, the *Tribune* reported, "The freshly waxed Ferrari, the one with the baby-blue North Carolina plates, purred down a corridor," into a sea of reporters, celebrating that Michael, miraculously, was not only alive, but ready to play! Jordan subsequently did his best to win the ring single-handedly for fifty-nine minutes and fifty-five seconds. He took 27 shots and converted 9.

The Bulls were struggling in the third, but a Buechler three turned the momentum briefly. The Jazz then came back to take a 9-point lead in the fourth, but the Bulls scrambled back. A Russell dunk tied it at 86. Jackson took a time-out with seventeen seconds left.

"It's Michael Jordan time!" Marv Albert told the world. Wrong. As would be the case in three of Jackson's six Bulls rings, it was little-guy time again.

"I remember missing a big shot back in Salt Lake, and I was extremely frustrated," Kerr recalls now. "And I remember in this game saying, *Screw it. Just let it fly.* I'd been thinking too much. In Seattle the year before, I'd been thinking too much of historic ramifications." (In that series, in one game, with thirty seconds left, Bulls down by one, he missed.)

In this quarter, he'd made 2 of 4 from the field and both of his foul shots. During the time-out, Jordan leaned over to his former sparring partner: "Stockton is going to double-team me," he said. "Be ready." In game four, Stockton had peeled off Harper at the end for a key steal off Jordan.

"I'll make it," Kerr said then. He says today, "I felt good. I said to myself, *If I get it, I'm going to shoot it.*" He got it. He shot it. He made it from fifteen. Game, set, match. The Drive for Five had succeeded.

When I asked Kerr if at that point he realized what he'd just done, or if, as athletes always say, "No, I just saw the basket, and it went in," Kerr laughed. "Oh, no . . . I appreciated it right away. I'm too big of a sports fan to have not been aware of what that meant. I felt it. And that shot changed my whole career. That's why I got the contract in San Antonio, why I have the TNT slot; that's why people know who I am. Because of that shot."

At the subsequent public celebration in downtown Chicago, Kerr took the podium for a monologue that foreshadowed the telegenic announcer he's become: "A lot of people have been asking about the shot," he told the crowd. "There have been some misconceptions. When we called time-out, see, Phil says, 'Michael, I want you to take the last shot.' But Michael said, 'I don't feel right, or real comfortable in these situations. Why not go to Steve?' I thought to myself, *I guess I got to bail Michael out again.*"

But for Jackson, the end was now in sight, five years after he'd first suggested it would be, even if there was one more ring to come. Jordan re-signed, Rodman re-signed, but Pippen was locked into the final year of the seven-year contract. Phil, unsigned, asking $7 million, claimed that Reinsdorf was offering $4 million. Eventually, Phil got $6 million for one more year—with a rider: Krause's office had to be moved out of the practice center.

The antagonism had been growing for years—ever since Sam Smith's book with its depiction of Krause as a man whom Pippen and Jordan would mock in front of the team. Krause's bald admission to me that he wanted to win one without Jordan—and I certainly doubt that I'd have been the only writer to whom he expressed that sentiment—was also a dis of Phil, with its implication that coaches don't win, GMs do. Halberstam's *Playing for Keeps* reported that "people in the organization" thought he was increasingly jealous of the publicity accorded Jackson—*his hire*, the man he'd rescued from Albany when no one else would touch the maverick. "Krause," wrote Halberstam, "seemed to believe that the turmoil within the organization was Jackson's fault and that he had failed some kind of loyalty test by allowing players to feel so negatively about Krause."

At the press conference announcing that Jackson would return, Krause made it clear that this was indeed for one year only. As reported by Halberstam, the wording from Krause to Jackson in a private conversation was that, after this year, "You're fucking gone."

When Krause's stepdaughter married, every Bulls coach except Jackson was invited. Tim Floyd, Iowa State head coach, was invited. What was left for Jackson? Other than a three-peat? But he already had one of those. Well, $6 million was a decent incentive.

TWENTY

Before that final season, Phil and June had decided that getting out of Chi-town and heading back to where it all started might be a wise move, a good strategy for dealing with whatever the future held in store. They bought a house near Woodstock. "We both believed," he would write, "that a new lifestyle would be good for us." It was in Bearsville, but it didn't resemble the modest ones they'd rented in the eighties. This was a large home with a guest house and a view of the distant Catskills, snow-capped much of the year. From the front of the house, the distant mountains furnished a Native American view of a virgin landscape.

The season began with the team's full knowledge that this would be the end of an era. They would not be lacking for a motive: to send their coach out with a historic bang. Well, most of them. Pippen had hurt his foot in the playoffs but, according to Jackson, put off the surgery until training camp to spite Krause for not paying him commensurate with his value—prompting Krause to utter the infamous statement that has albatrossed him ever since: "Players and coaches don't win championships; organizations do."

No, as Hodges had said a decade earlier, the system wins the championships. (And would continue to, for another decade.)

Without Pippen, the team lost 7 of 15. On their first West Coast trip, in Seattle, a pouting Pippen told reporters he wanted to be traded. He yelled at Krause on the bus over negotiations. Even Jackson was fraying. On the same trip, reviewing a player's mistake on the films, Jackson would later write, "I said, 'Everybody makes mistakes. And I made one coming back with this team this year.'" Later he would say he meant it to be "light-hearted." But Jordan had answered, "Me too," whereupon Longley took off on Jordan, taking his words as a criticism of the team.

According to Harper, bonds were dissolving. The old breakfast club that Jordan used to hold at his house for Pippen and Harper—weights and steam—had closed shop. Rodman was skipping practices. Management and coaches no longer dined together after games.

"The hard part," Harper says, "was nights when after we played, to see the guys get on the bus, then Phil gets on; the guys are really happy; then comes Krause, and you see Phil get off and get on the other bus. That wasn't fun to see."

They began the playoffs with newly minted T-shirts: THE LAST DANCE. "That would be our rallying cry," Harper says now, because he'd been saying it all season.

Before the first playoff round, Harper recalls, Jackson told his players to come to a meeting with a memory, written or spoken, about their time together. They would burn the papers in a coffee can. By all accounts, it was a moving day. Even Jordan wrote a poem. By Phil's account, it was Harper who stole the show. "I just talked about how cool it was to be on a winning family, to play any part," he says now, "instead of being a star in a messed-up one."

First up, in a fitting way, an ideological enemy: the Nets, led by John Calipari, the nomad ever in search of a buck. To prepare, Jackson spliced parts of John Singleton's *Higher Learning,* a film decrying racial stereotypes, and a James Taylor concert into film. This was sufficient for a sweep of New Jersey—but Phil could have spliced *The Last Picture Show* into his own film, for that week's *ESPN The Magazine* contained the first part of a four-part series: Jackson's diaries from the season, written with Chicago columnist Rick Telander. They were ugly.

Phil said he was supposed to get a final read. He would later say he didn't. Thirteen years after publishing a book he wishes he could have taken back, he'd done it again. And once again, no do-overs. He was critical of Krause. He described a riven team, saying he'd overstayed his time. He seemingly slammed Lakers coach Del Harris for an argument he had with Shaq on TV in a playoff game, which could have been interpreted as a veiled hint at the Lakers job.

Weirder yet, he talked about he and his wife wondering if they could make things work. He'd spent part of the season in a hotel room. Subsequent installments backtracked. Today, the online version has been edited.

The 51-31 Hornets presented an unusual challenge: Dave Cowens coaching, a man against whom Phil had played, plus Anthony Mason, Vlade Divac—and B. J. Armstrong, playing his butt off after being left open for the expansion draft and none too happy about it. Still, the Bulls took them apart in five, but this series had a speed bump too. On a bus ride to a second-game shootaround, Phil was tipped that Reinsdorf had given an extensive interview and that Phil should be prepared for questions about a response. A cluster awaited the bus, all asking, in essence, "Are you really the reason for the breakup of the Bulls?"

Which, of course, he was, but only because Krause and Reinsdorf had forced his hand. And Jordan wasn't going to stick around, he said, without Phil.

Indiana proved more challenging, and not only because Rodman, now losing interest, spent parts of the third game riding an exercise bike in the locker room and had to be summoned when Phil wanted to use him. Then the inevitable crisis: a *New Yorker* piece on Jordan portrayed the man as less than complimentary about Bulls management. The team subsequently refused to talk to the press.

They took the Pacers in six, but the aura was ugly.

All that remained was three-peat number two: the team against everyone else from outside the locker room looking for a chink in the armor.

They opened in Utah, the Jazz itching for revenge and the Bulls haunted by the threat that Rodman would not be back from Las Vegas in time for the first game. The Bulls split the first two.

(Harper laughed in the middle of our discussion of the series. "One night I walked down the hotel hallway. [Jackson] was there. 'Coach,' I say, 'it's two A.M.' He says, 'She kicked me out again.' I say, 'See you tomorrow, coach.'")

Back in Chicago for three games, Jackson's guys decided to go out with a bang. The Bulls won the third game 96–*54*. No NBA *game* had ever been decided by so wide a margin, let alone a final. The Bulls led 73–45 after three, then held the Jazz to 9. It was all over but for Rodman missing the next practice to go to Detroit to wrestle Hulk Hogan. But the next night, his 14 rebounds and 4 of 5 from the line in the stretch sealed an 86–82 victory.

They could have wrapped it up at home, where tickets were going for $6,000. Traffic was insane, and everyone was late. Still, down by one at the end, they could have won it. Phil called a play for Kukoč, who'd been 11 of 13 from the field. But Ostertag guarded Harper's inbound, and all he could see was Michael, whose three-pointer . . . missed. Given the chance to put a first-class stamp on his Bulls legacy in the town that worshiped him and go out on top with the ring winner, he missed.

Back in Utah, things sort of still hung in the balance. In a seesaw battle, a Stockton three gave the Jazz an 87–84 lead with forty-one seconds left. Jackson called a time-out, which was followed by this unforgettable sequence: A Jordan layup. A Jordan steal of Malone. Michael looks at Phil: time-out? No, Phil waves. Go!

The Bulls spread the floor; for the moment, the triangle had been retired. Everyone figured Jordan would drive. But at the top of the key, Jordan waited for Bryon Russell to swipe for the ball, then backed up and shot. Swish.

Ring Six.

Speaking to a reporter after the game, Krause said of him and Reinsdorf, "Jerry and I have done it six times."

In Phil's final diary installment the following week, the last line was "It's over."

"Krause didn't just drive *Phil* out," says Harper now. "Eventually he drove the whole team out."

★

Four days later, Jackson took his team to Jordan's steakhouse for the private good-byes. He thanked Harper, who, when Jordan came back, was willing to step back. Scottie toasted Jordan.

Three days later, on Sunday, June 21, Jackson said good-bye to his team publicly at the team's practice facility, open to writers. Somewhere in the same building were Jerry and Jerry—just not attending the session.

"I'm not going to speak about 'coulda, woulda, shoulda,'" he said. "It's my time to go. It's the right time. I don't know if there is a basketball challenge. I'll have to wait and see if one presents itself."

He climbed on his latest bike, glistening in black and red, signed by every player, and left Chicago for the last time.

★

At Tex Winter's induction into the Hall of Fame in 2011, Phil and Krause shook hands. When I reached Krause, the old scout who'd started with the White Sox, now scouting for the Arizona Diamondbacks, to ask him if, as had been suggested to me, the two had mended fences, he was driving from somewhere to somewhere. He spent twenty minutes telling me why he had no comment on Phil Jackson or his upcoming book or anything at all. It was actually sort of hard to get him to stop talking about why he was refusing to talk, and to tell him I understood him completely.

Before he said our conversation was off the record, he said, "There is no request Tex could make that I would turn down. So [Phil and I] shook hands and passed. We are not close. [Tex] would like us to get along, but it won't happen. My history with Phil has been well catalogued. No one knows the truth, because I'm not going to talk about it.

"Phil's a great coach. He did a great job for me. We had a fine relationship for a number of years. It won't be repaired. I don't see where I could help you. My life is fine. I was on the Hall of Fame ballot. I hope for my grandkids I get in there. I hope that a lot of young people in the game get started the way I did. It will be something good for them. It'd be nice. If it happens, great. If it doesn't, it doesn't. It's not important to me in my life. Fifteen years ago, I had a red ass in me. I got no red ass in me [anymore]."

When Phil left, Jordan retired again, saying he'd never play for anyone but Phil. Two years later, on a listless, low-profile basketball team, he was playing for Doug Collins, going out not with a bang but a whimper. Like Phil, he'd forever be unable to leave the game. Unlike Phil, who teaches others, Michael seems to be doing it all for no one but himself. He owns the worst franchise in NBA history, and unlike an extraordinary number of Phil's Bulls—from pro and college head coaches to GMs to truly happy adults—Jordan appears to be woefully incapable of finding a satisfying third act or of growing as a man (though in a thirty-seven-thousand-square-foot house, he has a lot of room to grow).

"He needs basketball," Hodges told me, "as much as basketball needs him." Or as the writer Wright Thompson said, on the occasion of Jordan's fiftieth birthday, "He thinks about the things Phil Jackson taught him. Jackson always understood him and wasn't afraid to poke around inside Jordan. It's a Zen koan Jordan needs now, in this new challenge: To find himself, he must lose himself."

TWENTY-ONE

Now the man who'd once said, "Who I really am is a mediator sitting at the edge of this culture and looking in," really *was* looking in from the outside. Now "in the middle of the journey that is my life," he would write, "I had lost my way." (And missing a chance to quote Dante: "Midway in our life's journey, I went astray from the straight road, and woke to find myself alone in a dark wood.")

With a half-dozen rings, should he decide to get back into the straight corporate-sport world, he wasn't going to be outside for very long. The unceasing wheel of change seemed destined to carry him back toward ol' Mannahatta, where in November, on the occasion of Red Holzman's death, Jackson and MSG VP Dave Checketts had talked.

Flash-forward to the following spring, near the end of a strike-shortened season in New York. Ewing, Allan Houston, Larry Johnson and Latrell Sprewell (who'd retire with a collective zero rings) had given up on Van Gundy at crunch time and had been eliminated three consecutive times in conference semis.

On April 19, the Knicks lost their fourth straight game, scoring 67 against the Sixers. At about the same time, Checketts was meeting again with Jackson. According to one published report, Jackson had said that he would consider taking the job if GM Ernie Grunfeld was axed. After Checketts met with Jackson, he let Grunfeld go. According to a source, Van Gundy, sensing the vibe, managed to somehow view listings from Checketts's appointment book, which confirmed that the meeting had taken place.

There was no love lost here. In 1995 Van Gundy referred to Jackson as "Big Chief Triangle" and said that to beat the Bulls, they'd have to "assemble as many Indian artifacts as we could." Thereafter, to Phil, he was Van Gumby, a man whose coaching karma seemed forever skewed. (In the spring of 2000, a jet blast from the Knick charter blew his car over, destroying the '95 Civic. He couldn't go home that night . . . because he couldn't get a ride.)

(Early postscript: After Jackson left the Lakers for good, an *L.A. Times* columnist said Van Gundy should be hired to coach the Lakers because he was such a good TV analyst, which is like saying that Simon Cowell should have gotten into producing U2 because he was funny on *American Idol*.)

The Knicks won six of their last eight. In the second round, they'd won three straight against the Hawks when Selena Roberts of the *New York Times* broke the Checketts story. Reporters asked Checketts if he really had met with Jackson. He insisted he hadn't. The next night, he admitted that, yes, he had: "I regret that I lied about that, that I misled the press and Jeff Van Gundy about that."

Now the team rallied around their little man, stunning Larry Bird's regular-season first-place Pacers. In the third game of the finals against the Spurs, a fan held up a sign that read, "Thanks, Phil, but we already have a coach," whereupon the Spurs crushed the Gumbies in five. (Jeff would last two more seasons. He would later coach Houston for four years, with Yao Ming and Tracy McGrady. No rings.)

Grizzlies coach Brian Hill threw himself into the fray, calling Phil "totally unethical, completely unprofessional . . . I can't think of anyone else in our league who would have done what he did. To openly solicit another guy's job is about as unethical as you get." This rant had nothing to do with Phil sweeping his Magic in four games four years earlier.

Ego? He stands accused. Enigmatic? For sure. Ethics? Well, try this hypothetical: You'd made a living as a star distributor of snack foods, which you loved, but after your boss at Cheez Whiz shut you out, and you quit, a rival

CEO calls. "Our Doritos guy is dropping the ball. I'd like to bring you in for an interview, maybe give you the entire Midwest region Doritos account, starting next third fiscal quarter. Interested?"

Would you say, "He still has a job; I can't consider it while he's still employed"? If you were one of Jesus's disciples, maybe you would. I wouldn't. (Five years later, Penny Hardaway led a player revolt that put old Brian Hill out on the street.)

Phil immersed himself in Bill Bradley's run for the White House, which was gathering steam after his endorsement by everyone from Mario Cuomo to Daniel Patrick Moynihan. If the Princetonian got the job, why not head of Bureau of Indian Affairs for his friend? But a drubbing in the Iowa caucuses nipped Bradley's run at the start. Charismatic he was not.

Equally unsuccessful was the Jacksons' attempt to save the marriage. They separated in May 1999.

"June felt that I was unable to commit to either my relationship or my family because my career was more important to me," he wrote in *More Than a Game*. And Phil? He needed something "to keep me goal-directed. . . . She saw me as mired in my fame and my day-to-day habits—a prisoner of my own past."

His ultimate rationale? "I felt that coaching was a gift and that if I didn't return to the NBA, I would be hiding my God-given talent."

"It's like a car," says Diane Mast now. "It is a thing [these] two people buy and get into and ride around in. It's new and clean in the beginning, and lots of friends get in the backseat and drive around with you. It is a great ride and everyone has a great time. But for no good reason, the car starts to wear out. You get the motor fixed and take it to the car wash. It runs for a long while.

"But one day the front tire falls off. June gets out and fixes it because she knows how. A few years later the other front tire falls off, and she tells Phil it's his tire to fix, so he gets out and fixes it. Then the back tire goes and there is an argument: 'It's your turn.' 'No it's your turn' . . . and finally they both get out and do it together but they are mad at each other . . . and they sort of don't get over that . . . and finally the last tire goes, wing nuts and all, and rolls away.

"Then comes the 'big' fight. The fur flies every which way, and this time neither wants to fix one more flat tire. They don't care about the rest of the car anymore either. They both get out and go their separate ways. They decide they are going to divorce.

"Friends start to weigh in: 'June should have fixed it.' 'No, Phil should have; he makes June do all that kind of stuff.' 'No, it was June's job because he was driving.'

"So it comes to a split over the next summer."

Today? Diane Mast smiles: "They should write the book on how to divorce and stay best friends. They are simply the archetype on how to do that."

★

"The last time I was in Los Angeles," Harper says now, "he told me, 'I'm going to drive to Montana. June will come down and drive back with me.' I say, 'Your ex-wife is going to drive with you and stay two or three weeks at your home?'" Harper guffaws. "OK, no problem. I can't understand that shit, but if you can, that's cool.

"Hey, that's Phil Jackson. He makes everything work. He always finds a way for it to work. To fit the parts together."

Salley has a counterintuitive take on the events of the time: He thinks that Phil, in leaving June and heading for L.A., showed character in making a difficult call: "To stay for the sake of your kids, even though your situation is one way . . . to be able to leave things when they're not right, or when you no longer think they're right for you . . . that takes a lot of courage. You just have to realize when people have had their time.

"It's like the old Chinese proverb: You got your feet in two different canoes. You're not looking forward. You're just trying to stay afloat."

Now it was déjà vu all over again. A call to Montana from his agent said that Los Angeles was interested. Kurt Rambis, the third coach of the disastrous previous season, was thought to have a chance. But not with Phil's availability, and Showtime Jerry Buss's addiction to trophies— young and female, and championship.

This is Phil's account of his first meeting with Jerry Buss:

JB: "I've had wonderful teams here in the eighties, but it's been a long time, and I'd really like to get one more championship."

PJ: "I think you should expect to win three or four."

How come everyone's math was always off by one?

The rumors had circled for a week. He'd been fishing for king salmon when the AP reported, "Phil Jackson stepped off a boat in an Alaskan village, and got the news from an Eskimo boy: 'I hear you're the coach of the Lakers.'" The perfect Hollywood lede. By one report, the kid was wearing a Bulls jersey.

"I think it was a marriage that was in the making," Jackson would say. "Of all the jobs out there, this was the one that piqued my interest." Not to mention the eventual balcony view from his beach house: bikinied beach volleyballers and the gentle Pacific.

"He always liked the beach," Charley Rosen says now, "and the water, and the sounds of the waves. In Tampa, we used to walk on the beach all the time, just to get away, shoot the shit, see if we could see dolphins. Once we even went to a topless beach just to fuck around."

The water. By the time it was over, Phil would play pro ball in a port city, coach on the banks of the Hudson, coach on the shore of Lake Michigan and coach on the Pacific—finding his annual downtime on the shore of one of the land's most stunning lakes.

The five-year $30-million contract held some allure, too. If you want the world to see you, as Rosen says, "There's no place like L.A. to show off what you have."

The press conference was held at the Beverly Hilton on June 16. Jackson, as Jerry West noted in his own confessional, *West on West,* wore sandals. Magic was blunt: "I'm tired of 'Go in to Shaq, go in to Shaq, go in to Shaq.' Everybody in America knows what the Lakers are going to do. There can't be any more excuses about the coach. We just got the best coach in the world."

★

Fitzgerald had it wrong: America is nothing if *not* second acts. Jackson was entering his. But why in hell *did* he come back? Yes, he had two great players, but there were no guarantees. On top of which, if Jackson couldn't pull it off with Kobe and Shaq, he risked harshing the mellow of the legacy in Chicago.

On the other hand, true monkdom is reserved for a select few in India and Burma. The rest of us have to be on the playing field of ego. "You can only settle down your mind by providing it a large pasture to run around in," he told *Tricycle.* "I certainly believe in boundaries, but I want my boundaries to be spacious enough to allow for extreme flexibility." But Phil Jackson, no matter how boundless his cerebral wanderings, would forever need to be in that basketball pasture.

I asked Sam Vincent, his point guard in 1989, with everything already accomplished, why he would choose a second act of life on the court over wife and kids. Vincent paused for a good ten seconds, then spoke virtually uninterrupted, issuing a statement I've come to think of as the Hoop Manifesto:

"We all genuinely love the game. We love the game because it's such an intricate part of our soul, spirit, heart and thought process that the connection is impossible to break. There's a magical realm around this sport that makes it unique. I don't know what the certain magical thing is. Is it the round shape of the ball? Is it the connection when it goes in the basket? Is it the teamwork of everyone being on the same page? All I know is, there's something mystical about the sport, something that provides power, confidence, security, happiness, sadness, laughter, joy. It takes you on a journey. And it is its own magical journey. Every time you play a game, every time you coach, every time you communicate, you go on a journey each time, and those journeys capture all of the senses in such an incredible way that when the journey's over, the smell, the sense, the feel, the touch, how the player communicates with the ball and the court, you want to feel that again, that same feeling, that incredible journey. That's what makes the next part of the journey better, in some other year, in the next season, that keeps you in love with the game—all of the time."

TWENTY-TWO

The first job was to assemble a coaching staff. Jimmy Rodgers was flattered but now enjoying retirement. Rosen? "It was never considered," says Charley now. "But I would have jumped at the chance. It was his rationale." In one of his books, Phil says Charley had already "found his calling as a writer." But then, he'd already found his calling as a writer as early as '78. Charley understood: Phil was now too far down the road in a corporation that doesn't welcome its radical disciples into the button-down business fold. Ones who'd rather wear the beat-up old Rockford Lightning jacket than the Armani.

Cleamons? On board. Tex? Obviously. Hamblen, the "man's man"? Three decades in the league? Signed. All knew the triangle. The only incumbent was Bill Bertka, who, except for a seven-year sabbatical in Utah in the seventies, had been with the Lakers for four decades. If there was a common denominator for all good things Laker, it was Bertka. When Phil was asked to keep him, he instantly obliged. At seventy-two, he was a bridge to the previous regimes, as unsteady as the recent one had been.

The team? Obviously underachieving. Shaq, Kobe in his second year, Rick Fox, Derek Harper, Derek Fisher and sharpshooter Glen Rice all had talent, but under Rambis they were slow. Fisher and Harper were the only sure-handed guys. (A midseason signing of Rodman had resulted in seven disastrous weeks before he was released.)

So Phil enlisted his Three Wise Men. They had thirty-seven years of experience.

After some work for NBC ("Stern told me, 'You can say anything you want about a player, but not about the league or an owner' "), Salley had been watching the Lakers blow their fourth straight playoff series. He called Phil. Phil told him to call West.

On the phone, West asked Salley if he was in shape. "Excellent shape," said John, who hadn't played in three years. West then told him Mitch Kupchak would be working him out against journeyman Benoit Benjamin for a roster spot. Salley made the cut.

Harper was home in Ohio when he got the call at the beginning of camp. Kobe had a hand injury. Rick Fox needed a new backcourt partner. Harper saw the caller ID and picked up.

"Hiya, Phil," said Ron.

"Ronnie," said the gravel voice, scraping the phonetic ocean's bottom.

"How you doing?" said Harper, smiling to himself.

"You'll start the first game," Jackson graveled back.

"Phil, I think I'm retired."

"Not yet you're not. Get out here as fast as you can. Our center is very good."

Harper arrived and watched a scrimmage. On one play, Harper watched Shaq pull down a rebound, decide to keep the ball, dribble to midcourt, spin between two defenders, dribble to the key, hop and slam.

Damn! Harper thought. *This might be fun.*

"Told you he was good," Phil said to his old quarterback.

And then there was Iron Man, A. C. Green: two rings with Riley in Showtime as an essential contributor, five seasons with a contender in Phoenix and one in Dallas for Cleamons.

"We knew he'd show the same leadership in Los Angeles as he had in Dallas," Cleamons says now. "With Ron and Salley, they were three essential pickups."

Green was more than reliable; he was the Cal Ripken of the NBA. He hadn't missed a game since 1987, literally. He set the record at 907 in '97. The streak ended at an insane 1,192. The more amazing streak was his lifelong sexual abstinence at age thirty-six. "You have to have some virtue in your life," he'd once said. And while that streak provided obvious cause for amusement ("Guys said that if you ever saw fireworks in a city the Lakers were playing in," Rosen laughs, "it was because Green had finally gotten laid"), he would marry in 2002 at the age of thirty-eight and find the pot of gold at the end of his rainbow. (Imagine the fireworks on that two-month honeymoon!)

"I had a huge amount of respect for Cleamons, friendship as much as player," Green says now. "So when he went back to Phil and they started looking for leadership guys, it was what had been missing. The core nucleus was there. For me, that Cleamons vote of confidence was, to Phil, the green light. And with Phil there was that spiritual background that we shared. We had talks about faith numerous times that helped us communicate in a deeper way. That was cool. Not everybody shared that same experience. I mean, that's not good or bad—just reality. But I would definitely agree that his other dimensions enhanced his abilities. Faiths can be different in details, but the principles are the same: being outside of yourself, seeking balance."

He'd start every game for Phil and have a hell of a season. Maybe there was something to be said for Woody Allen's reference to Balzac's presumably apocryphal quote after every orgasm: "There goes another novel."

Meantime, on the other side of the libidinal coin, Phil would be getting his paychecks from the sketchiest boss in sports history. I first saw Dr. Jerry Buss in the Forum halls at the age of fifty with a woman I assumed to be his young daughter. She wasn't. So what was Phil doing working with Captain Skeeve, the immodest ("At a relatively early age, I discovered that I was more intelligent, more creative and more competitive than the great bulk of people I ran into," he wrote) and megalomaniacal? ("Jerry's ambition is to conquer the world," said a former bunny girlfriend.) Other than bonding over their intense, arch-male competitive streaks? Why take a job with the NBA's Hef?

Start with upbringing: Both were born into the Western American out-back. As a four-year-old, Buss was standing in food lines in Kemmerer, a Wyoming coal town. Add an exceptional intellect. By the end of his senior year in high school, he was teaching the science class, and his teacher was backing the teenage hustler in a $50-a-game pool tournament. Having learned cards from his mother, he would eventually be judged one of the top fifty poker players in the world. Unlike Phil's religiously reserved deck, these cards definitely had faces on them.

At the University of Wyoming, like Phil, he married a woman he'd met as an undergrad and took a moonlighting job as a chemist for the Bureau of Mines. After graduating in two and a half years, he declined scholar-ship offers from Harvard and Yale to pursue a PhD in sunny SoCal. His dissertation was titled "The Bond Dissociation of Toluene"; he earned the doctorate at twenty-four.

A missile-lab job offered little glamour, so he turned his cerebrum toward mastering the alchemy that so many in the city of grand illusion had studied before him: turning real estate into cash. Two decades later, Buss had three office buildings, two hotels, more than a thousand houses and four thousand apartments, two homes, a chauffeur to drive him in his Rolls Royce Camargue (which replaced the Maserati Bora) and an empire: the Lakers, the Kings and the Forum, which together cost $67.5 million, the largest sports transaction in history at the time. That would be $200 million today, for teams that, sold by themselves, would bring seven times as much. The financing of the deal was so byzantine that *Sports Illustrated* hired accountants to parse it. They couldn't. It included a price tag of $24 million for the Lakers.

The sports world was hagiographic. *SI* described Buss as a man "reliv-ing almost with misty eyes" the exploits of old Trojan running backs. *People* revealed that he had once dated an eighteen-year-old who had decided to try prostitution. "I turned her over my knee and spanked her," he said, apparently with a straight face. Of the Forum? "I like to buy real estate that can't be replaced. It's effectively irreplaceable" (until it can be replaced), as would be the case with his next domicile, Pickfair, the twenty-five-room mansion built by Douglas Fairbanks and Mary Pickford on fifty-six acres of primo SoCal real estate from 1919 to 1924.

Pickfair had hosted the likes of Einstein, Babe Ruth, Lindbergh and Chaplin—a manse "only slightly less important than the White House, and much more fun," said a *Life* correspondent. It was on the market for ten mil at the time; Buss picked it up for five, but a few years later, he sold it to Pia Zadora, the woman who won a Golden Globe for a movie about incest. (Pia and her husband, thirty-one years her elder, vowed to never raze it, but they quickly did so and built a new mansion.)

"As for those teenaged girls," wrote Lakers watcher Roland Lazenby on his blog *Laker Noise* in early 2010, "Buss has long dated hundreds of them, usually once or twice each, and then collected their photos in albums. He has not been above boasting about his conquests to media and associates."

"I had started meeting those girls when I was about fourteen," daughter Jeanie would later write. "They were usually like twenty or twenty-one and treated me like a little sister. . . . When I reached my late teens and my dad's girlfriends were closer to me in age, we would go shopping together. They would do my hair, give me makeup tips and all that kind of stuff. . . . As I got much older than the women he was dating, however, it wasn't the same for me."

If Jeanie's *Laker Girl* reflects the woman's priorities and is not excellent satire, she is obsessed with tacky emblems; her book-long subplot of jewelry borders on the pornographic. The dramatic high point of her story? The morning she was robbed at the Forum on her way to work. "Give me all your jewelry," the man said at gunpoint. She parted with her engagement ring from volleyball player Steve Timmons, a diamond "tennis bracelet," a diamond Presidential Rolex, diamond earrings and a Lakers championship ring studded with diamonds. (Presumably the thief has been living in Monte Carlo ever since, sipping champagne on the beach.)

The low point of the book? Other than when Ryan Seacrest says, "I have a lot of respect for your dad's opinion about women"? Or the fact that she drops so many names that *Adam West* makes the cut? Her description of the *Playboy* shoot in 1986 and her, um, breasts: "Hef was very complimentary when he saw them." Dad had owned a Playboy Club in Phoenix when Jeanie was a teenager, but "I wanted to be in the magazine based on my own merits, not because of my dad's relationship with Hef." And when the art director said she didn't have to do anything with her breasts, such as enlarge them, "That was very flattering." Damn it, girl, be proud! You worked *hard* for those breasts! Oh, wait. No you didn't. (Check out @jeanie buss before you read further. Her Twitter portrait is from the *Playboy* shoot.) The book's footprint on literary history? I ordered it on Amazon for a penny, and the copy I received had been discarded from a library branch in the city of . . . Los Angeles.

But never judge a babe by her cover. As *Maverick* did, *Laker Girl* has a subtext. Beneath the shallow sparkles and unashamed tropism for jocks, from L.A. King Jay Wells to Dodger Mike Marshall to Timmons, lies a stone-serious businesswoman. She's served forcefully on the NBA Board of Governors forever. She's devoted her career to marketing the brand. On top of which, she clearly has the brains (when Magic says she should now be running the show instead of her brother Jim, that has to count for something). Unlike Wells and Marshall, Timmons, briefly her husband, was no average jock, if my night of Coronas with him a few years before his Jeanie fling means anything: His surf-slack punkish hairstyle disguised, like Phil's hair, his insane competitiveness. (In 2004, Perry Ellis bought Redsand, the beachwear company he founded in the eighties, for a nice chunk of change.)

To sell the product, Jeanie Buss will do everything: sponsor women's wrestling, send the dancers around the world and found a (failed) roller-derby league. A few years ago in the playoffs, she even unveiled the Jeanie cam, somehow convincing Phil to be interviewed on the way to games, from games and at home. It was boring. Phil was unmagnetic and clearly uncomfortable. Peeping Hoop didn't last long.

"Jeanie Buss took me in like a lost dog and nurtured and loved me," he would later write. She "balanced that teeter-totter love affair between the executive vice president and her partner, the coach."

"Hey," says Charley now. "He's a man." Meaning, among other things, what man would turn away the approval and ministrations, as his hair disappears, his eyesight fails, his heart weakens and his joints erode, of an alluring, much younger woman who can, not incidentally, kick ass in the workplace? (See: "Have your cake and eat it, too.")

I asked Mark Madsen, who would play for three years as Jeanie and Phil grew intimate, whether her sparkles were like the velvet glove in a rock-hard fist. "Absolutely right on," said the Stanford MBA. "Phil doesn't raise his voice. Jeanie doesn't raise her voice. I'd say this: They are proficient at what they do . . . and don't mess with either of them."

Jackson's first move was to write a personal letter to each man on the roster. Its emphasis? Welcome the triangle right out of the box, as in "my world, and welcome to it." For one thing, you don't fix what ain't broken. For another, this time around, he had a (very) big man who, still only twenty-seven, was mobile enough to add a new dimension to Winter's scheme. If Shaq could learn the basics of the weak side–strong side fluid dynamic of the triangle—with Salley tutoring—then, with good execution by point Harper and A.C., the big man could ideally find himself guarded by a single man, and Jackson would have his irresistible force.

The stars seemed aligned: That summer, Shaq had a rapping gig in, of all places, Kalispell, the largest city in northern Montana (ninety thousand, 0.02 percent of whom are African American) just north of Lakeside. He dropped down to meet his new boss. (And what a sight that must have been if he walked into the Homestead Café Bar & Casino to ask directions.)

Jackson's biggest challenge was to connect two dots: "The distance," wrote Phil Taylor in *SI*, "between their two most important points, guard Kobe Bryant and center Shaquille O'Neal." The cover of the issue? Slightly tacky: Phil posed as a hooded wizard, with his hands cradling a crystal ball in which a tiny Shaq was holding Kobe in his arms, accompanied by the cover line "What Does He See? Jackson Seeks Peace and Harmony in Los Angeles." It made the coach seem mystical, as if the players were his pawns.

One longtime former player, who requested anonymity, today finds the whole notion of Phil the magician/eccentric/philosopher maddening and insulting. "He's 'out of the box'? What's that mean? Is there a secret in the universe that he knows and we don't?

"I'll tell you the secret. Red had Russell. Riley had Magic and Kareem. Phil had Kobe and Jordan. Pop has Duncan. It's the players who score the points. That's your secret. Individual coaches are so-called geniuses? I haven't seen a coach, an owner or a scout score any points. There's only one group that's playing the game. That's the players. That's the ones doing the work. They're the ones laying it on the line day in and day out. The game doesn't belong to coaches. The game belongs to the game. To the kids on the playgrounds. The greatest lesson I ever learned as a player? The fundamentals. You know them, that's all you need to know. Those are the laws of the universe."

Two months before the season began, I met Bryant in a recording studio, where he'd decided to record. Just like Shaq. He opened a pizza box that had just been delivered and emptied an entire bag of potato chips on the other side of the box, and ate everything, the way any teenager would.

It soon became clear that he was a very intelligent young man (if a terrible rapper). His 1100 SAT could have gotten him a full ride anywhere. In his second season in Los Angeles, he told me he strolled the campus at UCLA, like a college kid he'd never been, and even signed up for some classes.

"When I walked around the campus the first day," he told me, "I thought, *This is cool!* I got my backpack ready. But I go to class, and there's only, like, twelve people. Where is everybody? 'Oh,' somebody says, 'they don't come to the first session of summer school.' I'm thinking I'm going to get the college experience, talk to some kids, hang out." He shook his head. "Nobody."

No audience? Then, hell, no college.

It so happened that at the same time, in the same building, a band called Tha Eastsidaz was shooting a music video. One of the backup dancers was a seventeen-year-old named Vanessa Cornejo, entering her senior year in high school in Huntington Beach. The next spring, she was wearing a diamond ring in high school. But not for long; she withdrew because of the media horde, and finished her diploma through independent study before they married.

At first, the transition was not smooth. Jackson's new group wasn't schooled in "alertness meditation." They weren't prepared for connecting some of the more-distant dots Phil had in mind. As he told *Tricycle,* "The common existence in this same now-ness is what connects everything, so that even the smallest microcosm in our particular world is connected to the most distant part of the universe."

The first team meeting? As if, after teaching an honors class in Chicago, he'd been given a group of ADHD kids. "It was impossible for my new players to concentrate on what I was saying," he would write. He obviously wasn't being treated as the master-teacher if he really had to say, "I want you to stop playing around with whatever's on the table in front of you."

Jackson had moved into a land as far removed as any colony could be from his coaching heritage, one as far from his childhood heritage as could be conceived. In the Plains and inland West, a man was stoic, rooted and stoic. In his new sprawltown, *no* one was original. All had fled something. Until now, his pilgrimage had taken him to cities founded on manufacturing, producing and representing, in one way or another, an aspect of the American ethic. Whether it was the Knicks, the Patroons or the Bulls, all were fond of the game as an embodiment of teamwork. The wives were friends, their kids were friends and, to rip off the '79 Pirates, "they were family."

This was not a Phil Jackson franchise—yet. Perhaps the first tipping point happened in an exhibition in Kansas City, in an arena that lay hard by where the stockyards had been. It was an exhibition. Kobe broke his finger. He would miss the first eighteen games of the season, which meant that the offense could immediately start relying on teamwork.

At least Frankie Jumpshot had been an adult. Kobe Bryant, named for a kind of beef (why not Lamborghini?), was a kid. Literally. Never having been taught, never having been contradicted, he was going to forever test Jackson's coaching chops. Anyone who insists that Jackson never won a title without two superstars didn't know Kobe the kid for those first few years with Jackson: the killer instinct of a black mamba, the maturity of a larval mayfly. Salley saw it from the start, but understood Kobe's confusion. He'd been there, albeit on a slightly less spectacular scale. If you grow up in a bubble, dysfunction is inevitable.

"Here it is in a nutshell," Salley says now. "First, you're eight years old, but they put you on an older team because you're so good. The man picks you up, says, 'You hungry? Here you go.' In high school, you're growing out of your pants. Someone says, 'You hungry? Here you go.' In college someone pays you. In the pros, someone gives you a credit card. Now you got a posse around you, and this guy, that guy, he looks like he knows how to buy food, buy cars, whatever. Manage your money. Run your life. And you want everything because you've always been able to have everything you want.

"So you leave it to them to do it all. All you do is say to someone, 'Just make it happen. I'm going upstairs and rest.'

"Because that's important. A pro athlete does three things: rest, play ball and have sex. That's it. When you cross them up, that's when you mess up. You can't rest, have sex and play ball. Gotta be rest, play ball, have sex."

It was the last part that would bite Bryant in the ass in a few years.

★

Gradually, Pavlovianly, they'd learned how to respond to the drum in their new training home, in the office, the Shinto figurines, the tobacco pouch, etc. As soon as Shaq heard the rhythmic pounding of the drum, he'd head for the fifteen-seat theater. "When you heard that 'doo, doo, doo' sound you better get moving—or else," O'Neal would later write.

It was always about the rhythm. "That was his thing," says Salley. "Phil called us the Grateful Dead. They had a rhythm. That was his thing, about how the Grateful Dead could get up there and jam for hours and be in rhythm. He wanted us to always find that rhythm."

Then out with the lights, and Phil would light some sage to smudge the room if he thought attitudes were going awry. It would be pitch-black, Shaq wrote. "So here comes the weed—oh, sorry, Phil, the *cousin* of weed— and then he'd tell us to lean back in our chairs and relax. Then he'd start talking with us about whatever was going on with our team. He'd say, 'Right now, there's some negativity going on, so let's release that.'

"A lot of days, you'd hear guys snoring, usually the ones who had been out late the night before. Certain days, even I'd fall asleep because I was tired. Other times I would try and listen to what he was saying, and other times I really would meditate." Then: deep breaths. "Some days I really think it helped me," said Shaq. "Other days it was a chance to catch a good nap."

Team meditation started at three minutes, then became five, then eventually became ten. It was a start.

The first round of books? For GM Jerry West, Phil's choice of *Confederates in the Attic* was a little tone-deaf. Just because West was from the mountains didn't mean he was a Civil War junkie. Just as Bryant, given *The White Boy Shuffle,* about a black kid raised in a Caucasian community who has trouble erasing the stigma of being an Uncle Tom, "thought Jackson assumed a bit too much about his upbringing so early in their relationship," the *New York Times* reported.

Bryant's alienation from Shaq did not surprise coach Frank Hamblen. "Well, Phil wanted it to be Shaq's team," says Hamblen now, and why wouldn't he? Shaq was more than ready to launch into the triangle. Bryant had no use for a scheme that would temper his showmanship. It was obvious to the new staff that coaching Bryant required a very specific approach.

"With Kobe you have to be careful, take the positive approach," says Jim Cleamons. "Someone else goes nine for twenty-six, you say, 'You had a bad night.' With Kobe—OK, you got a double standard there, but it's not, 'You missed seventeen,' it's 'Guess what! We can get you a better seventeen chances.'"

So what formed this ill-formed psyche? "His dad, Jellybean, always thought he was better than Erving and McGinnis," Cleamons says. Jellybean Bryant's stats: eight years, three teams, 8.7 points per game. He took the kid to Europe when Kobe was seven; the boy was practicing with Dad's teams at twelve.

"Kobe grew up in a household always hearing this . . . so Kobe vowed to himself, *I am not going to grow up and have to say that. I am going to* be *the best, and have documented proof.* His whole agenda is to psychologically not live the life his father did. He's vowed to go down swinging, the best of the best, with no bullets in the chamber, at high noon. Every game was going to be an Alamo for him . . . Kobe so much wants to be the alpha dog."

He'd played his first NBA game as an eighteen-year-old, a record at the time. He had one 17-for-47 evening. The next year, he was an all-star at nineteen, and by twenty had a $70 million contract. He was a *GQ* cover kid—and the antileader. From the start of 1999–2000, Harper ("the one who calmed down the team."—Jackson) turned his powers on the teenager.

"When I first got there, Kobe probably didn't have any friends," Harper says now. "All his teammates respected how he played hard, but he wasn't the most personable guy. Shaq probably didn't care for him, but he respected him because he worked so hard, because he respected that part. I mean, the guy would get a DVD after every game and review it. He studied. He studied opponents' weaknesses."

Harper had seen Jordan and Pippen bond. "So one day," Harper recalls, "Kobe and I had a talk. I said, 'Man, you just can't talk to your teammates any kinda damned way ... you're going to be around these guys six or eight months, and you can't be like this standoffish dude. These are guys you're gonna fight with, go to war with. *It's us as a whole.*"

It wasn't just Harper whom Phil asked to talk to Kobe. It was Magic. It was Jordan. "Eventually," Harper says, "he started coming around. Hey, he wasn't a bad guy. When he was a young kid, he just didn't have real friends."

The obvious priority was the big man. In practice, Salley, an inch shorter, seventy pounds lighter, would guard Shaq at the top of the key and actually tutor him on his next move. Salley had nothing to prove; he *wanted* Shaq to learn the scheme: Work from the weak side to the strong to the weak, until someone has a balanced, open shot. And in games, when Shaq bitched to Harper that, in the fourth quarter, he wasn't seeing the ball? "I'd say to Shaq, 'First, second and third quarters, I go to you first. Fourth quarter? Until you prove to me you can make free throws, I go the other way.' Shaq was totally cool with that, from the start. No attitude at all."

On the other hand, Salley noticed something different this time around: "In practice, Phil did a whole lot more yelling than he had in Chicago." Maybe Phil should have been reading more of those books himself.

They opened 8-4, including a rout of the 1-8 Bulls, whose own triangle, under Tim Floyd, would win them 17 games that year. ("Krause sold Tim a dream," says Ron Harper now.) Harper was in a groove: In Harper, Phil had his "on-court conscience," and they resumed their courtside rituals. "I'd be coming up and look over and he'd be filing his nails, and I'd say to myself, *I guess I better call the play. Phil's too cool to call it right now.* Or the other team's going on an 8–0 run, and I look over for the time-out; unh-unh, filing his nails: 'I'm not going to save you. Save yourself.'"

After Bryant's return, they won 15 of their next 16 and 30 of their first 35. But behind the scenes, chemistry was frayed. After barely winning against the Cavs after losing two of three, Jackson called for a meeting the next day, in which, Jackson would recall, Shaq said, "I have something to say. I think that Kobe is playing too selfishly for us to win."

"The trouble," Jackson wrote, "was that Kobe wanted to be a leader, but no one wanted to follow him." Why? Because off the court, he kept completely to himself.

After a fifteen-game winning streak, they suddenly lost 6 of 9. At the end of January, Jackson pulled a new psychological strategy out of his hat: self-revelation. He spoke of his own personal problems—a failed marriage, a ninety-two-year-old mother in the hospital, a transplant to a new city. Opening himself up to the team and perhaps to himself, he felt a new, first-time sense of family.

Phil would be the first to agree with the friends I talked to who say he is not the guy who wears his heart, or soul, on his sleeve. He's always kept us guessing, throwing out clues that suggest the recipient search for the answer.

This time, he felt the need to enter the circle as one of them. A few days after the meeting, the Lakers beat Utah by 46.

Another team was cohering too. "I would say very honestly," Jim Cleamons says, "that as a coaching staff, we mirrored our team roster. Collectively we were a very solid unit . . . but none of us wanted to be the head coach. Ever. *Phil* was the head coach. On some staffs, everyone is hustling to have the authority and the power. Not us. We were his assistants . . . and we all had certain things he'd empowered us to have a voice in."

In Chicago, Cleamons had thought he was the youngest member of the law firm of Jackson, Winter and Bach. Now he was still the youngest; all that had changed were the opposing teams he had to pay attention to (Jackson would give each coach different teams to scout) . . . and a new group of mentees.

"If they wanted to talk to Phil, I'd talk to them first. I'd tell them, 'Don't go in there ranting and raving.' Because these days, with players, with contracts, there's always the concern that no matter how much they love the game, they have to get their touches, their stats, so they can get their money. I'd say, 'Be pissed off with me. Have a logical reason before you go in. Present your concerns in a manner in which he's going to want to *hear* you. Make it productive.'"

The opening round of the playoffs featured an intense 3–2 defeat of Sacramento, most memorable for the first truly un-PC public remark of Jackson's career. It was no surprise that after a childhood of repression, he'd want to play out the final act on the beach with a babe. But it was surprising that, starting in L.A., his self-censoring mechanisms began to erode.

After the Kings took the fourth game in rocking Arco, Jackson was asked if the Kings' fans were the most raucous he'd ever seen. Phil cited Puerto Rico. Then, according to an ESPN account, he said, "We're talking about semicivilized in Sacramento. Those people are just maybe redneck in some form or fashion." In his latest book, he says, "I'd joked a few years earlier that the state capital was a semicivilized cow town." (On the other hand, if, as Charley Rosen says, near the end of his Chicago gig, he told his buddy that George Bush's presidency would eventually be graded with very high marks, there seemed to be a sea change occurring in the fifty-five-year-old man now living on the ocean.)

In game five, the Lakers took a 23-point lead after three and blew the Kings away, 113–86, sending Sac back home to a town to which Phil would also attach the sobriquet "cow town." That the Zen-Christian (their common denominator: compassion) was slurring a state capital known for an industry that his birth state of Montana was known for was very weird, indeed. (Maybe growing more conservative in his political leanings, he was giving a nod to the reported first recorded reference to Sacramento as a cow town, by Nancy Reagan, when her husband was governor.)

Phoenix rolled over in five, but the Blazers, led by Rasheed Wallace and now enhanced by a guy named Pippen, took them to seven. Los Angeles had broken to a 3–1 lead. Then, in Staples, the Lakers were poised to finish Dunleavy's boys off . . . until, with Pippen going 8 for 12 and leading a hounding lockdown defense, Kobe missed 9 of 13 shots and Glen Rice 8 of 9. Back in Portland, the Blazers held the Lakers to 45 percent from the field, and it was tied. Back at Staples, the Lakers turned up their own defense, held Pippen to a 3-for-13 night and won 89–84.

The Lakers' foe in the Finals? Reggie Miller's Pacers. After the Lakers romped in the first game, 104–87, the second was closely contested. Jalen Rose stuck out his foot to trip Bryant, and Kobe went down with a sprained ankle, but Harper coolly came on to score 21. Shaq was hacked, but the big man made 9 of 16 in the fourth quarter. The final was 111–104.

Jackson held Bryant out for game three, a loss, and put him back in for game four, a victory. Game five, in Indiana, produced an embarrassing loss—120-87, the worst finals loss in fifteen years. A quick glance at the box scores says it all: Kobe was 4 of 20 and went to the line . . . zero times. The ankle was hurting. So was the ego. Miller hit 7 of his 12 field-goal attempts.

Adjustments were called for. Harper would cover Miller, and A.C. would front the giant but less-than-mobile Rik Smits in the paint. The Lakers won game six with forty-eight minutes of focus, 116–111, and Buss and Nicholson had their ring. Shaq, Phil's man, Phil's mentee, had reached the pinnacle: He had his first of three consecutive finals MVPs.

What was the formula that had earned the ring right out of the box? A collective mind-set transplant. The late computer hacker Aaron Swartz liked

to cite the story of a GM plant in California that was a complete under-
achiever: striking workers, workers sabotaging the plant, even workers
dealing drugs. Toyota took it over, sent the workers to Japan to observe
Toyota factories, where workers considered themselves to be part of a
larger organism, sent them all back home—and put them back to work. It
became a very successful factory. The Lakers had seen the game and their
own individual goals through Jackson's new prism.

TWENTY-THREE

After forty-five years with the franchise, after being drafted by a team playing in the Minneapolis Auditorium (1927), a team named for the freighters that plied the Great Lakes, two months before training camp, Jerry West quit. It was as if the Dalai Lama had said, "*No más;* I'm going bowling."

He'd been the enduring emblem from the very beginning. By 1969, the NBA, trying to snuff the upstart ABA, unveiled a new logo: Jerry West dribbling. (To put Russell or Oscar on the logo would have made the league seem even *more* black when it was desperately trying to lure white fans).

That the former weed-smoker from the loft above the Big Bear shop could force out the icon from the Appalachians speaks of many things, including power, ego and competitive drive: attributes both possessed in spades. Two went into the Buss lair, one came out.

"Health reasons" fooled no one. He was walking away from $12 million. In West's public resignation he thanked Shaq and Kobe "for their belief in the Lakers," and Buss. No mention of Phil.

"West was great," Krause told me. "I don't believe he'll talk about Phil, and with me, that makes two GMs."

According to West's own account, he was confident in the man when he hired Phil, despite Krause's having told him that "we should stay away from him . . . that he had a large ego," and that Reinsdorf had "his own issues with Phil." As a GM, he landed Shaq. Then he got the Bryant kid. Then he picked up Rodman and traded for Glen Rice.

When Jackson came on, Buss was no longer coming to the office as often, West wrote, at which point, their relationship began to diminish, which wasn't insignificant to a man like West. ("In my house growing up, you didn't hear the words 'I love you,'" he'd write. He would subsequently look for love in the wrong places. When he was thirty-six and married with three kids, he met a college cheerleader, whom he would later marry after leaving his wife and moving into Pat Riley's house—and leaving behind his trophies: "Not rational," he would say of that decision, "but neither am I." No further questions, your honor.)

"Phil," he wrote, "would arrive in the morning, walk right past and never even bother to wave or duck his head in to say hello. . . . He would later say that he felt the need to stake out his 'territory.'" Then, with six rings, what did Jackson need to know about coaching from a ringless coach (145-101 in three years, with Kareem, including one trip to the finals).

It was officially over the night Phil threw Jerry out of the locker room.

"I honestly thought Phil was finished addressing the team, and so I walked in," West wrote. "As soon as I did, Phil barked, 'Jerry, get the fuck out. I'm not finished here yet,' and I immediately backed away, red-faced. . . . I vowed that I would never go in there again, and I didn't. I wasn't going to lower myself and get into a pissing contest with him. Phil's recollection is different; he says he didn't know who it was, that he didn't call me by name, but this is my version—corroborated by Tex, Bill [Bertka] and [general manager] Mitch [Kupchak], and I am sticking to it."

Under different circumstances, the two would have vibed from the start. In his wincingly honest memoir, the West Virginia native cites John Muir and Daniel Boone. And Joan Didion. He hiked the steep Alleghenies as a kid looking for some gestalt/preverbal way into the truth of such bountiful nature.

West's departure did not enhance the new coach in his city's eyes. (His exit would leave personnel matters now in the hands of Kupchak, who won a ring as a former Laker and then apprenticed with West for more than a decade: quiet, good with a draft board.)

In a transient town with few native heroes to call its own since Gary Cooper, a forty-five-year tenure made West as iconic as it got. Phil had driven out the king of our sovereign city-state! "The cunning Jackson has maneuvered himself into a position of unrivaled power," wrote columnist Doug Krikorian. "One must not underestimate the Machiavellian inclinations of Phil Jackson. This is no rube from North Dakota, but a shrewd calculating fellow . . . with a long history of pursuing a path that benefits him . . . [and] savors listening to himself talk even more than his audience."

In this latter matter, Krikorian wasn't completely off base. The next few years would be marked by *another* Jackson book, his third, and several off-the-cuff-isms that would land him in trouble. In Chicago, a city of substance, no one in the press had really taken off on his smudging and his tom-tom and the white buffalo in the hallway. They were happy to win and, as Midwesterners, were ineffably polite about the guy. The criticism in Los Angeles didn't faze him. He'd already—what was it Riordan had said?—comfortably "adapted" to Los Angeles.

"The fabric of his life doesn't rip and tear," Diane Mast says now. "It just gets bigger, and it incorporates all of us in his orbit. Every experience and every person keeps getting incorporated into it."

★

West's final draft pick was a Jackson type: center Madsen out of Stanford. Very smart, very tall, limited in talent. Free agent Stanislav Medvedenko was in too—at Salley's expense. Spider wasn't particularly happy with the ending: "I just wish I hadn't had to end my career on someone else's terms. [Phil] says, 'Sal, thanks for the year, I got no real estate for you. What are you going to do? What are your plans?'

"I say, 'I'm in the best shape I ever been. We're going to win championships for four years.'

"'Got no real estate, Sal.' And Madsen comes in, and Medvedenko. Now on the bench we got three white guys who don't play. Don't get me wrong— Madsen is a great guy. The year before, we had one white guy—Travis

Knight. He was asked if he was having a hard time; he had no one to hang with. Not that he didn't get along with black people. But the next year, Phil had no real estate?" (In Phil's latest book, he said three words of that year's new roster and Salley's departure: "John Salley retired.")

But Salley hardly holds a grudge. He unabashedly loves the man. "You know how Pope John Paul II came in and changed the Catholic Church? He was younger, he was energetic, he could walk around, he'd shake peoples hands? That's Phil. He changed the environment. Look, I got to meet the Dalai Lama. The guy walks into the room and the molecules change. I met Mandela. I met Bishop Desmond Tutu. And Phil brings that mentality."

Madsen? A man of strict faith—the Mormon faith. He'd done his time in Spain: not with Liga Endesa, but on a two-year Latter-Day mission. As A.C. said, faith can come in a lot of packages, but the principles never veer too far from one another. Madsen's canon was specific, but he had an omnivorous brain and found Jackson a delight.

"There's all these tremendous professors at the tops of their fields at Stanford," he says now, "and I figure he can't be any smarter than any of my professors. When I left three years later, I thought, *He could be teaching in any university.*"

Or monastery. "The first time he said, 'Let's meditate,' I thought, *You have to be kidding me.* Then I look over and Shaq has his eyes closed, and his tongue up against the roof of his mouth, and the next thing you know, you start to become a little calmer. Because like everything we did, it was always about the group.

"I'll never forget the time Phil said, 'Each and every one of you in this room has unique abilities to help us, to teach us to win the game.' To be mentioned in the same room as Kobe and Shaq? I felt I could do anything. I thought, *I do have unique talents and abilities.* He didn't tell me what they were. I searched within myself, and in that moment I suddenly knew: I can play with more energy than anyone, and I can get offensive rebounds . . .

"I've never before been on a team with so many open conversations. You could vent anger, frustration—everyone was open, and that adds up to true and honest conversation, a brilliant way of running a team. You were always included. And his comments to you . . . he had a way, when you needed a kick, he gave it to you. When you needed to be built up, he made you think you could take Mike Tyson and Ali in a boxing match."

Madsen also had never been on a team that practiced the way Phil and his staff did—a routine he's carried over to his own coaching years. "First off, [there were] no strength trainers stretching us. Phil took us through an entire intricate warm-up series that incorporated the spacing of the triangle, the rhythm, while giving you passing and dribbling drills, then back and forth, all loosey-goosey, with no ball, and then finally ending with the hard core. The whole process was like being in an orchestra that starts very, very softly, then goes up the perfect incline to energy, focus and intensity."

How intense was the Mormon? Ten years later, Shaq gave an interview in which he said that no one could ever beat him up on the court. Then he amended the thought: "There was Mark Madsen. In practice, he'd beat me up." His numbers were never impressive, but his energy infected the team. If he's telling the truth (and something tells me he's incapable of doing otherwise), even not playing had its rewards: "Phil would come over, shake my hand—he shook everyone's hand, win or lose; I never had a coach who *ever* did that—and say, 'Sorry I couldn't get you in tonight,' and it was unbelievable, man. Unbelievable. I never had a coach do that since."

Predictably, the next season began with the ritual Kobe crisis; he wasn't getting enough touches. Jackson asked if the kid (he'd have been a college senior) wanted to be traded. "The relationship between Kobe and me was becoming an issue," Jackson wrote. And the first few months were erratic in Staples. On January 15, O'Neal uttered the obvious: "Last year at this time we were thirty and seven, this year we're twenty-five and twelve."

The second year's books? Predictably, Shaq's was a success. He told

Phil that he'd read *Siddhartha,* and got its point, and even if it had been Cliffs Notes, the big guy made an effort.

Kobe's? *Corelli's Mandolin.* With Bryant having spent time in Europe, Jackson claims he thought Bryant might be interested in the tale of how the Greeks, while being controlled, managed to defy the Italian army's efforts at occupying their hearts and minds in World War II. Well, maybe in a TV documentary. But the tome? Try this:

> Dr. Iannis had enjoyed a satisfactory day in which none of his patients had died or got any worse. He had attended a surprisingly easy calving, lanced one abscess, extracted a molar, dosed one lady of easy virtue with Salvarsan [. . .] and had produced a miracle by a feat of medical prestidigitation.
>
> He chuckled to himself, for no doubt this miracle was already being touted as worthy of St. Gerasimos himself. He had gone to old man Stamatis' house, having been summoned to deal with an earache, and had found himself gazing down an aural orifice more dank, be-lichened and stalagmitic than even the Drogarati Cave.

To quote John Paxson, "That's just wack." Yes, teachers should want to broaden horizons. But to give a kid who never went to college a novel whose prose was dense as a thicket? Was that gesture about Kobe's needs— or Phil's? One of Bill Russell's no-nonsense books would have been a little more on the mark.

Perhaps the fates were punishing him when the *Mandolin* fallout landed. On a book tour, Jackson was asked by journalist Rick Telander, "Why *Corelli*?" This led into a discussion of Kobe's intense competitive nature. Then Jackson said that he'd heard that in high school Kobe would subvert games by playing less intensely than he had to, so that in the end, he could save the day. (Jackson would swear that that part of the interview was off the record. Telander did not respond to a message.)

The backlash was considerable. Some asked for his ouster. (That Jackson would refer to Telander as "his old friend" in the updated intro to the book begs a little credulity that there'd been a misunderstanding about the rules.)

In the midst of the mediocre play in this second season, according to Phil's recollection, was a team meeting that exposed all the frayed wires. "The thing that hurts us most about this season," Rick Fox said to Kobe and Shaq, "is that both of you have acted like you're apart from us, and that we're not any good. We've won championships together, and you turn your backs on us."

Shaq started to complain. "Quit your crying," Kobe said to the big man.

"You're as much to blame as Shaq is," Jackson said, "if not more."

"You're the one who should fucking talk," said Kobe.

And now another misstep for our man. In March 2001, still touting the book, Phil sat down for *60 Minutes II*. He would later tell a friend that he "wanted to be honest and was tired of lies that were being told." (He didn't specify what the lies were. No one had publicly accused him of anything.) When he was asked to do it, he thought, *Why not?*

Lots of not. Correspondent Carol Marin, in her fifth year with the program (she'd recently anchored a *60 Minutes* segment), would do the probing. Like Phil, she was represented by agent Todd Musburger.

With the soul patch and an open-neck shirt, he allowed the crew access to more than seemed seemly: Jeanie, for example, who said, "We're not Brad Pitt and Jennifer Aniston," looking annoyed (she expected questions about the Laker Girls?). "We're two adults who have lived long lives and had experiences. I really don't understand the fascination."

Now, cut to Phil walking in the halls of the Staples Center. "Basketball," Marin then intones, "has also left this fifty-five father of five with two broken marriages," as the screen now shows footage of June Jackson talking at an event. She is without makeup, guile or affect. It all added a Geraldo aura to this odd interlude. When Marin asked about the quotes in

More Than a Game about the dissolution of the marriage, Jackson said, "Well, I wrote those words. I can vouch that that is what she felt. Unfortunately I couldn't convince her otherwise."

When Marin had tried to put a word in his mouth to describe his philosophy as "unselfishness," he corrected: "selflessness." But he was now the one being selfish. It's one thing to write about the breakup in a book. It's another to talk about it to a national television audience after a week in which the interview repeatedly had been promoted on the network.

The crux of the breakup, he said, was having to commit exclusively to one or the other. "I carry this desire of my team or my group to be the best with me twenty-four hours a day." Why reveal it? Unless you want it on the record? And if you really do feel as if you have to use your "God-given talent," why not mention it now? Instead of leaving the impression that your job overruled your family?

To the viewer, he was taking advantage of his solo podium: June wasn't there to refute or debate or discuss or revise. She'd never commented on their relationship publicly. So why subject the kids to a public display of your failed marriage to millions of television viewers? At the very least, why not lay down some rules for the interview? The most cringe-worthy moment of the interview? The conclusion, when Marin says that he sounds like a "minister. Would you say that?"

"That's succinctly what I would say," says the basketball coach. "It's just a group of twelve instead of two hundred."

What happened to the prayer circle where there is no "I"?

Later that year, both Marin and her producer left the program to "start their own documentary company," according to Marin's Wiki bio.

★

On the other hand, say friends, "Phil really doesn't care a bean what people think of him," in Diane Mast's words, and Rosen wholly agrees. "It's what he thinks of himself—that's his foot fault."

So was he testing himself? Finding his footing in the land of illusion? In laying bare his own life, was he doing it not for the viewers, but himself? Was he trying on a new bespoke suit—the Hollywood celeb costume?

This is not to suggest that sitting on the balcony of your beach house in Playa del Rey with your girlfriend while you wait for the risotto to reach perfection isn't a good place to be. Knowing that in a few months, you can idly drive back highways to your breathtaking Montana retreat.

★

With Kobe and Harper hurt, Jackson asked Harper to come along anyway on a crucial four-game April road trip, just to provide a sense of leadership. The Lakers swept the series, then went home and swept the last four, and finished the season on that eight-game streak.

The day after the final game, Kobe married Vanessa. She was about to turn nineteen.

(An *L.A. Times* columnist would later say, "By all accounts, he treats marriage as if he wrote the manual.") His parents did not attend the ceremony, nor did any of his teammates.

★

Phil had obviously patched up the torn fabric of the team, though. They swept the Blazers, whereupon Shaq told the press that Kobe was the best player on the team. They swept the Kings. Then they swept the Spurs, with Kobe regularly dishing to the big man.

In the finals against Philly, Kobe wreaked revenge on Allen Iverson, who'd been the all-star-game MVP in a game where Kobe'd given the ball up on a key possession. According to Jackson, it was Harper's play in two of the five games against the 76ers in the finals that made the difference, although after losing one, they swept the next four; clearly, everyone had a hand.

The last game was the last game Harper would ever play. Five rings?

More than enough. "He'd always say when we were going to the playoffs, 'I'm gonna need you,'" Harper says now, "but hey, it wasn't me. And Kobe? Come on—he always loved Kobe. He did."

When I asked Mark Madsen what he thought had been the key to that season, he said, "A full, and sometimes you would call it stubborn, commitment to the triangle, but in a smart way. There were times—that season, every season—when it wasn't working well. And someone would always say, 'Man, this isn't working.' But Phil would never go away from the triangle. That shows serious guts and resolve. He had a system that he loved.

"The first time I asked him why, he answered instantly—his mind worked that way—'Because everyone is always touching the ball.'"

See *Holzman, Red; Knicks.*

TWENTY-FOUR

Numerologists could have seen the next ring from a mile away: In the land of the triangle, a third three-peat was ordained. And it would tie him with Auerbach . . . unless federal court testimony seven years hence is to be believed. But we're getting ahead of ourselves.

It had been a tough year. Jackson would later say that his team was "bored" and that Rick Fox, himself born into Pentecostalism, thought that by now certain players felt they knew more than the coaches. "The Big Moody" was growing larger, and would average 4 points fewer a game. Fox's numbers were down too. Journeyman Lindsey Hunter came in to replace Harper. Mitch Richmond, once a sharpshooting guard, now a shadow of his former self, came in to average just 4 points a game.

The team won 16 of 17, then slowed down, and went 52-23 the rest of the way.

Los Angeles cruised through Portland in the playoffs' first round. Then, after they split two with San Antonio, they won the next three. Tony Parker was a rookie, Tim Duncan was still growing and David Robinson (thirty-six) was worn down; he'd retire the next year.

★

Now, for the third time in three years, Sacramento loomed, with Arco and its fans clanging cowbells in derision of Phil's earlier slurs. From Peja Stojaković and Chris Webber down through Scot Pollard and Hedo Türkoğlu, Adelman's Kings were balanced. They had finished 61-21, and in the Western semis had run riot over Don Nelson's Mavs. In the fifth and deciding game, Arco rang with the anticipatory chant, "Beat L.A.! Beat L.A.!"

Los Angeles won the opener, but the Kings won three of the next four. Game six was in Arco. And Sacramento was set to put it away. And if convicted felon Tim Donaghy was telling the truth in his later trial, they did.

Donaghy was a thirteen-year ref who admitted to trying to fix games to pay off debts. He did eleven months behind bars and wrote a book trying to peel the layers off a long-simmering debate about whether refs knew whom to protect, whom to call fouls on, and what "the company" wanted.

In *United States v. Tim Donaghy,* his lawyer submitted an evidentiary document stating that, before game six, his client "learned from Referee A that Referees A and F wanted to extend the series to seven games. Tim knew Referees A and F to be 'company men,' always acting in the interest of the NBA, and that night, it was in the NBA's interest to add another game to the series."

Should a felon's word be taken as truth? Well, sometimes even the paranoid are being followed. In the previous five games, the Kings had gone to the line an average of 30 times. That night, they went to the stripe 18 times. In the previous five games, the Lakers had gone to the line an average of 22 times. That night, they went to the stripe 34 times, including 17 trips for Shaq and 11 for Kobe. L.A. took 18 foul shots in the fourth quarter alone.

In the final seconds, Kobe hacked Mike Bibby on a play that would have tied the game; it left Bibby bleeding. No foul. The Lakers won by four.

Six years later, with Donaghy's revelation, Jackson shrugged: "There's a lot of things going on in these games and they're suspicious, but I don't want to throw it back there. . . . A lot of things have happened in the course of the Tim Donaghy deposition . . . and we all think that referees should be under a separate entity than the NBA entirely."

Stern's reaction? That Donaghy, at the eye of the storm, was trying to throw things against the wall because the other things he'd said "haven't stuck." What he was saying was "baseless."

"I knew it," Scot Pollard would say. "Something wasn't right. . . . We didn't have a chance to win that game."

They didn't win the next night either, back in Staples. This game had sixteen ties and nineteen lead changes. The Kings were pumped but, ironically, terrible at the line (16 for 30) and, panicking, 2 for 20 from the three-point line. They still managed, thanks to two Bibby free throws, to take it to overtime, but lost.

The Lakers? All five starters in double figures. Triangle at work.

Now the Lakers faced their third different Eastern opponent in three years, the New Jersey Nets, who had emerged from nowhere thanks to Rod Thorn's acquisition of Jason Kidd from the Suns and his drafting of Kenyon Martin and Richard Jefferson. Under Byron Scott, they'd won 52. In their first playoff series in seventeen years, they needed a fifth-game double-OT win over Indiana to advance.

They then coasted through Charlotte and met the Celtics. In a game three for the books, the Nets had the Celtics by 21 in the fourth quarter but let Boston outscore them 41–16 in those twelve minutes—the greatest collapse in NBA playoff history. But thanks to Kidd's four triple-doubles, they took the Celts in six.

They'd clearly left some of it on the parquet checkerboard and, for game one of the finals, the rest on Los Angeles' 1-10. It's a good thing the Lakers were playing a neophyte. The Nets' traveling secretary had overlooked the obvious: If the game is starting at 5:50 PST, the L.A. freeways might be, um, slow. The Nets arrived late. By the time they got into a groove, they were down 42–19 midway through the second quarter. Shaq was being guarded by one Todd MacCulloch, the forty-seventh pick of the draft the year before.

In the second game, Shaq scored 40, MacCulloch 2, and it was 2–0. Back in New Jersey, in the warehouse of Continental Airlines Arena, the Nets put up a good but not good enough fight, losing the final two. The difference in game four was Kidd's 5 of 14 from the floor—and Shaq's 10 of 16 from the line.

Jackson now had three-peats in two cities. But slap an asterisk on this one.

★

On the other hand, take nothing away from the man who backboned all three: Shaq had his third finals MVP. Average points-per-game in those three finals: 35.5. Apparently the triangle suited the big man just fine.

★

There had been no four-peat since Red Auerbach's eight-peat. There would be none now. It was obvious from day one, in fact, when Phil's guys got off on the wrong foot—well, *no* foot, since Shaq had chosen to have toe surgery too close to the beginning of the season, at least in Kobe's opinion.

Phil's look had changed: no beard, no imperial, no facial hair of any kind (Jeanie preferred it that way). Lean and mean. The trouble was, without the big man at the beginning, the team was way *too* lean. So in a highly anticipated meeting with the Spurs in the season opener, Kobe decided to revert and take 29 shots, of which he made 9. The Lakers were blown out.

"Kobe looked to go one on one every time he touched the ball," Phil told the press. "His rare pass surprised his teammates." (That's how you knew he was really pissed. He was speaking eloquently.) "I can only promise that, even before Shaq returns, things will get better."

The collateral damage of the game was even worse. Charley Rosen was now writing for ESPN's website, and he was at the game. Tex Winter gave his old friend a ride back to the hotel, recounting his conversation with Kobe after the game.

"You played stupidly," Tex had said.

Kobe's answer, according to Tex? "You coached stupidly."

And then Tex attached a few adjectives to the kid: "Out of control, self-ish, stubborn, uncoachable." Unfortunately, Tex didn't know Charley was going to write it. But he did. Thereafter, Kobe and Charley were never again on the best of terms. Kobe wasn't real pleased with Mr. Winter, either.

★

It got worse. The Lakers lost 12 of their next 19 games—including one to Collins's Wizards. Double ouch.

Halfway through the season, they finally hit .500 at 23-23. The turn-ing point occurred in an inspiring double-overtime win over the Rockets, spurred by, of all people, Madsen, who, averaging fewer than fourteen minutes, came off the bench for twenty-eight minutes to score 9 points, pull in 5 rebounds, block 4 shots and dish off 2 assists. (In a few years, the Stanford biz guy would translate his energy, hustle and spark into a five-year, $10 million contract with the T-Wolves. Kevin McHale termed Madsen's intangibles "off the charts.")

Los Angeles now won 23 of its last 30 and knocked off the Wolves, set-ting up a meeting with the Spurs, which would turn out to be a painful experience, particularly for Jackson. The downtime in Montana had ap-parently not alleviated the stress of the time he'd annually spent court-side. Or maybe it was just all that fried food down in Pensacola all those years ago. But five decades of searching for inner peace through taking one breath at a time hadn't done its work. He was in pain in his upper torso.

After losing the first two games in San Antonio, the Lakers came home to win. The following day, Jackson underwent an angioplasty: An artery was 90 percent blocked. Cleamons coached the next one: an inspiring vic-tory. In the meantime, up in Sacramento, in his own series, Maverick coach Don Nelson showed up wearing a purple shirt and a tie. Asked why he was wearing Kings colors, he answered that they were Lakers colors, for Phil. "The stress is a ten," he said. "And most of it you put on yourself."

Jackson returned to coach the fifth game in San Antonio, with his cardiologist sitting across the floor and an ambulance at the ready. The Spurs won, and the series went back to Staples . . . where, in front of the home crowd, Shaq couldn't handle Duncan, no one could handle Parker, and the Spurs rolled with ease. (But then, Duncan and his gang stomped everyone that year—the first of three titles over the next five years.)

★

A week later, Jackson, who'd already contemplated retirement after the 2004 season, visited Jerry Buss in Hawaii. The Man asked if Jackson would stay two years; he revealed that he was going after Gary Payton, thirty-four, the slick vet late of Milwaukee. Karl Malone would be available, although thirty-nine. Hey, it's not the destination, it's the journey, right? So before his journey home, Jackson agreed.

This odyssey home took a long and winding path, including a stop in Eagle, Colorado, founded during the gold rush. A few days later, attending his fortieth Williston reunion, Phil took a call from Kupchak: Kobe, having knee surgery unbeknownst to the team, had been arrested . . . in Eagle, Colorado. A young woman who'd just finished her freshman year told authorities he'd raped her.

"Was I surprised?" Jackson later wrote. "Yes, but not entirely." Bryant, Jackson wrote, "can be consumed with surprising anger, which he's displayed toward me and toward his teammates."

★

This is what Kobe's bedroom featured in the Shangri-la of the Lodge & Spa at Cordillera: an Ansel Adams view of the snowcapped Sawatch Range, a stone fireplace, tapestry curtains, a bathroom with marble countertops, and four different kinds of drinking glasses. Two miles past the security gate, this is what was promised him: anything you'd like.

The evening when I checked in, a pretty and very young woman (not *that* young woman) did the credit-card work at a small table. A few minutes later, as I was waiting to be seated at the Restaurant Picasso, the same young woman quietly came up and lightly pressed her hand against the small of my back before assuring me that the maître d' would be out any second and I'd be quickly seated. The unexpectedly intimate gesture startled me.

Anything you'd like.

As I said, this was not the woman with whom Kobe had had sex nine days earlier, late at night, when she'd padded up the hotel's carpet through the silence, after the lobby pianist had gone back down to the valley, where the help lived. The sun-burnished golfers had long returned to their rooms.

Bryant was twenty-four, married, with an infant child, having professed his determination to be a great husband. The girl accusing Bryant? A nineteen-year-old who, in high school, had loved the stage: singing and acting. And had once driven a thousand miles to try out for *American Idol*.

On this night, she knocked on the door of room 35. Why? Well, it's not often that the kids from down in the valley get to ascend those stairs, already at 8,200 feet, now even higher and giddier. Quite far above the Eagle Ranch Development down in town, whose sales office featured a depiction of a Norman Rockwell portrait of a man painting the eagle atop a U.S. flagpole.

Sex had ensued, sex that resulted in blood on Kobe's T-shirt that was not menstrual. The next morning, she went to the Eagle County authorities and claimed rape. The next day, Bryant held a press conference with his wife by his side, confessing to adultery. A tear wound its crooked path down Vanessa Bryant's cheek.

From the start, it was apparent that a few "suicide" attempts in the accuser's past (seen by some who knew her as grabs for attention) and her general unpopularity were going to make the girl's case difficult. "Her background's going to eat her alive," a girl from her high school told me at the time. "I don't think she has a clue what she's done. I'd like to walk to her house and beat the crap out of her because I think she's making it harder for women who have really been raped to come forward."

A hotel employee concurred: Her reputation, he told me, might work against her.

Why had he taken the risk? Well, no one but Jackson had ever said no to him. His wife and child were a time zone away. And the Spa was the ultimate in discretion. And what of Wilt and his twenty thousand? Magic and his ur–sex drive? Emperor Buss and his girls? Role models all.

One morning at the Eagle County Courthouse, after he'd emptied his pockets into a plastic bowl, Kobe Bryant, most recently seen floating mid-air in yellow underwear with purple trim, now walked slowly beneath the cross-strut of a metal detector, just a six-foot-six man. A man who would have been king, but now simply the defendant. (When coaches tell their wayward troops, "Nothing good ever happens after midnight," they're usually right.)

I happened to be sitting next to a legal expert. When the charges were read, my colleague turned to me and said, "His career just ended." Bryant would face four years to life in jail if convicted of all counts. The arrest and the mess in the tabloid headlines all augured disarray for the Lakers' upcoming season. Hopefully, Malone and Payton would pick up leadership roles, but Shaq, Phil's guy, was no longer fat and happy, just fatter and asking for a $60 million extension. Kobe? Talking to other teams. Phil, by his own account, was finding himself at odds with Buss the elder: If only one of his two studs was going to stay, Phil wanted Shaq. Jerry wanted the black mamba.

Mark Madsen recalls another unusual and telling incident that clouded training camp. Since July, one of Jackson's former Bulls, Bison Dele, had been missing. He played one year for Phil, averaging fifteen minutes a game, leaving nary a footprint on the hoop landscape, but earning a ring against the Jazz, which made him family forever. Now, seven years later, after an FBI sting, came news that Dele's wayward brother, after using Bison's passport to gain access to his money, had probably shot and killed Dele and his girlfriend at sea.

"I could tell something was wrong," Madsen said, "and he told me.

When the news came out, I could tell it was a very difficult thing for him. Phil is all about family and relationships. He cared about everyone."

Despite the squabbles between Shaq and Kobe, this family won 19 of their first 24. But Malone injured a knee; he'd miss 39 games. And the relationship between Jackson and Kobe had gotten more estranged since the incident at the spa. In 2013, Jackson would reveal that in Chicago, his own daughter had been assaulted by a football player in school; thereafter, he would write, it would be hard for him to see Bryant the same way anymore. Nor could Bryant possibly have had a clear head (if he ever did); the prosecution was still gathering evidence and, as the season began, had not yet announced whether it would go forward.

Kobe was now twenty-five, no longer a kid, chronologically. Phil was fifty-eight, a professor unused to having geniuses metaphorically sit in the back of the class under hoodies with earphones on. Nothing could have been as frustrating as knowing that the man simply did not want to do the work to prepare, to learn the offense that, had he surrendered to it, as Michael had, would have made for a better basketball team. Whether it was the Williston Coyotes, the UND Fighting Sioux, the Patroons, the Bulls, the Lakers, Big Man Camp, Omega or a Monday-night run at the Evangeline Women's Home basement gym, the *team* was never more than a microsecond from Phil Jackson's mind. Now his second-most-gifted student simply refused to sublimate the ego for the good of the common cause, and it was unthinkable.

In late 2003, the Eagle County DA issued a statement: "It is alleged that he caused sexual penetration or intrusion, and he caused submission of the victim through actual physical force. . . . I feel after looking at the evidence that I can prove this case beyond a reasonable doubt."

It was on. Back in Los Angeles, Bryant held another press conference, with his wife by his side, and said, "I didn't force her to do anything against her will. I'm innocent . . . I sit here in front of you guys furious at myself. Disgusted at myself for making a mistake of adultery. I love my wife with all my heart. She's my backbone."

They lost six of the next eight. In February, Jackson approached Kupchak about trading the kid. But Buss clearly had other ideas. They did not include Phil Jackson. Apparently Kobe had talked to Buss, because a few days later, Jackson would recall, Derek Fisher told him that Kobe'd said to Fisher, "Your man's not coming back," referring to Phil. To know that he was not going to be rehired was bad enough. To hear it from a player who'd heard it from Kobe?

The rift had widened seemingly beyond repair if the tidbits about that year in Jackson's *The Last Season* are accurate.

- Kobe to Phil: "I'm not going to take any shit from Shaq this year. If he starts saying things in the press, I'll fire back. . . . I've had it."
- Kobe bitched about how the private jet the team was giving him to appear in Colorado—for a case that might lead to life imprisonment—wasn't good enough.
- Secondhand, Jackson had heard that Kobe was the only player in the entire league to vote against the changes in the collective-bargaining agreement because it meant he'd never make Shaq money.
- He'd stopped playing good defense.
- After Jackson said to Kobe of an errant pass, "You can't make that pass," Kobe answered, "Well, you better teach those mother-fuckers how to run the offense."

Phil to Kupchak: "I will not coach this team next year if he is still here. He won't listen to anyone. I've had it with this kid."

The Lakers suspended Phil's contract negotiations. But now he was free to teach without agenda, and after the all-star break, he and Kobe had a heart-to-heart; in retrospect, the long walk out of the valley had begun. Jackson's message to the young man: Start letting basketball be the refuge from your life's other problems in the same way it had been for Jordan.

According to Jackson, the final week of this discordant season included a game in which Kobe, some in the media believed, had "tanked" a game to help his negotiating position. "I don't know how we can forgive him," said a player, anonymously. The next day, Kobe demanded to know who the culprit was.

Nonetheless, they almost picked up a fourth ring. Houston, coached by Van Gumby, was up first: The first game was a slugfest, 72–71 L.A. In the second, Shaq smothered Yao (7 points), and the Lakers won in a rout. In the third, Kobe and Payton went 10 of 32, and the Rockets won. But the Lakers closed it out in the next two: first an OT thriller, and a fifth in which the Lakers held the Gumbies to 78, including 9 points in the third quarter. They then took the Wolves in six and Spurs in six.

In the finals, though, the wheel of change had come back to where it had often stopped so many years before: Detroit was the finals foe. A whole new roster wore the Piston uniform, but once again, as had been the case in Jackson's first finals as a coach, man for man, Larry Brown's Pistons seemed to want it more. Finals are won on defense, and Ben Wallace had emerged that season as a force: 246 blocks, 80 more than Shaq. On offense, Chauncey Billups and Richard Hamilton featured a perfectly balanced scoring backcourt. With Malone out with a sprained ankle, the Lakers went down in five . . .

. . . and Jackson was out. The headline: PURPLE DRAIN. Phil, said the *L.A. Times*, had "departed." Shaq was demanding a trade. Kobe had turned free agent. "The owner bluntly told his coach he would not be invited back," said one source to the *Times* writer.

This family had reached the nadir of dysfunctionality. Shaq insisted his need to move wasn't about Phil's departure; it was about "team"—or lack of it, since Buss had made it obvious that Kobe was his boy (having once called the kid his "son").

Asked what was next, Jackson said, "I'm going to the Greek Theater to see Garrison Keillor." One-liner-wise, he'd never miss a cue.

★

Shaq went to Miami for Caron Butler, Lamar Odom and Brian Grant. Phil went fishing—"run out of town," wrote the *Times*, "on the wrong end of the shotgun."

If in Chicago Krause had managed to drive away a coach and an entire team, six years later, Kobe had effectively managed to do the same thing.

TWENTY-FIVE

Kobe was now on a roll. In mid-July, Bryant had signed a seven-year, $136.4-million contract. Eight weeks later, more than a month prior to the season opener, the prosecution back in Eagle dropped its charges after the girl declined to testify. She sued in a civil case, and an undisclosed settlement was subsequently reached.

The takeaway? A gray area. Why would Kobe have settled, forever leaving doubt as to what happened in room 35, if the entire thing been so, even if X-rated, consensual?

But then, why not? For an unspecified amount of money (which he could now spend as Croesus did), he could make the entire thing go away. He could afford to give a middle-class girl from Colorado virtually any amount she asked for. And we have not heard from her since.

After the announcement of the dropping of the charges, Bryant's camp issued a statement attributed to Bryant. "Although I truly believe this encounter between us was consensual," it read, "I recognize now that she did not, and does not, view this incident the same way I did. After months of reviewing discovery, listening to her attorney, and even her testimony in person, I now understand how she feels that she did not consent to this encounter."

In other words, he was admitting, he could see the whole thing her way. If he was sincere, he was in a sense saying that he was trying to see her world as Jackson tried to see each of his player's, through the other person's eyes. Maybe that was the day when it became certain that Jackson and Bryant could go on to win more rings.

Then, in the same statement, Kobe said that the whole ordeal had been "incredibly difficult." Damn, yeah, it must have been tough. I mean, didn't we *all* feel for him?

★

Next season, 2004–05, was the Season of the Which—which of the two head coaches could get these guys to win?

After a one-year hiatus from the game to recover from bladder cancer, Rudy Tomjanovich came on board for a sweet $30 million for five years. He'd sent Bryant and his agent videos showing how well he'd done for other players at Kobe's position. Whereupon the ship began sinkin'. It wasn't that Rudy hadn't once been able to coach. He'd won two titles in Houston, a decade earlier, with guys named Olajuwon and Clyde the Glide, and compiled a 900-503 record. Then, in his last four years with the Rockets, he'd gone 150-178. He hadn't made the playoffs in his previous three years.

"I didn't know much about Tomjanovich," Brian Grant, one of the ex-Heat triumvirate shipped to the Pacific time zone, says now. "None of us did." Grant had broken into the league in Sacramento as a strong rebounder with an ability to physically intimidate. (Pat Riley had given Grant a stunning $86-million contract down in Miami: "the missing piece of the puzzle," Riley had said at the time.)

"I did find out immediately who the strongest guy on the team was," said Grant. "I was pulling three-quarters of the weights in the lap pools. Kobe said to me, 'That's good,' then jumped in and pulled the full weight." Grant, whose entire career had been built on his ability to muscle his way underneath to grab rebounds from taller and heavier men, was astounded.

"And it wasn't as if he didn't put out. In practice he worked as hard as he did in games. But as soon as we started to practice, I could tell it was going to be a rough year. The cohesion wasn't there. Rudy was trying to feel his way through a system that was left to him. And he was from a different era."

Inheriting a team that had won three titles under a coach who'd won nine, all using the triangle—Rudy scrapped it. The result? Free-form chaos. Did Kobe try to do too much? "If I'd been him, I think I would have thought I had to do more," Grant says. "He wanted to win. His attitude was right. But things weren't working that way.

"I'd done two horrible years with the Heat, and then we'd pulled it all together [Grant averaged 9 points, 7 rebounds, and thirty minutes a game for a playoff team in Miami], and now I looked around and thought, *Wow, it's happening all over again*. I mean, it was hard, because everyone was doing their thing—Lamar, Caron—but individuals weren't going to win on that team, even if they were bringing excitement . . . On top of which—and this was very weird—there were nights we were doing well, doing good things, and the place was quiet."

The star had been Kobe, but the likable star *power* had been Jackson and his Shaq-son. Now the last echoes of Showtime had died out, and, with the enigmatic and phlegmatic Bryant as the only star in uniform, Staples had the electricity of an office-supply store. And a mediocre team was bringing out Los Angeles's most notorious trait: indifference.

And then, out of the blue, Rudy quit, at 24-19. A recovering alcoholic, he was said to be having trouble with all the big-city pressures associated with coaching a team that had undergone such cataclysmic change. Or maybe people having gone face-to-face with mortality face it in different ways. Whatever the reason, the fire was apparently gone, and without it, he couldn't hope to balance the team with Kobe and whole-roster changes. Hamblen came into the slot, but the team lost 19 of its last 29.

"The cohesion was just never there," Grant said. "The guys weren't yelling. I didn't get it."

What no one was actually getting was Jackson's eternal curriculum: defense. The Laker starting rotation comprised small forwards, no agile big man and a superstar who, unlike Jordan, was not the most tenacious of defenders. They gave up 101 points per game—nearly 10 more than the previous season, twenty-seventh of thirty.

★

Meantime, Jackson did the thing that had always worked in the past to get another job: He went on an international bike odyssey. He visited Sydney and won $450 playing blackjack alongside Andy Roddick during the Australian Open. Down Under, he was asked, now that Lenny Wilkens had been fired, if he wanted to coach the Knicks. This was news to Phil. Via Jeanie, he had already heard that Rudy T was gone. But "I wondered if I was really prepared to return to the fray," he later said, likely telling the truth.

He visited with Luc Longley in Perth, where his former center now owned a team, and ran the triangle. He told Luc there was a fifty-fifty chance he'd be back, the perfectly imperfect Cheshire-cat-grin answer: He wouldn't even let a friend know who he was or what he thought.

He visited New Zealand, with its "perfect attitude," as he'd later tell Rosen in an account of his travels, in *Men's Journal*. The Kiwis are known for nothing if not for their love of visitors—and their dislike of swollen heads. Actress Lucy Lawless, a New Zealander, once described it to me as tall-poppy syndrome—if anyone feels the need to grow taller than everyone else, they're exiled and at least metaphorically beheaded.

Jackson's brothers and their wives joined him. They rode through wine country on the South Island and then to the rocky west on the Tasman Sea. They all took a jet boat up the Waikato River, the pilot driving like a madman—"just dangerous enough to be fun," as Phil the edge-seeker would later recall. They biked to the top of Mount Cook.

Then, alone, he went on to Tahiti, where, like Gauguin, perhaps, "I'd find an island woman who could be my soul mate." Hm. An interesting aside there. Meantime, "Whoever wins the Phil derby shouldn't look for him to report for duty until the 2005–2006 season," said agent Todd Musburger. "When he returns, it's a mix of family, business, charity, all the things that a guy who's worked his tail off for so many years would like to do."

Then back home, where he told Charley, "I wondered if, after forty years of competing as a player and a coach on a really high level, it might be time to step away from the arena. I also knew that if I wasn't going back, I needed to find a way to break free of the magnetism that the NBA exerts on my life."

Motivational speaking wasn't going to do it: "I'm not sure," he said, "that I'm capable of living a life that lacks a basic level of competition."

The conclusion? It was announced 363 days after he'd been fired that Dr. Jerry had laid down his arms and pleaded for his return. Now, *those* are terms a competitor can savor: "Looks like I won in the end, then, eh?"

"I decided to reinvent my future by returning to my past," he told Rosen. "If most of the players on the Lakers would be new to me, the game was still the same. The specific challenge posed by coaching in the NBA is to motivate a disparate group of highly talented people to sacrifice their talents in order to successfully pursue a common goal. Right now, that's where I have to be."

He could have said, "Right now . . . and forever." But maybe he didn't want to admit it. That would be to admit that the wheel of change was a hamster wheel where every revolution, no matter how long, returned you to the beginning.

(The *Times*'s account: "Phil Jackson is back in shackles, chained once more to the ball of confusion known as Laker basketball.")

Not surprisingly but most emphatically, a woman stood behind the turning of this wheel of life. The older a man who's comfortable in his own skin grows, the more comfortable he is with a woman being his driving wheel—especially a man who grew up in a nonpatriarchal household.

Oddly, Jackson made no mention of this in his latest memoir; he revealed on the book-promo circuit that it was Jeanie who was behind the return: both the Jeanie who helped run the team's business and the fiancée Jeanie, the woman who'd "saved" him. By his account in an interview with *Men's Journal,* she said, "Come on back and do this . . . it's important for me, and it's important for Kobe; he's gone through a really hard two years."

Their time apart, he said, had allowed them to test whether theirs had been a companionship that relied on geography, or the real thing. Apparently no Gauguin babes had wanted to sketch variations of the triangle on palm leaves. Apparently, as the sixtieth birthday approaches, being in the South Pacific soothes the mind, but even if you're slowing down, it's tough to finally turn your back on the spotlight. Or the business blonde.

"He's very attracted to her for all the right reasons," Diane Mast says now. "His companionship with Jeanie has been very strong and very loyal. They've been good partners. They've meted out territory. It isn't always him calling the shots. He has tremendous respect for her. Her business savvy is something he yields to. Phil is not a business guy. But she handles it with style and brains, and she has fun with it."

The man who returned to Los Angeles was a different guy: a scarred heart (only physically), increasingly brittle limbs and joints (he now has two artificial hips and an artificial knee) and seemingly more brittle ways of seeing the changing social landscape as, for five thousand years, men in charge have generally devolved with age. But he was returning to family: the woman he'd eventually propose to and the prodigy he'd been raising since a month after Kobe Bryant's twenty-first birthday, when his own young twins had turned twenty.

Ever since Jackson had made Eddie Mast's family feel he'd always be there for them, he was back at what he did best. Teach, coach, provide, care. Now all he needed was a team.

But that very uncertainty about this strange new Laker cast no doubt enhanced the appeal of the new job. Jackson could not only surpass Auerbach (and despite protestations to the contrary, one former player insists to do so would eventually give him "extreme pleasure"); he could do so without a superstar duo.

His attire at his final "Here's the new coach!" press conference? Charcoal suit, T-shirt, beads—and sandals. And soul patch. He looked pretty good for a fifty-nine-year-old limping his way through the later years.

"More than anything, the lessons were about stress," he told the press. "My kids all wanted to know why I wanted to come back to this stressful job . . . [but] I can manage the stress that comes along with this game."

As usual, as Diane Mast characterizes the man's decision making, he acted on instinct—immediate feelings. Two weeks earlier, he said he'd told his agent to not field Buss's offer. Two days later, he changed his mind. Maybe three years at something in the neighborhood of ten mil a year had something to do with it.

How could he command such exorbitant loot? Stars that had aligned: Coaching vacancies in Portland and Seattle provided some very fortuitous leverage. No one doubted that Jackson was amenable, if not eager, to re-enter the fray—not since he'd given an interview to an NBC reporter during the finals in which he'd stated that, despite the angioplasty, he had been certified "100 percent healthy"—a nice little advertorial, there.

The last thing Buss needed was Jackson on a rival divisional team. And who else was out there? Certainly no one who could override the owner's daughter, who was clearly weighing in heavily, for all sorts of reasons.

"Reconciliation, redemption and resiliency" were Jackson's stated catchwords this time. "And hopefully in March you won't see me with the kinds of bags under my eyes I was carrying around while I was in Australia." And if this rang a little self-referential, as if he was reveling in knowing how much he'd been missed, this time he was holding the shotgun. Or at least the bow and arrow.

"He'll hang that old Indian feather off the sprinkler nozzle in his office," reported the *Times,* "gather that familiar coaching staff, push that offense Jerry Buss came to despise. He's back. Who else would be wearing the sandals?"

Jackson revealed a couple of other thing in those first few days back: 1) that it wasn't about the money and 2) that beating Auerbach wasn't a factor. "I would be most amazed if at the end of the third year we had an opportunity to do that," he said.

Right. And perfectly acceptable utterances in the City of Illusion.

★

Obviously, the first thing on everyone's mind was how in the world he'd reconcile with Kobe, whom he'd trashed on his way out in . . . his *fourth* book. The hope was that Kobe, having seen his team finish behind the lowly Clippers, might see the light. On the other hand, a month before taking the job, Jackson had reached out to talk and Bryant had declined.

In retrospect, it would hardly be a stretch to say that Jackson's frustrations with Bryant were always those of a father with a wayward son, and that the scalding of Kobe in *The Last Season* represented nothing as much as a shot across Kobe's bow. The written word has a certain permanence and power, and even if Kobe hadn't read *Corelli's Mandolin,* you *know* he read quotes from *The Last Season.*

Add two other variables when equating Jackson's return. When Ron Harper told me, "Phil loved Kobe—he really did," this wasn't an off-the-cuff opinion; Harper was as close to Jackson as any player had ever been. Now add something Jackson said in 2013 on his book tour: that he was closer to Bryant than to any other player he ever coached in twenty years, including Jordan and Shaq. (Or was that just a sound bite to get him a third shot in L.A.?)

"The thing about Kobe," says John Salley now, "is everyone wants to talk about how he's the black mamba, and yeah, he's a good player. But that mentality came from Phil. No matter what Phil said about him in that book, Kobe let that shit go because Phil had given him so much more. And Phil probably wrote that on a bad day."

Bryant's response to the hiring, after saying a few months earlier that he'd "roll with it"? In a statement, he said that Jackson's return was "something I support. In Phil Jackson, they chose a proven winner." In private, he called Jackson to congratulate him.

Eighty percent of ESPN poll responders said Jackson would not get another ring. And Shaq, down in Florida? "I thank him for taking me to a level I couldn't get to myself. I wish him the best of luck. He'll need it."

TWENTY-SIX

s Tex liked to say, "You're only a success for the moment you've created a successful act"—the modern equivalent of the guy whispering in the returning conquering Roman general's ears, "All power is fleeting." And Jackson knew it. He now coached a decidedly different smudged locker room personnelwise. Butler and Grant were gone. (When I asked Brian how that had gone down with Phil, he said, "No comment.")

The three wise men had been replaced by three men who would never earn that adjectival modifier. His subsequent ability to at least corral, for a time, the likes of Kwame Brown, Lamar Odom and Andrew Bynum (and later, Ron Artest Jr./Metta World Peace) spoke perhaps more highly of Jackson's teaching skills than any previous era.

To note that as school began, the new crop's collective character did not mirror that of the '73 Knicks or, for that matter, the '91 Bulls, is to recognize and acknowledge the shifting slope of societal evolution. Some of Phil's immature new crop came from troubled circumstances, which was hardly their fault—nor was it their fault that the NBA was willing to let them into the adult club. (About now, Carmelo Anthony, after one year at Syracuse, was considered to be mature.) Without college, which is nothing if not the chance to ease into adulthood, no-fault style, it's pretty hard to expect a kid to arrive in his first workplace with his team values in place. Or to be receptive to an authority figure.

"The challenges that you ran into when Tex wrote the book, back when it was a team game," says Cleamons now, "were very, very different.

In today's culture, it's a 'me' game. Now the challenges are agents, lawyers, people doing the players' bidding, convincing teams how good their player is.

"It's not like we have to sit around, singing 'Kumbaya,' but you have to learn to appreciate each other's talents and skills. You *have* to have a solidarity."

In another time—see "New York Knicks, early seventies"—solidarity was a given. But to blame the new crop for not being the old crop would be irrational and ignorant. And that Jackson would now take home two more rings as an ever-aging man teaching ever-younger kids only reinforces the idea that, as a teacher, Phil Jackson was not all that bad, in the final assessment, at imparting his philosophy.

Then, it's not as if he didn't have practice at tutoring the immature. In his first Lakers stint, Jackson had been handed the youngest player to ever play in the NBA, a record that had since been eclipsed by Jonathan Bender (ticketed for going 120 miles per hour four months after being drafted) and Jermaine O'Neal. Now enter the record breaker, center Andrew Bynum, seventeen years, two hundred forty-four days old on draft day when Kupchak took him with the tenth pick, with Jackson's reported assent.

For a Bynum-esque perspective, remember where *you* were maturity-wise at seventeen. Now add the possibility of being raised for sixteen of those years by a single mother and shuffling among three high schools as just a piece of basketball machinery. Then out of the last school, being handed $2 million and having your boss say that the team was going to "fast-track" you in the company, as Phil said to Andrew; the triangle needed a big man who could move the ball.

But at first Bynum was an excitable boy. The first time he met Shaq that year, after Shaq had dunked over him, Andrew then insisted on dunking over Shaq, and then delivered an emphatic elbow to the elder. The ensuing scrap was broken up by Bryant (who one year later, when the Nets wanted to give up Jason Kidd to the Lakers for Bynum, let it be known that it should have happened. It didn't). A few years later, Bynum would commit a foul so flagrant on Bobcat Gerald Williams that Bynum fractured one of Williams's ribs and collapsed one of his lungs. A few years after that, young Andrew would be suspended for another flagrant foul—followed by a 50-rebound, 12-block three-game stretch.

When he was good, Bynum was good. When he was bad . . . well, he would eventually provide the ugliest moment in Phil Jackson's career, so that's got to be pretty bad. As in *bad* bad.

Then there was Kwame Brown, whose lineage was truly bizarre. He'd been the number-one pick in the 2001 draft by the Washington Wizards' director of personnel, one Michael Jordan. Straight out of high school. Chosen ahead of Pau Gasol, Shane Battier, Joe Johnson, Richard Jefferson and Gilbert Arenas. Not surprisingly, a kid with no college time didn't fit well with Jordan's coach . . . Doug Collins. Brown's three years in the capital gradually dissolved into a haze of boos and arguments with teammates and then arguments with coach Eddie Jordan (Collins had, of course, run his course with the Wizards).

In the *New York Daily News*'s list of the top ten worst number-one picks in history, Kwame Brown comes in at nine, just behind Michael Olowokandi. (Given that everyone above him is retired, he may yet climb up to rival Kent Benson and Joe Barry Carroll.) Kwame was not to be the big-man answer to the post-Shaq era in Staples. Dr. Buss's insistence on keeping Kobe and losing his two best big men—Shaq and Phil—had proved as acute as his taste in girls. Um, women.

In Brown's first game as a Laker in Washington, a Kobe pass bounced off his head into the stands, to the delight of the crowd. For Kwame, it was downhill from there. Six months later, he would be accused of rape and then cleared of all charges, but still, you have to hate it when that happens. In between, he was accused of assaulting a man with a cake. (You can't make this stuff up.) The following year, Brown would get hit with disorderly conduct and interfering with a police investigation after driving the wrong way down a one-way street. He is currently with his eighth team in a twelve-year career.

In the long run, Phil couldn't get inside Kwame's head, but Kwame ended up doing his part in changing the franchise: he would go to the Grizzlies in the trade for Pau Gasol.

Lamar Odom? He had this over the other two: he'd put in a year of college basketball. He was a superior athlete; at six-ten capable of pretty much doing it all. But in Odom, Phil had inherited a troubled kid, rocked by everything from his dad's smack addiction to his mother's death when he was twelve. A brief summer at UNLV came to an end when questions were raised in an *SI* story about his admission-test scores. It was later reported that he'd taken money from a booster, which led to an inquiry, which led to the firing of coach Bill Bayno, and the Runnin' Rebels slowing to a standstill: four years' probation for the UNLV's athletic program.

At URI, after having to sit out a year, he led the Rams to the conference championship and declared himself ready for the big time. Phil once said he had the potential skills of a Pippen but would never quite grok the triangle and would vanish mysteriously on the court at crucial times. But his game would grow over the years as the personnel evolved to allow him to play a more comfortable game.

Off the court, Odom obligatorily married a Kardashian, played himself on eight episodes of *Khloé & Lamar* and attended Carmelo Anthony's wedding to La La Vazquez. It was filmed by VH1. He has a film production company called Rich Soil, and as of this writing, *Star* magazine had run a story written by a woman who said she was his mistress.

In other words, this was not Phil's Cadillac of fifteen years ago in Chicago. On the other hand, taking on a new live crew fit the model: a new experience. A new challenge. New breaths. New universes. (Same blonde.) And to a man heading for the later years, there's no better way to stay young than by seeing the world through a new generation's eyes. Phil Jackson trying to Zen-out the new Lakers: the ultimate reality show.

The good news: Hamblen, Cleamons, Tex and Brian Shaw were back. Psych coach George Mumford, a regular in Chicago, was back, although less frequently. And not incidentally, Craig Hodges was on board now as a first-ever shooting coach, although no doubt the militant would speak his mind and share his life lessons about the culture to his young pupils. For Jackson, who would, some years later, call himself "fiscally conservative but socially progressive," an old buddy obsessed with inner-city entropy and the responsibility of society to get its act together could be a good guy to have around with such a new, un-politically-aware class—especially when, despite a total of six college and pro years being coached by Tex, the rest of the league had clearly blackballed him for more than a decade. At Phil's suggestion, Tex made the first call. Hodges, of course, was in, with his own mantra: "Communication is the biggest facet of winning."

To that end, the second draft pick bestowed on the new coach was a win. Center Ronny Turiaf, a native of Martinique, had attended the elite National Institute of Physical Education in Paris, where scholarship and athletics were meant to be in perfect balance, then gone to Gonzaga, where, after his senior year, he was named the West Coast Conference Player of the Year. Then, four weeks after the draft, he was discovered by a Lakers doctor to have an enlarged aortic root that would require open-heart surgery. Recovery was estimated at six months.

The team voided his contract but kept his rights in case of a return and paid for the surgery, the morning after which he awoke in his hospital bed to see Kupchak, who had brought him a Lakers jersey with his name and number on it. He awoke each day to see the jersey.

In January, he joined the team. Two weeks later, during a scrimmage, Jackson, disgusted with his play, tossed him. " 'Get off my court,' " Turiaf recalls now. "Those were his words. He told me I was the worst player in the scrimmage."

No, really, how *exactly* did he say that?

"Just like that," says the man they called Ro. "Get off my court."

Sounds as though Zen man, despite his surface laid-back demeanor, was losing some of the mellow. Turiaf's reaction? "It stimulated me psychologically [and] intellectually. He knew how to push my buttons. He put me in a situation where I could succeed," he says, measuring each word in that cool French-Caribbean accent. "I enjoyed the best three years of my career playing for him."

Used for his defensive rebounding and shot-blocking skills, Turiaf grew as a player and, to hear him tell it, as a person. A conversation with Ronny Turiaf is like a conversation with a college friend at midnight in front of a fireplace, over a bottle of wine. His references keep returning to the mentor. The tough love at the beginning quickly gave way to a jovial and convivial relationship, wherein whenever Jackson gave him grief for the French army's reputation, Ro would counter that he was actually Martiniquais.

"He always put me in a situation where I could succeed. He allowed me to reach places I hadn't reached. He found ways to use everyone's skill set with a system that explores every single part of a player's attributes, takes it down to the absolute bottom. When you have guys who can understand it, and think deeper than the surface level of stats, it makes the game very easy."

To an already thoughtful man, did the frippery of books and sage make a difference? "A huge influence," he says. "I consider myself a spiritual guy looking for better ways to see life's limitless options. To explore. As a better human and a better man. And at the same time to exponentially increase my basketball knowledge. I guess to find a way to better be in tune with myself.

"So many times in this world, athletes, we have a tendency to not see into ourselves, you know? He taught me how to find an equilibrium. A state of mind where you are detaching yourself emotionally from everything. You start looking at everything from *that moment*. He taught me of the immensity of the power of my brain. To understand what I was all about."

He would leave the Lakers for a $17-million deal with the Warriors, then earn a ring with LeBron's Heat. I asked: What's your next incarnation?

"Maybe you'll never hear about me again because I became a monk." He doesn't follow this with a laugh. This was clearly a student of Phil Jackson.

Two other new low-profile players fell quite within Jackson's radar: 2004 first-round pick Sasha Vujačić, a Slovenian, and Vladimir Radmanović, a Bosnia-Herzegovinian son of a Yugoslav People's Army officer. Having turned Toni Kukoč into a sixth-man winner, Jackson could not have been displeased at the chance to work with international players who arrive with at least one cherished talent: subscribing to the Holzmanesque insistence that everyone on offense touch the ball.

Vujačić could play either guard position, and while never known for his defense, would in two years set the Lakers free-throw record, although he was never quite as comfortable in the triangle as Jackson had hoped. Radmanović had been the Sonics' first pick, a big man who could also shoot the three. He'd been good, but not great, and when the time came for a free-agent signing with either of the Los Angeles teams, Jackson and the new Vlad's buddy Vlade Divac steered him to Jackson's triangle.

They lost 9 of their first 15. They finished eight games over .500 but bowed out to the Suns in the first round in uncharacteristic Phil-team fashion: with a 3–1 lead, they became the eighth team in history to give it up . . . with the final three losses by an average of . . . 18 points. In the final, a 121–90 blowout, the team shot 33 percent from the field. Kwame was 2 for 10.

Either the coaches weren't reaching the kids, or the kids had no understanding of team play. Or the generational drift was way too wide.

TWENTY-SEVEN

Before the 2006–07 season had begun, with Phil comfortably bonding with Jeanie, a year of beach basketball under his belt, and his bank account overflowing with goodwill, a Lakers linchpin underwent surgery. Just prior to camp (and just before Red Auerbach's death—in his final moments, Auerbach and Jackson were tied in ring tally), Jackson had hip-replacement surgery.

It's tough enough for humans to lose an organic part of themselves to age. A whole lot harder, psychologically, when (a) you're an athlete who relied on those legs, and (b) back when you broke in, surgery derailed what could have been a much cooler career.

"It's harrowing, to be an athlete and to think that you need an artificial joint, and then to think what it's going to do to your life," he told *Esquire*. "But diminishing returns set in. You can't play tennis or go hiking. Swimming and biking were my only activities—I couldn't even run anymore. And then, a few years ago, the pain started. It got to a certain level where I couldn't deal with it any longer."

He somehow managed to deal with the season, which included more injuries than a Jackson team had ever endured. Odom played just fifty-six games before undergoing shoulder surgery. Kwame was given the starting center spot over Chris Mihm and promptly injured his own shoulder, playing only half the season. Luke Walton, drafted in 2003, a Jackson kind of guy (he has a tattoo of four dancing Grateful Dead–style skeletons) turned in the only double-figure (11) points-per-game season of his career, but missed a quarter of the season.

Kobe? A streak of 50-point games. In other words, the whole thing had fallen apart. They lost eight of the last twelve, finished an inconceivable 42-40, and bowed out again, in five to the Suns, right after *Sports Illustrated*'s excerpt of Jack McCallum's book *Seven Seconds or Less* quoted Suns coach Mike D'Antoni as eviscerating the Lakers' talent.

Meanwhile, in Lakerland, all hell broke loose. Kobe very publicly demanded a trade. Weary of playing with men he considered second-rate, he wanted out. Anywhere, he said. Including Pluto. He went public with profanity, dissing Bynum and Kupchak. He suggested that Jerry West, of all people, come back to right the ship.

The team allowed exploratory talks with at least two teams, but they led to no satisfactory offers; Buss was not about to let go of the guy he'd banked the entire franchise on. Phil, who was entering his final contract year, let Kobe take some time off in training camp, and finally the waters stopped roiling.

"I think both Phil and I will be back," Kobe said. "Things are going to be all right. Don't go full bore just yet. Take a deep breath." Positively Buddha-like. Before long, Kobe would even be reading some of the books. Like *The Tao of Pooh,* which basically remains the best intro to Eastern thought out there (if a little more simplistic than *Sacred Hoops,* Jackson's best book about spirituality).

The 2007–08 season began with an essential Jackson acquisition, not without its own asterisk. Cool head Derek Fisher, who, during a spectacular playoff run in the spring with the Jazz, revealed that his daughter was afflicted with a degenerative eye cancer. With the breaking of the news, Kobe tweeted his support: "Go at 'em . . . do what you do best. . . . We're cut from the same cloth."

After they lost to the Warriors in the playoffs, Fisher asked to be released so that he could be in a city with proper medical care. Less than one month later, he signed a three-year deal with the Lakers.

"It did look funny when we just released Derek outright and, like, three weeks later, he signed with the Lakers," said Jazz owner Larry Miller at the time. "[But] I think he's a man of integrity. . . . He's for real unless there's something underhanded going on where he's getting paid somehow on the side. But I don't believe Derek would do that, and I don't believe Jerry Buss would do that. I mean, how are you going to tell a guy, 'No, you can't take care of your family, your child'? So I've made the conscious decision . . . just to assume that it was real."

Another bad omen? Kupchak's overrated first-round pick, Javaris Crittenton, who, despite attending Southwest Atlanta Christian Academy before doing a year at Georgia Tech, was beyond Jackson's salvation; by midseason he'd be gone. As of this writing, he's been indicted on murder charges.

Coby Karl was among the faces on the first day of training camp for the first prepractice meditation in September 2007. Son of coach George Karl, Coby was a walk-on who'd just finished his senior year at Boise State.

"But [Jackson] always treated me as well as Kobe," says Karl now, after finishing up a season with the Idaho Stampede. As I write this, he's been invited to Raptors camp and figures his career will end with about four more years overseas before he starts getting into his dad's business.

Coby had been operated on for thyroid cancer six months earlier, but hadn't announced it until after Boise State's season had ended. He made the team, signing a contract for $427,163. He made his debut on October 30, playing thirty-seven seconds. Shuttling between the Lakers and the D-Fenders, he played in seventeen regular-season games, averaging four minutes, 2 points and 1 rebound a game—and learning a style of coaching different from the one he'd been taught his entire life.

While his basketball contributions may have been minimal, his insight into Jackson remains unique: He was coming in from the outside with a preconception about the man forged over a lifetime. As a kid, following his dad's career, Coby saw his old man gain success with an engaging style: animated, excited, expressive, uncensored. As a kid, of course, he'd sided with his dad when he faced Phil. "Coaches are as competitive as players, and [with] my dad . . . it was always, '[Phil] has great players.' I was on my dad's side: 'My dad's a great coach; Phil's always had Jordan or Kobe, and that's why he wins.'

"With Phil, looking at him from afar, you see that air of . . . pretentiousness . . . that maybe he thinks he's better than everyone. And I went there with that perception—and then it becomes the complete opposite. There wasn't any pretension. It was real. It was the opposite from anything I'd dealt with. And I'd had so many intense coaches in high school and college, and obviously my biggest influence was Dad—an intense guy. I expected that to happen, but Coach Jackson had this calm demeanor, a quiet, good communicator, in a different way. Phil doesn't manhandle a practice. He doesn't strangle ingenuity. He lets players and coaches evolve. What's the word? Laissez-faire?

"That year, the thing that worked perfect for coach was that Kobe and Derek were 100 percent behind him. There was never a doubt. They were so completely grounded in the fundamentals of the triangle, and I just love the basicness of that offense.

"You know how in a family, sometimes you go to Mom, sometimes to Dad? With those guys, it was just coach. The perfect fit."

The first noteworthy event of the 2007–08 season was an unfortunate reprise of the increasingly loose-lipped Jackson's apparent love of his own wit. Six games in, routed by the Spurs, whose 13 three-point shots had exposed Phil's shaky perimeter defense, he said, "We call this a *Brokeback Mountain* game because there's so much penetration and kickouts," he said. Ouch.

That a sixty-two-year-old man who had spent more time inside a locker-room culture than out of it, raised by a fiery mother who schooled her flock in the Rapture, could dispense such a bad-taste one-liner is hardly surprising, if not particularly compassionate. The older he grew, now quite "free to be me," the more Phil liked to quip. Some of his snippets were bound to fall flat.

But it's a barometer of how swiftly society has changed that he could get away with it with a quick apology: "In retrospect it wasn't really funny. When you take it out of context, it wasn't funny. It was a poor attempt at humor, and I deserved to be reprimanded by the NBA." (Which also raises the question, In what context would it have been funny?) After noting that journalists laughed, as if to make his remark more understandable (as if the *wink-wink* wordpack is part of the old-boy network), according to ESPN, he said, "If I've offended any horses, Texans, cowboys or gays, I apologize."

Today, if he'd said it as a coach, the protests outside of Staples would be deafening. His words would have put a major asterisk next to the ringmaster. Context is all. Even in 2009, Kobe's calling an official a "faggot" lightened his wallet by $100,000.

It's a stretch to connect the next dot, but after that humiliation, maybe Phil decided to focus: The Lakers reeled off four straight wins, with Turiaf, Bynum, Vlad, Odom and second-year point guard Jordan Farmar all stepping up. In a key acquisition, Kupchak brought in Orlando's wingman, Trevor Ariza, coming into his own after the Knicks and Magic had somehow overlooked his versatility, in exchange for Brian Cook and Maurice Evans.

Then a few weeks later, Kupchak engineered the trade that would pave the way for the resurrection in Staplestown. Pau Gasol, twenty-seven, a national hero in Spain, after six solid years in Memphis, came over for Marc Gasol, his younger brother, and two future first-round picks, which would invariably be quite low. Gregg Popovich called it "beyond comprehension" and called for the NBA to institute a committee that could veto obviously one-sided trades motivated by salary dumping.

Jackson, hardly concerned with Memphis' motives, equated the trade to the franchise-shifting trade of Bellamy and Komives for the man named DeBusschere. (And Marc Gasol would become the 2013 Defensive Player of the Year in a delightful year for Memphis.)

Pau Gasol was an instant fit. Fisher, Phil's new Harper (who could also mediate between Kobe and Jackson when needed), would now be dishing off to the ever-hustling Renaissance man. At thirteen, Gasol wasn't playing pickup basketball in Catalonia; he was playing Tchaikovsky on the piano. The son of a medical doctor (his mother), he enrolled in med school at eighteen—a vocation that went by the wayside when he grew to seven feet. (In Los Angeles, in a few years, he would sit in on a pediatric surgery, as well as visit backstage with Placido Domingo.)

Jackson had the highest of hopes for his new, mobile, sure-handed big man. Most important, with a new backbone to this strange amalgam of a squad, Phil saw Odom start to feel more comfortable as a third, instead of second, option.

The first round of the playoffs brought Denver and Allen Iverson and Carmelo Anthony to town. Gasol's first playoff game produced 36 points, 16 rebounds, 8 assists and 3 blocks against the likes of Marcus Camby. The Lakers swept. Anthony accused his team of quitting. Funny how teams ousted by Jackson teams always bring out their finest whines.

(Coby played two minutes and recorded an assist, making the Karls the first father and son to ever face each other. Both had beaten cancer, but Coby would be the final cut the following October, to the dismay of a lot of Lakers fans. In Idaho over the next two years, he averaged 19 points, sneaking in three games for the Cavs and four for the Warriors before returning to Europe.)

Now Utah rolled in, then rolled out two games down. The Jazz took two at home, but back at Staples, Gasol and Odom (20 each) spurred a victory, and in Utah, the Lakers closed it out behind a Kobe show.

Next? A stunning 4–1 trouncing of the title-defending Spurs, including a 30-point rout of San Antonio in game two, in which Holzman's defense tattoo was applied: The Spurs scored just 71, only 14 in the fourth. They were 30 of 87 from the field.

Now, fittingly, the Celtics stood in the way, in their first final since 1987 . . . against Los Angeles. The hype was huge: two teams that had, in previous decades, defined the league. The chance for Jackson to pass Auerbach—maybe even in Boston. But the Celts possessed serious weaponry of all ages, from Ray Allen and Kevin Garnett to Paul Pierce and second-year man Rajon Rondo.

In game one, Pierce hit a bunch of key shots, then hurt his leg so badly colliding with Kendrick Perkins that he had to be wheeled to the locker room. Then he came back three minutes later to hit more shots that led to a Celtic victory. "Was Oral Roberts back there?" was Phil's reaction. No evangelists complained.

Game two saw Gasol and Odom struggle early, as did the Lakers' defense; after three, Los Angeles trailed by 21. Kobe seemed less than subtle about his dismay at his teammates' misses. The Lakers lost by 6.

Back in Los Angeles, Kobe took seven shots in the first quarter alone, but the Celtic scorers were ineffectual. Vujačić hit a key three with just under two to go, and it was 2–1. And that was all she wrote, for in game four, after leading 45–21, the Lakers folded the tent and gave up the biggest lead in finals history, allowed the Celtics subs ("the Bench Mob," a nickname for the times) to scrap, and lost the crucial fourth game, 97–91.

The Lakers took the fifth game, thanks to Bryant's steal off Pierce and subsequent dunk, which set the tone late in the game. "We wanted to go home," Doc Rivers said, holding his own in one-liner land. "We just didn't want to have to play."

But play they did, humiliating the Lakers, 131–92, in the least entrancing finals game in league history. Behind a 21-point performance by hobbling Rondo, the Celtics, in front of the likes of Bill Russell and John Havlicek, refused to let Jackson pass the ghost of Auerbach, which lit up a victory cigar somewhere in the reaches of the Celtics' new and dismayingly cookie-cutter arena, with its parquet floor seeming embarrassed by its surroundings.

But not as embarrassed as Phil. Which could only turn out to be a good thing.

TWENTY-EIGHT

O nly a romantic novelist would cite that day in Fargo a few months later as the bellwether, the happy augury, the laying of the foundation of the season that would vault Phil to the top. But to those of us looking for fanciful story lines, the dots must be connected.

Just before training camp, having been increasingly encumbered for forty years by real-world commercial entertainment demands, Philip Douglas Jackson turned back the clock.

It happened in his second non-basketball-related television appearance since his infamous CBS confessional six years earlier, but this time to a slightly smaller audience: channel 3 of Grand Forks' Midcontinent Communications cable television system. Witnessed by a few hundred cable watchers and by spectators in the half-empty Chester Fritz Auditorium at the University of North Dakota on the occasion of the university's annual convocation. In the heartland, star power remains irrelevant. Most of the folks in attendance would have been there if the speaker had been Grand Forks' deputy mayor.

This was as close as he'd ever get to the pulpit that always beckoned but could never get traction in Phil Jackson. On the 125th anniversary of the University of North Dakota's being granted a charter by the state, Jackson could try to educate not a dozen kids, but a generation. As Phil well knew, it was at just such a convocation that JFK had received his own doctorate in letters nearly half a century earlier.

A donor's private jet brought him in from Montana. He made no complaints about how uncool the jet was. He spent the morning touring the campus, was honored at the UND Indian Center and was given a beaded medallion in Lakers colors by the campus's Native Americans.

It was clear from the moment he strode down the aisle, single file with the school's faculty and administrators, that the bestowal of the state's highest academic award, voted not by some weird gumbo of sportswriters but by the high academic council of the state, had humbled the man.

Walking down the aisle with a slight limp to the somber tones of the Faculty Brass Quintet, behind a kid holding the mace, an ornately carved wooden staff, the baggy sleeves of his dark gray robe featured three diagonal black velvet stripes. Add the cap, and the effect was pure Henry VIII.

Jackson took his place onstage between the university president, Robert Kelley, to his right and the school's dean to his left. To her left sat the governor of North Dakota, John Hoeven. He did not look particularly sure of himself during the president's opening remarks; he kept smoothing his eyebrows. He looked old, wearied; no CBS makeup artists were on hand.

During the opening rendition of "God Bless America," as everyone stood, the president had to lean in and whisper to Phil, "Take off your hat," whereupon Jackson whipped it off with an embarrassed smile, to reveal anything but the glib Lakers look: The gray hair on the sides was unruly, and the nearly transparent thatch of wispy gray on top did nothing to hide the baldness of a sixty-three-year-old, weathered vet of a whole lot of peaceful wars.

"A recipient of an honorary degree," said Kelley, "reflects . . . an openness to the changing requirements of a diverse and complex world, and creativity and innovation through expression of a competitive and entrepreneurial spirit." Kelley then asked Jeanie Buss to stand. She was sitting out in the audience, next to the president's wife. When the camera found her, she seemed embarrassed. Equally cringey was the governor's quip: "After we award this doctorate, there's only going to be one Dr. Phil!" (Hoeven then called him "the first Sixth Man." Jackson tried to correct him; that honor would really have to go to one John Havlicek. Hoeven refused to take it back, and gave him a LUV ND license plate.)

Jackson took the podium holding his notes and faced the silence in the half-empty auditorium. He was about to turn and thank all the velvet robes, as protocol dictated, when a voice shouted out from the audience, "You gotta beat the Celtics!" For a second, you could tell that he was asking himself, *What to do? Follow the script or be Phil?* It was a no-brainer.

He smiled to the crowd. "Well, yeah, there's always that, isn't there?"

Then he opened with the third stanza of Housman's "To an Athlete Dying Young":

Smart lad, to slip betimes away
From fields where glory does not stay,
And early though the laurel grows
It withers quicker than the rose.

"I was three or four years out of basketball at that point," he said, "and I was seeing how quickly fame flees." Then he abbreviated a quote from the Danish philosopher Søren Kierkegaard—"Life is understood looking backward, but must *be lived looking forward*"—before offering a preface to his speech: "I want to take you on a little journey looking backwards to perhaps look forward."

It was typical Jacksonian conversation, ranging from Shropshire to Denmark. But where were the critical Los Angeles journalists who would have leaped at the chance to take off on his erudition? Or to at least see him in a more natural element? Not here in the outback. Anyway, if he *were* to say something outrageous, the chances of Grand Forks UND channel 3 releasing it to the wires were nil, as was the chance of some kid blogging out to the intertubes—not in North Dakota nice-land.

But he wasn't controversial. His body language, his expression, his nervousness all spoke of how long he'd been in the unreal world. Now the little kid was back among his Plains peeps, and he was not going to tall-poppy them. He was going to teach them how to question anything and everything, to never relinquish curiosity—the things he began his career believing in.

First he led the audience through a collage of the cultural tipping points that had opened his eyes to becoming a man on the outside looking in: "Little Rock. Birmingham. Joe McCarthy. Blacklist. Korea. H-bombs. Sputnik. *Catcher in the Rye.* The U-2 and Francis Gary Powers. Khrushchev. Castro. The Cuban Missile Crisis. Civil rights. The draft board." He evoked the somnolent, silent fifties, with "their customized sideburns, their customized cars, Elvis Presley. Their songs were"—and here he sang, to the crowd's delight, a slightly out of tune "How Much Is That Doggie in the Window?" before segueing into a stanza of Bob Dylan's lyrics from "My Back Pages, including its famous refrain,

> *Ah, but I was so much older then*
> *I'm younger than that now.*

In other words, unless you grow younger as you grow older, unless you keep exploring, you'll atrophy. He then cited the Beatles in a most interesting way: "Before the decade was over, they were singing about 'Lucy in the Sky with Diamonds.'" The man was willing to be younger than that now. Even if no one in the audience, the faculty or the administration got the reference to that acid trip back in Malibu, he did. It was as if, back in the haven of his youth, he was wishing for a wayback machine of his own, a mulligan, but he had to settle for trying to guide this generation.

"The overriding force that brought change about in those times," he said, was the fact "that issues that had been assumed to be right were challenged. Was Communism just evil for evil's sake? Or were the people of Vietnam willing and wanting to live under that kind of government? What was the justification for holding African Americans in disregard in one part of our country with Jim Crow laws when we'd fought a war one hundred years previous in part to free the slaves?"

He was on a roll. He was beginning to sound like one of the Chicago Seven rallying the Berkeley kids on Telegraph Avenue in 1967. "If a woman can do the same job as a man, why can't she be a fireman? Or a president? Those beliefs would change because light was brought to them. Change can happen swiftly. And gracefully."

The next citation? The voice he said he'd heard emerging from the "cacophony of voices": Maharishi Mahesh Yogi. "If ten percent of the world learned to meditate," he said, "the result would be peace on earth. . . . The Maharishi died this February sitting erect in the lotus position, peaceful at ninety-one, never seeing the fulfillment of that message. But the flame still burns with us today."

Then he paused and said, "Give peace a chance."

It was as if he were giving an intro, unashamedly, simplistically but lucidly, to Sixties 101. Because it wasn't being covered by KTLA or the *Times* and he didn't have to measure his words, he could publicly measure his heart, maybe to remind himself of what used to be burning at his core: Abbie, not Armani.

"Some of us went to Vietnam; some came back. Some became teachers, businessmen, but we all shared this desire to make our world better." Of course, it didn't work. "We grew up; we became parents. Then Madison Avenue co-opted our nerve and verve, and took us into slogans that embraced Levi's, and we drank Coca-Cola.

"[Then] a hopeful president [Carter], who spoke to humanitarian needs of our world, was being [considered] too soft to lead this country, and we moved back from embracing the world to confronting it. Then the decade of 'Me' came—and we enjoyed the process of eating at the trough of wealth.

"But family [read Sioux, Patroons, Bulls and Lakers as well as wives and children] became a dominant force in our lives. 'Teach your children well.' I hope we did. Now our children have grown, we've grown, we've become grandparents, and we've seen the circle of life almost completed.

"I hope I can share with you a few things: One: One group can be a strong voice in this country. Your youth, your group, can change the world. Two: Things that are big, like civil rights and war protests, have influences. Great influences. But it's the influence of the local interest group that's the strongest voice. If you want peace, start with yourself. Last: When issues appear that seem overwhelming, shed a little light on the problem."

But then, for his kicker, it got even better. As fortuitous timing would have it, he had a current political cause to weigh in on: the Fighting Sioux symbol. At the time, the NCAA was demanding that the school lose the mascot or be fined prohibitive amounts of bucks. The emblem of the whole controversy was the Ralph—a quarter-million-dollar Taj Mahal of hockey, built and paid for just over a decade before, a few blocks away, by the late casino-mogul alumnus Ralph Engelstad, who intentionally had his architects embed hundreds of Sioux symbols in the place as a protest, so that if the NCAA actually threatened the school with sanctions, they'd be unable to unembed those symbols in the floors and walls.

Phil had seen the Ralph for himself that morning, pronouncing it more glamorous than Staples, with its two home locker rooms and a kitchen for the players, its cherrywood seats, its marble floors . . . and the two huge Sioux-nation flags at the north end.

And thus did Phil have his cause. "I have been asked by tribal friends to speak out against the misnomer, the Fighting Sioux—our nickname for forty-five years. What is the peaceful solution to this dilemma? I think we all know through our political—through *your* political—consciousness that an objectification of people is limiting to ourselves and to the people we objectify. If they are two percent of the population, they are a minority unable to bring strength to their own cause. Money and donations can't make this issue right or justified.

"So I submit in this year of change being bandied about by all these presidential candidates, we have a chance to embrace change in a cycle of life. Above my desk in L.A., I have a quote attributed to the Buddha: 'Unceasing change turns the wheel of life so we may experience life in all its many forms. Peaceful dwelling in the midst of change brings sentient beings great joy.'

"This is one turn of the wheel I never expected. I never in my wildest dreams expected this was possible. But accepting this honor with great joy, I just want to thank you and accept it, and I want to ask you one favor: Please don't call me Dr. Phil."

Standing O. He quietly took his seat.

Postscript: Any chance for saving the symbol died when, three years later, one of the two Sioux nations in North Dakota voted to let UND keep the symbol and the nickname but the other refused to put it to a referendum, effectively killing the deal. A statewide referendum voted to put the Sioux to rest, and thus did it happen. No more Sioux merchandising. No more Sioux symbols on uniforms. And while the Fighting Sioux is officially a thing of the past, as a motel clerk told me, "To anyone in North Dakota, they'll always be the Fighting Sioux."

TWENTY-NINE

Having channeled his Mast/Walk–era self, Jackson had a team for the final act as balanced as it had ever been. With Pau starting, Odom could come off the bench and do his thing, as could multitooled Ariza. Vlad was healthy (after separating his shoulder snowboarding during the all-star break the year before) and was now a starter—another guy who knew how to pass, shoot and defend, as in game one, in which the Lakers allowed the Blazers 76 points.

They were missing a key starter, though. Tex, in failing health since 2007, would be with the team as a consultant, two weeks per month, then retire at the end of the year. No one was saying, "Win one for Winter," but that'd make a good subplot for the year of ring ten.

The highlight of the 2008–09 regular season came on Christmas, when, in Nielsen-rating heaven, they met the Celtics for the first time since the previous spring. Thanks to a few moments in which Pau scored seven straight, Jackson won his 1,000th, in his 1,423rd game, breaking the record for quickest to a grand held by Pat Riley . . . who'd done it in his 1,434th. Revenge is indeed best served cold.

The victory also snapped the Celts' record nineteen-game winning streak. "It's amazing," Rivers said of Phil's feat. "He's one of the greatest coaches of all time." (Of course, Doc could be gracious; he'd stomped Jackson's five.)

They were meshing: European ball, team ball, Fisher the new wise mind. Even Bynum seemed to be settling down. Not that Kobe would allow himself to be overshadowed: On February 2, in the Garden—as opposed to, say, EnergySolutions Arena—he scored 61 against the Knicks. Eight days later, they were 42-10. They clinched the division less than a month after the all-star game. When it was over, they'd had all of four back-to-back losses, never losing more than two in a row. They finished at 65-17, third best in franchise history.

As the 72-10 team in '86 was to Jackson's first NBA act, this would be his Los Angeles moment. Yes, his first L.A. team won more games, but it was with Shaq at his peak, Kobe on fire, Harper at quarterback and A.C. bringing back the Showtime energy.

But coachingwise? This was late-era Jackson's finest hour, considering that the Western Conference was the stronger league conference. First up? The outmatched Jazz. The Lakers won two of the first three, then scored 40 in the second quarter of game three, and that was it.

Adelman's Rockets shocked the Lakers in game one, but the Lakers took two of the next three, took a 3–1 lead in a laughable 118–78 rout, back-slid, then closed it out in seven at Staples with the perfect Jackson formula: on offense, four starters in double figures (Kobe took just 12 shots while dealing out 5 assists) and a lockdown defense: Houston scored 12 points in the first quarter. The final was 89–70.

Then on to George Karl's Nuggets, who'd won the Northwest Division behind unmellow 'Melo, Allen Iverson and Chauncey Billups. Denver scrapped to take game two at Staples because Phil had no answer for the 16-point off-the-bench mastery of 'Melo's backup, the immortal Linas Kleiza, a Lithuanian who had refined his craft at a Christian Academy in Maryland. The perfect NBA lab rat, Linas once scored 41 points in a game. Once.

But after a split in Denver, the Lakers won the fifth in Staples, and then back in Denver, behind Kobe, Gasol and Ariza's 17, the Lakers closed it out. Jackson was one more series from history.

★

If only it could have been the Auerbachsters! When Doc's 62-20 Celts drew a .500 Bulls team in the first round, you could see it coming: number

ten earned on the Celtics' home court, Auerbach's ghost, having material-
ized on the end of the bench, disappearing in a flash of sulfurous cigar
smoke.

But in the Eastern semifinals, the Magic pulled some magic out of Stan
Van Gundy's mustache. Trailing 3–2, Orlando won the sixth at home, and
then in the final—in Boston, yet—Pierce and Rondo went 8 for 23 while
the streaky Türkoğlu hit 9 of 12 for the Disneys. The legit Van Gundy's
unknowns seemed to be on a mission of their own. Rivers had been outcoached.

Orlando headed for Cleveland, where LeBron's (and technically coach
Mike Brown's) 66-16 Cavs, having dismissed Detroit and Atlanta in *eight
straight,* were ready to swat the Mouse out of the way, setting up an all-ego
finals: LeBron versus Bryant.

Dwight Howard spoiled the story line. The Magic snatched the first
game on the road. In the final two games, young LeBron, for whom the
fourth quarter in pressure games was still an albatross, was 19 of 44 from
the field. Howard had 40 points in each. Chalk it up to Mike Brown's inability to teach his child well.

We'll never know if Pau and Bynum and Jackson could've handled
the King.

We do know that, in the first game of the finals against Orlando, with
Phil facing an actual Van Gundy, no one could handle Kobe. In one stretch,
he scored 30—while the Magic scored 22. He singlehandedly snatched the
game. Well, when you're on, you're on.

With the Lakers' defense swarming him, Dwight managed 12. The
final score? An emphatic 100–75, followed by the inevitable letdown two
days later; the Magic were actually about to tie it when rookie shooting
guard Courtney Lee eluded Bryant to go in for the winning layup.

Maybe the lights reflected off Kanye's sunglasses at courtside. Maybe
the kid made the mistake of looking over at Jack Nicholson.

It rolled out. The Lakers won in OT. Hollow-point bullet dodged.

Game three was played in Amway Arena. The Magic shot an unheard-
of 75 percent from the field. But they couldn't pull away. Their grappling

108–104 victory was Pyrrhic; they escaped because Bryant missed some clutch shots at the end. The confetti fell on the Amway floor with two seconds remaining and the maintenance guys had to try to clean it up—not a good omen for the Mouse.

The good omen for Orlando was Howard, growing in fast-forward. In game four, with Howard going nuts—9 blocks! 21 rebounds!—none of his teammates stepped up to help him out. The other starting four shot under 30 percent. Still, the Magic led by 12 at the half, and with forty-five seconds left and the Magic holding an 87–82 lead, the series was all but tied—until Gasol hit a jump shot, Howard clanked two foul shots, Fisher called a time-out, Jackson pulled off a great move and Stan Van Gundy pulled a Gumby.

The details: Jackson decided to take the ball out in the backcourt instead of at half-court; it'd take the Magic longer to commit the inevitable foul . . . but Van Gundy decided not to foul, a decision that, he later said, "will haunt me forever." Bryant got the inbound pass from Fisher, shuffled it to Ariza, who got it back to Fisher, who in Paxsonesque fashion was wide open. The three tied it. In OT, it was a rout: 99–91 Lakers.

Back in Staples, it was all over but the confetti. A showmanlike dunk by Kobe at 36–31 led to a convincing run, and a majestic, floating, off-balance Bryant jumper led to a second run in the second half. In the end, it was fitting that Kobe was the MVP: "I was locked in a zone." The final was 99–86.

Auerbach was a second-place coach. Jackson's postgame comment? Pitch-perfect. High praise for his mentor and a dig at the old nemesis: "I'll smoke a cigar tonight for Red."

Bryant's quotes? Typically tin-eared. All about him. "I don't have to hear that idiotic criticism anymore," he said. "That's the biggest thing. I don't have to hear that stuff anymore. . . . L.A. is brutal, man. Now when I go to Disneyland, I can enjoy the moment. I don't have to answer questions about, 'What the hell happened?'"

The bottom line of the playoffs? Pau: 60 percent from the field, 120 shots in eleven games. Rebounding, defending, hustling, passing, weaving, loving the flow. A big man who, like his coach, played so that all of the skills were just part of a team game: move, pass, get open, shoot. Defend. Play basketball. Was he as tough as Phil had been? No. Was this a problem? Not yet.

THIRTY

Jackson's 2009 roster featured an intriguing and challenging new addition. To the average fan, the name Ron Artest was synonymous with "everything that's wrong with this league." Childhood friends with Odom in New York, he'd seen a teammate stabbed with a broken table leg—and later die—during a YMCA tournament in the city.

Krause drafted him the year after Jackson's departure. Under Tim Floyd, this proved to be a bad fit. But not an ugly one. That was with Indiana, when five years later, in the Palace at Auburn Hills, as a Pacer, he instigated what the Associated Press called "the most infamous brawl in NBA history." After he and immovable object Ben Wallace had gotten into a shoving match that resulted in an on-court brawl, while the refs were figuring out how to penalize everyone, Ron laid himself out on the scorer's table and ostentatiously put on a pair of headphones as if to give a live interview to Pacers broadcasters, at which point, in quick succession . . .

Wallace threw a headband at him, a fan lobbed a cup of Diet Coke on him and Ron sprang into the crowd looking for the culprit. The radio guy trying to hold him back got stepped on and suffered five fractured vertebrae. Pacer Stephen Jackson followed Artest into the stands and began hitting people. Fans went onto the court. In the stands, two fought with Artest, who punched on as Jermaine O'Neal (college: none) tried to attack another fan. O'Neal seemed propelled with such violent intent that Scot

Pollard later said he was afraid that O'Neal would kill the guy. Fortunately O'Neal slipped.

After the game, the police tried to board the Pacers' bus, unsuccessfully. Nine spectators were injured. Sixteen games into the next season, Ron demanded a trade, which landed him in Cowtown—the desertion pissing off all the guys who'd been fined for having his back the prior season.

He received just one suspension in Sacramento, for a flagrant foul in the playoffs, before going to Houston, where Yao said he hoped that Ron was through fighting people, whereupon Ron said that he understood why the center would say that, but as he told the *Houston Chronicle,* "I'm never going to change my culture. I don't think he's ever played with a black player that really represents his culture as much as I [do]."

A free agent, he now signed in Los Angeles and changed his number to 37, because it was the number of weeks Michael Jackson's *Thriller* was number-one on the album charts.

A notable sag encumbered the visible Jackson by now. With arthritic hips and knees, his body inevitably and increasingly slumping ever since the fusion operation, he would sit on the sideline on an orthopedic padded chair that only enhanced how much taller he appeared to be than the coaches around him: more fodder for critics who mistakenly saw this as an attempt to elevate himself. The truth was, he wanted to lessen the pain in his body, the better to coach his team. Besides: It had never been his style to jump up and meet the players coming off for a time-out or a break; that was the role of the coaches. His role was to look at you as you came to the sideline, assess your body language and intuit what your frame of mind was. "You get all these coaches in the game now, strutting their stuff," says Jim Cleamons, "trying to show the people how in charge they are. It's full of malarkey. You coach the team in practice, then you play the game like you played it in practice, and you practice like you play. If you want to wait till game time to turn it on, it's bull."

★

And yet if you can be off-kilter after winning 23 of 27, the Lakers were; they went a very mortal 23-14 over the next stretch. Kobe's MVP had seemingly gone to his head. By mid-March, Fisher was asking for more equitable "shot distribution," and Odom was saying, "Our aura comes off as soft right now," after the Raptors—the Raptors!—were trash-talking the Lakers in a game in which L.A. had barely beaten Toronto: "A couple of dudes talking to me," Odom went on, "if I'd talked to Charles Oakley like that, I would have been smacked in the face."

Other teams, Odom said, were "too confident" against them. "Now, at this point in the season, teams are like, 'Yeah, we can beat the Lakers.'" Odom was no inspirer; they went 10-7 the rest of the way.

Bryant was hurting: ankle, finger, a months-long troublesome knee. So Jackson made an unusual executive decision: Let the mamba sit out practices for the playoffs. The first time he'd favored a player to accommodate him as a special case was Edwin Pellot-Rosa, in Isabela in 1984, his all-star; if he showed up hungover, Phil would let him sleep through practice. Now Kobe could rest. And it would pay off.

These playoffs featured not one, but two Jackson controversies: a minor and a major, tasty chum for the sharks who'd long suspected his un-subtle idiosyncrasies to be a self-serving act. The first was just a verbal misstep. He dissed the refs as sucking up to Oklahoma City's Kevin Durant; they'd sent him to the line 26 times in two games. "I think a lot of the referees are treating him like a superstar," Phil said of the budding superstar. Larry Brown says it? A slap. But Phil? A $35,000 fine—with the implied threat of a possible suspension if his bitching were to continue one . . . more . . . step.

In the short run, his bark proved worth it, and then some. In the next game, in Staples, Durant went to the line only six times. The Lakers held the Thunder to 34 first-half points and won the series in six.

(Bottom line on ref-baiting during the Jackson career? "He wasn't a pain in the ass at all," Stern told me with a laugh. "He was Phil. Phil dances to the beat of his own inner drummer, which reflects his experience, his wisdom and his being. There have been some . . . disparate times, yes, because I'm the commissioner and he's the coach, and usually in some institutionally defined disciplinary scenario . . . but always in a good-natured way.")

Jackson's decision to rest Bryant proved a wise one; the Lakers, now in a groove, swept Jerry Sloan's Jazz in four. But then as Phil's band of brothers readied to take on the powerful Suns, things got decidedly weirder. Ever intrigued by national politics but occasionally impolitic, Jackson thrust his high-profile profile into very sensitive ground. Phil critics were ready to pounce.

In their previous round, the Suns, in sympathy with opponents of Arizona's strict anti-immigration policies, wore jerseys that said Los Suns. During a discussion about his future with the Lakers, a columnist asked Jackson about the jerseys. "Am I crazy," he asked, "or am I the only one that heard [the Arizona state legislature] say, 'We just took the United States immigration law and adapted it to our state? Gave it some teeth to be able to enforce it'?" His defining summation? "I don't think teams should get involved in the political stuff."

Aha! We knew it! The whole counterculture thing was a self-serving charade! "Boycott Phil Jackson," read the headline atop David Zirin's column in *The Nation*. Websites sparked into wildfires, calling him a racist. Protests outside Staples were peaceful but forceful. Fifteen local high-school students had their say. Even Al "Causes R Me" Sharpton tried to muscle into the spotlight.

When President Obama said in his Cinco de Mayo address, "I know that a lot of you would rather be watching tonight's game, the Spurs against Los Suns," the battle lines had been drawn: United States v. Phil.

Jackson's reply was measured: "I've been involved in a number of progressive political issues over the years, and I support those who stand up for their beliefs. It is what makes this country great. I have respect for those who oppose the new Arizona immigration law, but I am wary of putting entire sports organizations in the middle of political controversies. This was the message of my statement. I know others feel differently, even in the Lakers organization, but it was a personal statement. In this regard, it is my wish that this statement not be used by either side to rally activists."

Perhaps relevant, perhaps not: Six weeks earlier, down in border Cochise County, rancher Bob Krentz, who had a spread at the foot of the eleven-thousand-foot Chiricahua Mountains, was murdered. Krentz was known to be a Good Samaritan to illegals crossing his land; in 1999, in an interview with PBS after his home had been robbed, he'd said, "If they come ask for water, I'll still give them water."

The mountain passes were known as a drug channel. On March 26, Krentz's brother had stopped eight immigrants bringing more than 200 pounds of marijuana into Arizona. He had them arrested, and the drug was confiscated. The following day, Krentz was on his ATV at ten thirty in the morning when he called his brother and said, "I see an immigrant out here, and he appears to need help. Call the Border Patrol."

The patrol found Krentz dead. His rifle had not been taken off its rack. His dog had also been shot and later died. Police dogs tracked the apparent killer's trail back to the Mexican border. Days earlier, a 9mm Glock pistol had been stolen from a home in a nearby town. The bullet that killed Krentz, as well as the one that killed his dog, was a 9mm.

The morning of Jackson's controversial afternoon interview, the Associated Press had reported that law-enforcement sources had confirmed that the killer had been Mexican. If Jackson had read the paper that morning, he would have read that story, including the fact that the dog had been shot. A dog like Phil and June's old dog, whose death Phil and June had memorialized with a candlelight ceremony in Woodstock.

Jackson's statements were was popularly misread as the expression of a man talking for a team; after all, he led the team, so this was a Laker talking, right? No. Even a shallow study of Jackson's un-PC spouts shows that he never spoke for his team; it was always just Phil, the shoot-from-the-hip guy who'd told Cal Ramsay in 1971 that he was into "the occult."

Nor was this the biased screed of a "graying boomer," as one national columnist put it. They were words whose subtext was clear: Sport's power can be a very dangerous thing—as he'd learned the last time he'd used the NBA as a political forum, when he wore a Bradley pin in his lapel until the NBA told him to remove it. Since then? No political pronouncements, until now.

"It's interesting that Phil is not on the record politically, is he?" Diane Mast offered. "His politics are silent everywhere except the Bradley campaign. While the rest of us get into civil rights, women's rights, Nixon and Watergate, Phil finds a piece of peace in Lakota reservations, teaching basketball warriors amid sacred smoke and sweat lodges. Politics was not his thing."

But to the press, this was just another example of Phil seemingly deceiving us. The man was accused of everything from bias to obfuscation. "Frankly, Jackson's reputation as one of the NBA's deep thinkers has always seemed to me to owe more than a little to his impenetrably baroque syntax," wrote the *Times*'s Tim Rutten. "Take the time to untangle his sentences and what emerges usually ranges from the banal to the incomprehensible. Like the players in his fabled adaptation of Tex Winter's triangle offense, meaning is constantly, and elusively, in motion when Phil does the talking."

Wait. What's unclear about the statement "I am wary of putting entire sports organizations in the middle of political controversies"? What *is* clear is that if the writer was trying to imply that Phil was biased in any way, after a life spent (a) championing the rights of Native Americans and (b) winning basketball games by making disenfranchised African Americans love him, then he couldn't have been farther off base.

Which is not to suggest that Jackson was wise in opening the can of worms. Holzman would have kept it to "Why in the world are you asking me about politics?"

★

The Celtics had clinched their division a week after the Lakers had clinched theirs. With Pierce, Garnett, Ray Allen and Rondo all steeled in postseason pressure, they summarily dismissed Mike Brown's Cavs, who had won 11 more regular-season (i.e., nonpressure) games than the Celtics but, as had become a Mike Brown/LeBron James custom, folded under the postseason glare. The Celts then stomped the Magic, despite finishing with 9 fewer wins than Orlando, when they broke to a 3–0 lead by making sure Dwight was harassed into ineffectuality.

The finals would feature the new-school Lakers (a "finesse" team, according to Garnett) against the team Jackson was quoted characterizing as "roughhouse"—no doubt trying to get the refs oriented toward the Left Coast in advance. Whatever works, right?

In the first game, at Staples, Artest and Pierce wrestled within the first thirty seconds, both earning Ts, and a dynamic had immediately been established. As Teddy Roosevelt once said, to earn global peace, you have to "speak softly and carry a big stick." Artest had served notice: We have the talent, and we carry a stick.

In that opener, Gasol outplayed Kevin Garnett on both ends of the floor. Maybe he knew what this one meant to Phil. The Celts attempted a comeback, but in the fourth, when Artest blocked Big Baby Glen Davis, and Gasol dunked a few seconds later, the notice was served. The Lakers beat the Irish imposters in the first game, 102–89.

Two days later, Ray Allen hit his first seven three-pointers, set up by the maturing Rondo, and Doc Rivers's Celtics won by 9, whereupon Pierce foolishly pronounced that the series "ain't coming back to L.A."

But Fisher, now thirty-five, went into overdrive. He hounded Ray Allen into an 0-for-13 evening and made 5 of his 7 field goals in the fourth quarter—including a play in which, on a one on five, he decided, "What the hell," drove for a layup, made the basket and got fouled by Big Baby. Game over.

Wisdom had beaten youth. Decades ago, in Auerbach's steam-heat-radiator arena, it never would have happened. But these were new times.

Red had departed the quick, and his team was not nearly as quick as his old teams had been.

In game four, Big Baby and Nate Robinson convinced Rivers to keep the second unit on for most of the second half, combining for 30 points; when an ungainly big man and deft runt find a vibe outside the proscribed game plan, there's no way to defend it. Doc let the river run, and the series was tied at 2-2.

Game five turned out to be a Jackson nightmare. At one point Kobe scored 23 consecutive Lakers points—as Boston's lead went from 1 to 9. When it was over, it was 92–86, Celtics. Red's ghost followed the series out to L.A.—Red Holzman's. In game six, the Lakers held the Celtics to an unthinkable 31 points in the first half. Gasol hardened up and, tired of being flipped around by the other big guys, came up one assist short of a triple double, 17-13-9.

Artest threw elbows, and at one point, though illegally, Bynum knocked Kendrick Perkins out of the universe. Score: 89–67!

The next morning, before shootaround, Phil led his team through their longest meditation of the year. But when the game began, Bryant didn't pause to even take a breath. He started out 5 for 21. The Lakers were missing layups. They trailed 23–14 after one. They whittled it to 40–34.

But minutes into that pivotal third quarter, the Celtics used a 9–2 run to go up by 13. There was no time left to let them dig themselves out by themselves. Jackson called a twenty-second time-out. It worked. Bryant hit a couple of shots, Gasol converted two free throws, Odom had a tip-in and the third quarter ended 57—53, whereupon it was old man Fisher who addressed the team. The message? In essence, "Breathe. Just breathe."

Fisher hit an early three to tie it at 64. Another Bryant three and a lot of free throws gave them a 6-point lead with 1:30 remaining. Rasheed Wallace hit a three, but then the Peace Man hit a three, and that was the dagger. Allen hit a three, but Gasol rebounded Kobe's next miss and sent it back to Bryant, whereupon a Wallace foul sent Kobe to the line for two. Rondo hit a three, but the Celtics had to foul Sasha, who made both.

The war of attrition ended at 83–79. For Jackson watchers, this was not only the ring that made it all inarguable (*two* more than Auerbach), but it also came at the expense of the team he'd been bred since 1967 to dislike and still grumbled about, as any Knick forever would. For old Knick god Ned Irish's team, and ever since, no victory was ever as sweet as a stomping of the pompous Celtics, the greatness of Russell notwithstanding. As Luke Epplin recently wrote for the *Atlantic* about "Casey at the Bat," "Casey's downfall illustrates the enduring sports dictum that arrogance, both on and off the playing field, should never go unpunished." To Knicks fans—and to Jackson folk—Casey/Auerbach had been struck out.

Number eleven was the ultimate Jackson victory. As had always been the case with every ring, a ceremony ensued—this time in a small, spare locker room after the final whistle, where he gathered with family . . . including his former wife, June, wearing the same pair of "champagne slippers" she'd worn at every finals. Surrounded by their children. A decade after their divorce.

If a man is judged not by ego, not by victory, but by the company he keeps, the presence of the woman who'd remained his close friend for four decades now, here in a Buss building, spoke a whole lot of words.

THIRTY-ONE

For the purpose of this story line, it would be wonderful to be able to say that a few weeks later, when Phil the orator gave another sermon about the things in which he truly believed, freed of packs of digital recorders and tape recorders and notebooks and TV lights to whom he had to give meaningless answers to meaningless questions, this speech augured well for not only the following basketball season—the extra one, the one he'd agreed at Jerry Buss's imploring to oversee—but also for his own future post-hoop. New branches, new directions, new ways to change the world about which he'd been so curious were soon to beckon.

It didn't. But we're getting ahead of ourselves.

Standing at the podium of the Whitefish Performing Arts Center in Whitefish, Montana, thirty miles from his place on Flathead, giving the keynote speech at the hundredth annual Western Governors' Association meeting, Jackson's bold-faced audience included the likes of New Mexico governor Bill Richardson, Montana governor Brian Schweitzer and Colorado governor Bill Ritter: men in charge of the new American fracking West that was slowly destroying Phil Jackson's ancient Native American homeland.

If there were ever a time to deliver a meaningful manifesto, dealing from experiential strength, it was on this day when, despite a few more years in age since the UND convocation speech, he stood and spoke more confidently.

"This is really the place where I've always been, it seems like," he told his distinguished spectators. "I think [Flathead] is totally what's been able to sustain the energy I've had for [each] coming year: to come up here, grow a beard, let my hair down and sit around and not have to do anything. Not have to put a suit on, not put a tie on and just enjoy life."

There's the suit thing again: the still-unresolved duality of the naturalist climbing ice cliffs in Woodstock versus the man doing his job every night a few feet from Jack Nicholson and Kanye West and Snoop Dogg and Adam Sandler.

"It's a connected world, and one of the great things about living up here is cutting off and disconnecting from all those things," he said. . . . "Stop and look at what's here, and what about this nature that's so fragile and yet so harsh and beautiful."

Then, pressed about his desire to continue coaching, when it was now in the balance, Jackson told his audience, "Actually, I have a couple more rings as a player, so I guess thirteen is the natural number—which is a hard number to stop at when you think about it."

He smiled. The crowd applauded. (He'd forgotten Albany again. But then, the CBA couldn't afford rings. But it's too bad that, a quarter century later, he'd forgotten Lowes Moore and Derrick Rowland and Ralph McPherson and Frankie Jumpshot.)

But his subsequent words did say worlds about his past, present and future: a permanent mooring on Flathead, his parents interred across the lake. "I want my children's children to have the same experience that they've had on Flathead Lake, in this world, in this Western life that we so graciously think we are entitled to.

"We call this place 'the last best place on Earth,' but we don't know how long it's going to last," he said, from the metaphoric pulpit, infused with confidence. "It's changed so much in my lifetime. I'm a little bit afraid of what it's going to be like for my children's children." They sounded like the words of a man who might be getting close to making that decision about what to do with his remaining years. Thinking about the good he'd have done if he'd been in Bill Bradley's cabinet or taken a teaching job at, say, Valley City Teachers College.

And now he began to channel Charles and Elisabeth Jackson's son. He shifted into proselytizing gear. "Our government has to take away the money from corporate farming and put it back into local. We have to be able to feed ourselves here. Not have to go and have all these headquarters that are shipping food out to places. I've been coming back for almost forty years. It was my idea that, as I raised a family, my children should know what the West was like, what it meant to me, what it meant to be out of a metropolitan area, and what it meant to be part of the land. I felt that you had to *be* there. You had to be on the ground."

You had to be grounded. What was it Diane Mast had said about what the Buddha did when asked where enlightenment was? He'd pointed at the ground.

THIRTY-TWO

t was too bad he didn't stay grounded in Montana. It was too bad Buss had talked him into one more year. For now, back on the court, he couldn't get Pau to power up. Or Bynum. Or maybe himself.

As tends to happen in real-life epics, as opposed to novels, the denouement, to borrow from T. S. Eliot, would come "not with a bang but a whimper." If the Lakers had still been playing in the Forum, the two-faced Roman god Janus would have been the symbol for Jackson's final year. Despite retaining the players who mattered, winning just two fewer than the season before and clinching on March 20, the season felt atilt from the start.

A three-game losing streak, including an embarrassing rout at the hands of LeBron's Heat on Christmas Day, left them at 21-10. Wins came in clusters, but the three-game losing streak that included a 20-point loss to the Bobcats in February was an apt barometer of how, on this team, the old Kobe-esque imbalance had thrown a wrench into the works. A slice of a story on ESPNLA's website in mid-March spoke worlds. Hodges, the shooting coach, allowed writer Dave McMenamin to watch a game with him. On one play, a Kobe pass was picked off, and he didn't hustle back. McMenamin asked Hodges if "any player stands up to Kobe when he does something detrimental to the team."

"No," Hodges replied. "Not one. They all kiss his ass."

★

In the playoffs, after the second game of a 4–2 opening-series dissection of New Orleans, the *Times* ran a sort of Dewey-beats-Truman headline:

"Lakers' Andrew Bynum Has Grown Up and Grown Healthy—and Just in Time." Because now came the worst possible coda to Jackson's epic run: the series that no one who likes the man or likes to hate him will ever forget, against Rick Carlisle's Mavs.

It wasn't just the play that was ugly. It was the coach who, for the first time since Albany, boiled over. Down 2–0, during a time-out after an ugly couple of minutes in the third game, Phil vehemently berated Gasol; while no words could be heard on the television screen, with raw, uncompassionate anger etched on his face he threw a backhand slap at Gasol's chest. The big man looked stunned and bewildered.

The slap was ugly, but it was nothing compared to the next game . . . in which the Lakers gave up. With the Mavs up 100–68, Dallas's J. J. Barea went up for a layup. As he stretched his right arm high to lay the ball in, Bynum, standing under him, slammed his right elbow up into Barea's exposed underarm so violently that, as Barea fell to the floor, it would not have been surprising to learn that his shoulder had been knocked out of its socket.

On the replay, play-by-play man Mike Breen barked to a national television audience, "Oh! Look at that! That's one of the most bush-league things I've ever seen in a game! That's disgusting!"

He was speaking for all of us. It wasn't a flagrant foul. It was felonious. It could have easily ended Barea's career.

And then, in a final image of ignominy, when he was ejected, Bynum tore off his jersey to display a bare-chested, mindless, ugly, immature and decidedly un-Zen-like gesture of defiance to the Dallas crowd. Jackson had entirely lost control of his team. He had come to the end of this particular path.

"Everything that could possibly go wrong went wrong with that game," he told Stephen Rodrick of *Men's Journal* in 2013. "I realized that the forces against you sometimes are just overwhelming: home-court advantage, the right time and the right place for the team that won the championship. All those things were there for them." He called the ending "incomprehensible." "[But] at the end of the game, or somewhere in the last two minutes, I was able to just breathe through it and go into that area that you go into that you learn through meditation: 'Oh yes, I recognize this. This is life. This is how life goes, and these are the things that are right, and there's no reason to rail against it; this is OK.' So that was it."

A backlash had to ensue, and that it came from Scot Pollard, one of the most outspoken players of the era—and a King in the "Cowtown" days—was hardly surprising, even if he was three years out of the game. "Put him in charge of the Kings this year . . . on a team with no Hall-of-Famers on it, at least no one that has established themselves as a Hall-of-Famer already . . . put him as head coach of the Cleveland Cavaliers right now, and let's see how he does next year," Pollard said. "That's all I'm saying. He has never taken a team that wasn't a playoff team and turned them into a playoff team."

★

Yes, as Randy Newman sang, "It's lonely at the top." But he'd achieved the top: for his own Red and for himself. He'd passed the pompous Auerbach in his own Red's name.

He'd come into a transient city to raise Bryant from virtual childhood. He had endured ownership's schizophrenia.

As Jerry Garcia would have put it, he survived.

How?

The man had "found peace," says A. C. Green now—a man who knows from peace. "If you're successful with your own peace, then you can find energy in other places—spiritually, physically, emotionally. He'd found it all on that last part of his quest. He was a heck of a coach anyway, but you have to have some balance in your life to be that successful. And by then I think he'd found it."

Had he? In 2001, a Harvard Med School psychiatrist named George

Vaillant published a book called *Aging Well*. He'd inherited the results of two studies that had tracked the physical and emotional well-being of 824 men and women of all social strata from childhood to old age. His goal was to find out what made a happy old person happy and what made an unhappy old person unhappy. With such a large sample, it's safe to say that Dr. Vaillant's findings are as close to true social science as you can get.

He came up with predictors that contradict a lot of conventional wisdom. For example, low cholesterol at fifty does not necessarily correlate with happiness and healthiness at eighty. But the choices you make in life do. And here are four of his major takeaways of the common traits among those who were on top of the world in their later years.

1. They had one long-standing relationship with one partner. Phil doesn't make that cut by definition, but the fact that June could party with him in the Staples Club after ring number eleven, along with Jeanie, speaks pretty highly of him (and of her).

2. At some point, Vaillant's happiest oldsters had veered away from the professional path they'd taken, but not radically. Phil's going from coach to his current role as unofficial consultant (to the inevitable front-office job) fits that bill.

3. After achieving success in their chosen field, they'd relinquished their egos, intuiting that there comes a time in life when "being world-class should no longer be the issue." This one is tough to translate into the world of professional sports, where if you don't want to be the best, as long as you're part of a team in any capacity, you have no business being in the field. Moreover, Phil had been teaching for years already. But he'd hardly put aside the ego. He still had to be world-class.

4. The inevitable serious illness was no more than a speed bump. It did not define their character. Phil's prostate silence scores very high on that one, though asterisked by much talk in his own books of his bad knee, heart and hips.

And then there was Freud, some years earlier, who definitely had it right when he said that the only two things we must have in life are love and work. Not love *of* work. Not love *or* work. Love *and* work. Phil had both.

Of course, the peace did not last. A man trying to live on a revolving wheel of change could hardly expect that it would.

Phil was off to Montana again, but no one expected that this would be the final act. The Lakers hadn't triumphed after his last departure and surely wouldn't this time amid a Staples transition that represented one of the greatest Q-rating downgrades in entertainment history. They hired Mike Brown, who had led the Cavs to four consecutive winning seasons, one finals and a 61-21 season the year before in Quicken Loans Arena. But Brown didn't seem to have a clue, given a LeBron, on how to get a player to sublimate the ego for the good of the team.

Once the Cavs let him go, his next gig was as an assistant at the Lee Burneson Middle School in Westlake, Ohio, where his kid played. Then suddenly he was in Staples.

"Jimmy [Buss] has that old Krause thing—organizations win championships, not coaches," Charley Rosen says now. "He was tired of 'Phil, Phil, Phil.' And let's not forget that they got rid of Riley because the players—Magic—thought he was taking too much credit, right? Same with Phil.

"So Mike Brown had a great record at Cleveland because of giving the ball to LeBron, but Jimmy hired him because Jimmy loves numbers. Brown is a shitty coach. His time-outs were useless. His practices were too long. He made no adjustments in games or between games. He doesn't know what he's doing. His players ridiculed him behind his back, laughed at him. He couldn't stand up to LeBron, and Kobe did the same thing to him. Then he brings in Eddie Jordan to do the Princeton offense—and now you have an assistant knowing more about the offense than the head? A disaster."

In fairness, had Stern not vetoed the trade that would have brought Chris Paul to town, which could have created one of the most electric backcourts in history, who knows how far Brown could have taken them? He did take them to the playoffs in a strike-shortened season, despite Metta World Peace (né Ron Artest) coming in out of shape and hardly peaceful. In April, with no meditation to cool him out, he elbowed James Harden so peacefully that he gave the Thunder star a concussion. It was an ugly flashback to the early Artest. He absorbed a seven-game suspension.

Fortunately for Brown and his aging cast, after they'd blown a 3–1 lead and were facing elimination to the turnover-addicted Nuggets in the first round, Metta returned from his suspension and helped the team survive. But they were blown out in five by Oklahoma City.

Back in New York, the Knicks had fired D'Antoni in March. They elevated assistant Mike Woodson to the requisite interim slot. They did not call Phil. Woodson finished strong, and the Knicks hired him full-time.

Phil did not call the Knicks—which he revealed when, uncharacteristically, he let Andrea Kremer of HBO's *Real Sports* into his Montana sanctum; the resulting broadcast provided for a most uncomfortable segment/advertorial. Jackson seemed sorry he'd allowed the infomercial to happen, with its obvious subtext: I'm still around, folks.

When Kremer asked if the game had passed him by, there were no happy upslants or ironic self-reflective expressions to accompany his answer: "As much as I've been around this game, it doesn't happen. The game doesn't pass a person by."

Kremer: "Is sixty-six too old?"

"That's hogwash" came the quick answer.

When they took a stroll on the banks of the lake, Kremer noted that Jackson seldom let people this close to him, to which he answered, "I really didn't want you to even get this close. You're closer than I want you to be."

But then, why had he let her in? He then said he hoped that that particular quote would not be on the air, and of course, it turned out to be.

Another off-the-record on-the-record confusion. But even if HBO had overstepped its bounds, his response to Kremer was not exactly polite. Maybe he was just having a bad day.

Predictably, life's wheel began to spin again. Jackson met with Kupchak in September, before Brown's second season. The Lakers had acquired thirty-eight-year-old Steve Nash . . . and Dwight Howard. Physically, Howard was as good as it gets; but somehow, somewhere, a few microchips of desire seemed to be missing. (*The Onion:* "Scientists Theorize Existence of NBA Roster Capable of Supporting Dwight Howard.")

"We have a tremendous amount of pressure on us to succeed," the GM told the old coach, "and it's not going to be easy."

They lost four of their first five games—whereupon Buss and Kupchak et al fired Brown. Only in L.A. The fans, of course, chanted for Phil's return. Jeanie asked Phil if he'd talk to Jimmy, while Bernie Bickerstaff would roam the sideline for the next few games.

Kupchak and Jimmy Buss visited Phil on a Saturday. He was still recovering from knee replacement, and one of his Achilles tendons was hurting, but he was obviously intrigued. According to his close friend Kurt Rambis, quoted in *USA Today,* "They told Phil that it was his job, and they agreed to wait until Monday to allow him to digest whether or not he was the right coach to come and coach this team. Phil had made up his mind he wanted to coach this team."

"When it happened," Phil later told Stephen Rodrick, "Jeanie kind of stepped back and didn't get involved, but I knew how she felt. And I knew her brother had appealed to me from a deeper place, so I knew I had to take it seriously. I felt I could do this job, but it was going to be really difficult." He contemplated the rigors. He was contemplating dreamland at midnight on Sunday, when Kupchak called him to say that they'd hired Mike D'Antoni . . . who happened to share an agent with Mike Brown, Mike Legare.

The resultant chatter was deafening, and the speculation rampant.

"Phil Jackson was asking for the moon, according to a source familiar with the situation," wrote the *Times*. TNT's David Aldridge said that Phil wanted "total control." It was written that he'd asked for an eight-figure salary, the ability to skip road games and partial ownership of the team.

Charley Rosen shook his head when we subsequently sat down again. The leak about Phil's demands to the press—all false, he says—had to have come from someone in that room. And they hadn't come from Jackson. "All they did in that meeting was talk about the players on the team," he says. "Not one word was said about money. Nothing was said about a piece of the team. Nothing about not going on the road. Just the players. That's it. Pure and simple. What the team needed.

"[Agent Todd] Musburger took a red-eye Sunday to come in and talk about money, because they hadn't talked one word about money. He wanted 'eighteen million, no road games, a piece of the team'? Total fantasy. 'The triangle not suitable for the personnel'? The triangle is suitable for anyone! When they had Malone, they changed the focus from low to high post. Buss? Doesn't know a pick-and-roll from a Kaiser roll.

"Gasol is a genius in this offense. Now they don't know what to do with it. Kobe's a one-man offense, so they hire a big-name coach. D'Antoni had said earlier in the summer at an NBA-sponsored clinic, 'I do not want anyone in the low post. I want to keep the middle open.' So they give a running coach a team that's slow? That has no bench? To run you need a deep bench! Stupid, stupid, stupid. It's absurd.

"Then they call him up at midnight? What, they made up their minds at five to midnight? The whole thing is bad shit."

★

Jackson's reaction to Rodrick? "Relief." In the back his mind, he didn't know if they had the talent to win it all—"and I hate losing in the finals."

★

"By taking that off the table they almost did him a favor, in terms of him being able to really figure out something else," Diane Mast says now.

"Something different. Something that was there all along but, for whatever reason, he hadn't seen. They all cleared the dishes. I think they all had enough with that meal. When he walked away, he realized he was satisfied."

He had one more ring to go. Jeanie the jewel freak announced it on Twitter by posting a shot a few days into 2013. (It's a large emerald-cut diamond flanked by two smaller ones, should any of your Bud Lite buddies ask you in an NBA trivia game at the bar.)

Diane Mast had to ask Phil why he proposed after all this time. "He said, 'It kind of surprised me,'" she told me.

"I think there's a point in himself, in the way he lives his life, where he faces himself and knows what's right. He was at that point. He does what he wants. He's motivated by what he wants. He doesn't need to answer to anybody."

Except himself—with whom, we hope, he is still conversing, asking questions, listening to answers and embarking on this last act while not forgetting the lessons of a lifetime of accumulated wisdom that led to it.

POSTSCRIPT I

Obviously we haven't seen the last of him. When John Salley told me that the game is what keeps Phil alive, I began to think of the statement literally—to see Phil as Ed Wynn in that *Twilight Zone* episode where the old man with the grandfather clock tells his family, "If I can't wind this thing one day, make sure you do, because if it stops ticking, so will I." Of course, the family scoffs at him, it stops, and he goes on to Valhalla.

This much is certain: Phil is going to make sure that the basketball clock never goes unwound. But it doesn't take Rod Serling to see how the next chapter will likely unwind:

After Jim the Buss brother proves unable to jump-start the franchise, with Dr. Jerry gone and Magic more involved, the woman rightfully takes the reins of the team, gets Phil an office and pokes her head in the door one morning next year.

"What's up?" Jeanie asks. "Hey, I wanted to talk to you about Kobe. I think we might be able to get a couple of draft picks . . ."

"Wait, what's a six-letter word for 'baubly vegetables'?"

"Carats."

"Thanks. So I found this pretty good Thai halibut recipe for tonight, but I hate having to use canned coconut broth. I think I'll bop down to that place in Thai town to get it fresh. Maybe some lemongrass, too. You need anything?"

"A big man who can convert a fricking free throw. What about Kobe?"

"Oh, he'll be fine. I'll give him a few David Foster Wallace novels."

D'Antoni goes, of course. Cleamons comes in, maybe, with Madsen and Coby Karl and Hodges as assistants. The Lakers start to win again because Kobe's too old to dominate and turns into the consummate team player. And he finally reads Tex's book.

A few weeks later, a *Times* columnist mocks Phil because, at a salary of $11 million, he still comes to work in sandals, and, like, what's his real job? Does he have one? Because the writer's sources say that it was Jimmy Buss and Kupchak who actually pried big man Nerlens Noel away from the Cavs—and he somehow turns out to be amazingly quick as a big man picking up Cleamons's triangle.

And the trade that brought in Giannis Antetokounmpo, the Nigerian from Greece? Sources say that this was a Kupchak coup, after he'd been tipped off to the kid's skills by Jerry West. Or Jerry Krause. Or Jerry Buss's ghost.

Phil reads the column, torches some sage, leans back and puts his sandals on his desk.

What is the sound of one man laughing?

If you're in his office that day—and I intend to be—you'll know.

Phil matured enough to never settle for something as pat as rebellion for rebellion's sake. But he never relinquished the search, no matter where it took him. By studying and sifting and wrestling with the words of the elders of so many civilizations, he learned not only how to teach, but how to be taught—out on the fringe of the pasture but still within its fences. The natural desire to break away from a radically structured childhood, followed naturally by a self-serving few years in a Knick spotlight, gradually produced a man, not a caricature. Along the way, he gave athletes from every walk of life, many with their own agendas, a larger sense of perspective about their places on earth. And he will do so again.

But having channeled Red Holzman in so any ways, has he ever found Red's postcareer peace, wherein Selma Holzman and a scotch were all

that a Brooklyn kid needed in this mortal realm? Has he ever truly relinquished the need to be paid attention to—the logical endgame of a balanced man? Has he come to the perfect conjunction of body and mind?

No one does. He seems caught, as we all are, between the poles. But it's
hardly a stretch to suggest that the friction between the two caused the
spark that lit every one of those championships—because each and every
player, himself pressured by various pulls coming from all directions, was
playing for a human being. Not an automaton, or a martinet. A guy who
knows that that wheel of life turns unceasingly.

He was a teacher, and is there ever a higher compliment we can be-
stow? He erased a whole lot of life obstacles for the Lowes Moores and the
Craig Hodgeses. Skim the later-life résumés of the Salleys, the Kerrs, the
Paxsons and countless others. They found happiness and success after
playing for Phil.

On the other hand, he certainly seems to have bought into the eleven
rings. The house he lives in on Flathead? "Stained-glass portals appear
throughout the house," Andrea Kremer, way too close, told us, "each representing one of the eleven championships." He was not only counting; he
felt the need to memorialize the victories.

But then, think back: Has he ever said he had the answers that his
master thinkers had? No. They were guideposts steering him toward
whatever answer he craved. If he'd really thought he'd been imbued with
true wisdom, he'd have left the Bulls, returned to the West, taught basketball and life lessons to the Pine Ridge Lakota Sioux, taken a psychology-
teaching position at Valley State College and on the side written his *own*
spiritual manifesto instead of quoting from everyone else's. He'd have
given speeches to corporations for fees donated anonymously to any of a
thousand causes.

He would not have included a shot of himself in his kitchen in the latest book or, on the book tour, met a *New York Times* reporter at the
supermarket wherein the writer, intentionally or not, could see how me-

ticulously he sourced his food. But this is not to suggest that he acted inauthentically in anything he ever did. He was always, as Diane and Charley say, just Phil. Navigating the waters as best he could. Guided by voices and interpreting them as best he could.

At the beginning, it was trying to hear the voices that would allow him to speak in tongues. Then he grew to heed the voices of the sixties. And then he heeded Krause's summons, put on the suit and endorsed the Cadillac. And since then, heeding the voice of Something, because he insists that he stays in the arena because he has to use his "God-given gift," he's now worth more than the entire state of North Dakota.

The Buddha: "Unceasing change turns the wheel of life so we may experience life in all its many forms. Peaceful dwelling in the midst of change brings sentient beings great joy."

Or as Shunryu Suzuki said it a little more simply, "Everything changes."

POSTSCRIPT II

Jackson's most recent book carried the baldest title of any of them, *Eleven Rings* (why not just call it *I Won More Than Anyone!* and be done with it?), its cover featuring eleven diamond-crusted baubles that look as if they came from an ancient Persian king's chest of looted treasure.

In case you missed it, one day Jeanie tweeted that Phil was going to finally join the social media universe and would offer us his first tweet ever that night. And there it came: "11 champ;ipnsikp[ringhs."

Who took the bait? Well, for starters, Deadspin, of all sites ("Phil Jackson's First Tweet Didn't Turn Out So Well")—and, of course, the *Los Angeles Times*. Under the headline "Phil Jackson's First Tweet Is Very Profound," the writer said, "What you have to like about it, though, is that Jackson didn't delete the tweet and try again. He left it there. That is a sign of a person secure with himself. I guess winning 11 titles and being the greatest coach in NBA history will do that."

Had the newspaper learned *nothing* over the course of a decade? Did the *Times*'s writer honestly think that a meticulous man who (a) used ten ingredients in his pancakes, (b) showed his rookies what spot on the court they should make their cut *within inches*, and (c) was, from college on, a "neatnik," was going to issue a garbled tweet his first time out?

The next night, on the Web, Jackson spun around in his chair, facing the camera to reveal that it was tough to type with eleven rings on; the video went viral. Subsequently, on his book tour, he gave interviews to every media outlet but *Progressive Farmer* (and that one might still be in the pipeline) while managing all the while, in perfect Zen fashion, to reveal very little.

This is what we basically learned over the course of his book tour: (a) Michael was better than Kobe; (b) as aforementioned, he felt closer to Kobe than to anyone else he ever coached; (c) Bill Russell was the best player ever (stop the presses, if they still exist); and (d) he'd put off treatments for prostate cancer in his final year to keep coaching.

In other words, Jackson maintained the balance—or, if you will, balanced the duality. On the corporeal level, he spewed promotionally from *Oprah* to *Charlie Rose*, nurturing more fame and selling more books. On the spiritual/ethereal level, he avoided dissing anyone or giving up trade gossip, as most insecure celebs tend to do in their books and on the subsequent tours.

On the other hand, why yet *another* book? It was Jackson who once wrote of the two monks walking in the rain who come upon a woman who doesn't want to cross a puddle and get her gown wet. One carries her through the puddle, puts her down, and the two walk on. Hours later, the other monk breaks the silence and says, "We're not supposed to acknowledge or touch women! Why did you do that back there?" And the first monk stops and says, "I put her down. Why are you still carrying her?"

So why was he still carrying those eleven rings around? Why let them forever be displayed on a book cover? Isn't the stained glass enough? (Its back cover doesn't even feature the requisite quotes from former teammates or revered writers. It's just a huge picture of . . . Phil.)

Was it for the money? Despite his implying to Rodrick that he has to take commercial gigs because of the deterioration of his body and its uncertain future health, reportedly he is worth something in the range of $45 million—pending his next hiring, to the Lakers' or Knicks' or Pistons' front office . . . or a lucrative consulting deal wherein he could roam the globe and teach coaches in international leagues some of his wisdom. (Gilberto Benetton and other European owners would not be sparing on the bucks. . . .) That's a lot of coin for someone who might have to replace another joint. (Maybe he should smoke more of them.)

Perhaps he wants to leave the money to his heirs, although Child Psychology 101 would suggest that leaving millions to your kids and grandkids is not a healthy way to keep the Lakota/Zen/Christian meme alive or help them mature as actual citizens.

Literarily? To those who've read the previous tomes, the latest not only adds nothing; it subtracts. It's a primer of Jackson's canon. Purportedly, it's about the eleven championships he won as a coach, but at bottom it's a whitewashed autobiography (his second). William Maxwell once wrote, "In talking about the past we lie with every breath we draw," but that axiom doesn't apply here. This is just a malleable retelling that dismayingly reduces a once intriguing three-dimensional figure in the two-dimensional sports world into someone nearly equally two-dimensional.

Conspicuously absent: mention of LSD or weed or the loft. Of Rosen, Neal Walk or Eddie Mast. The Patroons merit *two paragraphs*—and not a single mention of any player. There's no mention of the Los Suns flap, Sacramento's "semi-civilized . . . rednecks" or *Brokeback Mountain*.

June Jackson? The word *divorce* does not appear. One page after the last of five references to the woman who stood by his side for three decades, he introduces Jeanie. ("Smart, attractive, with beautiful eyes. Things were definitely looking up.")

But the following *do* make appearances—in the first fifty pages: Suzuki, Lao-tzu, Satchel Paige, the Grateful Dead, Nikos Kazantzakis, Joel Goldsmith, William James, Rickie Lee Jones, Joseph Campbell (the mythologist, not the actor), an anonymous Japanese parable teller, some Dutch psychologists, a management consultant group and Pir Vilayat Inayat Khan. (Thereafter, the roster never lets up. Duke and Bird and David Byrne pop up; Gillespie bops up, too.)

Back in the day, there'd been no Jacksonian utterances like "Michael Jordan used to say that what he liked about my coaching style was . . ."; "Paxson once sent me a story that he said reminded him of me"; or "[Rodman] was so joyful . . . on some level, he reminded me of me." On not humiliating Pippen after he refused to take the playoff shot? "Some people applauded my clever management strategy." And "I discovered I had a gift for making adjustments and getting the most out of the talent on the roster."

It was his revered Black Elk who said that we start life in childhood and end life in childhood. Certainly Phil the psychologist, nearing enough credits for the master's, knows that one of the most obvious traits of the child, before passing into adolescence, is believing that the universe revolves around him, and that in life's final chapter, the organism regresses to that self-centric phase.

But to quote the Marine prosecutor played by Kevin Bacon in *A Few Good Men,* "Those are the facts . . . and they are not in dispute," and these facts are not in dispute: Phil Jackson is the greatest coach in not just NBA history but professional sports history, which means that, since we began keeping these championship records, he has coached a sporting team more effectively than any other American professional sports coach. Ever. In other words, if you're going to live your life based on sport's adherence to statistics, the numbers say that there's Phil Jackson, and then there's everyone else.

Truth be told, the most illuminating anecdote comes not from the book, but an interview on the book tour. *New York Times* writer Sam Anderson recounts the hour and a half Phil spent diagramming plays in a diner. Not ten minutes; an hour and a half. This observation led me back to my own notebooks, where I found the plays that Charley Rosen had diagrammed for me over a half-dozen sushi lunches. And the plays that Patroon point guard Lowes Moore diagrammed for me in his cluttered office in the Mount Vernon Boys and Girls Club. And I have no doubt that, had I been able to sit down personally with Jim Cleamons and Frank Hamblen and Craig Hodges, I'd have gone back to my own office with more diagrammed plays than I knew what to do with.

Not to mention how many plays I'd now know if I'd had the chance to share beers with Phil and Eddie Mast, in a pub, armed with a lot of quarters.

POSTSCRIPT III

So how close can we come to the essence of the man? To Plato-ian Jackson-ness? At this point, it's probably apt to turn to those who know him best.

"Phil?" says Ron Harper, with the Ron Harper laugh, a man possessed of five rings and a deep reverence for his friend. "Never gonna let any grass grow under him. And no matter where he is, he finds a way to make everything work."

"He's spirituality. He has the sense of community. And he has adaptability," says Neal Walk today. "Ghetto kids, single-parent kids, kids with criminal parents—he had a wide range of humanity he was trying to work with, and he reached them all because he's so adaptable. He doesn't need any trappings. Just the certainty that the strength of the wolf is in the pack, the strength of the pack is in the wolf."

"He wants to be part of the human dynamic," says Chris Thomforde. "When he says, 'This is what we're doing,' it's the same as saying, 'This is how I am.' There's a self-comfort. He doesn't have to be defensive. Because he has his passion. Mankind has an innate passion for the energy of how to live well and meaningfully. And Phil has it. He's 'What's in the flow?' His mother tongue was Evangelical Pentecostal Christianity, and since then he's learned a lot of languages, because he wants to communicate with a lot of people and get into their communities—whether it's an Indian reservation or Malibu. People think he's a 'Zen Buddhist,' all of those labels, and that he listens to one thing or the other thing? No. He listens to everything."

"A complicated guy, a mixed bag," says Danny Rudolph, the dentist who banged against him in the women's-shelter gym. "Too smart for his own good. Incredibly good friend who keeps you on your toes. Competing with you intellectually, but at the same time, has your back. The bottom line? Great friend and loyal to the end. Does he give you a jab now and then? You gotta keep on your toes. He isn't a docile guy. He's just one of the guys. What you see is what you get: a guy. A very intelligent guy."

Diane Mast laughs at my insistence to pin the man, to categorize. "Phil is just Phil," she says. "He always has been, and always will be. But getting Phil painted is a challenge. He likes fishing in the lake and swimming and floating in the Indian Ocean. He enjoys a rocker on the porch and being in charge of his cigar smoke. But honestly? Phil is just a good guy, period. He was always who he was. I've never known him as, like, this somebody, and then he became somebody else. He was always Phil. He still is Phil. And nobody's ever actually put that out there yet. He's not just a great coach or just a big tall guy who plays ball, or just the mystic man. No one has ever penetrated his center. Phil has managed to preserve his private self. What he is is a strong muscle-spirit of a man who was destined to become who he always was on any given day . . . a true good man, undivine and imperfect, but good."

AFTERWORD

Really, how could it have turned out otherwise? The chatter that he'd never commit to a mediocre team, lest his legend be tarnished, had vastly underestimated his need for a challenge. For more game. He had to finish the American round-trip journey: from New York, the global capital, to the Second City, the hub-anchor of the heartland; then on to the sunbathed Shangri-la to give the bones a rest across the street from the lapping Pacific; and then—ever the competitor reconnecting the final dot on the triangle—back where it all began. He had to go back to the town that had, in a few short years, grown him up: from prairie preacher searcher to a lover of art, architecture and culture of all kind.

Had New York changed in thirty-five years? Well, in the former Salvation Army's Evangeline Residence for Women, where he used to play with his buddies in the basement, condos are now going for $5 million. The abandoned elevated rail line a few blocks from his loft? It's called the High Line now, a new jewel, strewn with wildflowers—and surrounded by nineteen new condos and co-ops. In one, you can grab an apartment for $50 million.

Madison Square Garden? Unlike the team for the last decade and a half, it's undergone a nice renovation, priced at around $980 million—just a little more than Jim Dolan's paying Phil—including the spiffy Chase Square, where, on March 18, 2014, Cablevision did it up to the max to welcome him home with fanfare bordering on fawning. But why not? Between

February 1 and March 3, they'd won two games. The barbarians would have stormed the gates.

It was the Roman satirist Juvenal who observed, in 100 AD, that the Roman emperors kept the masses happy by giving them "bread and circuses." The Knicks delivered both: $12 million a year in the bread department for Phil, for five years, and an introduction that would have done Barnum and Bailey proud. This was not your usual "New exec sits at podium in front of some sagging curtain featuring the team logo and its sponsor."

This was, well, East Coast Showtime. Large placards featuring the Knick logo read, NY MADE: WELCOME HOME, and included different shots of the player in action back in the day. WELCOME HOME PHIL shouted a message board in the lobby. The team's marketing website was, as of that morning, offering Phil Jackson T-shirts featuring a caricature of the woolly-haired Fu Manchu guy. What Dolan was selling on this day was not the future, but a fuzzy memory.

But the man himself? Not a trace of the loft dweller to be seen. His short, white cropped hair was (as Warren Zevon would have put it) *perfect*; almost, in fact, what a Hollywood stylist would create for an aging but robust Roman emperor. Broad of beam, stouter of torso, cleanly shaven, he wore a perfectly tailored dark suit and dark tie against a white button-down shirt: Serious Manhattan Biz wear. His glasses were neither nerdy nor trendy; they made no statement. He was not wearing sandals. His demeanor suggested one thing, and one thing only: Act III: The Man.

As he posed in front of a large Knick logo, he was smiling like that cat who'd not only swallowed the canary but had already devoured an entire borough. He seemed to strike an almost larger-than-life figure, between his size and the dead-on look that said, *Yep. It's my team now.* It was as if the Williston High drama club guy who'd played a god had actually filled out to become one. The half-smile in the official Knick website portrait closely resembled the enigmatic half-smile he'd shown back in the University of North Dakota days; as in, *There's a whole lot more to me than what you're seeing.*

Perhaps all of the out-of-proportion pomp was designed to make us forget that he was, for once, inheriting a truly mediocre team. Or perhaps it was designed to make it clear from minute one that whatever virus had let the once glorious franchise unravel would find no purchase on a man this self-assured, accomplished and enormous. All that were missing were medals on his lapel.

Within about three seconds of taking the podium—without notes—he had the media crowd in the palm of his hand. He was quick to note that he was here to take over all basketball operations, from top to bottom. "The buck stops with me. That's the assurance I wanted to give Jim Dolan. I'm going to take care of this end of it: coaches, scouts, personnel, people in video, we're going to all have a direction in which we're funneling how to play the game." All the better to allow Jimmy the time he needs to be the Cable Guy.

The words that followed, unscripted but hardly spontaneous, weren't preacherly, but the tone was teacherly, and it brooked no disagreement. His mission statement was concise, self-assured and unemotional. Instead of dwelling on nostalgia, he spoke like a man who'd taken over an under-achieving factory in a friendly takeover, with a not-so-subtle message to his roster of workers. Asked about his "biggest challenge," he did not hesi-tate: "The players. Players on the floor have to have a certain sense about them. Remember [John McPhee's] book about Bradley? *A Sense of Where You Are*? Bill had this innate sense: 'Where are your players? Never turn your back on the ball, or your man.' These are features that have to come back."

Perhaps setting the stage for the events soon to follow, Phil spoke of his only true superstar much as if he were addressing Kobe back on that day when he returned to the Lakers: damning with faint praise. "There's no doubt about Carmelo being one of the top scorers in the league, maybe the best individual isolation player in the game," he told the crowd, in the bass voice that commands you to hear it. "I have no problem with committing to saying Carmelo is in the future plans."

I have no problem? Not quite a ringing endorsement, there, and a sign of things to come, where, as the days unfolded, Jackson used every opportunity he had to make it clear that Anthony was in no position to make demands or influence Jackson's thinking.

"There are a number of things I see Carmelo doing as he moves forward, and I think Carmelo, as great a player as he is, still has another level he can go to. I hope together with the team we create that he can get there." (As in, *Learn to play, you're welcome to stay, but if the Heat's in your heart, feel free to depart.*)

Then, whether Anthony was to move on or not, Jackson made it clear that everyone in a Knick uniform was going to have to step up his game. From day one in Chicago, Phil was a fundamentals man, exacting, and it was clear he was going to be the same man in New York: "A lot of our young players have jumped the fundamentals. They've gone from high school to one year of college and haven't mastered the skills. All of these are part of [my] vision of bringing basketball back."

And, of course, in his opening remarks he presented the requisite defense of the triangle, delivered with such confidence and clarity it was clear that the words were ingrained. The manifesto clearly lurks near the cerebellum's surface. He spoke without pause as he laid it all out: "So there's a number of times the triangle's been assailed as archaic and slow. But there are some real logical things that it does right: Offense to the boards. Defensive balance. It's not about the triangle offense. It's about a system. It's about the coach who doesn't have to jump up and say, 'Run the One'; the team knows what it's going to run, transition to flow to offense.

"There's no lull, no stop, so the defense can't get back and stop us in transition.

"You have chaos. Basketball is chaotic in itself. For the most part sets don't work in the NBA. They work a little bit in the first quarter, and the third—little special plays. But what matters is how you format your players on the floor so they can have the best ability to create. It's not one guy dribbling up and taking a shot." And that was it: Basketball 101. But then—this was Phil Jackson after all—he segued weirdly, without transition, to addressing the media about the media's role. The next few statements were as enigmatic as it gets. The Buddha couldn't have put them better himself.

"I'll be accessible," he said. Then immediately, without so much as an "and," "I'm gonna be removed."

Um, say what?

"I want to develop relationships with people here," he said. "This organization has suffered over the past few years by things that I think have been created by the press. We need your support, and the players need a positive attitude to play."

Uh-oh. Phil, this is 2014, and the days when the New York columnists pumped up your ego went out with Nixon. Larry Merchant isn't around anymore to let the world know how quirky and brilliant you are. It's been a good four decades since the press was allowed to sing a team's anthem. In fact, these days, a homer is likely to get a serious dressing-down from an editor.

Then it got weirder.

"There'll be some closed walls as far as media, as far as things that go on, and I think we have to accept that," he said, followed, inexplicably, by, "I'm reaching out to say we're going to have an open relationship and a good one. As we go forward we have a great chance and opportunity. This is the best place to play basketball. If you can make it here, you can make it anywhere. That's where the phrase started. We're going to make it here, and I ask for your support."

This was the unavoidable interpretation: That he wants a good relationship with the notoriously prickly New York media . . . on his own terms. That he'll let the press in when he wants them in, and shut them out when he wants them out, and yet still expects them to support the team. For a philosophy guy, this is a pretty untenable and downright bizarre paradox.

Clearly, Frank Isola of the *Daily News* wasn't paying attention. One month later, in a front-page story with the headline PARADISE LOST, Isola quoted sources saying that Jackson wanted to sweep so clean that some non-basketball-staff people would hit the street. And that Dolan was drawing a line in the sand. That was the last we heard of any friction between Jackson and ownership, but it surprised no one. Despite Dolan's insistence that he was "willingly and gratefully" ceding all basketball power to his new hire, no one ever questioned the likelihood of Dolan being every bit as difficult as Jerry Krause—or Jim Buss—had ever been. The Cable Guy is the most notoriously difficult owner in the league, if not all of sports—notorious for the revolving door through which he welcomes and then dispatches coaches and execs.

His father, Charles, had bought the team in 1994 with ITT and took full control in 1997, but by 1999, it was the son's team. He was an inexperienced, immature manager of a corporation with ambitions to run the Garden.

Dave Checketts knows the atmosphere well. It was Checketts who'd been caught in the middle of the first Phil flap, back when he huddled with Jackson while Jeff Van Gundy was still coach, and then fired general manager Ernie Grunfeld—reportedly at Phil's insistence.

In fact, Checketts says now that it was all Dolan's doing. Grunfeld and Van Gundy were at each other's throats, planting false stories about each other, but Checketts says he assured Dolan that they could both stay ("Phil and Krause didn't even talk to each other, and they won six rings"), but that Dolan demanded he ax Grunfeld.

"Jimmy? He's extremely complicated, irrational and difficult," Checketts told me after Jackson was hired. "I mean, I don't know what else to say."

But he actually did, as he went on to discuss how difficult Phil's task is going to be. Phil isn't working for Jerry Buss anymore, a private owner who lived and died for his team—sketchy of morals, perhaps, but fair as an owner, a self-made man with an IQ to match Phil's. Now he's working for a man ten years younger than he who inherited a sports team from a dad who made money in tech marketing and monopolizing. A man who admits, "I am by no means a basketball expert."

"The history of large corporate entities owning sports teams is not a good one," Checketts says, after working for four different owners for more than fourteen years in the Garden and producing 178 playoff games before Dolan jettisoned him. "This time, it's a little less about that—Jimmy is his own culture—but look at Fox's ownership of the Dodgers. Or Disney and the Ducks. Time Warner owned a lot of teams in Atlanta. They deliver a lot of things, but not sports.

"The arrangement doesn't tend to work because players and coaches want to know exactly who is at the top and who is making the decisions and who they have to please. When it is a large group of people, and some of those people feel as if they could be removed at any second, like what happened for so many for so long, it feels like a firing machine, which isn't good for the team. The players think: *This guy is not surviving. We don't have to work for him, play for him, respect him.*

"There's never been financial accountability [at the Garden]," Checketts continued. "So much money is coming from the cable side, there's never been a need to operate financially well on the sports side, so the result is bad trades. People running for their lives to keep their jobs."

That said, Checketts thinks that we may have reached a tipping point; that the hoi polloi were getting close to mutinying in mid-February and that Dolan sensed it.

"Phil just might be able to do it," he says. "It's perfect timing. There was a level of desperation that Jimmy brought about, and I think he knows it. I think Jimmy's gotten to where he can't interfere because he's invested—he's overinvested—but got a world-class guy. I think it might work this time."

In a rare interview with Mike Vaccaro of the *New York Post* in November 2013, Dolan came off as a tad self-deluded, asserting that he thought he was a "good owner" because he "watches out for the fans . . . [and tries] to give them a good product." That product had failed to make the playoffs eleven of the previous fourteen seasons and failed to get out of the first round in three of the four. In other words: one playoff-series victory in fourteen years.

Equally as troubling to true Knick fans who want to see Jackson succeed is Dolan's ongoing relationship with Isiah Thomas, whose winning record as a coach at the Garden was .341—fifth worst in team history. As president of basketball operations? He traded away a ton of draft picks for the immortal Eddy Curry—and some of those trades became lottery picks. Ever since Thomas led his team off the court before the final buzzer in the Bulls series, just about everything he's touched has failed. He bought the Continental Basketball Association in 1999, and two years later it declared bankruptcy. And the popcorn company he became a partner in had to recall contaminated kernels in 2012.

"I can tell you that he's a friend of mine," Dolan said. "We speak, but not as often as we used to because he's really involved in other things now. He actually uses me to bounce business ideas off of."

When Vaccaro asked him if he still consulted with Thomas about "basketball ideas," the answer was "Not really." Not too reassuring.

The first order of business as soon as the 2013–14 season ended was to thank Mike Woodson for his time and begin a search for a new coach. It seemed inevitable that no matter who Jackson would hire, that guy was going to be something of an apprentice to the wizard down the hall, the six-foot-eight gorilla in the room. Dolan didn't hire Jackson for his management expertise. He hired him for the aura. Just as Krause had hired Jackson for his rings, Dolan desperately needed a symbol of headier days, a beacon for coaches, players and fans alike. We weren't likely to see a neon coach come in.

Choosing Steve Kerr as coach was a no-brainer. Smart, but he'd never coached. He was, of course, a Phil man: an overachiever who hustled his butt off. Even after he'd gone to the Spurs, the two would have dinner when San Antonio played the Lakers. A few years back, Kerr attended Jackson's daughter's wedding.

And by mid-April, he let it be publicly known that he was more than willing to be in the running. On his radio show, Kerr said he figured he'd be "talking to Phil at some point."

"I know that philosophically we have a strong connection," Jackson said.

It was also in April when Jackson was asked whether losing Carmelo to free agency, should the man opt out on July 1, would leave a gaping wound. His predictable yin-yang response signaled that no one player meant a thing on the team he was going to mold over the next few years with free agents, draft choices and trades.

"I'm all about moving forward," he said. "Just deal with what is and move forward. If it's in the cards [that Anthony stays], man, are we fortunate. If it's not in the cards, man, are we fortunate. We're going forward, anyway." Maybe it was that second "If it's not in the cards" that convinced Carmelo to move forward, too.

But then things went awry. According to Isola, Kerr asked a friend, "Why do some people think I'd be crazy to do this?" Easy: Because the World's Most Famous Arena was now synonymous with the World's Most Fickle Arena, where coaches went to die—even really good coaches, from Mike D'Antoni to Lenny Wilkens to Larry Brown. Hardly the definition of stability.

And so, in a completely unforeseen move, one day after verbally committing to the job, in mid-May Kerr backed out, and took the head coach's job with the Warriors, getting a five-year commitment to replace Mark Jackson, whose own name had been inaccurately bandied about (as he was never considered).

Unpredictably, Phil had hit a public-relations speed bump right out of the gate. Dolan had, if indirectly, already dealt Phil his first setback with his reputation, spooking Steve.

In announcing the sequence of events, Phil was wondrously transparent. "I had to release him to go do this job," Jackson said, "to say, 'You have to do what's right for yourself.' This is something he thought would be a good fit for him. We're happy for him. It was California. And to be honest, that's a better team for him."

And then, true to contrarian form, Jackson said something completely antithetical to coachspeak: He admitted that the Knicks weren't as good as the team that had made the playoffs under Mark Jackson and were ousted in the first round.

"To be perfectly honest, they have a really good operating team right now. We're still a team that [has] to put together a roster. I'm not saying we have to rebuild per se, but we have to build a competitive team."

It was a tad unthinkable that Jackson would come in, hook his first pick and have the fish jump off the line. Now the pool suddenly looked a lot less inviting.

And now the interwebs were whispering, ever looking for a sliver of hypocrisy, that Phil was simply setting the stage for himself to be an interim coach. And when at one press conference he said, "I'm always interested in coaching; the question is whether I can do it physically," it was hardly great news for whoever was still in the circle of choices. "I have a big circle," Phil said. The man's body's broken, but he still wants to coach?

But Phil put the rumors to rest quickly, and immediately threw Derek Fisher's name out there—while Fisher was in the middle of a playoff series. Tampering with a Capital *T*. The fine? $25,000—more or less what Jackson earns in one morning. It was obviously worth the investment just to let Fisher know how serious Phil was, although he likely did already. They were as thick as thieves. He'd been a point guard on all five of Jackson's ring winners in Los Angeles, and his politics were suitably solid: He'd been president of the players' union during the stormy labor negotiations of 2010.

Of course, Fish jumped at the bait: $25 million over five years, but the money was clearly only one of the factors (the roster surely wasn't). Their opening press conference captured a tangible chemistry between two men that could never be faked. He had not only hired a man who brought his own rings; he hired a man who'd played in more playoff games, including his last a few days earlier, than any player in history. No one was going to think, as they might have of Kerr, that Fisher had been away from the game and the vibe of today's players. He'd been there only one week before.

During the opening remarks Phil spoke of the times Derek had played hurt. Of his understanding of how a team worked. Of how he'd always been able to sublimate his ego for the good of the team, and his "ability to speak the truth from what the sense of the group was."

Fisher looked on, with a serious look, sensing the high ceremony of the thing, dressed to the nines: purple shirt, silver tie, beige jacket.

But a few minutes later, they were sitting next to each other on stools, answering questions, and both seeming far more relaxed. And in answering one question about why the thirty-nine-year-old veteran of countless winning teams was his choice, Phil slipped into tone-deaf territory using the language of an out-of-touch, well, sixty-eight-year-old.

"I like the fact that he's current with the players," Phil said. "This is a generation that's a little different than the one I grew up with. Guys who were listening to the Grateful Dead aren't here anymore.

"And Derek has kind of gotten into that beat. He's 'hip-hop ready' to get going with this group of guys and their language."

Fisher's response to this lame old white guy's caricature? He looked at the crowd of writers, smiled widely, laughingly, pointed a thumb at his boss, and said, in a naturally complimentary way, "This guy is something." It was a guy talking about his buddy of many years. Brother to brother. A cowering coach wouldn't have made any such gesture to a new boss unless the relationship were a lifelong one and unless he was confident enough to know that he will be the boss on the court, not Phil.

I asked Charley Rosen, Phil's old buddy and the scribe of the league, the man who knows all, for his thoughts. Charley's take on the coaching outcome? That when Kerr opted for a better roster and a West Coast clime, the Knicks ended up with the right man.

"Kerr is a great guy," Charley told me. "Fucking brilliant, friendly, incredibly intelligent, knows the game, knows the triangle, knows personnel. And yeah, he stood up to Michael [Jordan], but that was different. For this? He doesn't have that edge.

"But Fisher? Maybe not as smart outside of *X*s and *O*s, and doesn't have the overall analytic knowledge, but he knows how to get guys to play.

Knows the game, knows the triangle inside and out. A great basketball mind. He is a leader.

"Listen, Kobe was young and stupid and no one would follow him, and he shunned everyone, but Fisher came in and connected with him. Worked out with him. Brought him into the corral, although he always had one foot over the fence. He's respected. He can relate better to NBA players than Kerr can."

Most significant? Fisher's a disciplinarian. Which means that Phil won't have to be. "He is a tough motherfucker. He can get some seven-foot, four-hundred-pound guy and say, 'Listen, you asshole: You got to rotate.'

"And whether you want to admit it or not," says the man whose latest novel is about an NBA scout and rings tellingly true, "he's black."

In other words, if it had been Kerr, when a player looked over at the coach, he'd be hearing Phil's words. Under Fisher, they'll be Fisher's words. "He won't be a puppet," says Rosen.

But who will they be? This roster? Does it really matter yet? He'll have a lot of people who like to shoot the ball, with varying degrees of success: Tim Hardaway Jr., J. R. Smith, Andrea Bargnani, Amar'e Stoudemire, Iman Shumpert (if the shooting guard hasn't been traded for a draft pick). He may or may not have Carmelo, as of this writing—but probably not. Yes, he'd be leaving $30 million on the table, but in Anthony's tax bracket, the dollars aren't a factor. The elusive ring is.

Jackson won't have a roster capable of threatening powerful teams. He will not have his requisite two superstars unless, in a longshot scenario, LeBron decides to join Melo. Jackson will build through the draft, and trades, and free agency.

This we know: He will gather guys who will be weaving and triangulating. And he'll have overachievers. He didn't win in Chicago because of Jordan and Pippen. He won because of Steve Kerr and Bobby Hansen and John Paxson and John Salley and Ron Harper and Jud Buechler.

Town to town, Jackson's cult-ees dive for loose balls and study game plans and bust their butts in every practice because they have come to know that they've arrived in the perfect workplace. They know that unless

Jackson wins, he dies inside. That sort of attitude tends to turn the Shumperts into what they promised they once would be.

"It'll work," says Charley Rosen. "The bottom line? Phil is a basketball genius. He's probably an all-around genius.

"All this bullshit about being in the front office and 'He's never done it before'? 'It's so hard'? Red Auerbach did it. Phil knows the game, he knows the players. He's been evaluating players from the beginning. He knows what players fit into the system, and he's a systems man.

"The other thing with Fish is that he wouldn't have taken the job until he knew what Phil's game plan is, what this team is going to look like in a year or two—full of smart players who've had a degree of success in the NBA but never won and are willing to bet that Phil can bring them to a championship.

"Because he's done it before. And he's going to do it again."

—Peter Richmond, June 2014

NOTES

Chapter One

For the history of Jackson's family, I referred to his own remembrances in his books *Maverick* (Playboy Press, 1975) and *Eleven Rings: The Soul of Success* (Penguin Press, 2013). For the circumstances of his birth, I relied on Jackson himself for clarification, through a mutual friend. For Jackson's childhood fascination with Native Americans, I obtained information from Bill Bradley's first book, *Life on the Run* (Quadrangle/New York Times Book Company, 1976).

For the history of Anaconda, Montana, I was fortunate to receive an impromptu and extensive oral history of the town, the copper industry, and all things Anaconda from proprietor Edith Fransen on my visit to the Anaconda Visitor Center, housed in the old railroad station. In addition, I referred to the *Anaconda Visitors Guide 2012*, published by the *Anaconda Leader*. Other details of Anaconda were from personal observation.

For the history of Miles City, Montana, I relied on resources from the Miles City Public Library, as well as the local office of the Bureau of Land Management of the U.S. Department of the Interior, just south of the Miles City Ranch Rodeo grounds.

Biographical data on Charles M. Russell came from the *Great Falls Tribune*'s tribute to the artist: http://www.greatfallstribune.com/multimedia/125newsmakers6/cmrussell1.html.

For additional insights into Jackson's upbringing, I referred to Jack McCallum's comprehensive profile in the November 11, 1991, issue of *Sports Illustrated*.

Chapter Two

For information on the current status of the fracking industry in Williston, North Dakota, I visited fracking wells in the area. In Williston, I also interviewed Jerry Zunich, a former roughneck and oilfield worker, and researched the involvement of Halliburton Company and Baker-Hughes through their websites.

In addition, "Greetings from Williston," Stephen Rodrick's thorough and riveting account of the impact of Williston's fracking industry in the July 13, 2012, edition of *Men's Journal*, paints a stunning picture of the boomtown. For information about Jackson's years as a high school student in Williston, I interviewed his classmates Barbara Sohlberg, Myron Oyloe and Pete Pornish, as well as Paul Presthus, the rival Rugby High School basketball captain at the time. I also tapped the brain of the Coyotes' current basketball coach, Mark Slotsve, who was kind enough to give me a tour of the gym where Phil played, including the Phil Jackson Fieldhouse, with its cases of Jackson memorabilia.

Regarding Jackson's decision to attend the University of North Dakota, interviews with his coach at UND, Bill Fitch, and Presthus were helpful, as were Jackson's own accounts from Jackson's book *Maverick*, as well as Roland Lazenby's thorough biography of Jackson, *Mindgames: Phil Jackson's Long Strange Journey* (McGraw-Hill, 2000).

Chapter Three

For information on Jackson's years as a student at the University of North Dakota, I was privileged to work with Jayson Hajdu, the university's media relations director in the Department of Athletics, as well as media intern Alison Copp.

Details about Jackson's performance as a college basketball player, as well as his personality as an undergraduate, are based on the recollections of Bill Fitch, his head coach, and Jimmy Rodgers, then an assistant.

For details of Jackson's basketball and baseball games throughout his college career, I relied on the all-inclusive and authoritative account *A Century of UND Sports: An Athletic History of the University of North Dakota* by Lee Bohnet (Lee Bohnet and the University of North Dakota Foundation, 1994).

I obtained details of the Sioux's postseason tournaments in 1966 and 1967 from the *Grand Forks Herald*.

For life on campus, as well as on the court and in the field house, I relied on the recollections of Jackson's teammate Pete Pornich.

For analysis of Jackson's thoughts about the likes of Martin Heidegger and Jean-Paul Sartre, as well as other philosophers Jackson studied during those undergraduate years, I referred to my own undergraduate studies of the same philosophers.

For details of Jackson's decision to go on to play for the Knicks, and analysis of his college talent, I relied on his own memoirs as well as Red Holzman's memoir *Red on Red* (Bantam, 1987).

Regarding Jackson's parting gift to Fitch, Fitch, in an interview, referred to the 1958 reprinting of *Leaves of Gold: An Anthology of Prayers, Inspirational Verse, and Prose*, edited by Clyde Francis Lytle (Coslett Publishing Co.).

For general information on Grand Forks, Fargo and the rest of eastern North Dakota at the time, I drew on personal notes from my own biography of the late singer Peggy Lee, *Fever: The Life and Music of Miss Peggy Lee* (Henry Holt, 2006).

Chapter Four

Information on Jackson's initial days in New York came from the recollections of former teammate Mike Riordan, Holzman's *Red on Red* and Jackson's *Maverick*.

For descriptions of the old Madison Square Garden, I depended on my own recollections—which, while distant, remain vivid—as well as those of Darrall Imhoff and former referee Norm Drucker, as well as Jackson's writings. Recollections of the new Garden are founded on years of personal experience.

Information on the New Yorker Hotel is based on the hotel's extensive historical archives.

For descriptions of Red Holzman and his coaching style, I interviewed Earl Monroe, Jerry Lucas, Henry Bibby, Bill Hosket, John Gianelli and Mike Riordan. I also relied on Holzman's *Red on Red*, as well as a personal interview with the man.

For further characterizations of Monroe, I relied on Woody Allen's story, "A Fan's Notes on Earl Monroe," in the November 1977 issue of *Sport* magazine.

Terry Pluto's *Tall Tales: The Glory Days of the NBA* (Simon & Schuster, 1992) and *Pioneers of the Hardwood: Indiana and the Birth of Professional Basketball* (Indiana University Press, 1998) by Todd Gould were essential and illuminating for descriptions of the early BAA.

For accounts of Jackson's first few seasons, beyond the recollections of his teammates, I used several clippings from the *New York Times* and *New York Post* and from *Sports Illustrated*'s Phil Jackson file. Bill Hosket provided information on Jackson's back surgery and the Knicks' physician, Kazuo Yanagisawa. Information on the rivalry with the Bullets came from interviews with Jack Marin and Earl Monroe, as well as my own recollections of the time.

Information about Jackson's relationship with Holzman in his off year came from *Maverick* and a story in April 2009 from the *New York Daily News*.

For the details of Jackson's friendship with Eddie Mast, I depended on several interviews with Diane Mast and Charley Rosen.

For Jackson's early love of motorcycles, I relied on his own recollections, as well as "New Zealand on Two Wheels," a story he cowrote with Rosen for the November 2005 issue of *Men's Journal*.

Chapter Five

I based initial descriptions of the loft on West Nineteenth Street on the memories of Diane Mast, Charley Rosen and Neal Walk. In addition, I relied on "Soul Brothers," Rosen's story for the December 1973 issue of *Sport* magazine.

For accounts of Jackson's marijuana use and marital difficulties, I referred to his own reports in *Maverick*.

In describing his role on the team as well as in the locker room, I depended on Bill Bradley's *Life on the Run*, as well as extensive memories from Jackson's friend and teammate Neal Walk. For Jackson's general style of play, I spoke with several former teammates.

Extensive newspaper accounts from all of the New York papers of the time, primarily the *Post* and the *Times*, provided specific details and quotes. The exhaustively comprehensive and invaluable website Probasketballreference.com confirmed the numbers of specific games, as they did for all of the games in the book.

For information on the Los Angeles Forum, I drew on personal experience in covering games.

My reference to Jackson's LSD experience is based on his book *Maverick*.

For information on the customs and beliefs of the Lakota Sioux Nation, I interviewed Virgil Bush and Rick Two Dogs. For information on the Sioux rituals involving tobacco, I relied on "No More Bull," Jackson's interview with Rosen for the September/October 1998 issue of *Cigar Aficionado*.

For further information on the reservation, I spoke with Jone Miller of Ulster County, New York, who runs an arts program on the reservation.

All details of current life on the Pine Ridge Reservation in South Dakota are from personal observation.

Chapter Six

For accounts of Jackson's spiritual explorations of the next few years, including his trip to New Haven, the memories of Chris Thomforde, former president of Moravian College and Theological Seminary, were particularly illuminating. Thomforde was also Bill Bradley's successor as Princeton's captain, a Knicks draftee who never played, and was able to fill out the Knick characterizations. For information on Bill Bradley's rough entrance into New York, I depended on Harvey Araton's riveting *When the Garden Was Eden* (Harper/HarperCollins, 2011).

For additional details on Jackson's state of mind in the loft, as well as the social scene, I relied on Diane Mast, Charley Rosen and Neal Walk.

I obtained accounts of the 1973–74 season from John Gianelli and Henry Bibby, as well as the *Christian Science Monitor* and New York newspapers.

Chapter Seven

Dr. Christopher Thomforde, who performed the ceremony, provided me with an account of Phil's wedding to June Perry.

Regarding Jackson and Bradley's cinema adventure in Houston, I relied on a dispatch from a *Sports Illustrated* correspondent, from that magazine's Jackson file.

For Jackson's blossoming friendship with Charley Rosen, I interviewed Rosen. For the biographical information on Rosen, I relied on several interviews with Rosen, Franz Lidz's "Basketball's Eclectic Basket Case" in the March 4, 1991, issue of *Sports Illustrated* and information from stories about him that have appeared in local media in Ulster County, New York.

Danny Rudolph and Charley Rosen gave accounts of Jackson's participation in pickup games in New York at the United Nations and the Markle Evangeline Residence for Women.

For the blossoming of Phil's friendship with Neal Walk, their explorations of New York and other cities, and their spiritual and literary explorations of the time, I relied on interviews with Walk. For my understanding of the distinctive relationship between Jackson and Holzman, Walk was also helpful.

The description of the postseason playoff–clinching party at Walt Frazier's apartment is reconstructed from Rosen's memories. Accounts of the writing of *Maverick* are from Rosen.

Jackson's quotes about his thoughts on having written *Maverick* are from our interview in Miami in February 1992, and from my own notes for my profile of Jackson in the April 29, 1990, edition of the *National Sports Daily*.

Accounts of the later years of Phil's career as a player were based on interviews with Jim Cleamons, Neal Walk and Kevin Loughery. I also relied on Jerry Lucas and a personal interview with Walt Frazier in 1990.

Chapter Eight

I obtained information on Jackson's two years with the Nets from interviews with Loughery, Walk and Rich Kelley, as well as newspaper accounts.

The recounting of Neal Walk's journey to Montana with Jackson is from interviews with Walk.

"New Woes in a New NBA Season," Jackson's *New York Times* story analyzing the state of the National Basketball Association during the summer, is from the September 14, 1980, edition.

Chapter Nine

The account of Jackson's years as coach of the Albany Patroons is based foremost on the extensive and joyous recollections of several people involved in Jackson's five years as a Continental Basketball Association coach, including Jackson himself, whom I interviewed at the Washington Avenue Armory in March 1987, his final year as the coach of the Patroons.

In those interviews, I drew on the memories of former Patroons Lowes Moore, Derrick Rowland, Rudy Macklin, Ralph McPherson, Andre Gaddy and David Magley, former Savannah Spirit media executive Craig Kilborn, and former Patroons executives James Coyne, Mike Sandman and Gary Holle, as well as the late former Patroons everyman Joe Hennessy.

I also drew upon Coyne's memoir, *Questions That Bother Him So!* (Kokomo Publications, 1992), as well as Patroons yearbooks and programs. Rosen's *Crazy Basketball: A Life In and Out of Bounds* (University of Nebraska Press, 2011) provided additional information, as did his novel *The Cockroach Basketball League* (Seven Stories Press, 1998).

I mined the memories of former Patroons beat writer Tim Layden, now a staff writer for *Sports Illustrated,* and Tim Wilkin, former Patroons beat writer for the *Albany Times-Union.* Former CBA commissioner Jim Drucker was particularly helpful in rounding out the picture. I also relied on microfilm accounts from the *Albany Times-Union* accessible through the Albany Public Library branch near the Armory.

Chapter Ten

My depiction of basketball in Puerto Rico in the Jackson summers relied largely on the memories of former referee Jack Nies and Charley Rosen, as well as several interviews with former Liga de Baloncesta Superior Nacional star Edwin Pellot-Rosa. I also referred to Jackson's own account in *Sacred Hoops: Spiritual Lessons of a Hardwood Warrior* (Hyperion, 1995).

Jackson's letter to Jim Coyne is from Coyne's personal files.

I also relied on Rosen's account experiences, as well as Holzman's *Red on Red,* for further insight into Puerto Rican hoops.

Chapter Eleven

Jimmy Rodgers shared with me his account of Jackson's near-miss hire onto the Knicks' staff, while Bill Fitch shared his recollections of Red Auerbach.

For accounts of Jackson's attempt to get the University of Minnesota job, I relied on the memories of Paul Presthus.

Diane Mast, Charley Rosen and former Milwaukee Buck Bobby Greacen contributed recollections for the section describing Big Man Camp.

For further insight into Jackson's final days in Albany, including his frustration at not being able to crack the Knicks hierarchy for a job, I referred to a personal interview with Jackson at the time, conducted at the Armory, which also allowed me to describe the Washington Avenue Armory from memory. I also relied on articles from the Schenectady *Daily Gazette*.

For accounts of Phil's second, and successful, hookup with the Bulls, I depended on "Phil Jackson: Then and Now," my interview with Jerry Krause for the April 29, 1990, edition of the *National Sports Daily*, as well as Rosen's recollection and accounts from *Maverick, More Than a Game,* and *Eleven Rings*.

Chapter Twelve

To obtain information regarding the Omega Institute for Holistic Studies, I spoke with cofounder Elizabeth Lesser and with Charley Rosen, in addition to visiting the institute and reading its literature.

For information regarding Jackson and Rosen's annual Beyond Basketball workshop at the institute, I relied on the memories of participants, in particular Rabbi Jonathan Kligler of Woodstock, New York. The wording of the Sioux prayer by Yellow Lark is from Kligler's personal files.

Jackson's *Sacred Hoops* provided insight into the Omega camps. For the experiences at the workshop after Jackson left, Rosen, who continues to teach the workshop, shared his knowledge.

Regarding the circumstances of Eddie Mast's death and funeral, I drew upon interviews with his widow, Diane, and Charley Rosen.

Chapter Thirteen

Information regarding Jackson's relationship to Johnny Bach in his first year in Chicago as an assistant, as well as Bach's appearance, is from a *Chicago Tribune* feature, "Coaching Odd Couple Teams Up for Bulls."

Chapter Fourteen

The account of the Bulls-76ers game in March 1990, and the following interview with Jackson, is from my personal research files for a profile of Jackson for the April 29, 1990, *National Sports Daily,* titled "Phil Jackson Then and Now," including unpublished quotes and scenes.

Subsequent conversations with Jerry Reinsdorf, Jerry Krause, Scottie Pippen, Bill Cartwright, and Michael Jordan come from the same file, as well as from interviews I conducted with them in Chicago the day after the March 1990 game. Later conversations and observations from Jackson's friends back in Woodstock come from those same notes and files.

I checked game accounts and box scores at Probasketballreference.com, as was frequently the case throughout the book. For specific games, I also relied on the *Chicago Tribune* and, in some cases, the *Chicago Sun-Times.*

Accounts of Scottie Pippen's migraine and Jackson's reaction come from David Halberstam's *Playing for Keeps* (Three Rivers Press, 2000).

The account of Krause barging into the locker room and berating the team comes from Jackson's latest book, *Eleven Rings.* Jordan's breaking down in the bus is drawn from Halberstam's *Playing for Keeps.*

Jerry Krause's first impression of Toni Kukoč comes from an interview I did with Krause in 1995 in Chicago. Further insight into the season and the man come from "For Whom the Bulls Toil," a November 11, 1991, *Sports Illustrated* story by Jack McCallum.

Accounts of Dennis Hopson's difficulties with Bill Fitch are based on my interview with Fitch.

The quotes from Gilberto Benetton are from a personal interview I did with him in Treviso, Italy, in 1995.

Accounts of the Perdue-Laimbeer fight are from YouTube viewings.

The section on coach Mike Dunleavy relies on a profile published in the June 9, 1991, edition of *Sporting News.*

Accounts of events from the finals, and subsequent riots and celebrations, are based on coverage by the *Chicago Tribune,* as well as a Bob Ryan column from the *Boston Globe.* Background came from *Chicago* magazine's April 2011 oral history of the season, "Inside the Championship Run," by Bryan Smith, as well as its retrospective twenty years later.

Krause's livid reaction to the publication of *The Jordan Rules: The Inside Story of One Turbulent Season with Michael Jordan and the Chicago Bulls* (Simon & Schuster, 1992) is from a personal interview.

My description of Lakeside, Montana, the village closest to Jackson's Montana home, comes from a personal visit to the town and the region.

Chapter Fifteen

Accounts of Jackson's demeanor in training camp and in practices came from my interview with Bobby Hansen, which touched on locker-room talks, readings and the relationship to the team.

The exploration of Jackson's enduring affiliation with the beliefs of the Lakota Sioux was greatly informed by the insights of Diane Mast, as well as my own discussions with Rick Two Dogs, Virgil Bush and Charley Rosen, supplemented by Jackson's own *Sacred Hoops.*

The Buddhism discussion draws heavily on the interview that Jackson gave to *Tricycle: The Buddhist Review* in its summer 1994 issue ("Buddha and the Bulls" by Hugh Delehanty). It was supplemented by my interview of the editor of the magazine, Alex Caring-Lobel.

June Jackson's characterization of Jackson's increasing conservatism came from "The Age of Jackson," Jeff Coplon's profile of Phil for the *New York Times Magazine* in its May 17, 1992, issue, as did Bill Bradley's comments.

Accounts of the 1992 finals, in particular Bobby Hansen's moment in the sun, rely on Hansen, Scott Williams, Will Perdue and other Bulls, as well as media coverage and Jackson's *Eleven Rings*. Accounts of the subsequent looting come from the *Chicago Tribune*.

The descriptions of Kukoč playing in the Italian League, his home, the region and the style of play all draw on my own visit to Split, Croatia, and Treviso, Italy, to see Kukoč and write a profile of him. The subsequent interviews about Kukoč with Jerry Krause and Jackson took place after my trip to Europe, in Chicago.

Subsequent accounts of Scottie Pippen, Michael Jordan and Kukoč in the Olympics rely on Melissa Isaacson's coverage in the *Chicago Tribune*.

The White House ceremony's unusual event was recreated for me by Craig Hodges.

Chapter Sixteen

The description of the beginnings of the 1993–94 season is based on my interviews with players, specifically new arrival Corey Williams. Charley Rosen relayed the anecdote involving Trent Tucker and Michael Jordan. In conversation, Scott Williams best articulated the chief characterizations of the mood on the team that year.

The account of Jackson's visit to Mike Riordan's restaurant was from my interview with Riordan.

Accounts of the Knicks' playoff series came from media sources and various players, as well as my own observations of the series. The description of Charles Smith's being blocked four times remains etched in my memory; subsequent YouTube tapes verified the sequence.

Johnny Bach's assertion that Jordan hoodwinked Charles Barkley into softening up for the playoffs is based on *Pro Sports Daily*'s account of a dinner with Bach at http://forums.prosportsdaily.com/showthread.php?614545-Dinner-with-Johnny-Bach.

The account of the circumstances surrounding the death of James Jordan, Michael Jordan's father, came from "Reasonable Doubt," an exhaustively reported and researched story of the murder by Scott Raab for *GQ* magazine (March 1994). As a veteran of thirteen years on staff at *GQ*, I can verify that its fact-checking teams are the best in the business, and Raab's account of the circumstances of the murder is definitive.

For Jackson's discussion of the gun situation on the team, I referred to his book *More Than a Game* (Seven Stories Press, 2001). Craig Hodges verified to me Jordan's propensity for going to the shooting range and his love of firearms.

Discussion of Jordan and gambling is recounted in *Michael and Me: Our Gambling Addiction, My Cry For Help* (Athletic Guidance Center Publishing, 1993) by Richard Esquinas and Dave Distel, and *Orlando Sentinel* writer Brian Schmitz's August 14, 1993, article, "Is Michael Somehow Tied to Dad's Bizarre Death?"

The implication that the league told Jordan to take time off comes from my personal interview with the late film producer Bert Schneider (*Five Easy Pieces*).

Biographical details of new arrival Steve Kerr, including the assassination of his father and the taunts at Arizona State, were largely obtained from "Fighting Back from Injury and Personal Tragedy, Steve Kerr Leads Arizona to the Top of the Heap" by Dan Knapp (*People*, February 8, 1988). Those details were filled in by my interview with him, which was, in addition, one of the most definitive confirmations of the sincerity of Jackson's lifelong search for knowledge and spiritual guidance.

Bill Wennington, Steve Kerr and others gave me their remembrances of the Jordan-less season.

Accounts of the distinctly different personalities (and verbal spats) of Pat Riley and Phil come Clifton Brown's *New York Times* April 12, 1993, story, "Age-Old Questions Divide Coaches." Jackson's decision to take his team on a trip around New York instead of practicing came from a George Vecsey column in the *New York Times* on May 11, 1994, titled "Phil Jackson Takes a Trip on Zen Ferry."

Steve Kerr described to me Scottie Pippen's refusal to enter in the last seconds of a playoff game; it is also mentioned in Jackson's *Eleven Rings*. The subsequent quotes about the strain between Pippen and the team being over are from a Bernie Lincicome column in the *Chicago Tribune*.

Characterizations of Jackson during this season also rely on a feature from the *Village Voice* titled "Phil Jackson: Crybaby or Hipster Genius?"

The events surrounding Phil's firing of Johnny Bach were described to me by a source who requested anonymity. Details about Jackson's not hiring Charley Rosen were provided by Rosen and by Jackson in *More Than a Game*.

Chapter Seventeen

Regarding the near-trade of Scottie Pippen for Shawn Kemp, I depended on *Chicago Tribune* accounts at the time, specifically "Sonic Fans Take to Airwaves to Keep Kemp" (June 30, 1994) and "Jordan Pushes Trade" (July 1, 1994).

Accounts of the meeting of Ron Harper, Jerry Krause and Phil Jackson are from my interviews with Harper in summer 1994.

I obtained information about the first part of the 1994–95 season primarily from my interviews with Jud Buechler and Steve Kerr in the months of November and December 1994. Brad Sellers, Buechler, and Kerr gave me insight into Jordan's aggressive habits during practice.

Information about the training camp fight between Kerr and Jordan comes from Kerr's account to me of that day. Bill Wennington provided information about Jordan's return and its influence on the team.

Author Scott Raab, supplementing his thorough profile of Dennis Rodman for "Reasonable Doubt" in the March 1994 *GQ*, provided me with specific details about Dennis Rodman at this time. In addition, Bruce Newman's story "Black, White—and Gray" (*Sports Illustrated*, May 2, 1988) was instructive, as were stories from "Dennis Rodman's Dad has 27 Kids and Runs Bar in the Philippines" in the September 23, 1996, issue of *Jet* magazine and the *Advocate*'s "Dennis the Menace" (January 21, 1997).

The description of the circumstances of the acquisition of Rodman is based on Jackson's account in *More Than a Game*.

Chapter Eighteen

Insight into the Bulls' state of mind at the start of the record-breaking 1995–96 season came most thoroughly from my interviews with John Salley, who joined the team midseason, and Ron Harper. Former Bulls radio commentator Harvey Catchings helped me fill in some details.

Accounts of the Heat-Bulls playoff series, with its subtext of Pat Riley's flight from New York, were drawn from my own personal interviews and reporting of the events at that time, including conversations with both Riley and Dave Checketts. Characterizations of Riley as a street-fighting kid come from my own interviews with Riley for my 1998 *GQ* magazine profile "Pat Riley's Looking for a Fight."

Characterizations of Don Nelson rely on my own interviews with him at the beginning of that 1995–96 season, before he quit the Knicks that season.

Accounts of the Bulls' playoff performance relied on many media outlets, predominantly coverage in the *Chicago Tribune*.

Further analytic insight into this team, which was arguably the best in the history of the game, was provided by Bill Simmons's definitive NBA tome *The Book of Basketball: The NBA According to the Sports Guy* (ESPN, 2009).

In addition, Rich Hoffer's "Sitting Bull" article (*Sports Illustrated*, May 27, 1996) was very helpful, as was Rich O'Corozine's profile of Jackson and Rosen, "A Tale of Two Coaches," for the winter edition of *Ulster* magazine.

Chapter Nineteen

For insight into the arrival in Chicago of assistant coach Frank Hamblen for the 1996–97 season, I depended on my interview with Hamblen, as well as Jackson's analysis of the man in *More Than a Game*.

The characterizations of Utah Jazz coach Jerry Sloan are based on definitive portraits of one of the game's most underappreciated coaches from several media accounts, most significantly Jack McCallum's story "Sloan's Straightforward Approach, and His Winning, Never Changed" (*Sports Illustrated* website, February 10, 2011).

The account of the Bulls-Jazz final relies primarily on Steve Kerr's memories. Further details were furnished by Halberstam's *Playing for Keeps*.

In describing the subsequent deterioration of Jackson's relationship with the Bulls, I drew largely upon Halberstam's recounting of the events, with additional insight provided by Jackson in *More Than a Game* and *Eleven Rings*.

Chapter Twenty

For descriptions of the final years of Jackson's marriage to June Jackson, I referred to his account in *More Than a Game*. In order to describe the home they bought back in Bearsville, I visited the site.

Diane Mast provided invaluable insight about Phil and June's lifelong and still ongoing relationship, as did Charley Rosen. I also referred to Jackson's interview with Carol Marin on the March 27, 2001, *60 Minutes II* broadcast about the details of the breakup of their marriage, from a DVD recording of the segment.

Ron Harper and John Salley, among others, provided me with descriptions of Jackson's final year with the Bulls. I also referred to Jackson's books.

For characterizations of playoff-foe coach John Calipari, I relied on personal interaction with Calipari.

For the controversy about Jackson's diary for *ESPN The Magazine*, I referred to the four-part series "The Last Running of the Bulls," published during the 1997–98 playoffs, which has since been edited to exclude his discussion of the state of his marriage at the time. Further analysis of the state of his marriage came from Ron Harper.

My description of his final playoff series with the Bulls was drawn from player and media information as well as *More Than a Game*.

The team's final dinner was recounted to me by Ron Harper and told by Jackson in *Eleven Rings*. The scene of his final press conference at the Berto Center came from the *Chicago Tribune*.

For confirmation of Jerry Krause and Phil Jackson shaking hands at Tex Winter's Hall of Fame induction, I relied on an interview with Krause.

For characterizations of Michael Jordan, I spoke with Craig Hodges and also relied on Wright Thompson's remarkable story in *ESPN The Magazine*, "Michael Jordan Has Not Left the Building" (February 22, 2013).

Chapter Twenty-One

My characterizations of Jackson's state of mind upon leaving the Bulls were derived from *More Than a Game*. The account of his meetings with Dave Checketts while Jeff Van Gundy still coached the Knicks was based on Selena Roberts's May 24, 1999, article for the *New York Times*, Jackson's description in *More Than a Game* and a source who requested anonymity. It was the same source who told me that Jackson would refer to Jeff as "Van Gumby."

The accounts of Jackson's learning that he had the Lakers job came from various media outlets, as well as Jackson's book *Eleven Rings*. The press conference was reported in the *Los Angeles Times;* his outfit was described by Jerry West in his own book, *West by West: My Charmed, Tormented Life* (Little, Brown, 2011).

Former Bulls player Sam Vincent provided definitive insight into Jackson and his return to basketball.

Chapter Twenty-Two

Insight into the assemblage of the new coaching staff came largely from my interviews with Jim Cleamons and Frank Hamblen, supplemented by Jackson's own account in *More Than a Game*.

My account of Jackson's recruiting of Ron Harper, John Salley and A. C. Green came from personal interviews with all three men.

For characterization of Jackson's moving to Los Angeles, I referred to Mark Rowland's *Los Angeles* magazine feature "Sports Guru Phil" (June 1, 2000).

I obtained biographical information about Jerry Buss from his daughter Jeanie's book, *Laker Girl* (Triumph Books, 2010); "Jerry Is Never Behind the Eight Ball" by William Oscar Johnson (*Sports Illustrated*, June 18, 1979); "Whether It's the L.A. Lakers or a Lovely Woman, Jerry Buss Is Interested in Champions" (Sue Ellen Jares, *People*, February 11, 1980); and John Ireland's May 2009 article "Jerry Buss: All in the Family" in the *Los Angeles Times Magazine*.

Regarding Buss's affinity for young women, and his habits, I relied on *Laker Girl,* as well as Roland Lazenby's blog entry on Lakernoise.com in early 2010, which is no longer on the Web. I also relied on personal interaction with Buss during the 1983 finals.

The accounts of Pickfair rely on information in *Laker Girl.*

For the life and times of Jeanie Buss, I relied on *Laker Girl.* I also referred to an old personal interview with her former fiancé Steve Timmons.

For information on Phil and Jeanie's relationship, I relied on *More Than a Game* and the observations of Mark Madsen. Further insight into Jeanie Buss came from Los Angeles writer Broderick Turner.

For information about Phil's first season in Los Angeles, I consulted with John Salley and relied on stories by Phil Taylor in *Sports Illustrated.* I also referred to his quotes in *Tricycle,* as well as his own recollections in *More Than a Game,* and Shaquille O'Neal's accounts in his book *Shaq Uncut: My Story* (Grand Central Publishing, 2011).

The criticism of Jackson as an "out-of-the-box" thinker came from an anonymous source who played for Jackson for many years.

My first characterizations about Kobe Bryant came from a personal interview in which I spent the day with him in a Manhattan recording studio for a December 1992 *GQ* magazine profile. In addition, John Salley provided insight, as did Jim Cleamons, about Bryant's psyche. Ron Harper was particularly astute regarding Bryant and his early alienation from the rest of the team.

For Jackson's initial letters to his team, I relied on *More Than a Game.* I obtained a list of the books he gave out from "Book 'em, Jacko," a Steve Rushin column in the April 3, 2000, issue of *Sports Illustrated.*

For Shaq's initial adjustment to the triangle, I spoke with John Salley and Charley Rosen.

Phil's slurs of the Sacramento fans were described in the *Los Angeles Times.* The account of the playoffs is also from the *Los Angeles Times.*

The reference to Aaron Swartz's theories comes from the March 11, 2013, story by Larissa MacFarquhar in *The New Yorker,* "Requiem for a Dream."

Chapter Twenty-Three

The depiction of the dissolution of relations between Jerry West and Phil Jackson at the beginning of the 2000–2001 season was obtained from several sources, including the June 17, 2013, *Los Angeles Times* story "Phil Jackson Recalls Night He Asked Jerry West to Leave Locker Room," but primarily from West's *West by West.* Further amplification came from Charley Rosen, Jerry Krause and Jackson's own recollections in *The Last Season: A Team in Search of Its Soul* (Penguin Press, 2004). The Doug Krikorian column lambasting Jackson appeared in the July 18, 2000, edition of the *Long Beach Press-Telegram.*

The differing accounts of John Salley's departure from the team are from Salley and *More Than a Game.*

John Salley and Mark Madsen gave their recollections of Jackson's methods in practice. The accounts of the flap over Jackson's implying that Bryant tanked games in high school came from Jackson's book *Eleven Rings* and from Rick Telander's story in the March 2001 *Chicago Tribune.* Jackson's subsequent explanation of his belief that his interview with Telander was off the record is from *The Last Season.*

The recounting of the Bryant-O'Neal-Fox locker room argument is Jackson's from *The Last Season.*

Chapter Twenty-Four

Reports of the controversy surrounding the events of the possibly fixed sixth game of the Western Conference finals are drawn from court filings by attorney John Lauro, specifically a lengthy letter to District Court Judge Carol Bagley Amon, re *U.S. v. Donaghy*; the *Boston Globe*; and several other media sources.

Accounts of the playoff series came from the *Los Angeles Times.* The description of the rocky beginning of the 2002–03 season is from Charley Rosen, *The Last Season,* and the *Los Angeles Times.* Rosen, both on ESPN.com and in personal interviews, recounted the events surrounding the confrontation between Tex Winter and Kobe Bryant.

Details of Jackson's angioplasty came from *The Last Season* and various media sources.

All accounts of the Lodge & Spa at Cordillera, and details about the rape charge against Bryant, are from on-the-ground reporting I did at the time of the events for a September 2003 *GQ* magazine piece titled "The Fall of Kobe." This included a stay in the hotel. I was also able to confirm Bryant's room number and observe the room.

Characterizations of the plaintiff's character and reputation came from my own interviewing of her high school classmates, as well as staff at the lodge, in the first week of July.

The description of his appearance at the time is from my own observations. Accounts of the courtroom are also my own, as are details of the town of Eagle, Colorado. Particulars about the prosecution's case come from firsthand interviews with the then-sheriff of Eagle County in the first week of July.

Accounts of Jackson's reaction to the news are his own, from *More Than a Game*.

Subsequent discussion of Jackson's daughter having been assaulted in high school comes from *Eleven Rings*.

The eroding relationship between Jackson and Bryant is outlined extensively in Jackson's *The Last Season*.

Following accounts of the final dissolution of the team, with Jackson fired, Shaq traded and Bryant re-signed, are from various stories and columns in the June 19, 2004, and June 20, 2004, *Los Angeles Times*.

Chapter Twenty-Five

After the charges were dropped, on September 2, 2004, the full text of Bryant's statement of apology, issued through his attorney, was reported by the Associated Press.

Characterization of the difficulties encountered by the team coached by Rudy Tomjanovich and Frank Hamblen relied extensively on an interview I conducted with then-Laker Brian Grant. I also interviewed Hamblen, who would succeed Tomjanovich after he abruptly quit.

For accounts of Jackson's year off, including his trip to the South Pacific, I depended largely on Charley Rosen's article "New Zealand on Two Wheels" with the man in the November 2005 issue of *Men's Journal*. The same article reveals Jackson's reasons, despite ambivalence, for returning to the game and accepting Buss's new offer.

Discussion of Phil's ability to reconcile with Kobe Bryant is based on the insights of John Salley and Ron Harper during interviews in the spring of 2013.

Extensive analysis of Jackson's decision to return was provided by transcripts from author Stephen Rodrick after his story for the July 2013 issue of *Men's Journal*, "Lord of the Rings." Further insight into that relationship came from Diane Mast and Mark Madsen. The account of Jackson's return press conference comes from the *Los Angeles Times*.

Chapter Twenty-Six

For Jackson's challenges in dealing with a new breed of modern player, I relied on Jim Cleamons's insights, as well as those of Craig Hodges, whom Phil had brought out to Los Angeles to be a shooting coach for the Lakers, and Frank Hamblen.

Background on Andrew Bynum is based on articles from the *Denver Post,* the *Trentonian*, and the *Los Angeles Times*.

For background on Kwame Brown, I referred to Sally Jenkins's *Washington Post Magazine* article "Growing Pains" (April 21, 2002), as well as the *Los Angeles Times*.

Details about Lamar Odom came from various media accounts, including "Another Sunny Day in Lamar's L.A." by Lee Jenkins in the March 23, 2009, issue of *Sports Illustrated*.

Further insight into the coaching methodologies Jackson used in his new and final regime came from an interview with Laker Ronny Turiaf. My understanding of the style of play of Sasha Vujačić and Vladimir Radmanović was enhanced by the games I watched Kukoč play in Europe.

Chapter Twenty-Seven

The account of Jackson's knee replacement came from his Mike Sager interview in *Esquire* ("Phil Jackson: What I've Learned," May 8, 2011).

For Bryant's wish that Bynum be traded, I relied on various sources, most specifically the YouTube clip: http://www.youtube.com/watch?v=FKI8K7GP3NM. For details on the subsequent flap about Derek Fisher's signing with the Lakers after he'd quit the Jazz, I relied on accounts in the July 13, 2007, *Salt Lake Tribune.* For Javaris Crittenton's murder charges, I relied on accounts from the April 2, 2013, *Atlanta Journal-Constitution.*

The account of Jackson's *Brokeback Mountain* controversy came from several media sources, including the November 14, 2007, ESPN website story "Jackson's Postgame Comments Get NBA's Attention."

My description of the Pau Gasol trade was based on *Los Angeles Times* coverage. Diane Mast and Charley Rosen provided insights into Phil's relationship with Gasol.

My account of the playoffs was drawn from various media outlets, notably the *Los Angeles Times* and *Sports Illustrated.*

Chapter Twenty-Eight

The recreation of Jackson's speech at the University of North Dakota's convocation ceremony relied on a DVD recording of the entire ceremony provided by the UND Athletic Media Relations Department.

Chapter Twenty-Nine

Details of the season in which Jackson won his tenth ring were based on that season's articles from the *Los Angeles Times.* Accounts of the championship series were taken from personal observation and Chris Ballard's "Following Their Star, the Lakers Are Champions Again" in the June 25, 2009, issue of *Sports Illustrated,* as well as accounts from the *Orlando Sentinel* and Jackson's own recollections in *Eleven Rings.*

Chapter Thirty

Background on Ron Artest came from several published sources, including my interview with Larry Bird two days after the infamous brawl between the Pacers and the Pistons in November 2004. Further insight into Artest's state of mind came from Jonathan Feigen's July 30, 2008, *Houston Chronicle* story, "Despite Yao's Comments, Artest Seems Happy About Future."

Accounts of Odom's assessment of the team's midseason status are from the *Los Angeles Times.*

Discussion of Jackson's controversial remarks regarding the anti-immigration policies of the state of Arizona was drawn from several sources, including specifically Dave Zirin's column for *The Nation.* Diane Mast and Charley Rosen provided me with insight into Jackson's own thinking on the subject.

Jackson's quotes are from J. A. Adande's column for ESPN's website, "Phil Jackson on His Future . . . and Leaving Politics in the Past," May 5, 2010.

My recreation of the murder of rancher Bob Krentz relied on Associated Press accounts of the crime. Characterization of the criticism of Jackson comes from the *Los Angeles Times,* most specifically a column by Tim Rutten, "Phil Jackson's Wrongheaded View of Arizona's Anti-Immigration Law," May 19, 2010.

My depiction of the subsequent playoffs, leading to ring eleven, is based on accounts from the *Los Angeles Times,* the *Boston Globe,* and *Sports Illustrated.* The references to June Jackson and her presence at the final party in Staples rely on a *Sports Illustrated* account by Lee Jenkins, "Dynasty: Beginning or Ending?" published on June 28, 2010.

Chapter Thirty-One

The account of Jackson's speech to the Western Governors' Association was based on Dillon Tabish's article in the June 28, 2010, edition of the *Daily Inter Lake.*

Chapter Thirty-Two

Accounts of the troubles of the Lakers in Jackson's final season relied on several sources. Dave McMenamin's interview with Craig Hodges for ESPNLA.com, published March 18, 2010, gave insight into Bryant's continued inability to meld with Jackson's vision.

Jackson's interview with Stephen Rodrick for the June 14, 2013, *Men's Journal* and with Andrea Kremer for HBO's *Real Sports with Bryant Gumbel* on June 28, 2012, revealed his thinking during the sweep at the hands of the Mavericks. Further insight into that last series comes from *Eleven Rings.*

My account of the HBO segment discussing Jackson's postretirement state of mind relies on a transcript of the entire segment.

The analysis of Harvard professor George Vaillant's metrics of later-life success relies on my study of the book for a piece I wrote for the May 2002 issue of *GQ*. References to Freud's predictors in life draw on my studies of Freud.

Charley Rosen shed light on Jackson's release and the subsequent hiring of Mike Brown.

My description of the Lakers' courting of Jackson but hiring of Mike D'Antoni depends primarily on Charley Rosen's account of the events. Further details are based on Kurt Rambis's interpretation of events in *USA Today* in 2012. I obtained further insight into the incident from personal interviews with Diane Mast and Stephen Rodrick.

The subsequent accounts of Jackson's engagement to Jeanie Buss come from my following Jeanie Buss on Twitter.

An index for this book is available at
www.penguin.com/philjacksonindex.